# China's New
# Political Economy

# CHINA'S NEW POLITICAL ECONOMY

## The Giant Awakes

**Susumu Yabuki**
*Translated by Stephen M. Harner*

**WESTVIEW PRESS**
*Boulder • San Francisco • Oxford*

Copyright © 1995 by Sososha Ltd.

English version published in 1995 in the United States of America by Westview Press, Inc., 5500 Central Avenue, Boulder, Colorado 80301-2877, and in the United Kingdom by Westview Press, 36 Lonsdale Road, Summertown, Oxford OX2 7EW

First published in Japanese in 1992, revised edition 1994, by Sososha Ltd.

Library of Congress Cataloging-in-Publication Data
Yabuki, Susumu, 1937–
  [Zusetsu Chūgoku no keizai. English]
  China's new political economy : the giant awakes / Susumu Yabuki ;
translated by Stephen M. Harner.
     p.   cm.
  Includes bibliographical references and index.
  ISBN 0-8133-2254-5. — ISBN 0-8133-2255-3 (pbk.)
  1. China—Economic policy—1976–   I. Title.
HC427.92.Y327813   1995
338.951—dc20                                                                                    94-28436
                                                                                                          CIP

Printed and bound in the United States of America

      The paper used in this publication meets the requirements
∞    of the American National Standard for Permanence of Paper
      for Printed Library Materials Z39.48-1984.

10    9    8    7    6    5    4    3    2    1

To the memory of Keiko Nakamura,
wife of Kimiyoshi Nakamura, president
of Sososha Ltd.,
whose last work was on
the English edition of this book

# Contents

# Tables and Boxes

# Illustrations

MAPS

ILLUSTRATIONS

# Author's Preface
## to the English-Language Edition

I am truly delighted to be presenting this book to readers in the English-speaking world by virtue of the translation provided by a young and talented "Japan and China hand," Stephen M. Harner. As a China watcher, I have heretofore often consulted the writings and views of U.S. and British researchers. In an open world, it is inappropriate that the products of intellectual labor should be imported only. It has thus been my desire to some day reciprocate the generosity shown to me.

It is my sincere hope that this book will, through deepening Americans' understanding of modern China's economic development, contribute in a small way to the advancement of U.S.-China relations.

*Susumu Yabuki*
*Tokyo*
*March 1994*

# Author's Preface
# to the Japanese Edition

It has been fifteen years since Deng Xiaoping instituted the reform and liberalization policy in the late 1970s. Initially this set of policies was regarded as a small step toward compensating for the deficiencies of the policies of Mao Zedong. However, it has constituted a critical step toward the conversion from a planned economy to a market economy.

The term "socialism" is still applied, but the reality is that these fifteen years have produced a decisive and irreversible change in the nature of the system. The old model for Chinese socialism, Soviet-style socialism, has disappeared from view and from mind, leaving only certain troublesome vestiges. In China, conservatives find little left to indulge their nostalgia.

How did the reform and liberalization policy evolve? And how did the consequent development—the conversion from a planned economy to a market economy—unfold and progress? What changed, and how? This book is an attempt to answer these questions, and to do so based on a rigorous review of the relevant data.

Reform and liberalization are presented as a duality, but in fact the liberalization policy was the starting point of everything. What awakened China from its "socialist delusion" was not the realization that it would never catch up with the developed countries (Japan, Europe, and the United States) but rather the examples of the newly industrializing Asian economies of Hong Kong, Taiwan, South Korea, and Singapore and later those of members of the Association of Southeast Asian Nations. The example of countries so close to China was the inescapable lesson. China's awakening has proceeded from the special economic zones to the fourteen coastal cities and from the coastal region to the Yangtze River; to the regions bordering on the former Soviet Union (the northeast and the northwest); to the regions bordering Vietnam, Thailand, and Myanmar; and now in all directions. It is also permeating vertically the multiple strata of the society and economy.

Statistical reporting has been keeping pace with this tremendous transformation. Symbolic (and also substantive) is the conversion effected in the "Statistical Communiqué of the State Statistical Bureau of the PRC on National Economic and Social Development in 1991," published in Beijing by the State Statistical Bureau in 1992. In this communiqué, summarized in *People's Daily*, February 29, 1992, the term "gross value and industrial and agricultural output" (GVIAO) disappeared and was replaced by "gross national product" (GNP). In the near future, we can expect a complete conversion from the socialist MPS (material products system) method to the Western SNA (system of national accounts) method.

This book relies heavily for basic data on *Statistical Yearbook of China*. Also employed is recent statistical information that has begun surging like floodwaters from sources such as provincial statistical yearbooks and *Foreign Economic and Trade Yearbook*. So abundant has statistical material from China become that it is necessary to consolidate and condense the information in order not to be inundated by it. This is one of the objectives of this book.

This book continues in the style of my previously published *The Economic Level of China: Illustrated* (Tokyo: Sososha, 1987) but is totally different in content, for two reasons. First, the subject, the economy of China, has undergone a major metamorphosis. Second, the statistical data necessary to describe the change have become available. Also to be mentioned are improvements in word processing and printing technology; advances in presentation media inevitably influence content.

When I reflect on the origin of this book, I begin with my article "Thirty-five Years of the New China in Figures," published in *Chuokoron*, November 1984. *The Economic Level of China: Illustrated* was an expansion of this idea. I continued this approach with new data in "China: Ten Years of Reform and Liberalization," *Sekai*, December 1988.

Bringing together data and figures from previous works, updating, and adding new material proved to be an extremely time-consuming and physically demanding project. I must apologize that I can only mention names of persons who directly helped me. They are Motohiro Kondo, editor of *Chuokoron;* Kan Yamazaki, editor of *Sekai;* Kiyoshi Inagaki, Mitsubishi Research Institute (senior researcher, International Trends Analysis Center); Hideo Ohashi (former researcher, Mitsubishi Research Institute, currently Senshu University associate professor); Hiroshi Waki (expert on Chinese personnel issues), who assisted in analyzing personal relationships; Akio Takahara (Oberlin University associate professor), who assisted on wages; Koji Kobayashi (former senior fellow, Institute of Developing Economies, currently Kansai University professor), who gave me the opportunity to organize data on the development of the liberalization policy; Tadayoshi Murata (professor, Yokohama National University), who assisted in using the FM.TOWNS personal computer; and Kazuyoshi Shiraishi (director, Research Office, Overseas Department, Agricultural Research Institute, Ministry of Agricultural and Water Resources), who provided his rigorous comments on the proofs.

Finally, the greatest contribution was from the editorial department of my publisher, Sososha, particularly Kimiyoshi Nakamura, Yuna Shimaguchi, and the late Keiko Takeda. Their efforts in gathering materials, producing illustrations, and proofreading were extraordinary. Of course, many of the illustrations were produced based on the comments and suggestions made by readers of my previous works. To all and for all of the above, my deepest gratitude.

*Susumu Yabuki*
*Personal Residence in the*
*Western Suburbs of Tokyo*
*March 1994*

# Translator's Preface
# to the English-Language Edition

China's continuing quiet revolution has implications for all the countries of the world and for its close neighbor, Japan, more than most. It is not surprising, then, that political and economic analysis on China in Japan is both abundant and of high quality. This book is an example.

As Japanese businesses survey the world today, China looms as an enormous and inevitable strategic challenge—in many ways the "Last Frontier." Their response to this challenge is proving worthy of it and typically Japanese—that is, involving painstaking, detailed, dispassionate research into the risks and potential rewards. This research is being conducted by the companies themselves, by industry associations and quasi-governmental agencies like JETRO, and by the academic community, often in business advisory roles.

It was in this context that the original version of this book was written by Professor Susumu Yabuki, in close cooperation with his longtime publisher, Sososha Ltd., which specializes in books and materials on China. Professor Yabuki is one of the most respected of Japan's younger, postwar generation of China scholars. This will be the first time one of his works has appeared in English. The book was initially directed toward Japanese corporate executives and students and was designed to provide a concise but in-depth overview of the major issues in China's political economy. The fundamental and highly estimable approach of the author and publisher was that "a picture is worth a thousand words"—hence the extensive use of charts and graphs based on the mass of statistics coming out of China. The book's original title was *The Economy of China: Illustrated* (Zusetsu: Chugoku no Keizai). The original work enjoyed three printings in Japan. A revised edition was published in January 1994.

For the current translation, Professor Yabuki, Sososha Ltd., and I, together with Westview Press, have completely updated the original Japanese book, using the most recently available statistics from China and Japan. In addition, we have added new chapters covering political and economic developments and trends through 1993 and into 1994 and incorporating thoughts on the post-Deng era and differing U.S. and Japanese approaches to China on the issue of human rights and development.

With the addition of the new material, especially, we feel that American readers will find in this book a uniquely comprehensive and yet clear and in-depth presentation of the key issues, challenges, and opportunities presented by China, whether the readers are approaching China as businesspersons, scholars, students, or generally interested individuals.

The translator's role is to give to an author a voice in another language, striving always to convey the author's message, and not to substitute the translator's. This I have tried to do faithfully. At the same time, however, I was asked by Professor Yabuki to assume the role of an American reader and to suggest changes to make the presentation interesting and accessible to American audiences. This I have also done, particularly in Chapters 19, 20, and 21. In all these endeavors I have been greatly assisted by and owe thanks to Susan L. McEachern, acquisitions editor at Westview Press, as well as Kimiyoshi Nakamura, president of Sososha Ltd., and of course, Professor Yabuki. Finally, I must thank my wife, Annie Lai Harner, whose patient support and efforts to educate me about China over twenty years of marriage deserve any credit for this translation.

*Stephen M. Harner*
*March 1994*

# 1

# Fifteen Years of Reform After Thirty Years of Utopian Socialism

The People's Republic of China (PRC) was established on October 1, 1949, and thus 1993 marked the forty-fourth year since its founding. Age forty-four in a human life would be the time of greatest vigor. From the perspective of China's long history, forty-four years is hardly more than the blink of an eye. For China, then, what has transpired during this period?

The history of communist China can be divided into the Mao Zedong era (1949 to 1976) and the Deng Xiaoping era (after 1979), with the Hua Guofeng interval sandwiched between them.

The twenty-seven years of the Mao Zedong era were most prominently marked by the Great Leap Forward (1958 to 1960) and the Cultural Revolution (1966 to 1976). In these two periods, Mao Zedong (it was subsequently learned) stepped forth personally as leader in campaigns to achieve "utopian socialism." The intervals immediately before these cataclysms—the mid-1950s and the early 1960s—were periods of stability and advancement, when figures like Zhou Enlai, Liu Shaoqi, Chen Yun, and Deng Xiaoping were prominently active. As the reader will come to see, the Mao Zedong era witnessed the interplay of the radicalism asserted by Mao and the moderately progressive line followed by formal position holders, with the former the dominant influence and the latter in the role of an opposition.

During the Deng Xiaoping era, "seeking truth from facts," "open-mindedness," and "reform and liberalization" came to express mainstream thinking, and utopian socialism was denounced. This new conceptual orientation advanced hesitantly at first and ran into opposition from those who felt it was going too far. However, its acceptance was clearly evidenced by the adoption by the Thirteenth Party Congress in October 1987 of the "Decision on the Early Stage of Socialist Development" and by the adoption by the Fourteenth Party Congress in October 1992 of the theory of the socialist market economy.

In the preamble to his report advocating the 1987 decision, Zhao Ziyang proclaimed that in the case of China, the idea "that socialism can be reached without first passing through a stage of capitalism development" is "a leftist error." He went further to emphasize that it is "utopian" and "leftist fallacy" to think that "it is possible to vault into the early stages of socialism without first building up great productive forces." From this time forward, the concept of "the early stage of socialism," which might earlier have been branded a leftist or rightist error, became a moderate "eclectic doctrine." What was rejected as a leftist error was the Maoist-era socialism that dismissed the need for a "huge build-up of productive forces" and advocated a quick "transition to communism."

The Thirteenth Congress of the Chinese Communist Party formally defined "the early stage of socialism" as the 100 years from the party's assumption of power in 1949 to the middle of the twenty-first century. The congress announced that during this period, wage labor, operator ownership of enterprises, and dividend-yielding stock ownership would be permitted. This decision was a theoretical breakthrough. Until that time, there had been virtually no apparent signs of change in the doctrine that socialism was achievable without an intervening capitalistic stage. No doubt the Communist Party could not have openly countenanced discussion on this issue.

The real evidence that China was at the early stage of socialism was the low level of its economic productivity—its material poverty. Further, because the backwardness of its economy was largely attributable to the structure of economic controls imposed in the name of socialism, the party's acceptance of the concept of an early stage of socialism can be said to constitute the party's declaration of defeat of its utopian socialist line. The reader can thus appreciate that the Chinese economy has begun a historic metamorphosis. The purpose of this book is to analyze the process and results and, to some degree, the future of this transformation.

Figure 1.1 illustrates the truly dizzying political vicissitudes since 1949 and provides a broad view of the historical currents of the People's Republic of China. A brief review of the major historical phases is as follows:

*Phase one: agricultural collectivization in the mid-1950s.* The first phase was the agricultural collectivization campaign launched in the mid-1950s. Individual farms were reorganized into low-level cooperatives, high-level cooperatives, and finally into people's communes. After lasting for more than twenty years, the policy was abandoned at the beginning of the 1980s and the farms were broken up and returned to individual family units under the "production responsibility system."

*Phase two: the 1958 to 1960 Great Leap Forward.* In the din of voices shouting the slogans "overtake and surpass Britain" and "the path to communism is near," the people's communes were organized; old peasant techniques, euphemistically called "Chinese traditional methods," were blindly introduced; and mass mobilization of labor was instituted—all in a frenetic pursuit of increased production. Mistakes in policy and natural disasters combined to create extreme food shortages, and deaths from starvation were recorded on a massive scale.

*Phase three: the "period of readjustment."* Remedial policies were implemented in response to the food and production crises. Deng Xiaoping's famous "White

Cat, Black Cat" doctrine (the cat that can catch the mouse is a good cat; the method that can raise production is a good method) expressed in bold terms the essence of the readjustment policies. (Indeed, it may be said that the party's adoption of the early-stage thesis is a revisitation of Deng's proposition, sometimes called the "productive forces doctrine," from the readjustment period.)

*Phase four: the 1966 to 1976 Cultural Revolution.* "Pure socialism"—involving the concepts of "class struggle" and "priority of productive relations"—was pursued by Mao's adherents as an antidote to revisionism; it reached extremes that greatly impeded economic development.

*Phase five: the Deng Xiaoping era.* The death of Mao in 1976 created the opportunity, after the interval of Hua Guofeng, for commencement of the Deng Xiaoping era in 1978 and 1979. The Deng era has lasted some fifteen years and has been marked by numerous twists and turns. Particularly important events have been the purge of Hu Yaobang in January 1987 and the purge (in connection with the Tiananmen Square student demonstrations) of Zhao Ziyang in June 1989. Both incidents constituted successful efforts of conservative forces to apply a brake to the pace of reform and liberalization. The pace of reform and liberalization slowed for two years following the Tiananmen incident. Sentiment toward such changes shifted to optimism and increased activity after Deng Xiaoping's visit to Guangdong province's special economic zones just before Spring Festival in 1992. Deng's exhortations for faster growth boosted confidence and real economic development and established the tone for policy as formalized at party and government levels in late 1993 and 1994.

Figure 1.1 Vicissitudes in Line since the Establishment of the PRC ——From the Mao Zedong Era to the Deng Xiaoping Era

| Year | Five Year Plan Period | Period | ⇐Left·Tilt | Line | Right·Tilt⇒ |
|---|---|---|---|---|---|
| 1949 | | Period of Recovery | | ["Tilt toward the USSR"] | Oct. 49 Establishment of the People's Republic of China |
| 1950 | | | Oct. 50 Oppose America Aid Korea Campaign | [Korean War] | |
| 1951 | | | Nov. 51 Three-Anti Five-Anti Campaign | | |
| 1952 | | | | | |
| 1953 | First Five Year Plan | | Aug. 53 General Line for transition period | | |
| 1954 | | | Dec. 53 Agricultural production cooperatives | | |
| 1955 | | | May 55 Criticism of Hu Feng Collectivization of agriculture | | |
| 1956 | | | | | May 56 "Hundred Flowers" |
| 1957 | | | June 57 Anti-Rightist struggle | | Sep. 56 Eighth Party Congress |
| 1958 | Second Five Year Plan | Great Leap Forward Period | Aug. 58 People's Commune Campaign | ["Overtake Britain"] | |
| 1959 | | | | | Apr. 59 Liu Shaoqi becomes president [Liu Shaoqi Line] |
| 1960 | | | | [Economic crisis, famine] ["Sino-Soviet Split"] | |
| 1961 | | | | | |
| 1962 | | | | | Jan. 62 Mao Zedong's self criticism. Debate over class struggle |
| 1963 | Period of Readjustment | | 63-64 Sino-Soviet Debate | | 62 Deng Xiaoping's 'White Cat, Black Cat' doctrine |
| 1964 | | | 64 Four Purity Campaign / Nov. 65 Criticism of "The Dismissal of Hai Rui" | | |
| 1965 | | | | | |
| 1966 | Third Five Year Plan | Cultural Revolution | Aug. 66 Decision on the Great Proletarian Cultural Revolution | ["Cultural Revolution"] [Liu Shaoqi, Deng Xiaoping are purged] | |
| 1967 | | | | | |
| 1968 | | | | | |
| 1969 | | | Apr. 69 Ninth Party Congress [Lin Biao designated successor] | | |
| 1970 | | | | | |
| 1971 | Fourth Five Year Plan | | | | Sep. 71 Lin Biao dies while escaping after attempted assassination of Mao Zedong |

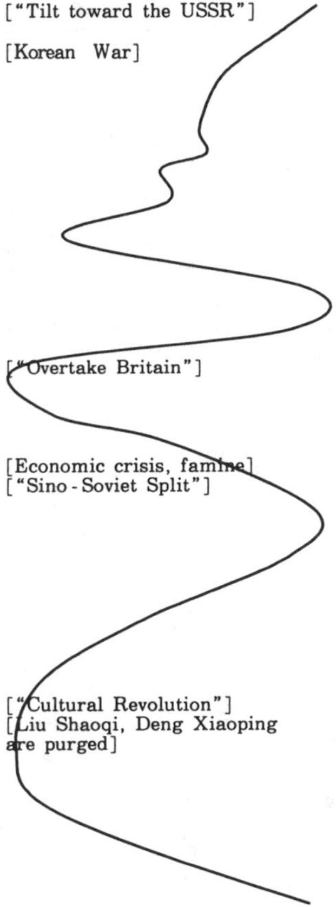

| year | Five Year Plan Period | Period | ⇐ Left Tilt ⇒ | Line | Right Tilt ⇔ |
|---|---|---|---|---|---|
| 1972 | Fourth Five Year Plan | Cultural Revolution | | [Sino-US Rapprochement] | Sep. 72 Japan and China restore diplomatic relations |
| 1973 | | | Aug. 73 Criticism of Confucius (The Gang of Four criticize Zhou Enlai) | | |
| 1974 | | | | | Oct. 74 Deng Xiaoping is rehabilitated |
| 1975 | | | Aug. 75 Criticism of The Water Margin (The Gang of Four criticize Deng Xiaoping) | | |
| 1976 | Fifth Five Year Plan | | Apr. 76 '76 Tiananmen Incident (Deng Xiaoping purged, Hua Guofeng designated Successor) | [Mao Zedong Dies] | Jan. 76 Zhou Enlai dies / Oct. 76 Gang of Four arrested |
| 1977 | | | | | Jul. 77 Deng Xiaoping rehabilitated |
| 1978 | | | | | Dec. 78 Third Plenum 11th Party Congress Central Committee |
| 1979 | | | Jan. 79 Four Basic Principles / Dec. 79 Democracy Wall prohibited | Deng Xiaoping Leads Main Faction [The Four Modernizations] [Foreign Opening, Domestic Revitalization] | Jul. 79 Special economic zones established |
| 1980 | | Deng Xiaoping Era | | | May 80 Liu Shaoqi's reputation restored |
| 1981 | Sixth Five Year Plan | | Apr. 81 Criticism of Bai Hua's "Kulian" | | Jun. 81 Historic decisions of the Sixth Plenum of the 11th Central Committee |
| 1982 | | | | | Sep. 82 12th Party Congress [Hu Yaobang made general secretary, Deng Xiaoping becomes chairman of Military Affairs Committee |
| 1983 | | | Oct. 83 Decision to reform the Party, oppose spiritual pollution | | |
| 1984 | | | | | Apr. 84 14 cities opened to foreign investment / Oct. 84 Decision on Reform of the Economic System |
| 1985 | | | | | Sep. 85 Party Congress |
| 1986 | Seventh Five Year Plan | | Oct. 86 Decision on spiritual culture / Dec. 86 Student demonstrations | | |
| 1987 | | | Jan. 87 Hu Yaobang purged, antibourgeois liberalism | | Oct. 87 13th Party Congress [Zhao Ziyang becomes general secretary, generational transfer of leadership] |
| 1988 | | | Summer 88 Erratic price movements, panic buying | | |
| 1989 | | | Jun. 89 Tiananmen Incident Zhao Ziyang purged, Jiang Zemin made general secretary | | |
| 1990 | | | | | Jan. 90 Martial law in Beijing lifted |
| 1991 | Eighth Five Year Plan | | Dec. 91 Soviet Union collapses | | |
| 1992 | | | | | 92 Promotion of reform and liberalization policy / Oct. 92 14th Party Congress liberalization policy |
| 1993 | | | | | Nov. 93 Third Plenum of 14th Party Congress Central Committee |

# 2

# The Population Explosion: An Intractable Problem

## The Chinese Population Pyramid

The fourth modern Chinese census was conducted on July 1, 1990. Previous censuses had been conducted in 1953, 1964, and 1982. The census result, based on a 10 percent sampling, was published in *Statistical Yearbook of China 1991*. The population pyramid described by the census (see Figure 2.1) has the following features:

*Generation born during the anti-Japanese war.* Previous censuses showed a significant compression of people who were born during this period. However, because this age cohort is already largely over fifty years old and natural deaths are increasing, it no longer exhibits the previous compression and simply appears not to have expanded compared with earlier cohorts.

*Bulge during the first five-year plan.* This was the postwar baby-boom period. Population grew rapidly after the end of the long war under conditions of political stability attending the establishment of a new nation and the rapid pace of economic reconstruction.

*Compression in the lower-middle range.* This was the period of "three continuous years of natural disasters" (actually manmade disasters) during and following the Great Leap Forward. Deaths from starvation were widespread, and the statistics indicate that newborns and weak persons succumbed in disproportionate numbers. On September 13, 1984, a spokesman for the China National Statistical Bureau admitted that "during the Great Leap period over ten million died of starvation brought about by human factors and natural disasters." Actually, the number is estimated to be several million more.

*Bulge during the Cultural Revolution.* After 1962 and through the first half of the Cultural Revolution, economic readjustment continued, and despite some politically inspired disorder, the birth rate climbed to a high level (the second baby

8

Figure 2.1  Population Pyramid from the 1990 Census
(10 percent sampling)

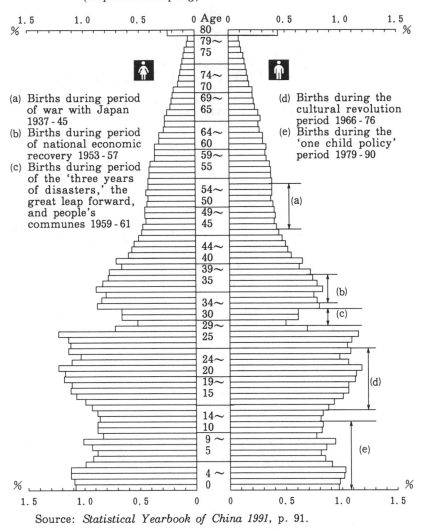

(a) Births during period
of war with Japan
1937-45
(b) Births during period
of national economic
recovery 1953-57
(c) Births during period
of the 'three years
of disasters,' the
great leap forward,
and people's
communes 1959-61

(d) Births during the
cultural revolution
period 1966-76
(e) Births during the
'one child policy'
period 1979-90

Source: *Statistical Yearbook of China 1991*, p. 91.

boom). In the second half of this period, the government introduced its birth restriction policy, and the effects of it started to become visible.

*Contraction resulting from the one-child policy.* In the first half of the Deng Xiaoping era that began in 1978, the government's one-child policy was vigorously implemented, and the population growth rate showed a remarkable decline. However, in the latter half of the 1980s, rural families whose first child was a girl were permitted to have a second child. Further, there was an increase in "black children" because some people disregarded the one-child policy (these children would not be included on the official register of members of the household). Thus, the government's policy of population restriction has been challenged. The principal reasons have been the enhanced prosperity of rural families and the heightened appreciation of the value of family labor in the countryside attending the introduction of the individual household responsibility system for agricultural production.

In the early 1980s the government adopted a plan to restrict the total population in the year 2000 to 1.2 billion. This plan apparently was later scrapped, and the actual target raised to 1.3 billion.

## Ma Yinchu's Warning Ignored

After the establishment of the PRC, an economist, Ma Yinchu, believing explosive population growth to be a crisis, began in the late 1950s to advocate a birth limitation policy (*People's Daily*, July 5, 1957, later Ma Yinchu 1979).

At the time, China was deep in the frenzy of the Great Leap Forward. Mao Zedong condemned Ma Yinchu as a "Malthusian." Mao's "mass line" theory maintained simplistically that every person has two hands and only one mouth, and a person's two hands can always produce enough to feed him. The possibilities of socialism were considered limitless, and consequently scarce resources were posited to present no constraints on economic growth. Furthermore, Mao Zedong believed that the outbreak of a nuclear World War III was possible, and that a consequence would be the deaths of about half of the Chinese population (comment to Prime Minister Nehru of India, October 19, 1954).

Figure 2.2 presents the growth of total population (rural and urban). From a base of 540 million in 1949, the Chinese population surpassed 600 million in 1954, 700 million in 1964, 800 million in 1969, 900 million in 1974, 1 billion in 1981, and 1.1 billion in 1988. By the end of 1992 it stood at 1.17 billion.

To construct a macro model of the increase in the PRC's population, we begin by sketching births: an annual average of 20 million during the 1950s (total 200 million), 25 million in the 1960s (total 250 million), 20 million in the 1970s (total 200 million), and 15 million in the 1980s (total 150 million), for an aggregate total of about 800 million births. From this we subtract deaths for a net increase of some 600 billion in forty years.

10

Figure 2.2   Overall Chinese Population Trends 1950 - 1992

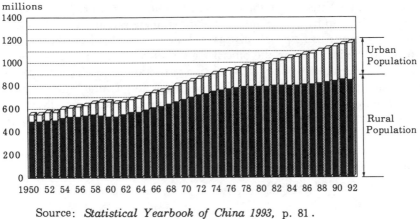

Source: *Statistical Yearbook of China 1993*, p. 81 .

Figure 2.3   Changes in Fertility, Mortality, and Rate of Natural
Increase (1949 - 1992)

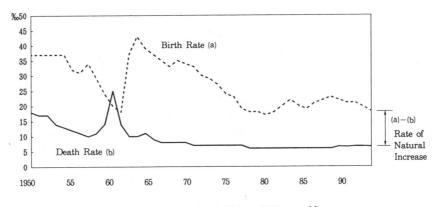

Source: *Statistical Yearbook of China 1993*, p. 82.

In Figure 2.3, which shows the natural population growth rate (birth rate minus death rate), we perceive four distinct phases. The first phase was 1949–1957, the first period of major population increase. The natural growth rate was at a high 2 percent per annum as the birth rate climbed and the death rate dropped sharply. The second phase, 1958 to 1961, was an abnormal period that included one year (1960) of negative growth resulting from economic crises and natural disasters. The third phase, 1962 to 1971, was the second period of substantial population growth. The birth rate rose, partly as a counteraction to the preceding period, and the death rate was stable. The result was a rate of natural increase as high as 3 percent per annum (this happens in the transition from a period of high births and high deaths to a period of low births and low deaths). The fourth phase, 1971 to 1990, was a period of stability at a low level of growth. The birth rate declined to the level prevailing in modern industrial countries.

It is generally accepted that with the advance of economic development, the tendency is for populations to move from a phase of high birth rates and high death rates to a period of low birth rates and low death rates. This was the case for China from 1950 to 1990, although perhaps its coercive population policy had the effect of compressing this process. However, during the 1980s, and particularly in the latter half of the decade, as the birth limitation policy was relaxed in the countryside, the overall population base increased and despite the limitation policy, the birth rate began an upward trend.

## Formulation of the One-Child Policy

The policy of birth limitation began in the late 1970s. In 1973, toward the end of the Mao Zedong era, the State Council Leading Group on Family Planning (birth limitation) was established, with Hua Guofeng as its head. Notwithstanding this move, the official line at the time remained antagonistic toward the concepts of population explosion and limits of economic growth. This could be seen in the statement of the Chinese delegate, Huang Shuze, at the Third United Nations World Population Conference (*Beijing Review*, no. 35, 1974).

However, the reality of a population explosion was becoming apparent to everyone by the mid-1970s, and soon thereafter the birth limitation policy was announced. In February 1978, Premier Hua Guofeng in his report on government activities to the National People's Congress announced the goal of "bringing down the rate of natural population increase to below 1 percent within three years." In the 1978 constitution ratified in March of that year, article 53 specified that "the state advocates and shall promote family planning." In June 1978, Vice Premier Chen Muhua was named head of the Leading Group for Family Planning under the State Council. The following January a meeting was convened of directors of national family planning offices. At this meeting, "the ideal family of a couple and one child" was strongly endorsed, and thus was born the one-child policy.

## The "Four-Two-One Syndrome"

The one-child policy was implemented relatively smoothly in the cities. This was related to the prevalence of couples both working outside the home, cramped living conditions, and the availability of a retirement pension for workers. In contrast, the policy encountered stiff resistance in the countryside. Traditional Chinese thinking that "four generations under one roof" (i.e., a big family) is the source of happiness and "the more sons, the more blessings" is deep-rooted. Illustration 2.1, "Happiness Fills the Entire Household" by Liu Jihou, aims to convey a message of family planning and is not intended to support the traditional attitude, but in effect it does perpetuate the large extended-family tradition.

In the countryside, the vicious cycle continues of bearing many children because of poverty and remaining in poverty under the burden of many children. Because a daughter leaves the house after marriage, peasants consider sons the

Illustration 2.1

sole source of support in old age. The desire for sons is almost desperate. People feel insecure with only one son and so want two or three. Moreover, under the household responsibility system of production (after the abandonment of the people's communes, individual households were given responsibility for production), even infants are more useful than cats (in some cases, they can be sold for a good price!). From the standpoint of the state, the population has already reached the saturation point, and birth limitation is a categorical imperative; to the peasants, however, children are support and sustenance now and in old age. It is a most complicated problem.

Prevailing in the urban areas of China now is a social malady known as the "four-two-one syndrome." This term denotes the various pathologies resulting from a family structure of four grandparents, two parents, and one child (see Illustration 2.2, "The Four-Two-One Pyramid" by Qiao Lin). The single children of indulgent parents are now the "little emperors." Illustration 2.3, "The Dragon Soars and the Tiger Leaps" by Wang Xiaolu, conveys these children's putative power. Is this not the same as the saying "hoping that the son becomes the emperor" (that the son achieves great success)?

## Population Forecast for the Year 2000

In making forecasts about population, researchers use the concept of "total fertility rate." This figure expresses the average number of children that a woman will

Illustration 2.2

Illustration 2.3

bear in her lifetime. A leading Chinese population researcher, Hu Angang (deputy researcher at the Research Center for Ecology and Environment, National Analysis Group, Academica Sinica), posited a number of cases in a comprehensive analysis published in 1989. His worst-case forecast was that population would reach 1.2 billion in 1994 and by 2000 would reach 1.26 billion at minimum and possibly exceed 1.3 billion, 100 million more than the goal of the Twelfth Party Congress set in 1982 (Hu Angang 1989, p. 59). The State Statistical Bureau announced in March 1994 that the Chinese population at the end of 1993 was 1.186 billion, an increase of 13.46 million over 1992. In the likely event that population increases in 1994 at a pace equal to that in 1992, the reality of China's population increase will exceed Hu Angang's worst-case prediction.

Table 2.1   Upward Revision of Total Population Figure
            Based on the 1990 Census   (in million)

| Year | Statistical Yearbook 1990 Edition | Statistical Yearbook 1991 Edition | Upward Revision |
|------|-----------------------------------|-----------------------------------|-----------------|
| 1981 | 1,000.7 | 1,000.7 | 0 |
| 1982 | 1,015.9 | 1,016.4 | 0.6 |
| 1983 | 1,027.6 | 1,030.1 | 2.4 |
| 1984 | 1,038.8 | 1,043.6 | 4.8 |
| 1985 | 1,051.4 | 1,058.5 | 8.1 |
| 1986 | 1,065.3 | 1,075.1 | 9.8 |
| 1987 | 1,080.7 | 1,093.0 | 12.3 |
| 1988 | 1,096.1 | 1,110.3 | 14.1 |
| 1989 | 1,111.9 | 1,127.0 | 15.1 |
| 1990 |         | 1,143.3 | 0 |

Note: The *Statistical Yearbook of China 1990* offered data
extrapolated from the 1980 census. The 1991 edition offered data
based on a 10 percent sampling of the 1990 census.
    Sources: *Statistical Yearbook of China 1990*, p. 89; and
*Statistical Yearbook of China 1991*, p. 79.

Another issue is the unregistered, hidden population ("black children"), as evidenced by Table 2.1. The *Statistical Yearbook of China* compiles official statistics. Before the 1990 census, *Statistical Yearbook* figures were based on the 1982 census, adjusted annually according to sample surveys to reach a total number. The population figures thus produced for the years 1981 to 1990 are the figures presented in the 1990 edition of *Statistical Yearbook*. The 1991 edition reflects the 1981 to 1990 figures readjusted based on a 10 percent random sampling of the 1990 census. There is a major problem with these numbers: the appearance of 150 million more people in the 1990 census numbers than in the aggregation of adjustments in the previous series. This disparity was remedied in *Statistical Yearbook 1991* by more or less equally adjusting upward the previous numbers for 1981 to 1989.

The upward revision obviously raises a question about the integrity of the statistics. But the more important issue is the unregistered, hidden population. The 1990 census managed to count and include in the statistics a part of the "black children." But it is believed that many more of them, perhaps numbering in the tens of millions, still escaped inclusion in the data.

Future issues concerning China's population were summarized by Hu Angang (1989) as follows:

- If the current rate of growth continues over the next 50 to 60 years, the basics of clothing, food, and shelter and such things as education, entertainment, and cultural activities will have to be assured for at least an additional 1.5 billion people;
- Over the next 30 to 40 years, work opportunities will have to be provided for some 300 million new entrants to the workforce;

- Over the next 20 to 30 years, work opportunities will need to be provided for 800 million workers;
- Over the next 50 to 60 years, social security support will need to be provided for 300 million old people;
- Over the next 50 to 60 years, basic commodities and foodstuffs and infrastructure will need to be provided to 700 to 800 million new urban residents; alternatively, measures will be necessary to hold down the increase;
- Over the next 20 to 30 years, it will be necessary to educate to basic literacy and raise the cultural level of over 200 million illiterate persons.

Figure 2.4 presents the population forecast (median forecast) of the United Nations Population Fund as compiled in *The World Population Report 1992*; China's share of global population is forecast to decline from 21.5 percent to 17.8 percent by 2025.

Figure 2.4   United Nations Projection for Global and Chinese Population Increase (median projection)

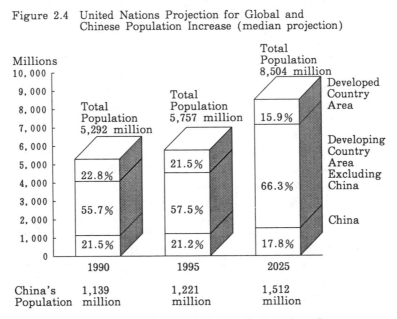

Note: Developed countries include North America, Japan, Europe, Australia, New Zealand, and the former Soviet Union. Developing countries include all Africa, Central and South America, all Asia (excluding Japan, Melanesia, Micronesia and Polynesia)

Source: U.N. Population Fund, *World Population Report 1992*.

# 3

# The Economic Consequences
# of Changing Political Tides

## Chinese Concepts of Output and Income

In January 1980 Deng Xiaoping said, "If by the end of the century we can achieve a GNP per capita of US$1,000, we will have become well off." At the time, China's per capita GNP (gross national product), measured in terms of Chinese currency renminbi (RMB), was estimated to be the equivalent of about $250 at the prevailing RMB/U.S. dollar rate. Thus he was envisioning a fourfold increase. Moreover, this was the first official use of the term "GNP" by a Chinese leader since the founding of the PRC. The use of international economic terminology was an indication that a policy of liberalization had been set.

To approximate the Western concept of GNP, the Chinese use the term "gross value of industrial and agricultural production" (GVIAO). This concept expresses the value of goods produced in five sectors—agriculture, industry, construction, transportation, and commerce. The difference between GVIAO and GNP is shown in Figure 3.1.

- GVIAO does not include culture, education, health, scientific research, defense, government administration, and other service activities (nongoods-producing sectors). These sectors are included in GNP.
- In GVIAO, for the five goods-producing sectors, the value of intermediate goods consumed in the production process, such as raw materials, fuel, and power (so-called transferred value), is included and thus double-counted with final goods. GNP does not include intermediate goods.
- Depreciation expense for fixed capital is calculated in GVIAO and GNP.

In other words, GVIAO is the total crude value of production from the sectors producing material goods. Subtracting from GVIAO the values of raw materials,

Figure 3.1  The Relationship Between Gross Value of Industrial and
Agricultural Output, GNP and National Income

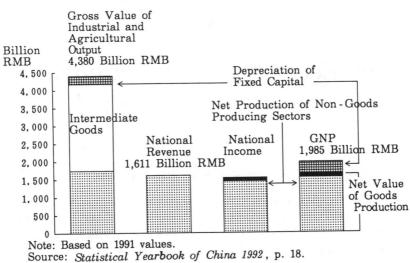

Note: Based on 1991 values.
Source: *Statistical Yearbook of China 1992*, p. 18.

Figure 3.2  Changes in Gross Value of Industrial and Agricultural
Output and National Income (1952-1992)

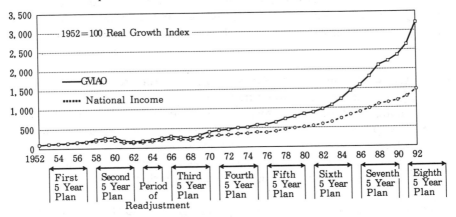

Source: *Statistical Yearbook of China 1993*, pp. 34, 51.

fuel, and power, as well as depreciation of fixed capital assets, gives "net production value." The Chinese concept of national income is net production value for a certain time period. The formula for converting Chinese national income to Western GNP is

GNP = Chinese national income + (a) + (b)

where (a) is the net value of production from nongoods-producing sectors and (b) is depreciation expense for fixed capital assets. Figure 3.2 presents GVIAO and national income with 1952 given the index value of 100 (constant values).

From the seventh five-year plan, China began to express target values in terms of GNP. However, it has not yet adopted the Western system of national accounts (SNA) method of accounting for national income as a complement to its material products system (MPS). China has indicated its intention to introduce the SNA method fully by 1995.

## Variations in Growth Rates for National Income

Figure 3.3 presents growth rates versus the previous year for national income and for its principal constituent elements, national agricultural income and national industrial income. Immediately evident from the figure is that in the process of growth, China's economy experienced two great depressions from which it later recovered. The first depression, from 1959 to 1961, was brought about by the policies of the Great Leap Forward; the second, from 1966 to 1967, was the product of the "rebellion and usurpation struggle" of the Cultural Revolution.

Let us look first at the growth of national agricultural income. The land reform of the early 1950s at first stirred the productive energies of the peasants, but soon this effect was lost. The collectivization of agriculture followed in 1955, but soon the limits of this policy also became evident. Then in 1958 and 1959 came the great experiment with the people's communes, which ended in devastating failure and led to drastic declines in production in 1959 and 1960. As previously noted, this series of failures can be said to be the product of utopian socialism.

Policy failures coupled with three years of natural disasters plunged the country into a food crisis, and an estimated 15 million persons died of starvation. Recovery followed a period of readjustment, but soon the influence of the struggles of the Cultural Revolution was felt. In the 1970s, growth declined markedly in the years 1971 and 1976. In the 1980s, agricultural production showed robust growth after the introduction of the agricultural production responsibility system.

Overall, the growth rate of national industrial income exceeded that of agriculture. However, particularly noticeable in Figure 3.3 is abnormal growth during the Great Leap Forward, then a sharp decline. Thereafter came recovery during the period of readjustment and then sharp declines attending the Cultural Revolution struggles. In the recovery that followed, there were deleterious effects on production of political incidents such as the ill-fated escape attempt of Lin Biao. In the

Figure 3.3   Vicissitudes in Growth Rates vs. Previous Year of
National Income and National Agricultural and
Industrial Income   (1953 - 1992)

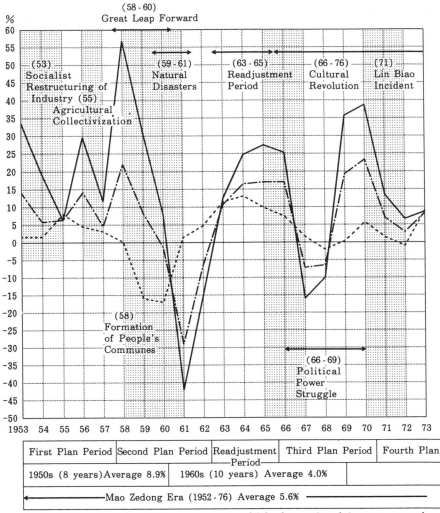

Note: Shaded areas indicate years in which the national income growth
rate fell.
Source: *Statistical Yearbook of China 1993*, p. 35.

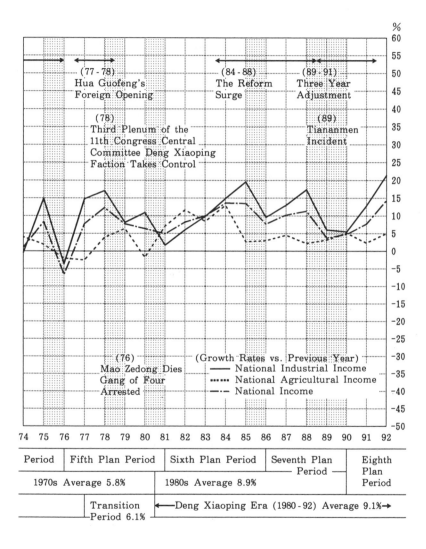

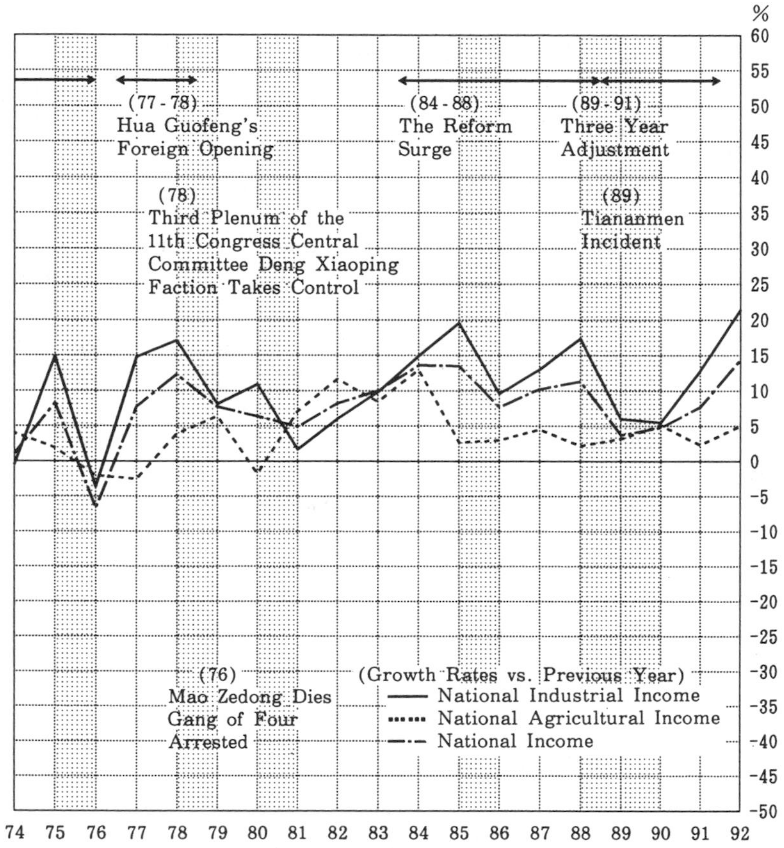
%
60
55
50
45
40
35
30
25
20
15
10
5
0
-5
-10
-15
-20
-25
-30
-35
-40
-45
-50
(77 - 78)
Hua Guofeng's
Foreign Opening
(84 - 88)
The Reform
Surge
(89 - 91)
Three Year
Adjustment
(78)
Third Plenum of the
11th Congress Central
Committee Deng Xiaoping
Faction Takes Control
(89)
Tiananmen
Incident
(76)
Mao Zedong Dies
Gang of Four
Arrested
(Growth Rates vs. Previous Year)
National Industrial Income
National Agricultural Income
National Income
74 75 76 77 78 79 80 81 82 83 84 85 86 87 88 89 90 91 92

| Period | Fifth Plan Period | Sixth Plan Period | Seventh Plan Period | Eighth Plan Period |
|---|---|---|---|---|
| 1970s Average 5.8% | | 1980s Average 8.9% | | |
| | Transition Period 6.1% | ←Deng Xiaoping Era (1980 - 92) Average 9.1%→ | | |

1970s both industry and agriculture achieved a relatively finely modulated stability. The two peaks in the 1985 to 1988 period evidence the stimulative effects of the "Leap Forward of Reform."

The relationship between agriculture and industry had a discernible pattern in the 1950s: Changes in agriculture were felt a year later in industry. For example, the decline in agricultural growth in 1952 to 1953 was mirrored by decline in industrial growth in 1953 to 1954. This clearly suggests that industrial growth was constrained by the growth of agriculture because of, inter alia, the reliance of industry, especially light industry, on agriculture for raw materials and the constraint that lagging food production exercised in growth in the industrial worker population. In this sense, the primary factor behind significant year-to-year economic fluctuations has been agriculture's low productivity and susceptibility to effects of weather.

The second factor has been shifts in government policy. The disruption of the economy due to government policy (e.g., the Great Leap Forward and its collapse, the turmoil of the Cultural Revolution) is clearly evident. The Great Leap Forward—Mao Zedong's pursuit of a Chinese brand of socialist construction as an alternative to the Soviet socialist model that he was denouncing—produced tragically devastating results. Living conditions of material backwardness and deprivation have intensified the desire of modern China's leadership for wealth and prosperity. But this focus has tended to give rise to policy drives emphasizing "subjective activism," which have led to absolutism and extremism and invited a backlash. The Cultural Revolution had a dual character: the effort to reassert the premises of the Great Leap Forward and the construction of strategic bases in preparation for a third world war (the "third-front defense base" construction strategy). The military bias in the policy line sanctioned keeping the living standard of the people at a low level.

## Chinese Business Cycles

It is well known that there are cycles of capital investment in capitalist economies. Normally occurring in seven- to eight-year periods, they are called Juglar cycles after the Frenchman, Joseph Clement Juglar (1879–1905), who identified them. Because the economic lives of machinery and equipment average around ten years, the need to replace them gives rise to fluctuations in capital investment.

Figure 3.4 presents an approximation of cycles of fixed asset investment in the case of China. Definite cycles appear for increases or decreases versus the previous year in fixed asset investment (state-owned sector only, historical values). Specifically, these were the first cycle of five years, 1953–1957; the second cycle of five years, 1958–1962; the third cycle of six years, 1963–1968; the fourth cycle of four years, 1969–1972; the fifth cycle of four years, 1973–1976; the sixth cycle of five years, 1977–1981; and the seventh cycle of eight years, 1982–1989.

Figure 3.4  Cycles of Capital Investment (1952-1991)

Bar graph presents value of fixed capital investment of state-owned sector at historical prices (billion RMB). Line graph presents rate of growth vs. previous year (percent).

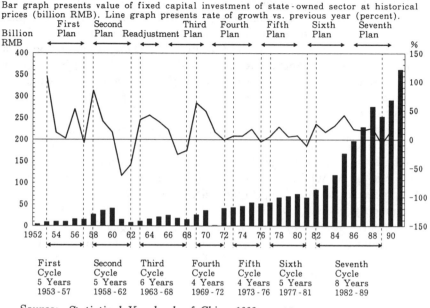

Source: *Statistical Yearbook of China 1992*, p. 145.

Figure 3.5  The Share of the State-Owned Sector in Total Fixed Capital Investment (1982-1991)

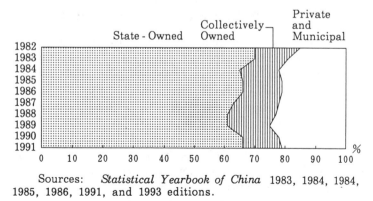

Sources: *Statistical Yearbook of China* 1983, 1984, 1984, 1985, 1986, 1991, and 1993 editions.

Most cycles lasted four to five years. The most conspicuous exception was the seventh cycle of eight years, a duration related to the decline in the proportionate share of the state-owned sector; see Figure 3.5. Furthermore, except for the third and fourth cycles—from the interval from the readjustment period through the early period of the Cultural Revolution—the cycles fairly well track five-year plan periods. From this one observes that Chinese capital investment cycles are in essence planned equipment cycles based on five-year plans. By the midpoint in a plan period, budget expenditures reach peak levels, and soon the economy begins to overheat. Shortages appear in such basic construction materials as cement and steel, and internal competition for resources places a brake on economic expansion.

Research in China on economic cycles made its appearance in 1992 in the work of Lu Jian (1992). Table 3.1 presents the six cycles (average 6.7 years) Lu Jian detected based on a methodology of plotting the three-year moving average of the growth rate of GVIAO (Figure 3.6). From this he reached conclusions diametrically opposed to the prevailing (Communist Party) view that "economic cycles are common phenomena which transcend systems and levels of development" (Institute of Political Economy 1954). Rather, he observed that China's highly centralized planned economy experienced much greater economic volatility than Western economies in the same periods. This was because the West had implemented successful countercyclical policies, but China lacked such economic policies. Based on this finding, Lu advocated that China develop policies in response to the economic cycles: In a period of economic expansion, measures such as reform of the labor employment system and enforcement of bankruptcy legislation (to close down insolvent businesses) should be implemented; in a period of economic contraction, price reforms should be implemented. He warned that getting this wrong could lead to disproportionate, severe economic fluctuations.

## Periods of Economic Construction

Figure 3.7 presents the growth rate in the value of industrial and agricultural production during the period of each five-year plan; Figure 3.8 makes the same presentation for the growth of light and heavy industry. Table 3.2 presents growth in the national income; Table 3.3 shows the rate of growth for per capita national income. The following discussion summarizes the distinctive features of each period of economic construction in the nearly forty-five years since the establishment of the PRC:

*Economic recovery (1949–1952).* This was a period of over three years of revival and rehabilitation for the Chinese economy following the end of the Chinese civil war (1946 to 1949) and the anti-Japanese war (1937 to 1945). The economy had suffered severe damage during these war periods, but recovery to prewar levels was generally achieved by the end of 1952.

Table 3.1  Chinese Economic Cycles According to the Analysis
        of Lu Jian

| Cycle | Period | Duration | Period of Economic Recession | Period of Economic Growth |
|---|---|---|---|---|
| First Cycle | 1950~1956 | 6 years | (5 years | 1 years) |
| Second Cycle | 1956~1961 | 5 years | (4 years | 1 years) |
| Third Cycle | 1961~1967 | 6 years | (2 years | 4 years) |
| Fourth Cycle | 1967~1975 | 8 years | (5 years | 3 years) |
| Fifth Cycle | 1975~1980 | 5 years | (2 years | 3 years) |
| Sixth Cycle | 1980~1990 | 10 years | (6 years | 4 years) |

Source: Lu Jian, *Positive Research on China's Economic Cycles*
(Beijing: Chinese Financial and Economic Press, 1992) .

Figure 3.6  Cycles of Gross Value of Industrial and Agricultural
        Output and Capital Investment

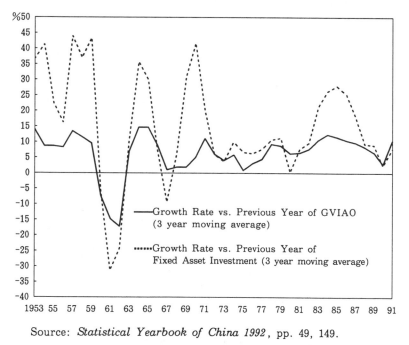

Source: *Statistical Yearbook of China 1992*, pp. 49, 149.

26

Figure 3.7  Changes in Average Annual Growth Rates for Agricultural and
Industrial Output in Successive Five Year Plan Periods

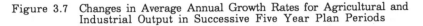

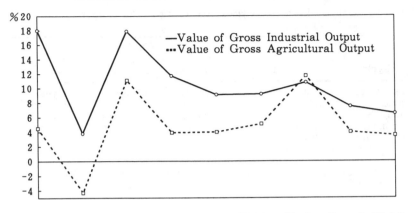

First      Second     Period    Third    Fourth   Fifth    Sixth    Seventh  Eighth
5 Year   5 Year   of Read-  5 Year   5 Year   5 Year   5 Year   5 Year   5 Year
Plan       Plan      justment  Plan     Plan     Plan     Plan     Plan     Plan

Sources: *Statistical Yearbook of China 1991*, p. 56 and
The National Ten Year Plan and "Eight Five" Plan.

Figure 3.8  Changes in Average Annual Growth Rates for Light and
Heavy Industrial Output in Successive Five Year
Plan Periods

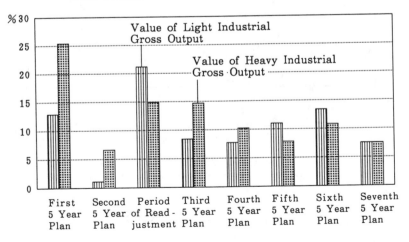

First      Second     Period    Third    Fourth   Fifth    Sixth    Seventh
5 Year   5 Year   of Read-  5 Year   5 Year   5 Year   5 Year   5 Year
Plan       Plan      justment  Plan     Plan     Plan     Plan     Plan

Source: *Statistical Yearbook of China 1991*, p. 56.

Table 3.2  Real Rates of Growth in National Income by Period
(annual percentage rate)

| Five Year Plan Periods | Real Rate of Growth of National Income | of which | | | | |
|---|---|---|---|---|---|---|
| | | Agriculture | Industry | Construction | Transportation | Commerce |
| 53~57 First Plan Period | 8.9 | 3.7 | 19.6 | 19.4 | 12.0 | 8.0 |
| 58~62 Second Plan Period | -3.1 | -5.9 | 1.8 | -7.8 | -0.5 | -4.3 |
| 63~65 Readjustment | 14.7 | 11.5 | 21.3 | 20.9 | 15.1 | 2.8 |
| 66~70 Third Plan Period | 8.3 | 2.6 | 12.6 | 8.0 | 5.6 | 9.2 |
| 71~75 Fourth Plan Period | 5.5 | 3.0 | 8.5 | 5.2 | 5.3 | 2.1 |
| 76~80 Fifth Plan Period | 6.1 | 0.7 | 9.2 | 6.9 | 5.6 | 7.6 |
| 81~85 Sixth Plan Period | 10.0 | 8.5 | 10.2 | 11.6 | 11.9 | 13.2 |
| 86~90 Seventh Plan Period | 7.5 | 4.1 | 10.2 | 5.6 | 9.4 | 2.9 |
| 1953~92 40 years since founding | 7.0 | 3.1 | 11.3 | 8.3 | 7.6 | 5.2 |
| 1979~92 Deng Xiaoping Era | 8.8 | 5.3 | 11.1 | 10.9 | 9.3 | 6.8 |

Source: *Statistical Yearbook of China 1993*, p. 35.

Table 3.3  The Real Growth Rate in National Income and
the Population Growth Rate (annual percentage rate)

| Period | Real National Income Growth Rate | Population Increase | Per Capita Growth Rate |
|---|---|---|---|
| 1953~60 | 9.0 | 1.8 | 7.2 |
| 1961~70 | 4.0 | 2.3 | 1.7 |
| 1971~80 | 5.8 | 1.7 | 4.1 |
| 1981~90 | 8.7 | 1.5 | 7.2 |
| 1953~92 | 7.0 | 1.8 | 5.2 |

Source: For economic growth rate *Statistical Yearbook of China 1993*, p. 35; for population growth rate, p. 81.

*The first five-year plan (1953–1957).* Collectivization of agriculture commenced, and the socialist transformation of private industrial and commercial enterprises was pushed forward. Further, the planned economy model of the Soviet Union was adopted, and a centralized economic planning system was established. The rate of economic growth (real rate of growth of national income) for the period was 8.9 percent per annum, with industry and agriculture growing at highly commendable rates of 19.6 percent and 3.7 percent, respectively.

*The second five-year plan (1958–1962).* The Great Leap Forward was launched. The aim was to "catch up with and surpass England in fifteen years" in steel production. In the countryside, the movement to create the people's communes was unleashed. In 1958 and 1959 production appeared to make great advances, but this was due in part to bogus reporting. In 1960 and 1961 the country plunged into economic crisis. Inclement weather and the abrupt termination of Soviet assistance accompanying heightened tensions in Sino-Soviet relations were contributing factors in the crisis, but the fundamental cause was the disastrous consequences of mass movements that totally disregarded economic principles.

*Readjustment (1963–1965).* As the collapse of the Great Leap Forward led to economic crises in which some 15 million persons died of starvation, the five-year plan was abandoned, and the Chinese economy was forced to readjust itself. In the countryside, the level of distribution (accounting unit) for the harvest of the people's communes was lowered to the "production team" (old village) level in order to revive the peasants' motivation to work. Construction work on industrial projects was halted in order to concentrate on production.

*The third five-year plan (1966–1970).* Liberalization of economic policies during the readjustment period resulted in recovery of production in the countryside. However, there also appeared a tendency toward polarization among the peasantry (an obvious gap opened between rich peasants whose wealth was rapidly increasing and poor peasants falling deeper into poverty). Mao Zedong, who harbored a crisis mentality with regard to reported incidences of black market trading and "exploitation" of poor peasants by rich peasants, judged that China was changing into a "revisionist society." At the same time as the Sino-Soviet dispute was escalating into a split, Mao Zedong vilified Liu Shaoqi, Deng Xiaoping, and other first-line members of the party leadership as "bosses walking the capitalist road" and "Chinese revisionists" and launched the Cultural Revolution. Although there ensued a certain amount of turmoil in the economy, the annual economic growth rate fell only slightly to 8.3 percent.

*The fourth five-year plan (1971–1975).* In the early 1970s the Cultural Revolution was for a time subdued, and Zhou Enlai among others set about improving relations with the United States and Japan. Indications of stabilization in the economy were also present. However, the "Gang of Four" (Jiang Qing, Wang Hongwen, Zhang Chunqiao, Yao Wenyuan), opposing the revisionist line taken by Zhou Enlai, sought to seize power by reigniting the spirit of the Cultural Revolution. Against this, an enfeebled Mao Zedong wavered between the two camps, and all the political upheaval had a negative effect on economic development.

*The fifth five-year plan (1976–1980).* Hua Guofeng, assuming the position of party chairman upon the death of Mao Zedong in 1976, pledged to uphold the Mao Zedong line. However, after the Third Plenum of the Chinese Communist Party's Eleventh Congress in December 1978, Deng Xiaoping seized leadership of the "Party Central." ("Party Central" [*dang zhongyang*] is a term used ubiquitously in Chinese materials. It is meant to encompass and convey the meaning of the top leadership organs of the Chinese Communist Party, including organs controlling the civilian government and the PLA.) This plan period was the latter half of the ten-year Cultural Revolution; it was also the transition period from the Mao Zedong era to the Deng Xiaoping era.

*The sixth five-year plan (1981–1985).* This was the first half of the "ten years of reform and liberalization" guided by Deng Xiaoping. In the countryside, peasant motivation to increase production was greatly enhanced by expansion of the system of allowing individual peasant households to take responsibility for production. As a result, in 1984 grain production for the first time in history exceeded

400 million tons. In industry, experimentation in economic reform was carried out in cities as well. Thus, through reform the Chinese economy began to revitalize itself.

*The seventh five-year plan (1986–1990).* This was the second half of Deng's reform and liberalization program. The fall 1984 "Decision on Reform of the Economic System" established the policy of liberalization and set the economy on a high-growth track. Thereafter economic reform proceeded apace in the cities and in industry, and by 1988 the economy had overheated, manifesting double-digit inflation. Panic buying and runs on banks occurred. In response, in fall 1988 the government decided to shelve reform temporarily and to implement economic adjustment measures. Notwithstanding this, by 1989 inflation had not been brought under control. On the pretext of the sudden death of the party's previous first secretary, Hu Yaobang, a democratization movement led by students and intellectuals arose. It was suppressed by the authorities through mobilization of the People's Liberation Army. There ensued a political tightening and a parallel "rectification" on the economic front. Policy revisions aimed to curb excessive economic reforms were implemented, and in consequence growth declined from 11.3 percent in 1988 to 4.4 percent in 1989 and to 4.1 percent in 1990 (see Table 3.2).

*Summary.* In the more than forty years of the PRC economy, extremist political agitation—not confined to the mass mobilization movements of the Great Leap Forward, the people's communes, and the Cultural Revolution—has exercised enormous influence on economic construction; the result has been wide fluctuations in growth. Moreover, in this period the population explosion has occurred, and much of economic growth has been offset by the increase in population. As shown in Table 3.3, during the 1950s and 1980s, the per capita growth rate was maintained at over 7 percent. But this was only because the actual growth rate during these two periods was about 9 percent. In contrast, the difference between economic growth rates and population growth rates in the 1960s and 1970s was under 4.1 percent. The average economic growth rate over the PRC's forty-plus years is 7.0 percent. The population growth rate is just under 2 percent, so the per capita growth rate is about 5 percent. To reiterate, notwithstanding that real growth was depressed to 4 percent as a consequence of the collapse of the Great Leap Forward in the 1960s and the Cultural Revolution, one of the greatest failures of the Mao Zedong era was the explosive increase in population.

# 4

# Obstacles to Reform in China's Planned Economy

## "The Superiority of the Socialist Economy"

In the 1950s China imported the Soviet Union's system of economic planning. In such a system, called a centralized planned economy or a command economy, the fundamental tenet is that all economic activities should be removed from the "commodity economy" (where market principles prevail); all activities, from material goods production through final distribution, are undertaken according to and included in the plan. Whereas in a capitalist economy adjustment is accomplished by the market after the fact, a planned economy seeks to accomplish adjustment before the fact through planning. Because such prior adjustment is presumed to be more efficient, claims are made of "the superiority of the socialist economy."

In a capitalist economy (market economy), resource distribution is accomplished through economic activity carried on by individuals, families, and enterprises making decisions individually and freely. In a command economy, the plan takes over all these activities and functions. Some persons have maintained that advanced computer technology could make processing this information possible. However, it has been proved empirically through failed experiments that the state is unable to aggregate and process all the information disseminated by the market.

## Managing Resources in a Planned Economy

Before the economic reforms of the 1980s, China managed resources by drawing a sharp distinction between resources used in production, on the one hand, and resources used in consumption, on the other. The former were termed "materials" and the latter "commodities." Materials were divided into three categories depending upon their importance, as follows:

1. *Centrally controlled materials.* These were materials of primary importance to the national economy, such as steel, nonferrous metal raw materials and products, lumber, cement, coal, petroleum, rubber, sulfuric acid, caustic soda, trucks, and machine tools. For these materials a detailed materials balance and input-output allocation plan would be drafted by the State Materials Bureau (currently the Ministry of Materials and Equipment) under the direction of the State Planning Commission. After this "directive plan" received State Council approval, it would be issued by the State Planning Commission.

2. *Ministry-managed materials.* These were materials of critical importance as inputs for the centrally controlled materials. The balanced distribution of these materials was the responsibility of the relevant ministries under the State Council. For example, responsibility for textile machinery and equipment lay with the Ministry of Textiles; for coking coal and iron alloys, the Ministry of Metallurgy. When enterprises or provinces had need of these resources, they had to apply to the ministries for an allocation (see Figure 4.1).

3. *Category 3 materials (those not included in categories 1 or 2).* This group encompassed construction materials such as bricks, tiles, ash, sand, and stone; machinery and electrical equipment such as small-scale machinery, electrical tools, measuring instruments, parts, and tools; chemical industrial products such as dyes, medicinal raw materials, cosmetics, and rubber products; metallic raw materials such as crude copper, waste aluminum, and raw nonferrous metal ores. This category included a multitude of materials produced in widely dispersed areas. Most were produced and used locally (*Contemporary Chinese Economic Management,* 1985, p. 290).

In September 1984 the State Council approved "Some Temporary Decisions on Improving the Planning System" drafted by the State Planning Commission. Management of materials under the plan was modified as follows:

1.  A system of state-directed "planned allocation" was implemented for a portion of the important materials. Centrally allocated materials were again designated to include coal, petroleum, steel, nonferrous metals, lumber, cement, basic chemical raw materials, and important electrical products. They would be allocated under a "directive plan" (a sample plan for steel appears in Table 4.1).

2.  The directive plan would still govern allocation of important industrial products, but enterprises would also be permitted—after consideration of supplies of materials, energy availability, and market demand—to take the initiative to produce and trade the goods subject to the directive plan.

3.  Goods outside the state plan would be subject to regulation through the market mechanism, and enterprises were free to produce and trade them.

Figure 4.1 Vicissitudes of Centralization and Decentralization of Management of Key Materials

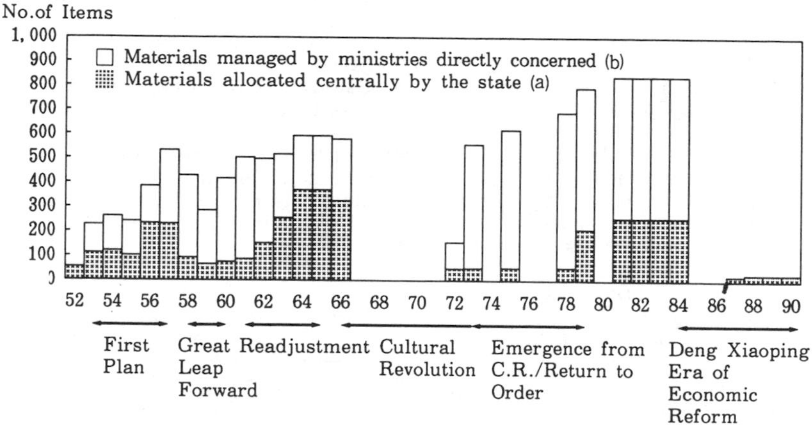
No.of Items
1, 000
900
800
700
600
500
400
300
200
100
0
Materials managed by ministries directly concerned (b)
Materials allocated centrally by the state (a)
52 54 56 58 60 62 64 66 68 70 72 74 76 78 80 82 84 86 88 90
First Plan
Great Leap Forward
Readjustment
Cultural Revolution
Emergence from C.R./Return to Order
Deng Xiaoping Era of Economic Reform

| | Number of Centrally Allocated Materials (a) | Number of Materials Managed by Concerned Ministries (b) | (a)+(b) | | Number of Centrally Allocated Materials (a) | Number of Materials Managed by Concerned Ministries (b) | (a)+(b) |
|---|---|---|---|---|---|---|---|
| 1952 | 55 | | | 1972 | 49 | 168 | 217 |
| 1953 | 112 | 115 | 227 | 1973 | 50 | 567 | 617 |
| 1954 | 121 | 140 | 261 | 1974 | — | — | — |
| 1955 | 162 | 139 | 301 | 1975 | 52 | 565 | 617 |
| 1956 | 234 | 151 | 385 | 1976 | — | — | — |
| 1957 | 231 | 301 | 532 | 1977 | — | — | — |
| 1958 | 93 | 336 | 429 | 1978 | 53 | 636 | 689 |
| 1959 | 67 | 218 | 285 | 1979 | 210 | 581 | 791 |
| 1960 | 75 | 342 | 417 | 1980 | — | — | — |
| 1961 | 87 | 416 | 503 | 1981 | 256 | 581 | 837 |
| 1962 | 153 | 345 | 498 | 1982 | 256 | 581 | 837 |
| 1963 | 256 | 260 | 516 | 1983 | 256 | 581 | 837 |
| 1964 | 370 | 222 | 592 | 1984 | 256 | 581 | 837 |
| 1965 | 370 | 222 | 592 | 1985 | — | — | — |
| 1966 | 326 | 253 | 579 | 1986 | — | — | — |
| 1967 | — | — | — | 1987 | 26 | — | — |
| 1968 | — | — | — | 1988 | 26 | — | — |
| 1969 | — | — | — | 1989 | 26 | — | — |
| 1970 | — | — | — | 1990 | 26 | — | — |
| 1971 | — | — | — | | | | |

Sources: 1952-86 *Contemporary Chinese Economic Management* (Beijing: Chinese Social Sciences Press, 1985), p. 291; 1987 and after *Economic Encyclopedia-Planning*· (Shanghai: Shanghai Dictionary Publishing Co., August 1990), p. 144.

Table 4.1  Comprehensive Materials Planning

| | |
|---|---|
| [Applied for Four Types of Materials: Steel, Timber, Cement, Coal] | |
| Example: Items for Steel Materials | |
| 1. Gross Resources Account | (3) Production repair |
| (1) State distribution | (4) Expenditure - science & technology |
| (2) Regional enterprise production | (5) Metal products and packaging |
| (3) Steel from key steel mills withheld by regions | (6) Machinery manufacturing |
| (4) Scrap iron | (7) Fixed asset investment |
| (5) Inventory utilization | (8) Geological investigation |
| (6) Sourcing from affiliated factories | (9) Production repairs for defense industries |
| (7) Steel purchased for re-sale | (10) Exports and foreign aid |
| (8) Materials imported by regions with foreign currency | (11) Out-sourcing by affiliates |
| (9) Processing on consignment | (12) Materials returned from processing |
| (10) Other | (13) Increase in inventory |
| 2. Consumption (Demand) Account | (14) Other |
| (1) Agriculture | Attachment: Inventory At Year Start |
| (2) Light industrial market | Inventory At Year End |

Source: *Compendium of Regulations of the Plan of the PRC 1986-1987* (Beijing: Chinese Financial and Economic Press, 1989), pp. 15-16.

In 1984, about two-thirds of gross production of steel products, half of coal production, and about 30 percent of cement were subject to central allocation under the state plan. Centrally allocated materials were produced in state-owned large enterprises, called "unified enterprises." Plans for allocation of materials coming under directive plans were drawn up according to the following procedures. First, the state would hand down unified numerical targets representing annual production tasks. At the levels of the ministries and agencies under the State Council and of each province, the targets were specifically assigned among basic units (factories). The basic units applied to their main management department for the materials needed to complete the production tasks. The main management department compiled this information and produced a draft plan, which was reviewed by the State Planning Commission. Adjustments were made at the level of each province, at the ministries and agencies under the State Council, and at the State Planning Commission through measures to increase production or imports of materials in short supply, and to increase use or exports of materials in excess supply or limit their production. Finally, a draft materials allocation plan would be adopted by the State Planning Commission and implemented after approval by the State Council. This plan comprised only the aggregate allocation targets of the ministries and agencies under the State Council and of the provinces (at a provincial level of aggregation). Actual allocations to the basic units were effected later at the ministry, agency, and provincial levels (*Contemporary Chinese Economic Management*, pp. 292–293).

*Categories 1, 2, and 3 Commodities.* Consumer goods, called "commodities," were managed separately from industrial materials and separated into three categories. In Category 1 were 38 items, including grain, edible oils, raw cotton, cotton yarn, tobacco, and processed sugar (categories in 1959). Items in this category came under State Council management with actual work assumed by relevant ministries. Category 2 commodities comprised 293 items, including jute, ramie, tea, slaughter hogs, eggs, cocoons, chemical fertilizer, herbicides, and bicycles (categories in 1959), managed by various ministries. Category 3 commodities were goods not in the other two categories. These commodities were large in number but small in importance; management was left to the provinces. It increasingly became the policy to monitor demand and supply conditions for these commodities, and, according to circumstances, to remove them from the direct allocation plan.

## Enterprise Organization in China

State-owned enterprises, the foundation of the planned economic system, are like gears in the national economic machine. In relation to the totality of a particular industry, any individual enterprise is only one component of the whole mechanism. In the framework of a planned economy, each enterprise is expected to modulate its activities so as to mesh with other gears in the system. Independent initiative is neither expected nor welcomed and is in any event made virtually impossible.

In the case of state-owned industries, raw materials are allocated through the Ministry of Materials and Equipment under the State Council. All products are bought by the Ministry of Commerce (in the case of consumer goods) or the Ministry of Materials and Equipment (in the case of goods used in production). It follows that management effort has not been required in state-owned enterprises, and that there is little appreciation of competition among enterprises.

The Chinese economic model was nurtured in the "liberated areas" (guerrilla bases) during wartime, and as a consequence, self-reliance came to assume a high priority. Thus the emphasis in enterprises has been on production from parts to final assembly, or "one unit-ism" (producing the entire production in one place). The slogan "small and complete, large and complete" means that each enterprise, regardless of size, would produce all parts on-site, so that production could be carried on independently.

Theoretical support for "one unit-ism" has been provided by the one-unit approach on the battlefield and by the reality that enterprises and society are closely knit. When a large enterprise is established, it often forms subsidiaries to provide nurseries, schools (kindergartens all the way to universities), hospitals, and stores for its workers. The reason (if we are not to attribute everything to the self-sufficiency policy of the guerrilla period) has been to give employees adrift in a society of deprivation a secure environment in which to work. This approach to solving social problems bears a close resemblance to the self-reliant supply of products.

The battlefield mentality of assuming full responsibility for workers' basic societal needs has made modernization difficult, if not impossible. Enterprises have begun to see the need to cut back or spin off these service departments in order to reduce the cost of administration. However, such a move is not feasible unless local governments are prepared to take the services over. Thus, China's "one unitism" ultimately has served as a shackle on modernization.

The presence of Communist Party organs within enterprises also was an impediment to improvement. Under the planned economy system, the party secretary within the enterprises had ultimate authority to manage production, personnel, and finances. (Labor resources were also allocated; see Table 4.2). However, after enterprise reform, the factory manager was accorded substantial responsibilities, and the role of the party secretary was dramatically reduced (see Figure 4.2 [3]).

After the Tiananmen incident of June 1989, a tendency to enhance the role of the party secretary was again observable. The position of the factory manager was substantially eroded in the Enterprises Law, to the extent that the party secretary was even given authority to dismiss him (see Figure 4.2 [4]). There were cases of party secretaries impeding reforms being pushed by enthusiastic, reform-minded factory managers. However, since Deng Xiaoping's talks in spring 1992, enterprise reform has once again come to the fore.

## "Third-Front" Construction

A major factor that severely distorted the Chinese planned economy, apart from the irrationality of economic planning, was the war-economy mentality of the leadership. During the Cultural Revolution, fears of war with the United States and with the Soviet Union were prevalent, which caused additional emphasis to be placed on self-reliance. The concept of defensive "third-front" construction informed the strategy of self-reliance in this period. According to the strategic division of the country at the time, the coastal regions and the northeast region were called the first front; the interior areas of the southwest and northwest (excepting

Table 4.2   Proposed Allocation Program for Labor Resources of Cities and Rural Areas

| | |
|---|---|
| 1. Total Labor Resources | Finance, insurance |
| 2. Labor Resource Allocation | State organs, social organizations |
| (a) Social labor force | Others |
| Agricultural, forestry, animal husbandry, | (b) Urban residents awaiting assignments |
| Fishing, water supply sectors | (c) Other labor resources |
| Industry | Students over 16 years old |
| Geological survey, investigation | Homemakers |
| Construction | Attachment: |
| Transport, postal & telecommunications | New Labor Force Population |
| Trading, food service | Excess Rural Labor Force |
| Real estate management, service, etc. | Excess Rural Labor Force as Percent |
| Health, physical fitness, social welfare | of Total Rural Labor Force |
| Education, cultural arts, broadcasting | Labor Force Movement from Rural to |
| Scientific research | Urban Areas |

Source: *Compendium of Regulations of the Plan of the PRC 1986 - 1987*, pp. 18 - 19.

Figure 4.2   Vicissitudes of the Communist Party's Method of
Enterprise Management

(1) System of Factory Manager Responsibility under Party
Committee Leadership (1956 to 1966)

The enterprise's party committee was the key leadership
organ in the enterprise. All important matters concerning
the enterprise would be decided through discussion in the
Party Committee; the factory manager would be responseble
for implementation. This system was operative from 1956 to
1966.

During the Cultural Revolution period Party and government leadership structures were "unified." After the fall of
the Gang of Four, the "System of Factory Manager Responsibility under Party Committee Leadership" was revived.

(2) System of Staff and Worker Representative Committees
under the Leadership of the Party Committee

After the fall of the Gang of Four, some small and
medium sized enterprises implemented on an experimental
basis a system of enterprise management in which staff and
workers representatives committees under the leadership of
the Party Committee decided important matters, and the factory manager took responsibility for implementation. This
was a transitional method until the factory manager responsibility system was approved at the Third Plenum of the
12th Party Congress Central Committee.

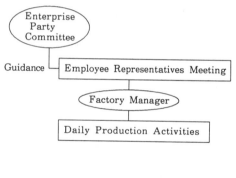

(3) Factory Manager Responsibility System

The decision to implement the "factory manager responsibility system" was contained in the October 1984 "Decision
on Reform of the Economic System." It was formally stipulated in the "State-Owned Industrial Enterprise Law of the
PRC" promulgated on April 13, 1988. The state entrusted to
the factory manager full powers to direct production and
carry out enterprise management. Factory managers were even
accorded authority to appoint and dismiss cadres responsible for providing administrative guidance to the enterprise.

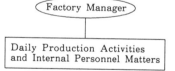

(4) The Duality of the "Nuclear Position" of the Party Organization and the "Central Position" of the Factory Manager

The conservative faction that dominated decision-making
after the Tiananmen Incident of June 4, 1989, supported a
roll-back of "factory manager dictatorship." This became the
parallel implementation of a duality: "party as nucleus,
factory manager as center." However, after Deng Xiaoping's
"Important Talk" during the 1992 Spring Festival, the mood
of state enterprise reform began to flourish again, and the
tendency has been back toward the factory manager responsibility system.

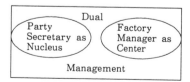

Tibet and Xinjiang) were the third front; and the region between the two was the second front.

From the mid-1960s to the early 1970s, in order to prepare for war, China undertook a massive construction program in the "strategic rear areas" (the third front). The construction was primarily in such heavy industries as defense, metallurgy, energy and machinery, and railway transport (see Table 4.3 for data on railroad construction).

Third-front construction (also called interior construction) in turn had a geographical breakdown based on designation of the "large third front" and the "small third front." In the draft fourth five-year plan adopted in 1970, the "large third front" was specified to be the vast region to the south of the Great Wall and to the west of the Beijing-Hankow railway line; this comprised Sichuan, Guizhou, and Yunnan in the southwest; and the largest part of Shaanxi, Qinghai, and Gansu in the northwest; the western part of Henan and Hubei in the central plain; western Hunan, northern Guangdong, and northwestern Guangxi; and Shanxi and Hebei in the north. The "small third front" was given as the remote parts of the interiors of each province. In general, third-front construction refers to construction in the areas of the large third front.

In August 1964 the Central Committee set the basic policy for construction in the third front, and this was incorporated in the third and fourth five-year plans. The policy was to establish quickly a relatively complete economic system in the southwest and northwest regions. However, because investment was concentrated in the extremely backward interior, economic efficiency was low. After 1971, as the international situation surrounding China improved, the urgency felt about building up for war was lost, and in 1973 large-scale construction in the third front entered a lull (*Economic Encyclopedia: Planning*, 1990, pp. 620–621).

Thus, in total disregard of economic efficiency, China strenuously pursued a policy of developing industrial bases in interior areas where industry had been scarce. The achievements of this policy in making possible the movement of other industry to the interior regions should be acknowledged, and it should be understood that the initial purpose of the policy was to prepare for war, not to achieve economic efficiency. From this perspective, it is inappropriate now to make retrospective judgments about the economic efficiency of this policy. Nevertheless, it was one of the major factors in the backwardness of the Chinese economy.

As can be seen in Map 4.1, third-front construction is one reason Sichuan province is beset with problems of sulfurous acid gas emissions and acid rain. Third-front construction stands as a symbol of the war-mobilization character of the so-called planned economy.

Table 4.3  Railways Completed During the Cultural Revolution Period

| Railway Name | Starting Point - Terminus | Distance (km) | Construction Started | Construction Completed |
|---|---|---|---|---|
| (1) Lanqing Railway | Helounan - Ketu | 302 | 5.1958 | 12.1966 |
| (2) Guikou Railway | Guiyang - Kunming | 467 | 8.1958 | 11.1966 |
| (3) Tongrang Railway | Tongliao - Ranghulu | 411 | 7.1964 | 12.1966 |
| (4) Handan Railway | Xinjiangan - Danjiakou | 416 | 10.1958 | 12.1966 |
| (5) Gouhai Railway | Goubangzi - Tangwangshan | 102 | 2.1960 | 12.1970 |
| (6) Chengkun Railway | Chengdudong - Kunming | 1,086 | 7.1958 | 12.1970 |
| Total Trunk Lines during the Third Five Year Plan Period | | 2,784 | Opened 1966 to 1970 | |
| (7) Houxi Railway | Yumenkou - Yenliang | 211 | 9.1958 | 5.1971 |
| (8) Jinyuan Railway | Shijingshannan - Yuanping | 4 | 1.1958 | 1.1972 |
| (9) Hangchang Railway | Genshanmen - Nintoushan | 156 | 4.1959 | 1.1973 |
| (10) Liaoxi Railway | Weizhangzi - Taian | 254 | 11.1970 | 12.1973 |
| (11) Xintai Railway | Xindian - Taian | 157 | 4.1970 | 10.1974 |
| (12) Xiangqian Railway | Xiantan - Guiding | 802 | 1.1953 | 1.1975 |
| (13) Jiaozhi Railway | Jiaozuo - Zhicheng | 825 | 10.1969 | 7.1976 |
| (14) Tonggn Railway | Tongxian - Tuozitou | 206 | 12.1972 | 8.1975 |
| Total Trunk Lines during the Fourth Five Year Plan Period | | 3,025 | Opened 1971 to 1975 | |

Source: *Transportation Grid of China* (Beijing: Scientific Press, 1986), pp. 97, 100.

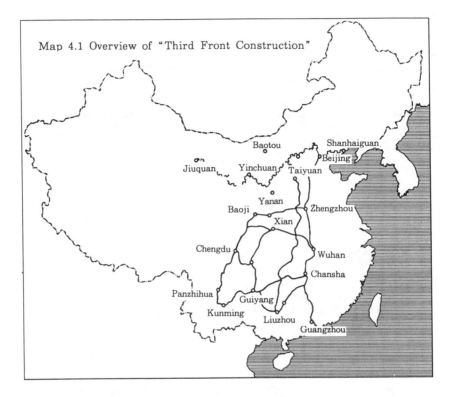

Map 4.1 Overview of "Third Front Construction"

(1) "Third front construction" comprises large third front construction and small third front construction. The former was an effort to build in the interior large scale industrial bases, principally of heavy and defense industries. The latter aimed at building a system to supply small armaments based on small and medium scale steel plants at the provincial and county levels.

(2) The center of large third front construction was the Panjihua region (Dukou city) at the southern tip of Sichuan province. Here the aim was to establish a major steel making complex supported by extensive mining operations in Yunnan and Guizhou provinces.

(3) Areas of concentration of major projects included, in addition to the Panjihua area, the Jiuquan area (surrounding the Yumen oilfield in Gansu province) and Chongqing, among others. Included among the major projects were building of five large iron and steel complexes (Panjihua, Jiuquan, Wuhan, Baotou, Taiyuan); coal mine development with emphasis on Guizhou province; and construction of hydroelectric power generation stations in Sichuan, Gansu, Jiangxi and other provinces, and thermoelectric power plants.

(4) Of the RMB 85 million in basic capital construction investment in the third five year plan (1966 to 1970), it has been estimated that investments in third front construction projects took about 42 percent, or RMB 36 million of the total. However, the actual share of third front construction expenditures in total capital construction investment was 52.7 percent (Economic Chronicles, and my work, Modern Chinese History 1949-1985 (Tokyo: Yuhikaku 1986), pp. 219-221.

# 5

# The Irreversible Transformation from a Planned to a Market Economy

For some thirty years from the 1950s through the late 1970s, China operated under a system of economic planning. From the beginning of the 1980s, it began to abandon this approach and to find ways to convert to a market system. The change was clearly heralded by the endorsement of the "socialist market economy system" by the Fourteenth Party Congress in fall 1992.

## The Third Plenum of the Eleventh Party Congress

The first step toward this transformation was taken in December 1978 when the Chinese Communist Party Central adopted the policy of economic reform with emphasis on enterprise reform at the Third Plenum of the Eleventh Party Congress. The basic themes were fleshed out in five documents issued by the State Council in mid-1979. These were (1) "Some Experimental Methodologies Concerning the Expansion of Enterprise Sovereignty"; (2) "Experimental Regulations on Rewards and Punishments for Staff and Workers"; (3) "Initial Reform Program for the Financial Management System"; (4) "Regulations Governing Foreign Trade Management and Allocation of Foreign Exchange"; and (5) "New Methodology for Progressive Bank Loans for Basic Capital Construction Investments."

## Evolution of Economic Concepts

### The Birdcage Economy

In spring 1982 the vice chairman of the Communist Party, Chen Yun, announced a policy shift toward "taking the planned economy as primary and market adjust-

Figure 5.1  Evolution of China's Economy

| | |
|---|---|
| The Universal Planned Economy (a) | Mao Zedong Era [ The universal planned economy model: the 'commodity economy' was attacked as the 'tail of capitalism.'] |

Economic planning to be practiced in all areas (Planned economy system) ── Commodity economy regarded as 'Capitalism's tail'

Sources:
Mao Zedong, "On Theoretical Issues," *People's Daily*, Dec. 26, 1974;
Mao Zedong, "Notes on Readings in Soviet Political Economy," Dec. 1959 - Feb. 1960.

| | |
|---|---|
| The Birdcage Economy (b) | Early Deng Xiaoping Period [Introduce the commodity economy partially into the planned economy structure ] |

Planned economy remains primary (Planned economy system) ── Market adjustment mechanism is secondary

Sources:
"Problems of Planning and Markets," March 8, 1979, *Selected Works of Chen Yun*, pp. 220 - 223.
"Some Questions on Realizing the Stratigic Objection Set by the 12th Party Congress," December 2, 1982, *Selected Works Chen Yun*, pp. 286 - 287.

| | |
|---|---|
| The Socialist Commodity Economy (c) | Middle Deng Xiaoping Period [Planned commodity economy ] |

Plan adjustment ── Commodity economy (Commodity economy system)

Sources:
Third Plenum of 12th Congress Central Committee "Decision on Reform of the Economic System," October 1984;
"The State to Control the Market, the Market to Lead Enterprises," Zhao Ziyang's Report to the 13th Party Congress, October 1987;

| | |
|---|---|
| Socialist Market Economy (d) | Late Deng Xiaoping Period [Socialist market economy ] |

Socialism ── Market economy (Market economy system)

Sources:
"Report by Jiang Zemin at the 14th Party Congress," November 1992.
Third Plenum of the 14th Congress Central Committee, "Decision on Some Issues Concerning the Establishment of the Socialist Market Economic System," November 1993.

ment as secondary" (*People's Daily,* January 26, 1982). The concept was presented analogously by likening the planned economy to a cage within which the market adjustment mechanism, like a bird, could fly freely, thus vitalizing the economy; this concept was commonly called the "birdcage economy" (see Figure 5.1). At the Twelfth Party Congress in September 1982, the report by General Secretary Hu Yaobang on political work included language expressing the concept:

> Correctly and thoroughly implementing the principle of taking the planned economy as primary and market adjustment as secondary is a fundamental issue in reform of the economic system. ... Directive plans, advisory plans, market adjustment, each should be correctly differentiated in its appropriate sphere and area. ... Reforming the method of price management and the price system, reforming the wage and salary systems ... are all essential.

The Chinese economy in the first half of the 1980s was directed essentially according to the concept of the birdcage economy: The system of economic planning continued as the basis for activity, but market forces were introduced and allowed to play an increasingly larger adjustment role.

### The Planned Commodity Economy

Introducing a market adjustment mechanism leads directly to contradictions with a planned economy structure. The Third Plenum of the Twelfth Party Congress in October 1984 adopted the "Decision on Reform of the Economic System," thus ratifying the concept of a "planned commodity (market) economy." With this action the theretofore doctrinal belief that socialism equals a planned economy was abandoned and replaced by the notion that socialism equals a commodity (market) economy. After adoption of this resolution, the pace of economic reform dramatically quickened (Table 5.1).

The concept of the planned commodity economy was elucidated at the Thirteenth Party Congress in October 1987. Its meaning and goals in terms of the economic system were expressed as "the state controls the market, and the market guides enterprises." On this basis, emphasis was placed on market guidance of enterprises, and the state withdrew from direct intervention in their activities. The state concluded that it was better to exert control over enterprises indirectly through its control of the market (Figure 5.2).

# Inflation, Repression, and the Revival of Reform

### The 1988 Commodity Price Panic and the Tiananmen Incident

After the Thirteenth Party Congress, economic reform made dramatic advances. At the beginning of 1988 it became evident that implementation of the policy of

Table 5.1  Various Models of the Chinese Economy

| Economic System Model | Macro - Economic Decision - Making | Enterprise Daily Activities Decision - Making | Individual, Household Economic Decision - Making |
|---|---|---|---|
| I   Military - Communist Command Economy | Centralized Physical goods - based | Centralized Physical goods - based | Centralized Physical goods - based |
| II   Traditional Centrally Planned Economy | Centralized | Centralized | Dispersed |
| III   Improved Centrally Planned Economy | Centralized | Centralized (Larger part) Dispersed (Smaller part) | Dispersed |
| IV   Market - Adjusted Planned Economy | Centralized | Dispersed | Dispersed |
| V   Market Socialism [Close to Capitalism] | Market - based Dispersed | Market - based Dispersed | Market - based Dispersed |

Note: Model III can be considered Chen Yun's birdcage economy model. Model IV is the aim of the October 1984 "Decision on Reform of the Economic System."

Source: Yisui and Ayin, "Capital Economic Theorists Discuss Problems of Reform of the Economic System," in *Currents in Economics*, February 1982 issue.

price system reform had begun. However, some urban residents, fearing that such reform would ignite inflation, began to speculate in and to hoard goods. Lines formed at banks as people sought to withdraw money in order to pursue these activities, and bank runs occurred in some regional areas. With this, the issue of inflation became a political problem, and the Third Plenum of the Thirteenth Party Congress in fall 1988 occasioned a shift to a policy of economic adjustment.

Economic adjustment stalled, and a two-price system provided opportunities for *guandao* (official profiteering). Common people's anger at such unsavory activities grew, and in May and June 1989 a democratic "rebellion" arose and spread. The government responded by instituting martial law and mobilizing the People's Liberation Army to carry out armed suppression.

## Three Years of Reorganization and Rectification

The Party Central and the government announced after the Tiananmen incident that they would firmly hold to the policy of reform and liberalization. However, in the period 1989 to 1990 it seemed that these tenets remained in name only. There was a severe tightening not only in the political sphere but also in the economic sphere. Although inflation was contained, the country fell into a condition of "market exhaustion." In the three years following fall 1988, employment expansion stalled, and a severe problem of unemployment became apparent.

Figure 5.2   Differences in the Commodity Economy and the Planned Economy

(a) Planned Economy (Bureaucratic Adjustment or Vertical Adjustment)

(b) Commodity Economy (Market Adjustment or Horizontal Adjustment)

Source: Yanos Kornai, *The Possibility of Economic Reform* (Tokyo: Iwanami Shoten, 1986), p. 7.

## Deepening Reform and Making a Quantum Leap in Liberalization

The Eighth Plenum of the Thirteenth Party Congress in fall 1991 (November 25–29) became the occasion for publicly declaring the end of contradictory policies. Behind this decision were the problems of unemployment and deficits of state-owned enterprises. The emphasis in economic policy on maintaining a stable social order had led to unlimited advances of funds to money-losing state enterprises in order to support continued production and to disregard of accumulations of dead stock and excess inventories. The severity of the deficit situation in state enterprises was manifested in the form of the triangle debt problem (see Chapter 6).

In spring 1992 Deng Xiaoping made an inspection tour in the south and called for an acceleration of reform and liberalization. The Party Central issued in 1992 Document No. 2 (talks by Deng Xiaoping); Document No. 4 (opening cities along the Yangtze and border cities); and Document No. 5 (developing tertiary industries), thereby concretely accelerating reform and liberalization and aiming toward realization of a socialist market economy (Table 5.1).

# 6

# Economic Momentum Shifts to the Nonstate Sector

## The Decline of State-Owned Enterprises

The Eighth Plenum of the Thirteenth Party Congress held in November 1991 endorsed the proposition that China's urgent problem is "the contradiction between advanced socialist productive relations and backward productive forces." This constituted a victory of the Deng Xiaoping reformist line against conservatives who had been advocating "peaceful evolution."

The decline of state-owned enterprises (which could be said to embody "socialist productive relations") is all too clear in Figure 6.1. In the late 1970s state-owned enterprises contributed nearly 80 percent of production. By 1990 their contribution had declined to around 50 percent. Official statistics for 1992 indicate that the share of gross value of industrial production contributed by state-owned enterprises had fallen to 48.1 percent of total. This decline is from a level of 74 percent ten years earlier.

In contrast to the stalled state enterprises, nonstate-owned foreign-invested enterprises and individual enterprises are showing remarkable growth, together approaching the 10 percent level. From a zero base to 10 percent in the five years of the second half of the 1980s was a dramatic advance. The share of collectively owned enterprises has also increased, but this reflects the strides of township and village enterprises (small and medium-sized factories in rural villages that are successors to the people's commune industries).

The indicator of whether an industry is in decline is labor productivity, which is compared in Figure 6.2 for the different types of enterprises. At the time that Deng Xiaoping's policies were inaugurated, the labor productivity of collectively owned enterprises was only half that of state-owned enterprises. This was an indication that advanced equipment was allocated almost exclusively to state-owned enterprises, and collectively owned (i.e., township and village) enterprises oper-

48

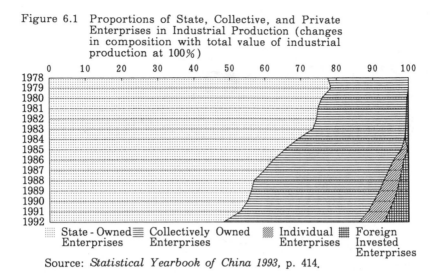

Figure 6.1 Proportions of State, Collective, and Private
Enterprises in Industrial Production (changes
in composition with total value of industrial
production at 100%)

State - Owned≣ Collectively Owned ▨ Individual ▦ Foreign
Enterprises      Enterprises          Enterprises   Invested
                                                    Enterprises

Source: *Statistical Yearbook of China 1993*, p. 414.

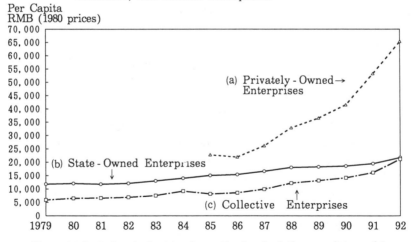

Figure 6.2 Differences in Labor Productivity of State,
Collective, and Private Enterprises

Per Capita
RMB (1980 prices)

Note: (c) Includes industry above the level of the rural township
only after 1984. Until 1985 urban collective industry was also
included.
Source: *Statistical Yearbook of China 1993*, p. 431

ated with an extremely low ratio of installed capital. However, because they were accorded management autonomy, collectively owned enterprises developed new vitality. Rationalization of operations served to compensate for the low ratio of installed capital, and in ten years these enterprises advanced to two-thirds the productivity levels of state-owned enterprises. This is an average figure for township and village enterprises, so there can be no doubt that many excellent rural enterprises have long since surpassed the level of state-owned enterprises.

The labor productivity of the nonstate-sector foreign-invested and individually operated enterprises is over three times that of state-owned enterprises. Indeed, the private and collectively owned enterprises are today supporting the vitality of the Chinese economy. If this labor productivity can be sustained, this sector's share will continue to expand, and the accelerating decline of the state-owned sector will become obvious. Clearly, reform of the state-guaranteed management style of state-owned enterprises is a critically urgent task. Moreover, in the tightening after the Tiananmen incident, the deficit problem of state-owned enterprises was exposed. It is said that 30 to 50 percent of them are operating at a loss and accumulating deficits. Major surgery is unavoidable.

## Deficits in State-Owned Enterprises

The deteriorating operating efficiency of state-owned enterprises is evidenced in their financial indicators. Chinese "return on capital" is the equivalent of the Western gross return on capital (pretax). The formula for return on capital is (C + D) / (A + B) where A is fixed capital, B is liquid funds, C is profits, and D is taxes (Figure 6.3).

Figure 6.3 shows that the "tax and profit return on funds" dropped from 24 percent to almost half this level from 1981 to 1990. When the tax element is subtracted from this numerator to obtain "return (profitability) on funds," there is clearly a deteriorating trend: a precipitous decline from 15 percent in 1981 to 3 percent in 1990. This performance accompanied a conversion from the system of remitting total profits and taxes to higher authorities, to one of remitting only taxes due. In sum, profits retained at the enterprise declined drastically. Also remarkable was the deterioration in the efficiency of funds.

An internal document, "Causes of the Huge Losses of State Enterprises" (Yen Wenguang 1990), exposed the continuing increase in the proportion of Chinese state-owned enterprises operating at a loss. The author's penetrating analysis of the situation and its causes was much talked about. He pointed out that (1) money-losing state enterprises had reached 30 percent of all such enterprises; (2) the aggregate annual deficit had risen to RMB 20 billion in 1990; (3) the deficit phenomenon had spread from some enterprises within an industry to entire industries, and the trend was continuing; and (4) subsidies to deficit enterprises had reached the level of half the value of all industrial profits.

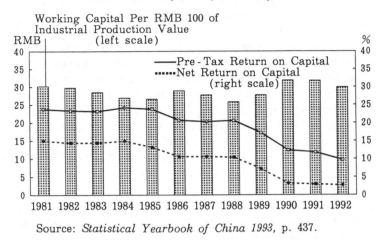

Figure 6.3   Changes in Financial Indicators in State - Owned
Industrial Enterprises (1981 - 1992)

Source: *Statistical Yearbook of China 1993*, p. 437.

This phenomenon has since become well known. The *Yearbook of Chinese In-dustrial and Economic Statistics 1991* included an extensive analysis of the deficit problem of state-owned enterprises. As is evident from Table 6.1, deficits of these enterprises expanded rapidly in the second half of the 1980s, particularly during the tightening after the Tiananmen incident. Table 6.2 shows which industries were earning significant profits and paying significant taxes.

The deficit problem entails not only the magnitude of the financial burden but also the critically depressed morale and motivation of the staff and workers of these enterprises. The result has been a drastic decline in labor productivity and economic efficiency.

Yen Wenguang (1990) offered the following reasons why the deficits of state-owned enterprises arose.

- Rising costs for raw materials, personnel, welfare allowances, and enter-prise management
- Losses in the transfer of enterprise profits to other departments and di-visions
- Damage to operations from shortages of energy and raw materials
- Slack enterprise management and waste
- Management errors at the enterprise level

The severity of the deficit problem of state-owned enterprises is evident even from this cursory introduction. However, because the data presented here are the "reported figures" designed to put the best and not necessarily an accurate light on matters, it is reasonable to conclude that the actual or potential deficit is far greater than that indicated.

Table 6.1  Trends of Deficits of State - Owned Industrial Enterprises (1985 - 1990)

| | No. of enterprises (a) | Deficit enterprises (b) | (b)/(a) | Deficit (c) | Gross profits and taxes (d) | (c)/(d) | Value of subsidies to deficit enterprises (e) | (e)/(d) |
|---|---|---|---|---|---|---|---|---|
| | (units) | (units) | (%) | (billion RMB) | (billion RMB) | (%) | (billion RMB) | (%) |
| 1985 | 70,342 | 6,749 | 9.6 | — | 134 | — | — | — |
| 1986 | 70,511 | 9,221 | 13.1 | 5.5 | 134 | 4.1 | 32.5 | 24.2 |
| 1987 | 72,803 | 9,459 | 13.0 | 6.1 | 151 | 4.0 | 37.6 | 24.9 |
| 1988 | 72,494 | 7,912 | 10.9 | 8.2 | 177 | 4.6 | 44.6 | 25.2 |
| 1989 | 73,501 | 11,785 | 16.0 | 18.0 | 177 | 10.2 | 59.9 | 33.8 |
| 1990 | 74,775 | 20,603 | 27.6 | 34.9 | 150 | 23.2 | 57.9 | 38.5 |

Sources: *Statistical Yearbook for China's Industrial Economy 1991* (Beijing: Statistical Press, 1991), pp. 97, 124. *Statistical Yearbook of China 1991*, p. 212.

Table 6.2  The Deficit Situation by Sector of State - Owned Industrial Enterprises (1990)

| | Gross value of profit & taxes | | Deficit value of deficit enterprises | | (b)/(a) | Net contribution (a)−(b) |
|---|---|---|---|---|---|---|
| | (billion RMB) (a) | (%) | (billion RMB) (b) | (%) | (%) | (billion RMB) |
| Food processing | 40.6 | 20.9 | 5.0 | 11.0 | 12.3 | 35.7 |
| Machinery | 34.5 | 17.7 | 8.7 | 19.1 | 25.2 | 25.8 |
| Chemicals | 27.0 | 13.9 | 3.1 | 6.8 | 11.4 | 23.9 |
| Metallurgy | 24.6 | 12.6 | 2.2 | 4.8 | 8.9 | 22.4 |
| Textiles | 19.2 | 9.9 | 4.7 | 10.5 | 24.7 | 14.5 |
| Electric power | 17.6 | 9.1 | 1.7 | 3.8 | 9.7 | 15.9 |
| Petroleum | 9.9 | 5.1 | 4.9 | 10.8 | 49.5 | 5.0 |
| Construction materials | 7.9 | 4.1 | 2.5 | 5.5 | 31.4 | 5.4 |
| Other | 4.9 | 2.5 | 1.4 | 3.0 | 28.2 | 3.5 |
| Education - related | 4.4 | 2.3 | 0.4 | 0.9 | 9.4 | 4.0 |
| Sewing | 2.7 | 1.4 | 0.5 | 1.1 | 17.5 | 2.3 |
| Paper | 2.5 | 1.3 | 0.8 | 1.7 | 6.8 | 1.7 |
| Forestry | 1.8 | 0.9 | 1.0 | 2.2 | 24.5 | 0.8 |
| Tanning | 0.7 | 0.4 | 0.6 | 1.3 | 18.3 | 0.1 |
| Coking coal | -3.8 | -2.0 | 7.9 | 17.4 | — | -11.7 |
| Total | 194.6 | 100.0 | 45.4 | 100.0 | 23.3 | 149.2 |

Source: *Statistical Yearbook for China's Industrial Economy 1991*, pp. 74 - 77.

# The "Triangle Debt" Scandal

"Triangle debt" means that a chain of enterprises cannot pay their debts to others (banks, general creditors, and suppliers, including other companies in the chain) because they cannot collect receivables from each other; the result of this linkage is that illiquidity spreads generally through the system. The phenomenon is also called "interlocking debts" and "rolling debts." The source of triangle debt is losses by state-owned enterprises. In the process of financial tightening, funds stopped circulating; the situation suddenly was exposed and became a major topic of conversation.

China's economy is one of scarcity. Consequently it is fundamentally a seller's market with the seller in a stronger position. However, in the actual conduct of transactions, the buyer is overwhelmingly favored in the methods of settlement. The seller must present to the bank an invoice evidencing that a sales transaction has been executed. The bank then undertakes to collect settlement proceeds from the buyer. It is by means of this established mechanism that trade settlements between state-owned enterprises have heretofore been carried out. Every state enterprise has an account with the People's Bank, and all settlements have been required to be effected via transfers between these accounts. An operating premise has been that the People's Bank will collect the sales proceeds according to the expectations of the seller.

However, as economic reform has advanced, this premise has been increasingly eroded in practice. First, the People's Bank has been transforming itself into more of a central bank, leaving standard transactions to the Industrial and Commercial Bank of China, the Agricultural Bank of China, and the Construction Bank of China. Also, the structure of enterprises is changing and becoming more diverse as forms other than complete state ownership are being tried. In this context, there has been a proliferation of cases in which the seller has transferred goods and been left with no alternative but to plead earnest with the buyer for payment when the buyer arrogantly refused to pay. In the aftermath of the Tiananmen incident, priority was placed on maintaining political stability, including stable employment. Consequently, lending continued to be expanded even to deficit enterprises; thus their deficits—and their triangle debts—increased (Table 6.3).

On February 1, 1992, an announcement was made of the achievements of the State Council Leading Group for Liquidation of Triangle Debt (group head, Vice Premier Zhu Rongji) (*People's Daily,* February 9, 1992). According to the report, in 1991 unpaid debts of RMB 136 billion were liquidated through a combination of RMB 30.6 billion in bank loans and RMB 2.5 billion in enterprise (department) funds. Thus, for every RMB 1.00 of funds invested, RMB 4.1 of unpaid debts were liquidated.

In several cases public pressure against nonpaying enterprises resulted in payment being made (see Table 6.4). The debtor enterprises made a variety of excuses, but as reported in the press, the Leading Group for Liquidation of Triangle Debt pointed out that none of the excuses was a valued reason for nonpayment. For example, "the responsible person is on a business trip" was determined to be simply a problem of the enterprise itself. Having excess inventory of coking coal also could not be a reason for refusing payment. "The goods have not arrived" was another excuse given for nonpayment, but as noted in the article, under the payment-upon-request system payment was due upon presentation of a "dispatch order" even if the goods had not been delivered. In the case of "insufficient funds," officials suggested installment payments or payment with overdue interest (*People's Daily,* October 30, 1991).

Table 6.3　The Situation of Triangle Debt Arrangements of Each Province and Municipality (April 15 to May 31, 1992)

| | (a) Actual Rate of Bank Lending (vs. Plan) | | | | (b) Actual Rate of Reinvestment of Funds (vs. Plan) | | | | (c) Gross Value of Triangle Debt Arrangements | | |
|---|---|---|---|---|---|---|---|---|---|---|---|
| | (a) % | (b) % | (c) Billions RMB | | (a) % | (b) % | (c) Billions RMB | | (a) % | (b) % | (c) Billions RMB |
| Henan | 96.8 | 32.1 | 30.6 | Shaanxi | 93.4 | 87.4 | 11.1 | Guizhou | 74.9 | 20.7 | 4.1 |
| Hebei | 100.0 | 86.3 | 28.3 | Heilong | 89.4 | 105.1 | 11.0 | Gansu | 71.8 | 20.1 | 3.2 |
| Tianjin | 106.0 | 35.3 | 27.9 | Beijing | 100.0 | 5.1 | 10.9 | Xinjiang | 85.0 | 0.0 | 3.2 |
| Hubei | 100.0 | 88.9 | 27.5 | Jiangxi | 90.7 | 11.7 | 10.6 | Changchun | 100.0 | 98.9 | 3.0 |
| Jiangsu | 99.3 | 65.9 | 25.6 | Guangxi | 85.5 | 63.2 | 10.0 | Guangzhou | 85.1 | 18.3 | 2.6 |
| Shandong | 95.4 | 20.5 | 23.5 | Jilin | 94.3 | 27.4 | 8.5 | Ningxia | 74.4 | 10.9 | 1.9 |
| Sichuan | 97.0 | 0.8 | 23.5 | Harbin | 90.6 | 70.1 | 7.9 | Qinghai | 92.4 | 61.1 | 1.8 |
| Zhejiang | 96.5 | 119.0 | 20.4 | Chengdu | 98.0 | 70.5 | 7.4 | Dalian | 99.8 | 9.1 | 1.6 |
| Anhui | 99.9 | 69.1 | 18.7 | Liaoning | 73.2 | 37.1 | 7.1 | Shenzhen | 32.8 | 0.0 | 1.1 |
| Chongqing | 102.7 | 11.7 | 18.4 | Shenyang | 73.2 | 101.5 | 6.0 | Ningbo | 95.6 | 77.6 | 0.5 |
| Hunan | 97.8 | 106.7 | 17.6 | Wuhan | 83.3 | 29.5 | 5.8 | Fujian | 109.4 | 1.9 | 0.4 |
| Shanghai | 59.9 | 7.3 | 15.0 | Guangdong | 90.1 | 105.1 | 5.4 | Hainan | 5.1 | — | 0.3 |
| Shanxi | 99.5 | 20.3 | 13.1 | Qingdao | 99.9 | — | 5.3 | Xiamen | — | 0.0 | 0.1 |
| Inner Mongolia | 84.5 | 8.4 | 11.7 | Xian | 78.6 | 56.3 | 4.6 | | | | |
| Yunnan | 94.2 | 7.5 | 11.4 | Nanjing | 100.0 | 120.8 | 4.2 | Total | 92.9 | 36.6 | 452.9 |

Source: *People's Daily*, June 25, 1992.

# Growth of Township and Village Enterprises

The term "township and village enterprises" first appeared in a party and government notice that confirmed the March 1984 "Report on Opening of a New Phase for Commune and Brigade Enterprises of the State Council Ministry of Agriculture, Animal Husbandry, and Fisheries." This notice announced the breakup of the people's communes and a name change of the former "commune and brigade enterprises" to "township and village enterprises." It also contained four policy statements:

1.  Excess farm labor should be fully employed, production of goods for the market should be developed, and funds needed for the modernization of agriculture should be saved.
2.  Former "commune and brigade enterprises," peasants' "joint capital enterprises" (which pool capital of several peasants), and "individual enterprises" were all important constituents of a diversified enterprise structure and were important sources of revenue for the state.
3.  Township and village enterprises, in comparison with state-owned large and medium-sized enterprises, possessed old equipment, obsolete technology, and outdated information and were vulnerable to error. However, because of individual unit accountability, these enterprises were competitively strong and would be able to adjust quickly to meet the needs of the market.
4.  Administrative management of township and village enterprises should be left to each province.

Table 6.4   Enterprises Refusing to Pay Debts as Reported in the Press

| Repayment Refused | | Repayment Refused | | | Name of Creditor Enterprises |
| --- | --- | --- | --- | --- | --- |
| Name of Enterprises | Relationship Bank | Date | Amount RMB | Reason | |
| Agricultural Equipment Company of Ninghai County, Ningbo City | Agricultural Bank Ninghai County Branch | Sept. 9 1991 | 2,014 | Responsible person is traveling on business | Saihuan Factory Ningbo Municipality |
| Pingxiang Steel Mill Jiangxi Province | Industrial and Commercial Bank Jiangxi Pingxiang City, Xiashankou Office | Sept. 9 1991 | 332,257 | Stocks of coking coal were adequate | Head Office,Shaoxing City Materials Sales Company Zhejiang Province |
| High Pressure Switch Factory Pingdingshan City, Henan Province | Industrial and Commercial Bank,Henan Province, Pingdingshan City, Railway Terminal Office | Sept. 9 1991 | 22,894 | Voucher did not have stamp from tax office | Shanghai Copper Materials Factory |
| Chinese Medicine Tablet Factory Tonghanchun Tang, Shanghai | Agricultural Bank Pudong Branch Shanghai | Sept. 7 1991 | 24,867 | Goods had not yet arrived | Chinese Medicinal Materials Sales Dept  Medicinal Materials Company, Ningbo Municipality |
| Carburetor Factory Hubei Province | Agricultural Bank Yingshan County Branch Hubei Province | Sept. 19 1991 | 13,247 | Goods had not yet arrived | Hangzhou General Tool Factory |
| Guangzhou Office, Hainan Drug Trading Company, Hainan Province | Construction Bank Guangzhou No.2 Branch | Sept. 25 1991 | 52,180 | Goods had not been received | Jiangxi Chinese Medicine Factory |
| Electric Post Value Unit Set Department Shanghai Electrical Unit Company | Construction Bank Shanghai No.2 Branch | Sept. 24 1991 | 5,021 | Goods had not been received | Ningbo Valve Factory |
| Xinhua Sewing Machine Shop, Shijiazhuang | Beidajiecheng Municipal Credit Cooperative, Shijiazhuang | Sept. 25 1991 | 1,050 | Lack of funds | PLA Unit 81065 Low Pressure Electrical Equipment Factory |
| No.2 Electrical Equipment Factory, Dalian | Industrial and Commercial Bank, Dalian Shahekou, Xinghai Branch | Sept. 20 1991 | 47,223 | Lack of contract | Shanghai Copper Materials Factory |
| No.2 Chemical Factory, Nantong Jiangsu | Industrial and Commercial Bank, Tangban, Nantong, Jiangsu | Oct. 4 1991 | 55,140 | Lack of contract | Nanjing Hard Alloy Factory |

Source: *People's Daily,* October, 30, 1991.

Thus, after liberalization, China officially accepted the individual peasant enterprises and joint capital enterprises that succeeded the commune and brigade industries. As a consequence, the position of rural industries in village society was greatly enhanced. Recently, they have also become remarkably active producers of goods for export.

At the close of 1992 rural enterprises numbered 20.8 million and had 105.8 million employees (Figure 6.4). In the counterreformist mood prevailing after the Tiananmen incident, individually operated enterprises were criticized as bourgeois, and some township and village enterprises were similarly maligned. This political factor, in addition to the effects of economic tightening, explains the leveling off of employment in the nonstate sector from 1988 through 1991.

Figure 6.4  Trends in Number of Enterprises, Numbers of
Staff and Workers, and Gross Production for
Township and Village Enterprises

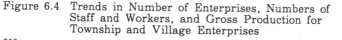

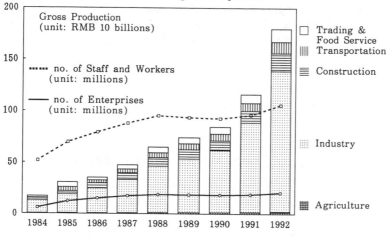

Source: *Statistical Yearbook of China 1993*, pp. 395-396.

Figure 6.5  Relative Share Position of Township and Village
Enterprises in Total Rural Production and Total
Industrial Production by Value

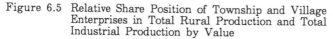

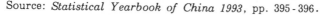

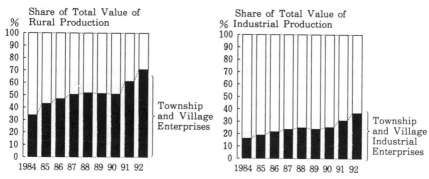

Source: *Statistical Yearbook of China 1993*: Gross value of rural
production, p. 333; gross value of township and village enterprise
production, p. 396; gross value of industrial production, p. 412.

In 1992 enterprises under "ownership of the entire people" (i.e., state-owned) had 108.9 million employees, and employment in collectively owned enterprises under municipalities was 36.2 million. Thus, township and village enterprises employed nearly three times as many workers as municipal collectives and almost as many as the state-owned sector (*Statistical Yearbook of China 1993*, p. 97).

Figure 6.5 presents a comparison of the value of production of township and village enterprises, value of gross agricultural production, and value of gross industrial production. The fact that township and village enterprises account for over 70 percent of overall gross agricultural production testifies to their enormously important role in Chinese rural society.

Township and village enterprises now contribute nearly 40 percent of the total value of industrial production. During his 1992 southern inspection, Deng Xiaoping described township and village industries approvingly as "appearing out of nowhere."

## The Upsurge of Foreign-Invested Enterprises

Foreign-affiliated enterprises in China are commonly called "three capital enterprises." The "three" denotes (1) Chinese-foreign joint ventures, (2) Chinese-foreign contractual joint ventures, and (3) 100 percent foreign capital enterprises. [Translator's note: Chinese define and differentiate (1) and (2) as follows. A Chinese-foreign joint venture operates under joint Chinese-foreign management in a limited liability joint stock company structure, with profits and losses allocated according to the percentage of stock ownership. A Chinese foreign contractual joint venture is operated under a *contract* between the Chinese and foreign parties. Most key issues between the contracting parties with respect to the enterprise—rights and obligations, proportion of profit distribution or share of risks and liabilities, management structure, and settlement of assets—are negotiated and stipulated in the contract.]

In 1992 there were 48,852 new foreign-affiliated enterprises established, compared with 13,086 in 1991. New capital commitments on a contract basis were $58.1 billion, a figure that exceeded the cumulative capital commitments during the entire period 1979–1991. Moreover, in 1993 new contracted investment commitments rose to $110 billion, nearly double the 1992 figure.

This growth brought the total number of foreign-affiliated enterprises by the end of 1992 to 90,676 (Figure 6.6). The contractual value of cumulative investments was $191.1 billion, and the cumulative amount actually disbursed was $98.8 billion (*Statistical Yearbook of China 1993*, p. 647).

As shown in Figure 6.6, joint ventures are the most numerous form of enterprise with 58,875 companies (64.9 percent); next are contractual joint ventures, including petroleum development companies, with 16,831 (18.6 percent); wholly foreign companies number 14,970 (16.5 percent). Of these enterprises, 95 percent are engaged in manufacturing. Industries are mainly in infrastructure, such as

Figure 6.6   Trends in Establishment of Foreign Invested Enterprises in China

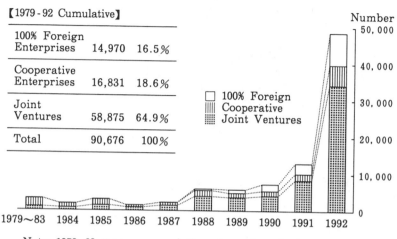

【1979-92 Cumulative】

| | | |
|---|---|---|
| 100% Foreign Enterprises | 14,970 | 16.5% |
| Cooperative Enterprises | 16,831 | 18.6% |
| Joint Ventures | 58,875 | 64.9% |
| Total | 90,676 | 100% |

Note: 1979-83 5 years cumulative. Annual totals for establishment after 1984.
Source: Mitsubishi Research Institute, *Digest of Foreign Companies in China,* 1993 edition (Tokyo: Sososha Ltd., 1993), p. 33. (Original material from Chinese Ministry of Foreign Economic Relations and Trade.)

Figure 6.7   Proportion of Total Chinese Export Volume Contributed by Foreign Invested Enterprises

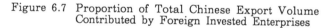

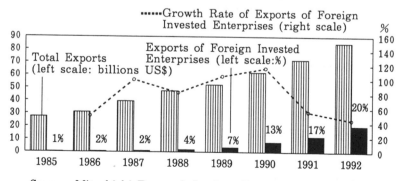

Source: Mitsubishi Research Institute International Trend Analysis Center (Original material from *China Statistical Report,* annual reports).

Figure 6.8   Proportion of Individual Operations in Cities and
Rural Areas

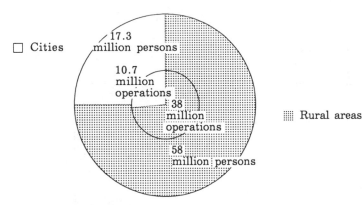

Note: Inner circle shows number of operations. Outer circle shows
number of employees.
Source: State Council Individual and Private Economy Research Group,
ed. *China's Individual and Private Economy* (Beijing: Reform Press,
November 1990), p. 2.

Figure 6.9   Sectoral Breakdown of Individual Operations

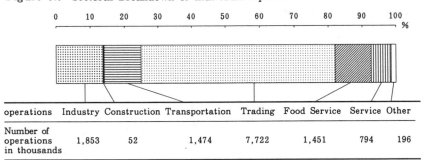

| operations | Industry | Construction | Transportation | Trading | Food Service | Service | Other |
|---|---|---|---|---|---|---|---|
| Number of operations in thousands | 1,853 | 52 | 1,474 | 7,722 | 1,451 | 794 | 196 |

Source: *China's Individual and Private Economy*, p. 2.

energy, transportation, communications, and export (foreign exchange earning
or import substituting).

The way foreign-affiliated enterprises contribute to the Chinese economy is
implied in Deng Xiaoping's "four windows" concept. "The special economic
zones are windows. They are windows for technology, windows for management,
windows for knowledge, and windows for foreign policy" (Deng Xiaoping 1987, p.
40). Although his comment "windows for foreign policy" is vague, the important
point is the rapid rise in the export share of foreign-affiliated enterprises.

Figure 6.7 shows the contribution of foreign-affiliated enterprises to exports.
From 1985 to 1986 these enterprises were just getting established, had not yet de-

Table 6.5  Origin of Operators of Privately Owned Enterprises

| Merchants | Laborers | Workmen | Individual Operators | Cadres | Peasants | Teachers/ Soldiers |
|-----------|----------|---------|---------------------|--------|----------|--------------------|
| 22.1% | 17.9% | 15.2% | 6.95% | 15.2% | 14.0% | 9.3% |

Source: Yang Kezhang, editor, *Investigation into the Privately Operated Economy at the Current Phase in China* (Shanghai: Fudan University Press, 1990), p. 274.

veloped overseas markets, and were contributing only about 1 percent of exports. However, the products they sought to produce in China were competitive in export markets. Thus, as production increased they began to make a significant contribution to China's foreign exchange earnings. In 1990 the foreign-affiliate export share was 12.5 percent; by 1992 it was 20.4 percent. This role can be expected to increase in the future.

Foreign-affiliated enterprises got their start in the special economic zones. Later they expanded to the fourteen open coastal cities. Eventually they will spread from these points to the Pearl River delta, to the Minnan (Fujian) triangle region, to the Yangtze River delta, and to the Bohai rim area.

# Potential for Development of the Private Economy

Individual business operators are called "entrepreneurs" (*ge ti hu*). Together with privately owned enterprises, they form the private economy, which China finally accepted in the 1980s. On July 7, 1981, the government promulgated "Policy Provisions of the State Council on Urban Non-Agricultural Individual Economy." These regulations recognized the existence of "individual enterprise which does not exploit the labor of others" and thus signaled official toleration. The line between exploitation and nonexploitation was clarified in article 5 of the eighteen-article regulations: employing "one or two persons as helpers and two or three persons as apprentices" was acceptable, but "apprentices are not to number more than five." Thus, it was considered permissible to employ up to seven persons. Figure 6.8 presents the urban-rural breakdown for individual enterprise, and Figure 6.9 indicates the sectoral distribution.

It is clear that behind the approval given to individual enterprise was the problem of unemployment in the cities. On July 1, 1988, the "Provisional Regulations Governing Private Enterprises in the People's Republic of China" were promulgated (administrative regulations were issued February 1, 1989). This law applied to private enterprises employing eight persons or more (fewer persons would be treated as individual enterprises). Private enterprises were divided into three categories based on number of investors: "sole proprietor enterprise" (a single investor), "partnership" (two or more), and "limited liability company" (two or more but fewer than thirty). A restriction was that the monthly salary of factory managers of private enterprises could not exceed ten times the average wage of the workers. Operators of these enterprises came from varied backgrounds (Table 6.5).

Along with the recognition of private enterprises, the government amended article 11 of the constitution (promulgated December 4, 1982) on December 12, 1988, as follows: "The state approves the existence and development of private enterprise within the sphere set out in laws and regulations. The private economy is a supplement to the socialist economic system of public ownership. The state shall protect the legal rights and profits of the private economy, and will carry out guidance, supervision, and management of the private economy." This constitutional amendment gave the private economy a legal existence.

The development of individual enterprise and the private economy has passed through four stages:

1. *Recovery (1979–1981).* The employment problem, principally in the cities, of "persons awaiting work assignments" (the unemployed) and "leisure personnel" (unemployable) was solved. Nationwide the number of urban individual industrial or commercial operations increased from 310,000 in 1979 to 1.1 million in 1981, an increase of 8.1 percent a year.

2. *High growth (1982–1985).* The growth of individual and commercial operations in the cities was paralleled in the countryside, where similar operations in combination numbered 11.7 million in 1985 with 17.6 million employees. The annual growth rates were 64 percent and 77 percent, respectively.

3. *Stable growth (1986–1988).* By the end of 1988 nationwide the number of urban individual commercial and industrial operations had risen to 14.6 million, and employees to 23 million. Annual growth rates were 9.5 percent and 11.7 percent, respectively.

4. *Tiananmen-related decline, then recovery.* At the end of 1989 individual industrial and commercial operations had decreased to 19.4 million. Private enterprises had decreased from 90,581 operations in the first half of the year to 76,581 (8,000 businesses ceased operations, and 4,000 businesses changed occupations [State Council Individual and Private Economy Research Group 1990, p. 2]). By the end of 1992 total employment in individual industrial and commercial operations and private enterprises had reached a level of some 27 million, up from 24 million at the end of 1991. In 1992 the number of private enterprises grew to 140,000, up from 100,000 at the end of 1991 (*Statistical Yearbook of China 1993*, pp. 113–114).

# 7

# Wage Reform and the Rise of China's Power Elite

## Average Worker Wages

The average wage for workers is presented in Figure 7.1. Employment in the sector of state-owned enterprises and organizations at the end of 1992 was 108.9 million persons. In comparison, employment in the municipal collective sector, where conditions are somewhat worse, was 36.2 million. (*Statistical Yearbook of China 1993*, p. 97.) For the relatively fortunate workers of the state-owned sector, the per capita annual wage increased from RMB 446 in 1952 to RMB 2,878 in 1992, a 6.5-fold increase in nominal terms. However, the great enemy of wages is price increases. Using the "general index of staff and worker living costs" (a cost-of-living index) to deflate nominal wages to real wages, we see a drastic reduction. In 1980 and 1982 real wages finally recovered the peak of RMB 581 reached in 1957, and this advance (which continued) marked the true beginning of the Deng Xiaoping era. The emphasis he placed on ending the long stagnation in real wages had profound political implications.

During the Mao Zedong era, China gave priority to production over living standards. The policy program was designed to force the maximum amount of savings possible by drastically suppressing consumption in order to support the priority position of heavy industry. However, as the era drew to a close, so did this policy. When the Deng Xiaoping era began, material incentives (rejected during the Cultural Revolution period, in particular, as revisionism) in the form of wage increases were widely instituted as a means of countering low morale: The people had grown unresponsive to spiritual incentives to work and had become deeply skeptical about socialism.

Afterward, as a consequence of the emphasis on "distribution according to work" and a policy of material incentives, real wages finally began to rise, and a major improvement of the living standards of the people commenced. However, a new problem accompanied economic reform—general price inflation.

Figure 7.1 Changes in Per Capita Nominal and Real Wages (1952-1992)

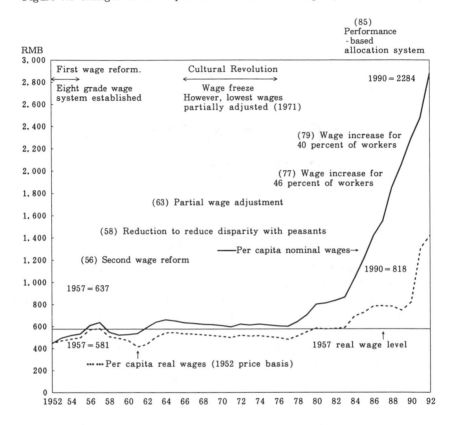

Note: Figure for per capita nominal wages is the average for staff and workers in state-owned enterprises. Real wages are derived from applying the general index of worker and staff daily living costs deflator.

Sources: *Statistical Yearbook of China 1993*, pp. 122, 238; for wage reform: *China's Wage System*, pp. 17-76.

Since the beginning of the Deng Xiaoping era, wage increases have been paced and sometimes exceeded by price rises. Especially in 1988, prices rose at double-digit rates, which dealt a heavy blow to workers' living standards. Although public dissatisfaction with price increases was at the bottom of the Tiananmen demonstrations in 1989, people were angered even more by profiteering practices, such as holding goods off the market and side-streaming of goods of enterprises and government agencies by "official brokers" (*guandao*). During the period of tightening after the Tiananmen incident, prices stabilized but unemployment rose.

Table 7.3   Monthly Wage of Workers in State Institutions: Central and Provincial Levels, Established June 1985. RMB.

| (Grade=G) | G-1 | G-2 | G-3 | G-4 | G-5 | G-6 | G-7 | G-8 | G-9 | G-10 |
|---|---|---|---|---|---|---|---|---|---|---|
| Technical workers | 113 | 105 | 97 | 89 | 82 | 76 | 70 | 64 | 58 | 52 |
| Regular workers | 89 | 82 | 76 | 70 | 64 | 58 | 52 | 46 | | |

Original source note: Following a period of apprenticeship, technical workers meeting qualifications are first paid RMB 52 at grade 10; this is adjusted to grade 9 RMB 58 at the grading period. The same applies to graduates of technical schools. Regular workers are assigned to grade 8 and paid RMB 46 in the first year after completing apprenticeship; the following year at the grading period they are promoted to grade 7 and RMB 52.

Source: *China's Wage System*, p. 155.

Table 7.4   Monthly Salary of Civil Servants of Eight Large Municipalities: Central and Provincial Levels. Established June 1985. RMB.

| (Grade=G) | G-1 | G-2 | G-3 | G-4 | G-5 | G-6 |
|---|---|---|---|---|---|---|
| Mayor | 255 | 230 | 205 | 190 | 180 | |
| Deputy mayor | 205 | 190 | 180 | 170 | 160 | |
| Bureau director | 180 | 170 | 160 | 150 | 140 | |
| Bureau deputy director | 170 | 160 | 150 | 140 | 131 | 122 |
| Office director | 160 | 150 | 140 | 131 | 122 | 113 |
| Office deputy director | 140 | 131 | 122 | 113 | 105 | 97 |
| Section chief, senior section staff | 131 | 122 | 113 | 105 | 97 | 89 |
| Deputy section chief, deputy senior section staff | 113 | 105 | 97 | 89 | 82 | 76 |
| Section staff | 97 | 89 | 82 | 76 | 70 | 64 |
| Staff | 82 | 76 | 70 | 64 | 58 | 52 |

Original source note: Cities are Guangzhou, Wuhan, Chongqing, Shenyang, Dalian, Harbin, Xian, and Nanjing.

Source: *China's Wage System*, p. 156.

plans to convert to noncombat-related operations (i.e., factories). Table 7.6 indicates the correspondence between military positions and titles and civilian positions and provides a reference point for this transition to civilian undertakings. The payment of allowances was widely used so that actual take-home income was not reduced.

# The Wage System in Large and Medium-Sized State Enterprises

In 1985 the Ministry of Labor and Personnel drafted standard wage scales applicable to workers and cadres in state-owned large and medium-sized enterprises (Tables 7.7 and 7.8) and sent them to state-owned enterprises nationwide for refeence during wage reform.

Table 7.5   The Chinese Civil Service Wage Structure   (1985)
(state institutions from common workers to premier)

| RMB | State Civil Service Administrative Positions | | | | | | | | | | | | Civil Servants in the Eight Large Municipalities | | | | | | | |
|---|---|---|---|---|---|---|---|---|---|---|---|---|---|---|---|---|---|---|---|---|
| | Chairman · Vice Chairman · Premier | Vice premier · Member-State Council | Minister · Provincial gov. | Vice min. · Vice gov. | Bureau dir. · Provincial dept. dir. | Provincial dept.dep.dir. · Dep. bureau dir. | Office dir. | Dep. office dir. | Sec. chief · Sen. sec. | Dep. sec. chief · Dep. senior sec. chief | Section staff | Staff | Mayor | Deputy mayor | Bureau director | Office dir. | Dep. Ooffice dir. | Section chief · Senior section chief | Section staff | Staff |
| 530 | G-1 | | | | | | | | | | | | | | | | | | | |
| 450 | G-2 | | | | | | | | | | | | | | | | | | | |
| 380 | G-3 | G-1 | | | | | | | | | | | | | | | | | | |
| 340 | | G-2 | | | | | | | | | | | | | | | | | | |
| 310 | | G-3 | G-1 | | | | | | | | | | | | | | | | | |
| 280 | | | G-2 | | | | | | | | | | | | | | | | | |
| 255 | | | G-3 | G-1 | | | | | | | | | G-1 | | | | | | | |
| 230 | | | G-4 | G-2 | | | | | | | | | G-2 | | | | | | | |
| 205 | | | G-5 | G-3 | G-1 | | | | | | | | G-3 | G-1 | | | | | | |
| 190 | | | | G-4 | G-2 | | | | | | | | G-4 | G-2 | | | | | | |
| 180 | | | | G-5 | G-3 | G-1 | | | | | | | G-5 | G-3 | G-1 | | | | | |
| 170 | | | | | G-4 | G-2 | G-1 | | | | | | | G-4 | G-2 | | | | | |
| 160 | | | | | G-5 | G-3 | G-2 | | | | | | | G-5 | G-3 | G-1 | | | | |
| 150 | | | | | | G-4 | G-3 | G-1 | | | | | | | G-4 | G-2 | | | | |
| 140 | | | | | | G-5 | G-4 | G-2 | | | | | | | G-5 | G-3 | G-1 | | | |
| 131 | | | | | | | G-5 | G-3 | G-1 | | | | | | | G-4 | G-2 | G-1 | | |
| 122 | | | | | | | G-6 | G-4 | G-2 | | | | | | | G-5 | G-3 | G-2 | | |
| 113 | | | | | | | | G-5 | G-3 | G-1 | | | | | | G-6 | G-4 | G-3 | | |
| 105 | | | | | | | | G-6 | G-4 | G-2 | | | | | | | G-5 | G-4 | | |
| 97 | | | | | | | | | G-5 | G-3 | G-1 | | | | | | G-6 | G-5 | G-1 | |
| 89 | | | | | | | | | G-6 | G-4 | G-2 | | | | | | | G-6 | G-2 | |
| 82 | | | | | | | | | | G-5 | G-3 | G-1 | | | | | | | G-3 | G-1 |
| 76 | | | | | | | | | | G-6 | G-4 | G-2 | | | | | | | G-4 | G-2 |
| 70 | | | | | | | | | | | G-5 | G-3 | | | | | | | G-5 | G-3 |
| 64 | | | | | | | | | | | G-6 | G-4 | | | | | | | G-6 | G-4 |
| 58 | | | | | | | | | | | | G-5 | | | | | | | | G-5 |
| 52 | | | | | | | | | | | | G-6 | | | | | | | | G-6 |
| 46 | | | | | | | | | | | | | | | | | | | | |

Source: Li Wei, *China's Wage System*, pp. 154, 155.

| Admin | Ministry dep. general engineer | Ministry Dep. general engineer | Bureau general engineer | Engineer | Assistant engineer | Technician | Technical worker | Common worker | RMB |
|---|---|---|---|---|---|---|---|---|---|
| | | | | | | | | | 530 |
| | | | | | | | | | 450 |
| | | | | | | | | | 380 |
| | | | | | | | | | 340 |
| | | | | | | | | | 310 |
| | | | | | | | | | 280 |
| | G-1 | | | | | | | | 255 |
| | G-2 | | | | | | | | 230 |
| | G-3 | G-1 | | | | | | | 205 |
| | G-4 | G-2 | | | | | | | 190 |
| | G-5 | G-3 | G-1 | | | | | | 180 |
| G-1 | | G-4 | G-2 | | | | | | 170 |
| G-2 | | G-5 | G-3 | | | | | | 160 |
| G-3 | | | G-4 | | | | | | 150 |
| G-4 | | | G-5 | G-1 | | | | | 140 |
| G-5 | | | | G-2 | | | | | 131 |
| G-6 | | | | G-3 | | | | | 122 |
| G-1 | | | | G-4 | | | G-1 | | 113 |
| G-2 | | | | G-5 | | | G-2 | | 105 |
| G-3 | | | | G-6 | | | G-3 | | 97 |
| G-4 | | | | | G-1 | | G-4 | G-1 | 89 |
| G-5 | | | | | G-2 | | G-5 | G-2 | 82 |
| G-6 | | | | | G-3 | G-1 | G-6 | G-3 | 76 |
| | | | | | G-4 | G-2 | G-7 | G-4 | 70 |
| | | | | | G-5 | G-3 | G-8 | G-5 | 64 |
| | | | | | | G-4 | G-9 | G-6 | 58 |
| | | | | | | G-5 | G-10 | G-7 | 52 |
| | | | | | | | | G-8 | 46 |

Left admin vertical labels: Dep. senior section staff · Deputy section chief · Dep. section · Dep. bureau dir. Top spanning headers: Technicians | Workers | RMB.

68

Table 7.6 Correspondence of Salary Structure of the Chinese People's Liberation Army and Civilian Administrative Positions (1985)

| | | Monthly wage (a) + (b) | Position wage (a) | Admin. level-based wage (b) | Military Scientists Authors | Military Athletes |
|---|---|---|---|---|---|---|
| Military Affairs Commission | Military Chairman and Vice Chairman | 580 | 340 | 240 | | |
| | Standing Committee Member | 420 | 220 | 200 | | |
| | Full Military Region Commander | 390 | 206 | 184 | G-1 | |
| Army Level | Second Military Region Commander | 356 | 186 | 170 | G-2 | |
| | Second Army Commander | 326 | 170 | 156 | G-3 | |
| Corps Level | Full corps leader | 300 | 156 | 144 | G-4 | |
| | Second corps leader | 277 | 143 | 134 | G-5 | G-1 |
| | Third corps leader | — | — | 126 | — | — |
| Division Level | Full division leader | 248 | 130 | 118 | G-6 | G-2 |
| | Second division leader | 227 | 117 | 110 | G-7 | G-3 |
| | Third division leader | — | — | 102 | — | — |
| Regiment Level | Full regiment leader | 199 | 105 | 94 | G-8 | G-4 |
| | Second regiment leader | 180 | 94 | 86 | G-9 | G-5 |
| | Third regiment leader | — | — | 78 | — | — |
| Brigade Level | Full brigade leader | 153 | 83 | 70 | G-10 | G-6 |
| | Second brigade leader | 137 | 74 | 63 | G-11 | G-7 |
| Company Level | Full company leader | 122 | 66 | 56 | G-12 | G-8 |
| | Second company leader | 108 | 58 | 50 | G-13 | G-9 |
| Platoon Level | Full platoon leader | 94 | 50 | 44 | G-14 | G-10 |
| | Second platoon leader | 81 | 42 | 39 | G-15 | G-11 |
| Squad Level | Full squad leader | | | 34 | | |
| | Second squad leader | | | | | |
| Soldiers | Old soldier | | | | | |
| | New soldier | | | | | |

Sources: *Military: Outline of the Cadre System* (Military Science Press 1988-internal distribution), p. 313. Administrative: *China's Wage System*, pp. 153, 224.

| Corresponding Civilian Administrative Post | Corresponding Administrative Monthly Wage | Old Adminis- trative Grade | Technical Position | | Current Ranking | Current Wage |
|---|---|---|---|---|---|---|
| Premier | 380 - 530 | Grade 1 - 3 | | | 1 | 530 |
| | | Grade 4 | | | 2 | 450 |
| Vice Premier | 310 - 380 | Grade 5 | | | 3 | 380 |
| | | Grade 6 | | | 4 | 340 |
| Minister | 205 - 310 | Grade 7 | | | 5 | 310 |
| | | Grade 8 | | | 6 | 280 |
| Vice Minister | 180 - 255 | Grade 9 | Ministry -level general engineers -5 grades | | 7 | 255 |
| | | Grade 10 | | | 8 | 230 |
| Bureau director | 160 - 205 | Grade 11 | | | 9 | 205 |
| Dep. bureau dir. | 140 - 180 | Grade 12 | | | 10 | 190 |
| — | | Grade 13 | | Bureau -level general engineers -5 grades | 11 | 180 |
| Office director | 122 - 170 | Grade 14 | | | 12 | 170 |
| Dep. office dir. | 105 - 150 | Grade 15 | | | 13 | 160 |
| — | | Grade 16 | | | 14 | 150 |
| Section chief | 89 - 131 | Grade 17 | Engineers -6 grades | | 15 | 140 |
| Dep.section chief | - 113 | Grade 18 | | | 16 | 131 |
| Section staff | 64 - 97 | Grade 19 | | | 17 | 122 |
| | | Grade 20 | | Technical workers grades 1 - 10 | 18 | 113 |
| Staff | 52 - 82 | Grade 21 | | | 19 | 105 |
| | | Grade 22 | | | 20 | 97 |
| Common workers | | Grade 23 | Common workers grades 1 - 8 | | 21 | 89 |
| | | Grade 24 | | | 22 | 82 |
| | | Grade 25 | | | 23 | 76 |
| | | Grade 26 | | | 24 | 70 |
| | | Grade 27 | | | 25 | 64 |
| | | Grade 28 | | | 26 | 58 |
| | | Grade 29 | | | 27 | 52 |
| | | Grade 30 | | | 28 | 46 |

Table 7.7  Standard Wage Scale of Workers in State-Owned Large and Medium Sized Enterprises (RMB)

| | ⇐ Light labor · Low price regions | | | | | | Heavy labor · High price regions⇒ | | | | |
|---|---|---|---|---|---|---|---|---|---|---|---|
| Grade | I | II | III | IV | V | VI | VII | VIII | IX | X | X I |
| 15 | 99 | 102 | 105 | 108 | 111 | 114 | 117 | 120 | 123 | 126 | 129 |
| 14 | 93 | 96 | 98 | 101 | 104 | 107 | 110 | 112 | 115 | 118 | 121 |
| 13 | 87 | 90 | 92 | 94 | 97 | 100 | 103 | 105 | 108 | 110 | 113 |
| 12 | 81 | 84 | 86 | 88 | 90 | 93 | 96 | 98 | 101 | 103 | 105 |
| 11 | 76 | 78 | 80 | 82 | 84 | 87 | 90 | 91 | 94 | 96 | 98 |
| 10 | 71 | 73 | 74 | 76 | 78 | 81 | 84 | 85 | 87 | 89 | 91 |
| 9 | 66 | 68 | 69 | 70 | 72 | 75 | 78 | 79 | 81 | 82 | 84 |
| 8 | 61 | 63 | 64 | 65 | 66 | 69 | 72 | 73 | 75 | 76 | 78 |
| 7 | 56 | 58 | 59 | 60 | 61 | 64 | 67 | 68 | 69 | 70 | 72 |
| 6 | 52 | 53 | 54 | 55 | 56 | 59 | 62 | 63 | 64 | 65 | 66 |
| 5 | 48 | 49 | 50 | 51 | 52 | 54 | 57 | 58 | 59 | 60 | 61 |
| 4 | 44 | 45 | 46 | 47 | 48 | 49 | 52 | 53 | 54 | 55 | 56 |
| 3 | 40 | 41 | 42 | 43 | 44 | 45 | 47 | 48 | 49 | 50 | 51 |
| 2 | 36 | 37 | 38 | 39 | 40 | 41 | 43 | 44 | 45 | 46 | 47 |
| 1 | 33 | 34 | 35 | 36 | 37 | 38 | 39 | 40 | 41 | 42 | 43 |

Note: The standard wage area is that of columns II −VI of this table. The premium wage area involving remote area allowances would be columns VII − IX.

Sources: *China's Wage System*, p. 117; Liu Jiesan, ed., *Practical Manual of Enterprise Wage Reform* (Beijing: China Urban Economic Society Press, 1988), p. 312.

Table 7.8  Standard Salary Scale for Cadres in State-Owned Large and Medium Sized Enterprises (RMB)

| | ⇐ Light labor · Low price regions | | | | | Heavy labor · High price regions⇒ | | | |
|---|---|---|---|---|---|---|---|---|---|
| Grade | I | II | III | IV | V | VI | VII | VIII | IX |
| 1 | 248 | 255 | 263 | 270 | 277 | 285 | 292 | 299 | 306 |
| 2 | 224 | 230 | 236 | 243 | 250 | 256 | 263 | 269 | 276 |
| 3 | 202 | 208 | 214 | 220 | 226 | 231 | 237 | 243 | 249 |
| 4 | 185 | 190 | 196 | 201 | 207 | 212 | 217 | 222 | 227 |
| 5 | 170 | 175 | 180 | 185 | 190 | 195 | 199 | 204 | 209 |
| 6 | 155 | 160 | 165 | 169 | 173 | 178 | 182 | 187 | 192 |
| 7 | 141 | 145 | 150 | 154 | 158 | 162 | 166 | 170 | 175 |
| 8 | 128 | 131 | 136 | 139 | 143 | 147 | 150 | 154 | 158 |
| 9 | 115 | 118 | 122 | 125 | 128 | 132 | 135 | 138 | 142 |
| 10 | 102 | 105 | 108 | 111 | 114 | 117 | 120 | 123 | 126 |
| 10' | 96 | 98 | 101 | 104 | 107 | 110 | 112 | 115 | 118 |
| 11 | 98 | 92 | 94 | 97 | 100 | 103 | 105 | 108 | 110 |
| 11' | 84 | 86 | 88 | 90 | 93 | 96 | 98 | 101 | 103 |
| 12 | 78 | 80 | 82 | 84 | 87 | 90 | 91 | 94 | 96 |
| 12' | 73 | 74 | 76 | 78 | 81 | 84 | 85 | 87 | 89 |
| 13 | 68 | 69 | 70 | 72 | 75 | 78 | 79 | 81 | 82 |
| 13' | 63 | 64 | 65 | 66 | 69 | 72 | 73 | 75 | 76 |
| 14 | 58 | 59 | 60 | 61 | 64 | 67 | 68 | 69 | 70 |
| 14' | 53 | 54 | 55 | 56 | 59 | 62 | 63 | 64 | 65 |
| 15 | 49 | 50 | 51 | 52 | 54 | 57 | 58 | 59 | 60 |
| 15' | 45 | 46 | 47 | 48 | 49 | 52 | 53 | 54 | 55 |
| 16 | 41 | 42 | 43 | 44 | 45 | 47 | 48 | 49 | 50 |
| 16' | 37 | 38 | 39 | 40 | 41 | 43 | 44 | 45 | 46 |
| 17 | 34 | 35 | 36 | 37 | 38 | 39 | 40 | 41 | 42 |

Note: The standard wage area is that of columns II −VI of this table. The premium wage area involving remote area allowances would be columns VII − IX.

Sources: *China's Wage System*, p. 117; *Practical Manual of Enterprise Wage Reform*, p. 312.

## Wage Scale for Workers

As shown in Table 7.7, the system differentiated according to geographic place of employment and type of work. Regions neither remote nor in high-cost cities were considered standard areas. This standard case includes columns two through six in the table. Columns two through four are for light labor industries, such as wheat or rice milling. columns three through five include labor considered between light and heavy, such as in the machinery, construction, transport, textiles, electric power, petroleum refining, and chemical industries. Columns four through six are for heavy labor industries such as metallurgy, coal mining, petroleum extraction, and logging.

## Wage Scale for Cadres

In the case of cadres in state-owned enterprises (Table 7.8), the "position ranking wage system" was employed; each position was divided into various salary grades. Administrative and technical positions received the same wages. Positions in the standard wage area are included in columns two through six. Leading cadres in large unified enterprises were assigned grades one to six; leading cadres in large enterprises were given grades three to eight; and leading cadres in medium-sized enterprises were assigned grades five to ten.

If the standard area is removed from these two tables, the result is Table 7.9. This presents the highest salary level in heavy industry for cadres and the highest level of heavy labor for workers.

# China's Privileged Class

There are two meanings for "cadres" in the Chinese language. The broad meaning is state institution and military "civil servants" (the term is not applied to "workers," such as soldiers and guards, clerks, and drivers). The narrow meaning is persons engaged in "certain specified leadership work or management work" (e.g., organization cadres and enterprise cadres); these individuals are China's privileged stratum. In 1981 Communist Party conservative ideologue Deng Liqun (former head of the party's central propaganda department) defended this stratum:

> There are nationally about 80,000 cadres above the deputy bureau director level and cadres above the military deputy division commander level [senior cadres]. We do not have accurate figures about their average wages, but we can make two calculations. The first would be a high estimate of a monthly wage of RMB 200, annualized to RMB 2400. In this case, their aggregate wages would be RMB 190 million. Another calculation would be a monthly wage of RMB 160, and an aggregate RMB 140 million. ... According to the remnant theory of the "Gang of Four," this is a privileged stratum, a highly paid stratum. However, how large are their wages in comparison with wages paid in the whole country—a mere 0.2 percent or even less. If you put the people re-

Table 7.9  Standard Wages in State - Owned Large and Medium Sized Enterprises

(a) Cadres (highest in standard area)   (b) Workers  (heavy labor in standard area)

| New 24 Grades | Monthly Amount | Old 17 Grades | New 15 Grades | Monthly Amount | Old 18 Grades |
|---|---|---|---|---|---|
| G-1 | RMB 270 | G-1 | Grade 15 | 114 (RMB) | Grade 8 |
| G-2 | 243 | G-2 | Grade 14 | 107 | |
| G-3 | 220 | G-3 | | | |
| G-4 | 201 | G-4 | Grade 13 | 100 | Grade 7 |
| G-5 | 185 | G-5 | Grade 12 | 93 | |
| G-6 | 169 | G-6 | | | |
| G-7 | 154 | G-7 | Grade 11 | 87 | Grade 6 |
| G-8 | 139 | G-8 | Grade 10 | 81 | |
| G-9 | 125 | G-9 | | | |
| G-10 | 111 | G-10 | Grade 9 | 75 | Grade 5 |
| G-11 | 104 | G-10' | Grade 8 | 69 | |
| G-12 | 97 | G-11 | | | |
| G-13 | 90 | G-11' | Grade 7 | 64 | Grade 4 |
| G-14 | 84 | G-12 | Grade 6 | 59 | |
| G-15 | 78 | G-12' | | | |
| G-16 | 72 | G-13 | Grade 5 | 54 | Grade 3 |
| G-17 | 66 | G-13' | Grade 4 | 49 | |
| G-18 | 61 | G-14 | | | |
| G-19 | 56 | G-14' | Grade 3 | 45 | Grade 2 |
| G-20 | 52 | G-15 | Grade 2 | 41 | |
| G-21 | 48 | G-15' | | | |
| G-22 | 44 | G-16 | Grade 1 | 38 | Grade 1 |
| G-23 | 40 | G-16' | | | |
| G-24 | 37 | G-17 | | | |

Source: *China's Wage System*, pp. 117-119; *Practical Manual of Enterprise Wage Reform*, p. 313.

Table 7.10  The Percentage of China's Power Elite

|  | (1987 year-end) | | | (1990 year-end) | |
|---|---|---|---|---|---|
| Class | Number | Percentage | Class | Number | Percentage |
| Senior Cadres    more than | 0.10 million | 0.01% | workers | 140 million | 2.2 % |
| All Cadres | 29.0 million | 2.5 % | peasants | 420 million | 39.1 % |
| of which | | | | | |
| administrative organs | 5.5 million | 0.5 % | Total | 1,150 million | 100.0 % |
| business units | 6.2 million | 0.5 % | | | |
| enterprise units | 10.8 million | 0.9 % | | | |
| middle and elementary schools | 6.5 million | 0.6 % | | | |
| Communist Party members | 47.8 million | 4.5 % | | | |
| Communist youth league members | 60.0 million | 5.2 % | | | |

Source: *History of Organizational Work of the Chinese Communist Party* (internal distribution), p. 454.

ceiving these wages in the numerator, and you put 800 million peasants in the denominator, you will get less than 0.1 percent. (*Xinhua Wenzhai 1981*, no. 5)

More than ten years later the number of senior cadres probably had roughly doubled, but their position as rulers of the people had not changed.

In fall 1982 the director of the Organization Department of the Party Central, Song Renqiong (currently deputy director of the Advisory Committee to the Party Central) disclosed the following facts about cadres. At the time (1) there were approximately 11 million in the 35–55 age range; (2) approximately 12 million had assumed responsible positions in the period from the victory in the war with Japan to the beginning of the Cultural Revolution (1945 to 1965); (3) approximately 12 million had educational levels of high school or higher; and (4) approximately 8.3 million were specialized technical cadres (*Red Flag* 1982, no. 19).

Table 7.10 summarizes China's 1987 class composition, from peasants to the privileged stratum. Included are the 47.8 million Communist Party members who constituted 4.5 percent of the population. (The party's basic organization units numbered over 2.9 million; Zhao Bo and Pan Tianshun 1966, p. 454.) Table 7.11 provides data for 1987 from restricted Chinese sources (and therefore not updatable) on a separate powerful class of cadres even within government organizations; this group included the full-time staff of the organizations' party committees.

## Communist Party Cadres Are Shaken by Reform

The *People's Daily* reported on September 20, 1989, that Communist Party membership had increased nationally from 4.5 million in the early years of the PRC to 48 million; basic-level party organizational units had increased over the same period from 200,000 to just under 3 million. At the end of 1988 there were 7.97 million worker (noncadre) members, an increase of 71.2 times the figure in 1949. The proportion of worker members had increased from 2.5 percent in 1949 to 17 percent. Party members with educations of high school or above numbered 14.8 million, or 30.4 percent of the total, 362 times more than in 1949. In the "party rectification" after 1983, evaluation of persons who had joined the party during the Cultural Revolution period had resulted in 330,000 persons being expelled and over 90,000 being refused membership renewal. Further, in 1988 and 1989 (in connection with the Tiananmen incident), the number of persons who quit the party after being advised to do so or who were expelled rose to over 60,000.

The *People's Daily* of September 16, 1989, pointed out three major changes that had occurred in the cadre ranks since the early PRC period.

1. *Enlargement of scale.* In the early years of the PRC, there were fewer than 1.7 million cadres, 400,000 of them former officials of the Kuomintang government who were accepted into the cadre ranks. In 1989 there were 30 million, 95 percent of whom had become cadres after 1949.
2. *Expansion of the technocrat stratum.* In 1954 there were only 570,000 "specialized technical cadres" (8.6 percent of total cadres); by 1988 these had increased to 21 million (67 percent).
3. *Elevation of cadres' educational level.* In 1988 cadres with high school or higher educations numbered 23.04 million, or 75 percent. Of these, cadres with college-level or higher educations totaled 8.61 million, or 28 percent of the total.

Table 7.11   Central Government Staffing and Full-Time Party
Committee Staff (1987)

| State Council Ministries and Committees | Budgeted Staff Level | Actual Staff Serving | of which Full-Time Party Committee |
|---|---|---|---|
| State Council General Office | 984 | 953 | 17 |
| Ministry of Foreign Affairs | 2,621 | 2,827 | 42 |
| Ministry of National Defense | | [Secret ] | |
| State Planning Commission | 1,490 | 1,544 | 74 |
| State Economic Commission | 1,090 | 1,018 | 25 |
| Internal organs | 592 | 611 | 11 |
| State Committee on Economic System Reform | 195 | 162 | |
| State Athletic Commission | 819 | 763 | 22 |
| State Commission Science & Technology | | [Secret ] | |
| State Commission of Science, Technology and Industry for National Defense | | [Secret ] | |
| State Commission Nationalities Affairs | 183 | 230 | 10 |
| Ministry of Public Security | | [Secret ] | |
| Ministry of State Security | | [Secret ] | |
| Ministry of Supervision | - 620 | 221 | 2 |
| Ministry of Civil Affairs | 425 | 448 | 7 |
| Ministry of Justice | 495 | 467 | 7 |
| Ministry of Finance | 1,121 | 1,308 | 32 |
| Ministry of Labor | 644 | 748 | 10 |
| Ministry of Geology and Mineral Resources | 690 | 753 | 20 |
| Ministry of Coal Industry | 908 | 1,078 | 60 |
| Ministry of Petroleum Industry | 703 | 704 | 24 |
| Ministry of Railways | 1,291 | 1,362 | 22 |
| Ministry of Transportation | 861 | 1,240 | 35 |
| State Committee on Machinery Industry | 1,300 | 1,251 | 42 |
| Ministry of Nuclear Industry | 842 | 885 | 28 |
| Ministry of Aeronautical Industry | 807 | 816 | 25 |
| Ministry of Astronautics Industry | 649 | 717 | 69 |
| Ministry of Metallurgical Industry | 896 | 1,012 | 19 |
| Ministry of Electrical Industry | 956 | 1,032 | 39 |
| Ministry of Chemical Industry | 737 | 824 | 21 |
| Ministry of Light Industry | 936 | 928 | 29 |
| Ministry of Textile Industry | 571 | 615 | 18 |
| Ministry of Posts and Telecommunications | 638 | 794 | 25 |
| Ministry of Water Conservancy & Electric Power | 1,016 | 998 | 24 |
| Ministry of City and Rural Construction Environmental Protection | 944 | 1,002 | 23 |
| Ministry of Agriculture, Animal Husbandry & Fishery | 1,428 | 1,560 | 21 |
| Ministry of Forestry | 647 | 790 | 18 |
| Ministry of Commerce | 2,090 | 2,545 | 40 |
| Ministry of Foreign Economic Relations and Trade | 1,472 | 1,643 | 33 |
| Internal organs | 140 | 145 | |
| Ministry of Culture | 1,025 | 1,194 | 31 |
| Ministry of Radio, Film and Television | 586 | 560 | 24 |
| Ministry of Health | 576 | 583 | 21 |
| State Physical Culture & Sports Commission | 510 | 493 | 12 |
| State Family Planning Commission | 140 | 134 | 5 |
| People's Bank of China | 731 | 742 | 16 |
| Auditing Administration | 800 | 663 | 13 |
| Subtotal | 36,169 | 38,366 | 1,016 |

| Direct Organs of the State Council | Budgeted Staff Level | Actual Staff Serving | of which Full-Time Party Committee |
|---|---|---|---|
| State Statistical Bureau | 580 | 620 | 14 |
| State Administration of Commodity Prices | 537 | 181 | 4 |
| State Materials Bureau | 445 | 493 | 17 |
| State Administration of Building Materials Industry | 476 | 434 | 15 |
| State Administration for Industry and Commerce | 356 | 333 | 9 |
| General Administration of Customs | 325 | 317 | 4 |
| State Press & Publications Administration | 300 | 229 | 9 |
| State Meteorological Administration | 260 | 287 | 20 |
| Civil Aviation Administration of China | 549 | 842 | 28 |
| State Air Traffic Control Bureau | 70 | 61 | 1 |
| State Land Administration Bureau | 170 | 146 | 2 |
| State Oceanography Bureau | | | |
| State Seismological Bureau | 150 | 138 | 15 |
| National Tourism Administration | 231 | 207 | 8 |
| State Pharmaceutical Administration | 80 | 70 | 8 |
| State Language Work Committee | 65 | 65 | 3 |
| State Council Bureau of Legislative Affairs | 100 | 85 | |
| State Bureau of Archives | 135 | 99 | 3 |
| State Council Religious Affairs Bureau | 57 | 72 | 3 |
| State Council Counsellors' Office | 36 | 31 | |
| State Council Government Office Administration | 1,027 | 907 | 21 |
| State Council Office of Overseas Chinese Affairs | 300 | 275 | 5 |
| State Council Office of Hong Kong & Macao Affairs | 100 | 82 | |
| State Council Office of Special Zones Affairs | 42 | 36 | |
| State Commission for Restructuring Economy | 20 | 15 | |
| Subtotal | 6,761 | 6,379 | 208 |
| Grand Total | 42,930 | 44,745 | 1,224 |

Note: Non-professional, manual workers are not included.
Source: Ministry of Labor, Organization Bureau, ed. *Overview of Organizational Structure of the State Council 1987* (Internal distribution only. 1988).

As the Fourteenth Party Congress in fall 1992 approached, a major issue was the generational transfer among the ranks of cadres. From 1982 to 1988, 640,000 younger, middle-level cadres assumed positions at the provincial or office director or higher levels (see Table 7.6); at the same time, 3.4 million older cadres retired. At the provincial, regional, and county levels, 90 percent of members of all levels of party committees and leaders in government departments were selected after 1982 (*People's Daily,* September 17, 1989).

Thus the party has been acquiring a more youthful character, but attending this shift is the contradiction between economic reform and the bureaucratic system. Critics are focusing on the "iron wages" system of guaranteed wage payments regardless of a worker's actual production, and the "iron armchair" system of cadres receiving guaranteed positions regardless of performance. The totality of this is called the "iron rice bowl." As the focus of economic reform begins to shift to reform of state-owned enterprises, the party bureaucrats who had staked out this territory as a place to idle away time are being tagged as obsolete. The Communist

Party is being forced to transform itself from a party dedicated first to political work into one engaged in economic construction. But this metamorphosis may be too challenging for many party members individually.

In contrast, privileged senior cadres are converting their political power into economic niches and frenetically trying to transfer vested interests to second or third generations. The early 1990s have witnessed the phenomenon of cadre "incorporation"—the practice of cadres setting up companies through which to "privatize" their official duties for personal and family profit. Such activities have since mid-1993 been the target of the official anticorruption campaign under the titular leadership of Jiang Zemin (see Chapter 19).

## From State- to Enterprise-Determined Wages

After the Third Plenum of the Eleventh Party Congress in 1978, reform of the wage management system was commenced in connection with reform of the economic system. In 1982 the Party Central and the State Council issued "Regulations on the Work of Factory Managers in State-Owned Factories." This document gave factory managers authority to raise wages 1 percent every year. This ceiling was increased to 3 percent in May 1984 when the State Council issued "Temporary Regulations on Further Expanding the Sovereignty of State-Owned Industrial Enterprises."

In 1983 the first stage of reform of the tax payment system was implemented. In the second stage in 1984, limitations on enterprise payments of bonuses were removed, and a tax was applied on the payment of excessive bonuses. Thus enterprises were given full sovereignty in the method of distributing bonuses, and the way was opened for strictly performance-based and piecework compensation systems. Further, raises and position-related allowances were left to the discretion of the enterprises.

The "Decision on Reform of the Economic System" was adopted at the Third Plenum of the Twelfth Party Congress in October 1984. The policy thus set, the State Council in January 1985 issued the "Notice Concerning the Problem of Wage Reform of State-Owned Enterprises," in which it was stipulated that "with respect to enterprises wages, the state shall adopt a system of multi-level management" (i.e., at the appropriate level of authority). This policy provided another boost to the sovereignty of enterprises in wage reform.

In December 1986 the State Council issued "Some Regulations on Deepening Enterprise Reform and Strengthening Enterprise Vitality," which further broadened enterprises' independence: "Within the limits of policy and total wage payments established by the state, enterprises will have sovereign authority to decide and pay wages and bonuses, and to decide the time and recipients of wage raises within the enterprise; the state will no longer lay down unified rules."

The "State-Owned Enterprise Law of the People's Republic of China" adopted in April 1988 was another step to reform. Article 3 pertaining to rights and duties of enterprises stated that "enterprises possess the sovereign authority over incentive award payments and the form of wages as appropriate to the conditions of the particular enterprise." This provision was the first confirmation in legal form of the sovereignty of enterprises over internal distributions.

The preceding discussion shows clearly the step-by-step progression from wage determination by the state to wage determination by enterprises. Establishing the sovereignty of the enterprise in the area of wages was a critical pillar in the general expansion of enterprise sovereignty.

This liberalization of wage decisionmaking brought change in the wage structure, as shown in Figure 7.2. In state-owned enterprises in 1978, hourly wages constituted 85 percent of the total, but by 1992 this had declined precipitously to 45 percent. Allowances in 1978 amounted to less than 10 percent of compensation; by 1992 these had risen to 24 percent, and incentive payments constituted nearly another 20 percent. As seen in Figure 7.3, the wage level in private and joint venture enterprises was high.

## Constraining Wage Levels Through Full Employment Policies

Chinese wages were fixed for an extraordinarily long period—over thirty years. Chinese workers managed to sustain their livelihoods during this time through multiple employment.

From the standpoint of government, the burden of providing employment for an expanding population of workers was already great enough; the state could not also increase wages. In response, workers put the whole family to work. The trend toward full family employment was in line with the idea that "if one does not work, one does not eat," and the notion that providing work in society to women would allow them to liberate themselves from the shackles of the household. However, some observers regret that the priority placed on full employment led to overemployment and to a belief that it was acceptable to ignore labor productivity. Nevertheless, urban family incomes did increase (Figure 7.4).

In 1985 household members of urban families numbered 3.9 persons, wage earners numbered 2.2 persons, and dependents 1.7 persons. By 1992 the numbers had declined to 3.4 members, 2.0 workers, and 1.4 dependents (Figure 7.5).

The situation in the countryside between 1985 and 1992 was one of more moderate change (Figure 7.6). Average household members numbered 5.5 persons in 1985 and declined to 4.7 in 1992. Workers declined slightly from 2.9 to 2.8. Dependents declined from 2.6 to 1.9 persons (*Statistical Yearbook of China 1993*).

The reason for the larger size of agricultural households is that there have traditionally been two "workers." In recent years, as a result of the one-child policy,

78

Figure 7.2   Changes in the Composition of Wage
Payments of State - Owned Enterprises
(1978 - 1992)

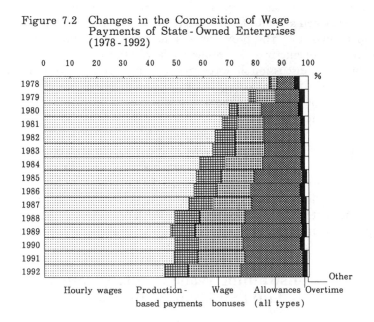

Sources: *Statistical Yearbook of China 1993*, p. 127,
and *Statistical Yearbook of China 1986*, p. 644.

Figure 7.3   Trends in Average Wages in Enterprises by
Ownership Category (1985 - 1992)

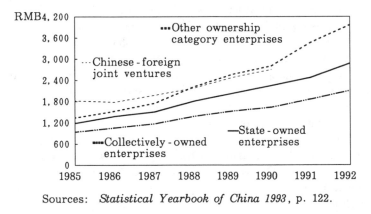

Sources: *Statistical Yearbook of China 1993*, p. 122.

Figure 7.4  Urban Family Income Structure: Percentage of
Urban Households by Per Capita Monthly Income

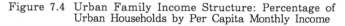

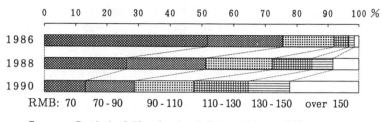

RMB: 70    70-90    90-110    110-130   130-150   over 150

Source: *Statistical Yearbook of China 1991*, p. 276.

Figure 7.5  Changes in the Number of Members and Wage Earners in Urban
Households

【1985】
Family members 4.4 persons

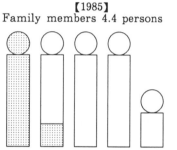

Wage earners 1.3 persons
Annual household per capita income
253.6 RMB

【1992】
Family members 3.4 persons

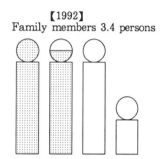

Wage earners 1.9 persons
Annual household per capita income
2,032 RMB

Source: *Statistical Yearbook of China 1993*, p. 287.

Figure 7.6  Changes in the Number of Members and Laborers
in Peasant Households

【1985】
Family members 5.5 persons

【1992】
Family members 4.7 persons

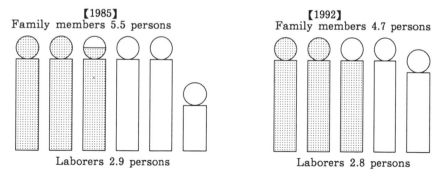

Laborers 2.9 persons                Laborers 2.8 persons

Note: Annual household income per capita is deflated by the staff and
worker living cost index.
Source: *Statistical Yearbook of China 1993*, p. 311 (sample survey).

households have been getting smaller. However, under the system of giving the individual agricultural household responsibility for production, additional household labor is useful, and this has been discouraging people from family planning.

The problems of unemployment and employment are extremely vexing for China. Since the establishment of the PRC, a sustaining notion has been that under socialism there is no unemployment, and all efforts have been made to expand employment and create jobs. The consequences of this approach have been a pernicious egalitarianism in the distribution of income, a resulting demotivation of labor, and long-term stagnation of labor productivity. Deng Xiaoping's reforms started with toleration of the income gaps entailed in breaking out of this destructive syndrome; his policy became "it is acceptable that some people will get rich ahead of others."

# 8

# National and
# Per Capita Income

## China's GNP and GNP Growth Rate

According to *World Bank Atlas 1994* (World Bank 1994), China ranked ninth internationally in 1992 in terms of GNP with $442.3 billion ($424.0 billion in 1991). The eight countries ahead of China were (1) the United States $5,904.8 billion; (2) Japan $3,507.8 billion; (3) Germany $1,846.1 billion; (4) France $1,278.6 billion; (5) Italy $1,186.6 billion; (6) United Kingdom $1,024.7 billion; (7) Canada $565.7 billion; and (8) Spain $547.9 billion (Figure 8.1). After ninth place were (10) Brazil $425.4 billion; (11) Russian Federation $397.8 billion; (12) the Netherlands $312.3 billion; (13) Australia $299.3 billion; and (14) Republic of Korea $296.3 billion.

International comparisons of growth of GNP (Figure 8.2) (1985 to 1992 real growth rate) place China in tenth place with 6.0 percent, behind such countries as the Republic of Korea with 8.5 percent and Thailand 8.3 percent (World Bank 1994). Taiwan was not included in the World Bank's data. In *Taiwan Statistical Data Book 1992,* the figure was 6.5 percent.

It is important to note that among the top ten countries in terms of GNP growth are several countries—the Maldives, Botswana, Swaziland, Belize, and Mauritius—with small populations. The ability of China, with its huge population, to sustain high levels of growth, even in comparison with these small countries, is remarkable. Among the top fifteen countries are the Asian NIEs (newly industrializing economies) of Korea, Taiwan, Singapore, Malaysia, Thailand, and Hong Kong. Fifteen years ago when Deng advocated the policy of reform and liberalization, he drew encouragement from the growth performance of the Asian NIEs. Since then their continued rapid advance has served to pull China further toward reform and liberalization. More than a few voices are prophesying that the twenty-first century will be the century of Asia. The fundamental element of Asia's advance has been its rapid growth of GNP.

Figure 8.1  Top Countries in Terms of GNP (1992)

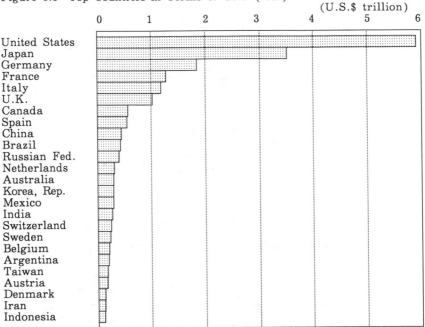

Sources: *The World Bank Atlas, 1994; Taiwan Statistical Data Book, 1992.*

# Per Capita GNP

In terms of GNP, which is an overall indicator of a country's strength, China is an economic power. However, it has a huge population, and when GNP is converted to GNP per capita, China's rank drops drastically. Of the 129 countries in the world with populations over 1 million, China ranks 103rd in per capita GNP. The *World Bank Atlas 1992* calculated China's per capita GNP in 1991 at $370 (in 1990 it was $350—the same as in 1989 due to RMB depreciation).

This low figure reflects both population increase and the steady depreciation of the RMB exchange rate against the U.S. dollar. If we look instead at real purchasing power, we can calculate an increase in China's GNP of 300 percent, or a per capita GNP of around $1,000.

Figure 8.3 provides a comparison of GNP per capita in the Asia and Pacific region, including China. From lowest to highest are (1) India $330; (2) China $370; (3) Pakistan $400; (4) Sri Lanka $500; (5) Indonesia $610; (6) Philippines $740; (7) Thailand $1,580; (8) Malaysia $2,490; (9) South Korea $6,340; (10) Taiwan $8,815; (11) Hong Kong $13,200; (12) Singapore $12,890; and (13) Japan $26,920. The World Bank categorizes countries by per capita income as follows: $500 or less, low in-

Figure 8.2   Top Countries in Terms of GNP Per Capita Growth Rate
(1985 to 1992 average)

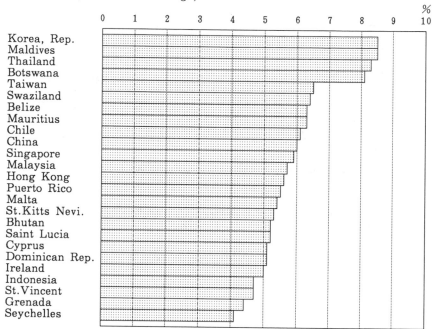

Note: Taiwan Data for 1980 - 1991
Sources: *The World Bank Atlas, 1994; Taiwan Statistical Data
Book, 1992.*

come; $500 to $6,000, middle income; and over $6,000, high income. According to this scale, China ranks with India and Sri Lanka as a low-income country; the group between Indonesia (5) and South Korea (9) includes middle-income countries; and Taiwan, Hong Kong, Singapore, and Japan are high-income countries.

In times of war, GNP as a measure of national strength is most relevant, but in times of peace and economic development and cooperation, GNP per capita is most important because it clearly expresses living standards. Figure 8.4 shows how China's GNP and GNP per capita have increased during the Deng Xiaoping era.

One symbolic event marking the commencement of the reform and liberalization policies of the Deng Xiaoping era was the adoption of the GNP indicator, which had previously been rejected as a vulgar conceit of bourgeois economists. In the early 1980s China abandoned its self-absorbed isolationism and converted to measures of economic growth performance that the West commonly used.

When 1980 is indexed as 100, GNP doubled by 1987–1988, and per capita GNP doubled two years later (1989–1990). The two-year lag for GNP per capita was of course because population growth offset part of absolute GNP growth. In 1992

Figure 8.3   Per Capita GNP of China and Other Asian
Countries (1992)

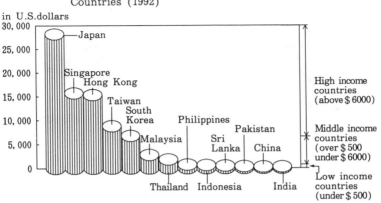

Sources: *The World Bank Atlas, 1994; Taiwan Statistical
Data Book, 1992.*

Figure 8.4   Trends in China's GNP and Per Capita GNP
Growth (1978 - 1992)

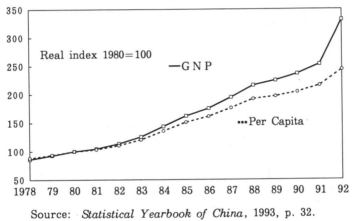

Source:   *Statistical Yearbook of China*, 1993, p. 32.

GNP was RMB 2,206 billion (current prices), and GNP per capita was RMB 2,063
(*Statistical Yearbook of China 1993*, pp. 31–32).

# Disparities in Per Capita GNP at the Provincial Level

China is a vast country with great regional disparities. Figure 8.5 presents for China's various special (centrally administered) municipalities, provinces, and autonomous regions (hereafter, provinces) 1990 GNP per capita figures (obtained by
dividing GNP by their respective populations).

Figure 8.5   Per Capita GNP of All Provinces, Municipalities, and
Autonomous Regions (1990)

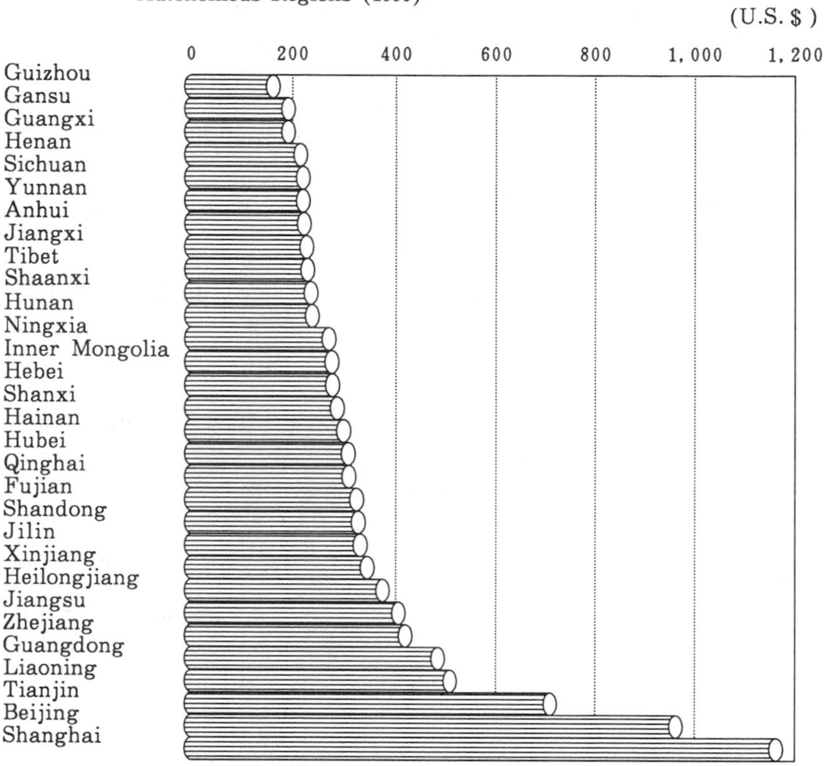

(U.S. $ )

Source:   *Statistical Yearbook of China 1991*, p. 36.

At the official rate of $1.00 = RMB 4.78375, Shanghai leads the list at $1,164, followed by (2) Beijing $963, and (3) Tianjin $710. These three centrally administered
cities are old industrial cities; furthermore, the inflow of population has been rigidly restricted. Their populations are consequently small in relation to their production, and GNP per capita is high. Next are (4) Liaoning $508 and (5)
Guangdong $484; both are near the $500 benchmark set by the World Bank for dividing low-income from middle-income countries. It may thus be ventured that
in China, the three cities and two provinces of Shanghai, Beijing, Tianjin, Liaoning, and Guangdong are at middle-income status and that the two provinces of
Zhejiang and Jiangsu are approaching this level. The remaining provinces are low-
income regions.

The poorest five provinces are (2) Guizhou $162, (2) Gansu $192, (3) Guangxi
$192, (4) Henan $216, and (5) Sichuan $221. The first three are border regions pop-
ulated by many minorities. Henan is in the Yellow River basin and includes large
areas of wasteland. The population of Sichuan exceeds 100 million persons.

The disparity ratio shown in Figure 8.5 between the most prosperous provincial unit, Shanghai, and the poorest, Guizhou, is approximately 6:1. It should be noted that at the close of the Mao Zedong era, 1977, the disparity was 15:1. This is evidence that, contrary to much recent commentary, income disparities have been closing rather than widening during the Deng Xiaoping era. The principal reason is the greater mobility of labor that allows workers from interior provinces to travel to and work in the booming coastal provinces, remitting earnings and purchasing power back to their families.

Figure 8.6 shows per capita GNP on the vertical axis (similarly to Figure 8.5) and GNP growth rate on the horizontal axis (1980 to 1990). The per capita GNP of Shanghai, Tianjin, and Beijing is high, but a high rate of growth does not necessarily follow. If we view these industrialized cities together with Liaoning, we begin to observe the inherent contradictions in concentrations of state-owned enterprises. Numerous state-owned industries in these cities have helped to produce a high per capita GNP figure, but because growth has been stagnating, their share of industrial production has been declining.

In contrast to these cities are Guangdong, Zhejiang, and Jiangsu provinces. With per capita incomes of under $500, they are in transition from the low- to the middle-income stage. The principal driving force behind their rapid growth rates is township and village enterprises. The contribution of foreign-invested and joint venture enterprises is also significant, particularly in Guangdong where Hong Kong capital has been decisive. The development of these rural and foreign-affiliated enterprises has been possible because of the liberalization policy. The result has been an increasingly larger economic gap between the interior regions and the coastal regions, the latter developing rapidly through economic integration with the East Asia economic zone.

With regard to this problem, Deng Xiaoping in his talks before Spring Festival 1992 pointed out that there will be no way to prevent a widening of economic disparities in this century. Only through major development of the coastal region will assistance to the interior become possible. Thus it is critical to reject the pernicious egalitarianism that would seek to rein in the coastal regions. Deng Xiaoping's tolerance of having certain regions become rich in advance of others is a realistic strategy. The question is whether it will be possible to maintain political stability in the transitional period required to reduce the resulting disparities.

## Disparities in Per Capita GDP at the Municipal Level

Figure 8.7 presents calculations of per capita GDP (gross domestic production) for principal Chinese cities. According to the previously mentioned categories of the World Bank, GNP (gross national production) of $6,000 or more defines a high-income country. At $5,693 Shenzhen is a breath away from this level. Closely following are the special economic zone cities of Zhuhai $2,010 and Xiamen $1,590.

Figure 8.6   Comparative Per Capita GNP and Per Capita GNP
             Growth Rates of Provinces, Municipalities, and
             Autonomous Regions

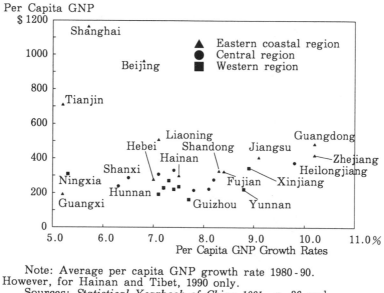

Note: Average per capita GNP growth rate 1980-90.
However, for Hainan and Tibet, 1990 only.
   Sources: *Statistical Yearbook of China 1991*, p. 36 and
*Compendium of Historical Statistical Materials for All
Provinces, Autonomous Regions, and Special Municipalities,*
p. 46.

Next come Guangzhou $1,510, Shanghai $1,365, Nantong $1,353, Beijing $1,337, Hangzhou 1,328, Dalian $1,183, Qinhuangdao $1,084, Nanjing $1,077, Urumchi $1,056, Ningbo $1,040, and Weihai $1,024, all of them in the $1,000 to $2,000 range. Except for Urumchi and Hangzhou, all fourteen cities are along the coast.

The twelve cities of Haikou, Kunming, Qingdao, Tianjin, Lanzhou, Shijiazhuang, Changsha, Shenyang, Jinan, Taiyuan, Fuzhou, and Lianyungang are in the $800 to $1,000 range. The seventeen cities of Wenzhou, Hefei, Harbin, Chengdu, Beihai, Shantou, Nanning, Yinchuan, Wuhan, Chongqing, Nanchang, Zhengzhou, Zhanjiang, Guiyang, Xian, Huhehot, and Changchun are in the $500 to $800 range. Yantai at $428 is approaching the $500 level. Thus it can be said that some forty-three cities exist at the middle-income level of $500 and above (conversion rate of $1.00 = RMB 4.783, or RMB 1.00 = $0.209). They comprise a population of 81.92 million.

It may be a bold statement, but these data indicate that something less than 10 percent of China's population has approached the economic "takeoff" stage. One issue, however, is the appropriate conversion rate of the RMB to the U.S. dollar. As an element of the opening policy, China has repeatedly devalued the RMB in order to sustain an export drive aimed at acquiring foreign exchange. The official RMB/

88

Figure 8.7  Per Capita GDP of Principal Cities (1990)

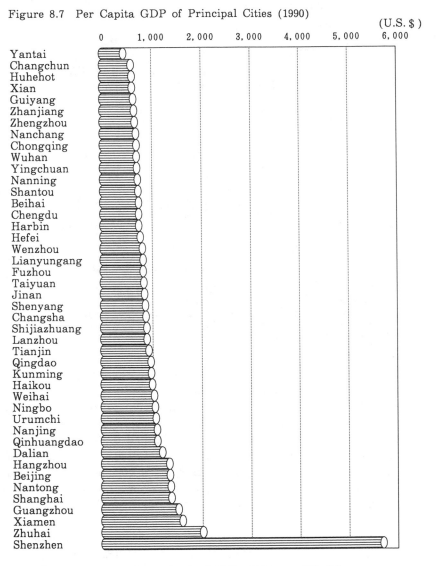

Source: *Statistical Yearbook of China 1991*, pp. 659 - 667.

U.S. dollar exchange rate declined from 1.68 in 1978, to 2.32 in 1984, to 3.45 in 1986, to 4.78 in 1990, to 5.51 in 1992. To buy one U.S. dollar now requires three times as many RMB.

[Translator's note: The official rate continued to depreciate to about 5.75 in 1993. The managed quasi-market rate depreciated dramatically in 1993 from about 6.00 to 10.00 before recovering to approximately 8.8 after financial rectification measures were introduced in July 1993. As a step toward more rational foreign exchange management, the dual rate system was unified effective January 1, 1994. The official rate was abolished, leaving the managed market rate determined through daily trading under Central Bank supervision. Through the first quarter of 1994 the RMB was being traded in domestic markets at a fairly stable rate of about RMB 8.6 to US$1.00. See Chapters 19 and 22.]

As a consequence, it is undeniable that in converting China's GNP into U.S. dollars there is a danger of underestimating it. Further, considering the real purchasing power of the RMB, there is an increasingly widely held view that in order to indicate accurately the current income level, the figure resulting from conversion to U.S. dollars increased severalfold. Here it is appropriate to reiterate a point previously made: It is a gross oversimplification to think that because in the 1980s GNP per capita was about $250 and in the 1990s it is around $300, growth has been only about $50. It cannot be doubted that real GNP growth per capita (correcting for price rises) from 1980 to 1990 was about 100 percent. Expressing these values in U.S. dollars at the current exchange rate undervalues this performance.

In sum, because China has a huge population, figures expressed in per capita terms are small. Also, there are enormous disparities between regions. It remains a big question whether the motive power of the advanced cities can lead the rest of the country to the takeoff stage.

# 9

# The Never-Ending Struggle
# to Feed 1.2 Billion People

## Supply of and Demand for Grain

Grain production stagnated after reaching a peak of 407 million tons in 1984, a level not recovered until 1989. In 1990 production totaled 446 million tons, but flooding held the harvest to 435 million tons in 1991. In 1992 production was 443 million tons. Grain holdings (not consumption) per capita (grain production divided by the average of previous year-end and current year-end population) reached 390 kilograms in 1984. This level was finally exceeded in 1990, then the figure fell to 376 kilograms in 1991 and to 338 kilograms in 1992 (see Figure 9.1).

The Chinese leadership has established 400 kilograms as the goal for per capita grain holdings. Reaching this goal will be difficult. Production targets are 455 million tons in 1995 (eighth five-year plan) and 500 million tons in 2000 (ten-year plan ending 2000). Even if China reaches these targets, grain production per capita will not reach 400 kilograms after the expected increase in population.

Experts have offered five reasons why demand for grain will increase: population increase, increased requirements for livestock feed, demand from the brewing industry, the mobile and "underground" populations, and the excessively cheap ration distribution price for grain (Japan International Cooperation Agency 1991, pp. 97–98). The analysis is as follows:

1. *Population increase.* If we posit an annual increase in population of 15 million persons and a per capita grain requirement of 390 kilograms, then an annual increase in production of 5.85 million tons is required.
2. *Requirements for livestock feed.* Grain used for animal feed increased from over 30 million tons (12 percent of grain production) in 1978 to 77.34 million tons (about 20 percent) in 1988 (*Farmer's Daily*, March 4, 1989.

Figure 9.1   Changes in Grain Production and Per Capita
            Grain Holdings (1952 - 1992)

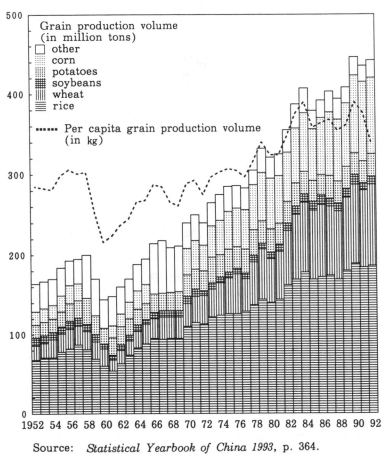

Source:   *Statistical Yearbook of China 1993*, p. 364.

3. *Requirements for brewing.* Production of alcoholic beverages in 1979 totaled 3.1 million tons, of which 520,000 tons was beer. In 1989 the figure
   was 12.85 million tons (of which beer, 6.43 million tons), more than a
   fourfold increase. Of this, production of Chinese spirits ("white liquor") was consuming 11 million tons of grain (*Market Report,* June 17,
   1991).

4. *Mobile and "underground" populations.* There are several estimates of
   China's mobile population; one estimate is 50 million persons. Added to
   this would be the "underground" population ("black children"). The
   former would increase the demand for grain in the cities, and the latter
   would be a factor in raising demand nationwide.

5. *Waste resulting from underpricing.* The ration distribution price for grain to the cities is kept low through price subsidies. The result is a general feeling that grain is cheap, and there is widespread waste (approximately 200 million persons receive ration distribution of grain).

Nationally the supply-and-demand situation for grain is tight. In some areas freight congestion and grain spoilage are exacerbating the situation. An urgent need exists for improvements in transport systems and increases in storage and processing equipment.

# Land and Labor Productivity

## An Exploding Population and Diminishing Cultivated Land

Figure 9.2 presents the relationship between the increase in population and cultivated land and planted area. Population was 574 million in 1952; by 1992 this had about doubled to 1.17 billion. Cultivated area in 1952 was 107 million hectares, and this increased to 111 million hectares in 1957; thereafter, it evidenced a steadily diminishing trend, and in 1990 was at the level of 95 million hectares. On the one hand, there have been some efforts to increase cultivated area by recovering wastelands and draining swamps; on the other hand, the active forces of industrialization and urbanization and activities such as roadbuilding and regulation of rivers and waterways have taken land out of cultivation. Overall, the trend toward reducing land under cultivation has continued.

## Advances in Multiple Cropping

Planted area in 1952 was 141 million hectares; this increased by 1956 to 159 million hectares. Thereafter, however, as with cultivated area, planted area continued to evidence a slowly diminishing trend. The multiple-cropping index, obtained by dividing planted area by cultivated area, shows a figure of 1.31. in 1952 (i.e., a piece of land was used to produce harvested crops 1.31 times on average during the year). In 1960 this figure peaked at 1.44; in the period 1976–1978 this peak was regained; and in the 1980s the figure increased from 1.47 to 1.55 (1990) (Figure 9.3). From this it can be seen that the shortage of cultivated land was compensated for through an increase in planted area, as is indicated in a rise in the multiple-cropping index. However, in the context of small reductions in cultivated land and planted area, the per capita measures of cultivated area and planted area evidenced an unrelenting downward trend.

94

Figure 9.2  Trends in Population Increase and Decrease
in Cultivated Land (1952-1990)

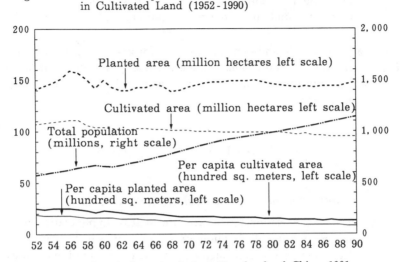

Sources: Population: *Statistical Yearbook of China 1991*,
p. 79; Cultivated area: *China in the Year 2000*, p. 60 and *Rural
Statistics Yearbook of China*, pp. 88-90; Planted area: *Complete
Rural Economic Statistics of China*, p. 314, and *Statistical
Yearbook of China* 1991, p. 79.

Figure 9.3  Labor and Land Productivity in
Grain Production (1952-1992)

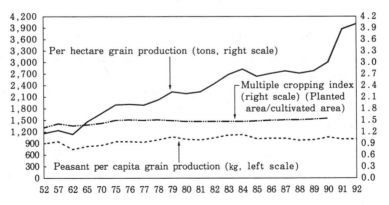

Sources: Grain planted area: *Statistical Yearbook of China 1993*,
p. 358; food production volume, p. 364; rural laborers, p. 7.

## Rising Land Productivity

Notwithstanding the successive diminution of planted area (and cultivated area), grain production increased by approximately 3.4 times. In 1952 production was 163 million tons, and in 1992 it was 443 million tons. Increased production was possible because China's peasants meticulously cultivated the limited land they had available. Unit productivity (grain production divided by planted area) in the 1950s was 1.1 to 1.3 tons per hectare. By 1992 the yield had risen to 4.0 tons.

## Stagnation of Labor Productivity

Per capita productivity for agricultural labor (grain production volume divided by the agricultural labor force) was 800 to 900 kilograms in the 1950s, remained almost unchanged through the 1960s and 1970s, and in the 1980s finally rose to the level of 1.0 to 1.1 ton. Increasing numbers of agricultural laborers were kept on the land, in a sense bound tightly to a narrow piece of cultivated earth, with the result that labor productivity stagnated. In the 1980s agricultural reform was implemented, and ancillary employment and township and village enterprises developed. As a consequence, the labor force dedicated to agriculture declined, and there was a modest rise in labor productivity.

In sum, although cultivated land (planted area) remained practically unchanged, both grain production and productivity of land increased two to three times; however, the agricultural labor force increased from under 200 million to over 400 million, so labor productivity changed little.

# Pessimistic Outlook for the Future of Agriculture

Postulating that China's population will be 1.3 billion persons at the end of the twentieth century and 1.5 billion by the year 2020, certain researchers have described a future scenario as follows.

- Total cultivated area will be less than 100 million hectares; cultivated land per capita of 970 square meters in 2000 will become 850 square meters in 2020; thus cultivated area will continue to diminish on both an absolute basis and on a per capita basis.
- Forested area and the forest coverage ratio will increase to some degree on both an absolute basis and on a per capita basis. In 2000 forested land will increase from 144 million hectares to 153 million hectares, and the forest coverage ratio will be 15 to 16 percent (against 12 percent in 1989). Forested land per capita will reach some 11,300 square meters. Timber supplies will fall short of requirements by 30 to 50 million cubic meters annually (fuel requirements not included).

Table 9.1  Estimated Historical Population Levels in China

| Year | Period | Population (millions) | Annual Percentage Increase — Peak to Peak | Per Capita Cultivated Land (m²) | Source |
|---|---|---|---|---|---|
| 350 B.C. | Peak of Warring States Period | 60 million level | | | |
| 205 B.C. | Demise of Qin, Early Han | | | | |
| 1 A.D. | Zenith of Western Han Dynasty | | | 9,300 | Book of Han, Geography |
| 25 | Early Eastern Han | 25 | | | |
| 150 | Late Eastern Han | 60 | | 9,200 | Cefuyuanbi |
| 215 | Three Kingdoms | 15 | | | |
| 290 | Western Jin | 25 | 0.4% (752 years) | | |
| 510 | Peak of Northern & Southern Dynasties | 47 | | | |
| 581 | Early Sui Dynasty | 35 | | | |
| 608 | Zenith of Sui | 50 | | 28,200 | Book of Sui, Geography |
| 620 | Early Tang Dynasty | 25 | | | |
| 752 | Zenith of Tang | 80 | | 18,000 | Tongzhi |
| | | 80 million level | | | |
| 760 | An Shan-Shi Siming Chaos | 50 | | | |
| 850 | Late Tang Period | 60 | 0.6% (350 years) | | |
| 980 | Early Sung Dynasty | 40 | | | |
| 1110 | Zenith of Northern Sung Dynasty | 100 | | | |
| | | 110 million level | | | |
| 1210 | Period of Sung, Jin Contention | 115 | | 23,200 | Jin History • Foodstuffs |
| 1290 | Yuan Dynasty | 85 | 0.7% (460 years) | 23,500 | Yuan History • Geography |
| 1370 | Beginning of Ming Dynasty | 60 | | | |
| 1570 | Zenith of Ming | 140 | | 7,700 | Xuwenxian Tongkao |
| | | 140 million level | | | |
| 1640 | Demise of Ming Dynasty | 75 | 3.9% (270 years) | | |
| 1840 | Opium War | 410 million level | | 2,000 | |
| 1911 | Demise of the Qing Dynasty | 370 | 0.25% (109 years) | 1,800 | Statistical Abstract |
| 1949 | | 542 | | | |
| | | 540 million level | | | |
| 1981 | | 1,001 | 1.8% (42 years) | 1,000 | Statistical Yearbook of China 1990 |
| 1992 | | 1,172 | | 800 | Statistical Yearbook of China 1993 |
| | | 1,172 million level | | | |

Source: Hu Huanyong, ed., *The Population Geography of China* (Shanghai: East China Normal University Press, 1984), p. 10.

- Total grassland area will rise slightly to 320 to 330 million hectares; however, on a per capita basis it will decline to 2,500 to 2,600 square meters.
- River flow per capita will decline more, and water supplies will approach a crisis point. Nationally, water usage demand will be 820 billion cubic meters, or 634 tons per capita annually. This is below the average (900 tons per person) for developing countries. Water availability per capita will decline to 2,200 cubic meters. Newly developed water sources will add 660 to 670 billion cubic meters, but the water shortfall will be 48 to 106 billion cubic meters. For the country overall, water shortages will remain in the early stages, but some regions and many cities will find themselves in the grip of crisis. The seriousness of the shortage in water resources is second only to the shortage of cultivated land and constitutes for China's natural resources "the second crisis."

In summary, population increase, reduction in cultivated land, and water shortages in many cities—these are the fundamental structural contradictions between China's population and its resources. As China's population continues to grow, and as the economy enters a period of rapid expansion, these problems will increasingly become critical contradictions (Hu Angang and Wang Yi 1989, p. 27).

The current capacity of China's land resources (calculated from research materials of a joint study group of the State Statistical Bureau and the Chinese Academy of Sciences) can be expressed as an annual biological production volume of approximately 3.2 billion tons (dried materials, including 380 million tons of grain). This productive capacity translates into a "population support capacity" of 950 million persons. The excess of population over capacity is thus 130 million. Even if in 2000 the productive capacity of land resources increases to 3.5 billion tons (dried materials, including 460 million tons of grain), the reasonable population support capacity will be 1.16 billion people, 140 million short of predicted population. The potential natural productive capacity of China's land resources is 7.26 billion tons (dried materials) annually, which theoretically could support 1.5 to 1.6 billion people. Even with extremely strict population control, China in 2030 will be reaching the absolute limit of its resources. However, at the current rate of population increase, this limit will be reached in 2015. Thereafter, either the pressure on agricultural resources will have to be alleviated through large-scale imports of agricultural products, or there will be a large-scale "population export" to the other countries of the world (Hu Angang and Wang Yi 1989, pp. 29–30). Table 9.1 presents the problem of population and cultivated area in a historical context. China may be a vast country, but it cannot support an unbearable burden of population.

# 10

# The New Focus on Tertiary Industry

## China's Distorted Industrialization

China's industrial structure is reflected in the sectoral composition of national income. Figure 10.1 shows that the principal generator of national income has changed from the agricultural sector to the industrial sector (including construction). In 1952, 58 percent of national income was generated by agriculture; industry and construction accounted for no more than 20 percent. However, by 1992 the contribution of agriculture had fallen to 29 percent, and industry and construction had reached 57 percent. It would appear from this that the Chinese economy's transition from agriculture to industry has been a normal one. However, there are a number of qualifications.

First, the peak level of industrialization reached around 1980 (after which the industrialization ratio declined slightly) is overstated because of the price system. The government's mandate of agricultural prices in comparison with high industrial prices tended to exaggerate the ratio of industrialization.

The second qualification stems from the definition of national income. As previously explained in the discussion of the difference between the MPS and SNA methods of income accounting, apart from "services such as transport and trade that are directly connected with material production," the pure service sector is not included in Chinese national income. Consequently, in this sense the service sector is understated, and the industrial and construction sector is again overstated.

We can avoid these two biases by looking at the structure of employment in terms of the primary, secondary, and tertiary sectors as presented in Figure 10.1 (right-hand side). In the 1950s and 1960s, 80 percent of employment was in agriculture; less than 10 percent was in industry and construction. By the 1980s agriculture was providing 60 percent of employment and the share of industry and

Figure 10.1   Changes in the Structure of Primary, Secondary, and
              Tertiary Industry (1952 - 1992)

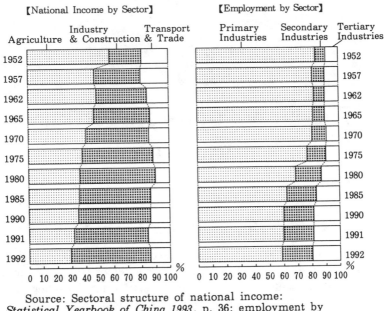

Source: Sectoral structure of national income:
*Statistical Yearbook of China 1993*, p. 36; employment by
sector: p. 101.

construction had risen to over 20 percent. During the Cultural Revolution service
activities were criticized as capitalistic, and the resulting slowdown in this sector
can be seen in employment. After having surpassed the 10 percent level, employment in transport and trade declined in this period. Growth finally began again in
the 1980s, but employment remained below the 20 percent level.

Here the distortions in China's industrialization become manifest. Normally,
industrialization is accompanied by a parallel development of service industries.
In this sense, the case of China is highly unusual. As we can see from Figure 10.2,
the weight of industrialization in China is extremely high in comparison with not
only other low-income countries but also advanced countries.

## Defining Industry and Scale and Share of Enterprises

In China "industry" is defined as the sector engaged in material production
through the processing or reprocessing of agricultural products and extraction
and aggregation of natural resources. Specifically, the definition includes

1.  Mining, salt milling, and logging (but not hunting and fishery)
2.  Food processing, cotton spinning, silk thread manufacture, textiles,
    leather, and other processing of secondary agricultural crops

Figure 10.2   Comparison of Industrial Structures of Key Countries (1990, GDP base)

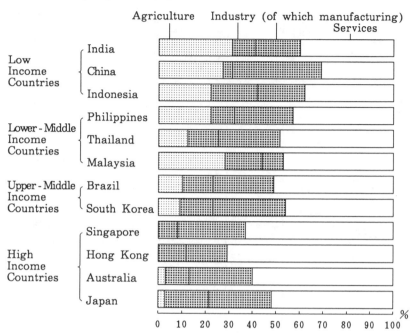

Source: World Bank, *World Development Report 1992*, pp. 222, 223.

3. Iron making, steel making, rolling process, chemicals, petroleum processing, machinery manufacturing, wood processing, and production and supply of electric power, water, and gas
4. Machinery and equipment repair and transport equipment repair

This list would equate in Japan to the term "industrial and mining industries."

Before 1984 industrial activities at or below the level of farming villages were categorized as agriculture. After 1984 these were reclassified as industry.

Thus, an "independent industrial enterprise" meets three criteria: (1) It is an administratively independent organization; (2) it is an economically independent unit with discrete profit-and-loss accounting that produces an independent statement of assets and liabilities (balance sheet); (3) it has authority to enter into contracts with other enterprises and to maintain an independent bank account. Conversely, a "nonindependent enterprise" is one that does not meet these three criteria. Included would be state institutions, military units, scientific research organizations, schools, peoples groups, and industrial activities and units under state-owned enterprises.

"Enterprises under ownership by the whole people" means state-owned enterprises. These are divided into enterprises operated by central government organs

Table 10.1  Categorization Standards for Enterprise Scale in Key Industries

| | Unit | Large Enterprises | Medium Enterprises | Small Enterprises |
|---|---|---|---|---|
| Steel complexes | Annual output crude steel | over 1 mil/tons | 0.1-1 mil/tons | under 100 thou/tons |
| Coal mines (Coal Mining Bureau) | Annual output coal | over 5 mil/tons | 2-5 mil/tons | under 2 mil/tons |
| Refineries | Annual refining | over 2.5 mil/tons | 0.5-2.5 mil/tons | under 500 thou/tons |
| Sulfuric acid plants | Annual production capacity | over 160 thou/tons | 80-160 thou/tons | under 80 thou/tons |
| Electric power plants | Electric power gen. capacity | over 250 thou kWh | 25-250 thou kWh | under 25 thou kWh |
| Large scale machinery equipment factories | Annual production capacity | over 20 thou/tons | 5-20 thou/tons | under 5 thou/tons |
| Automobile plants | Annual production capacity | over 50 thou gen. vehicles / over 3 thou large vehicles | 5-50 thou gen. vehicles / 1-3 thou large vehicles | under 5 thou vehicles / under 1 thou vehicles |
| Cement plants | Annual production capacity | over 1 mil/tons | 0.2-1 mil/tons | under 200 thou/tons |
| Cotton textile factories | Spindles · 10,000 | over 100 thou spindles | 50-100 thou spindles | under 50 thou spindles |
| Wristwatch factories | Annual production capacity | over 1 mil units | 0.4-1.0 mil units | under 400 thou units |

Source: *The Current Situation of Chinese Industry*, State Council Leading Group for Industrial Surveys (Beijing: People's Press 1990), p. 69.

Table 10.2  Enterprise Scale Structure of Chinese Industry (1985 industrial census)

| | Total | Large & Medium Enterprises | | Small Scale Enterprises | |
|---|---|---|---|---|---|
| | | absolute nos. | % | absolute nos. | % |
| Number of enterprises (companies) | 358,701 | 8,320 | 2.32 | 350,381 | 97.7 |
| Gross value of industrial production(1980 prices) | 792 mil RMB | 388 mil RMB | 49.0 | 404 mil RMB | 51.0 |
| Net value of industrial production(current prices) | 274 mil RMB | 151 mil RMB | 55.3 | 122 mil RMB | 44.7 |
| Number of workers | 66 mil persons | 22 mil persons | 33.4 | 44 mil persons | 66.6 |
| Fixed assets held (current prices) | 472 mil RMB | 301 mil RMB | 63.7 | 171 mil RMB | 36.3 |
| Total value of profits and taxes (current prices) | 166 mil RMB | 104 mil RMB | 62.7 | 62 mil RMB | 37.3 |

Source: *The Current Situation of Chinese Industry*, p. 70.
Original source: *1985 PRC Industrial Survey Materials* (Beijing: Chinese Statistical Press, 1988), Vol. 3.

Table 10.3  Enterprise Scale Structure of Chinese Industry (1990 industrial census)

| | Total | Large Scale Enterprises | | Medium Scale Enterprises | | Small Scale Enterprises | |
|---|---|---|---|---|---|---|---|
| | | absolute nos. | % | absolute nos. | % | absolute nos. | % |
| Number of enterprises (companies) | 417,082 | 3,965 | 0.95 | 9,450 | 2.26 | 403,667 | 96.8 |
| Gross value of industrial production | 1,869 mil RMB | 651 mil RMB | 34.8 | 369 mil RMB | 19.7 | 850 mil RMB | 45.3 |
| Net value of industrial production | 509 mil RMB | 200 mil RMB | 39.2 | 96 mil RMB | 18.9 | 213 mil RMB | 41.8 |
| Sales turn over | 1,679 mil RMB | 612 mil RMB | 36.5 | 335 mil RMB | 19.9 | 732 mil RMB | 43.5 |

Source: *Statistical Yearbook of China 1991*, p. 399.

Table 10.4  Production Concentration of Key Industrial Products
(1985 industrial census) (percent)

| | Top 3 companies | Top 5 companies | | Top 3 companies | Top 5 companies |
|---|---|---|---|---|---|
| Coal | 7.06 | 10.34 | Cement | 2.47 | 3.88 |
| Electric power | 4.69 | 7.01 | Flat glass | 52.13 | 58.77 |
| Crude oil | 74.17 | 85.78 | Caustic soda | 16.03 | 22.09 |
| Pig iron | 31.31 | 40.26 | Trucks | 56.83 | 66.96 |
| Crude steel | 27.86 | 34.93 | Paper | 5.09 | 7.15 |

Source: *The Current Situation of Chinese Industry*, p. 75.

Table 10.5  Changes in Industrial Structure as Observed from Employment
Trends

| | 1985 | | 1990 | | 85 - 90 | |
|---|---|---|---|---|---|---|
| | millions of persons | % | millions of persons | % | increase millions of persons | % p.a. |
| National total | 55.6 | 100 | 63.8 | 100 | 8.2 | 2.8 |
| of which central industry | 8.7 | 15.6 | 9.9 | 15.6 | 1.3 | 2.8 |
| local industry | 46.9 | 84.4 | 53.9 | 84.4 | 6.9 | 2.8 |
| Light industry | 22.7 | 40.9 | 26.5 | 41.6 | 3.8 | 3.1 |
| Heavy industry | 32.8 | 59.1 | 37.2 | 58.4 | 4.4 | 2.6 |

Source: *The Current Situation of Chinese Industry*, p. 152; *Statistical Yearbook of China 1991*, p. 392.

Figure 10.3  Changes in the Sectoral Structure of Industrial
Production by Value (1952 - 1990)

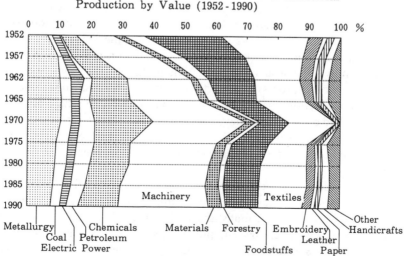

Source: *Statistical Yearbook of China 1991*, pp. 72 - 73.

and enterprises operated by regional government organs (the latter are divided into province level, regional level, county and city level, and subcounty levels).

Between state-owned enterprises and the private ownership sector are "industries under collective ownership." These include (1) enterprises operated by collectives (e.g., "street committees") under cities and counties and (2) industries operated by villages and townships.

In connection with the national industrial survey (census) in 1985, the State Council Leading Group for the National Industrial Survey and the State Statistical Bureau issued standard categories by scale (large, medium, and small) for industrial enterprises. Table 10.1 presents the standards established in this document. The categories were established essentially on the basis of annual production capacity.

The shares of large- and medium-scale enterprises as determined by the 1985 census are presented in Table 10.2. These enterprises constitute only about 2 percent of total enterprises but account for 30 percent of worker employment and 55 percent of gross production value. Table 10.3 presents the shares of large-, medium-, and small-scale enterprises established in the 1990 census.

Table 10.4 shows the degree of concentration of production of key industrial products. Concentration in production of crude petroleum, flat glass, and trucks is extremely high. By contrast, the concentration in cement, electric power, and paper is low.

## Changes in the Sectoral Structure of Industry

Figure 10.3 presents a view of total value of industrial production in terms of contributions of various sectors. From the 1950s to the 1970s, the momentum behind heavy industrialization was strong. The main sector was machinery, followed by chemicals. Until 1970 the sectors whose shares were most diminished by the growth of heavy chemical industries were textiles and foodstuffs.

However, heavy chemical industrialization peaked in the 1970s and subsequently experienced a process of correction. As policy changed from a one-sided emphasis on production to allowing also for consumption, the share of light industry, which had once fallen below 30 percent of total output, recovered to some 40 percent. This point is illustrated in Table 10.5. In 1985 and 1990 approximately 60 percent of employment was in heavy industry and approximately 40 percent in light industry.

Table 10.6 presents the sectoral structure of industry from the perspective of employment. Sectoral employment in 1990 comprised, most notably, in light industry, textiles 11.7 percent and foodstuffs and beverages 6.7 percent; and, in heavy industry, machinery and electric equipment 24.8 percent, building materials 6.1 percent, chemicals 6.0 percent, and iron making 4.7 percent. The three largest

Table 10.6   Changes in Employment by Industry

| | 1985 | | 1990 | | 85 - 90 | |
|---|---|---|---|---|---|---|
| | millions of persons | % | millions of persons | % | increase millions of persons | % p.a |
| Extractive Industries | 7.4 | 13.3 | 9.1 | 14.3 | 1.7 | 4.2 |
| 1. Mining | 6.2 | 11.1 | 7.6 | 12.0 | 1.5 | 4.3 |
| 2. Timber, bamboo | 1.1 | 1.9 | 1.2 | 1.9 | 0.2 | 2.7 |
| 3. Waterways | 0.2 | 0.3 | 0.3 | 0.4 | 0.1 | 8.1 |
| Manufacturing Industries | 42.1 | 75.8 | 54.7 | 85.7 | 12.6 | 5.4 |
| 1. Food stuffs, beverages, cigarettes | 3.1 | 5.7 | 4.3 | 6.7 | 1.2 | 6.4 |
| 2. Animal feed | 0.4 | 0.7 | 0.1 | 0.2 | -0.2 | -17.7 |
| 3. Textiles | 5.7 | 10.3 | 7.5 | 11.7 | 1.8 | 5.5 |
| 4. Embroidery | 1.2 | 2.1 | 1.7 | 2.6 | 0.5 | 7.5 |
| 5. Leather, furs | 0.6 | 1.1 | 0.8 | 1.2 | 0.2 | 6.0 |
| 6. Wood products (bamboo, rattan) | 0.4 | 0.8 | 0.7 | 1.1 | 0.3 | 10.8 |
| 7. Furniture | 0.4 | 0.7 | 0.4 | 0.7 | 0.0 | 1.5 |
| 8. Paper & paper products | 0.8 | 1.5 | 1.2 | 1.9 | 0.4 | 7.9 |
| 9. Printing | 0.7 | 1.2 | 1.0 | 1.5 | 0.3 | 7.3 |
| 10. Education and sports products | 0.2 | 0.4 | 0.3 | 0.5 | 0.1 | 3.9 |
| 11. Handicrafts & arts | 0.4 | 0.8 | 0.7 | 1.1 | 0.3 | 9.4 |
| 12. Electric power, steam, water supply | 1.2 | 2.1 | 1.6 | 2.6 | 0.5 | 6.8 |
| 13. Petroleum processing | 0.3 | 0.6 | 0.5 | 0.8 | 0.2 | 10.5 |
| 14. Coke, coal gas | 0.2 | 0.3 | 0.3 | 0.4 | 0.1 | 10.8 |
| 15. Chemical industry | 2.9 | 5.3 | 3.7 | 6.0 | 0.9 | 5.4 |
| 16. Medical industry | 0.5 | 1.0 | 0.8 | 1.3 | 0.3 | 8.9 |
| 17. Chemical fibers | 0.2 | 0.4 | 0.3 | 0.5 | 0.1 | 7.2 |
| 18. Rubber products | 0.6 | 1.0 | 0.8 | 1.2 | 0.2 | 5.6 |
| 19. Plastic products | 0.7 | 1.2 | 1.0 | 1.6 | 0.3 | 8.3 |
| 20. Building materials | 3.2 | 5.7 | 3.9 | 6.1 | 0.7 | 4.3 |
| 21. Iron & steel | 2.4 | 4.4 | 3.0 | 4.7 | 0.6 | 4.3 |
| 22. Non - ferrous metals | 0.6 | 1.0 | 0.9 | 1.3 | 0.3 | 8.2 |
| 23. Metal products | 1.3 | 2.5 | 1.8 | 2.9 | 0.4 | 5.5 |
| 24. Machinery, electrical equipment | 13.3 | 23.9 | 15.8 | 24.8 | 2.5 | 3.5 |
| 25. Other industry | 0.7 | 1.3 | 1.6 | 2.5 | 0.8 | 16.4 |

Source: *Statistical Yearbook of China 1991*, p. 392.

sectoral generators of new employment from 1985 to 1990 were machinery and electric equipment 2.52 million; textiles 1.75 million; and foodstuffs 1.15 million.

# Regional Structure of Industrial Production

Figure 10.4 presents regional production for various important industrial manufactures (1990). The upper section is consumer products; the lower section is industrial products.

Let us look first at consumer goods. For cotton cloth, the largest regional share is held by Huadong (east China), of which Shanghai is the key contributor; next is the central region, which is where cotton raw material is produced.

For nylon the share of Shanghai in east China is overwhelming, which evidences Shanghai's status as an industrial city.

For sugar the southern region, particularly Guangdong and Guangxi, has the largest share. The south is where sugarcane is produced. In the northeast sugar is made from sugar beets. For paper the share of the central region is relatively large, but production is fairly evenly dispersed throughout the country. This is no doubt

Figure 10.4   Regional Distribution of Principal Industrial
Manufactures (Volume basis)

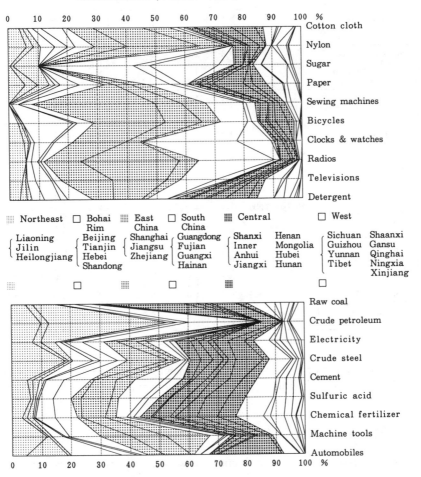

Source: *Statistical Yearbook of China 1991*, pp. 422-427.

because raw materials are widely available throughout the country, and the technology involved is relatively simple.

In sewing machine production, Shanghai is by far the largest production location. For bicycles, Shanghai and Tianjin have the largest shares. The brand-name bicycles produced in these cities enjoy high and steady popularity.

For clocks and watches the share of Guangdong is large. For radios the leader is Jiangsu, followed by Guangdong. In televisions, Jiangsu and Shanghai are strongest. Production of detergent is spread throughout the country.

The lower section of Figure 10.4 shows regional distribution for heavy industrial products. First, for coal, the position of Shanxi in the central region is overwhelming. The expression that "the entire subsoil of Shanxi is coal" suggests the importance of this location.

In crude petroleum Heilongjiang's share is large, reflecting of course the presence of the Daqing oil field. Next is Shandong where the Shengli oilfield is located.

Electricity production is dispersed throughout the country. However, in general, in the south hydroelectric power generation is common, whereas in the north thermoelectric power prevails. When the Three Gorges dam project is completed, the share of Hubei province can be expected to increase greatly.

Crude steel production is concentrated first in Liaoning, then Shanghai. The extent of production concentration in cement is low. Sulfuric acid production is dispersed nationwide.

Chemical fertilizer production is also dispersed nationally, but modern urea-based technology and traditional technologies coexist, and production of highly effective chemical fertilizer is limited to a number of plants. In machine tools, the largest shares are held by Liaoning and by Shanghai, Jiangsu, and Zhejiang in the east China region. For automobiles Hubei and Jilin dominate. For the former this is because of the Number Two Automobile Plant (Shiyan); for the latter it is explained by the Number One Automobile Plant (Changchun).

In policy about industrial location, China's leadership has vacillated between taking a national perspective on the one hand—viewing the country as a great playing field and establishing industries in the most rational location (the original Chinese phrase is "the entire country as one great chess board")—and taking a regional perspective on the other—trying to establish independent local industrial systems. Now, with the establishment of economic zones, policymaking has entered a new phase.

## Promoting the Development of Tertiary Industry

On June 16, 1992, the Party Central and State Council announced the policy of accelerating development of tertiary industry (*People's Daily,* June 30, see Appendix 3). This decision called for raising the growth rate for tertiary industry above that for primary and secondary industries, and for the weight of tertiary industry in China's GNP and employment structure to "reach the average level of developing countries."

Document No. 4 of the Party Central (see Appendix 2) established the expanded policy that "areas allowed to make direct use of foreign capital will include finance, trade, commerce, transport, and tourism." Further, "a certain number of cities that have been specifically designated are each authorized to approve one or two retail commercial enterprises invested by foreign banks and foreign capitalists. Shanghai can approve the operation of one foreign capital invested insurance company on an experimental basis." [Translator's note: The insurance company is

Figure 10.5   Provincial Level Industrial Structure:
              Position of Tertiary Industry (1990)

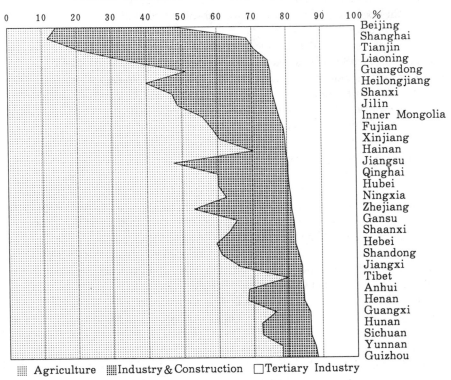

▓ Agriculture  ▓Industry & Construction  ☐Tertiary Industry

Source: *Statistical Yearbook of China 1992,* p. 100.

American Insurance Group [AIG] of the United States.] The main objective of the decision to introduce foreign capital as far as the financial, insurance, and retail industries was to reform the tertiary sector. An obvious hypothesis is that development of the tertiary sector is seen as a means of expanding employment.

Let us here take a macro view of China's tertiary sector. In the first half of the 1980s, agricultural production rose along with introduction of the system of giving farming households responsibility for production; in terms of ratio of GNP, it remained about 33 percent—33.9 percent in 1982, 33.7 percent in 1983, 33.0 percent in 1984. At the same time, the tertiary sector's share of GNP was about 20 percent—20.0 percent in 1982, 20.3 percent in 1983, and 21.9 percent in 1984. In the second half of the 1980s, agriculture's share was in the 26–27 percent range, industry's was 44–45 percent, and the tertiary sector finally reached 27 percent, thus finally tending to exceed the primary sector. This may justly be called a historic transformation for the Chinese economy.

It would be appropriate to make provincial-level comparisons of the tertiary sector; however, GNP-based data are not available. As an alternative, Figure 10.5

Figure 10.6   Correlation of Secondary and Tertiary Industry
at the Province Level

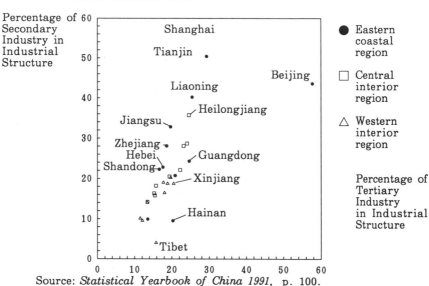

Source: *Statistical Yearbook of China 1991*, p. 100.

presents employment data for the primary, secondary, and tertiary sectors at the provincial level. Nationally, tertiary-sector employment accounts for 18.2 percent of total employment. The five highest provinces are Beijing 57.7 percent, Shanghai 31.5 percent, Tianjin 29.3 percent, Liaoning 25.4 percent, and Guangdong 24.6 percent; at the low end are Guizhou 11.5 percent, Yunnan 12.1 percent, and Sichuan 13.4 percent. Figure 10.6, on the same employment basis, presents a comparison of the correlation of secondary and tertiary sectors at the provincial level. In short, provinces that score high in share of tertiary industry also possess a high share of secondary industry, which reveals a basic correlation between these two sectors. However, for Jiangsu and Zhejiang, whereas the secondary sector has been growing rapidly in the form of township and village enterprises, the tertiary sector remains behind. The same phenomenon is observed in Hebei and Shandong. In contrast are Xinjiang and Hainan, where the tertiary sector is relatively highly developed, and the secondary sector lags behind.

In retrospect, the "dream of industrialization" was the starting point of China's revolution. China's revolutionary leaders—harboring the notion that in the century after the Opium War, it was because China possessed only agriculture that she was colonized by industrialized countries—devoted maximum energy to industrialization after they had gained power. As a result of this effort, China succeeded in establishing an estimable industrial base. However, excessive heavy and chemical industrialization, combined with a war-preparation economic system, brought forth extreme inefficiencies.

# 11

## Accumulating Deficits and Central-Regional Competition for Financial Resources

### Aggressive Deficit Budgeting Begins in the Deng Era

Figure 11.1 presents changes in fiscal revenues and fiscal expenditures over the history of the PRC. During the Mao Zedong era, great efforts were made to maintain a balance of government receipts and outlays. Basically, government expenditures were adjusted to remain within fiscal revenues, so that when deficits occurred (as during the Great Leap Forward) they were the result of exceptional circumstances.

By contrast, the Deng Xiaoping era brought a change to an activist fiscal policy of issuing government debt and borrowing from abroad and, when the growth of fiscal receipts slowed in consequence of economic reform, of consistently running huge fiscal deficits.

Aggregate deficits over the five-year periods corresponding to the five-year plans are as follows: RMB 28.6 billion for the fifth plan period (1976–1980), RMB 12.1 billion for the sixth (1981–1985), and RMB 46.0 billion for the seventh (1986–1990) (*Statistical Yearbook of China, 1993*, p. 215). These statistics classify funds garnered from domestic and foreign borrowing as revenues; such "revenue" is indicated by the blackened area on the lower section of Figure 11.1, "fiscal balance." Adding this deficit financing figure to the official deficit indicated by the dotted area gives the real deficit. This real deficit exceeded RMB 50.0 billion in 1990, grew to RMB 66.6 billion in 1991 (government bond issuance of RMB 28.1 billion, foreign borrowing of RMB 17.4 billion, and a nominal deficit of RMB 21.1 billion), and topped RMB 90 billion in 1992.

A noteworthy trend during the Deng Xiaoping era was a decline in government revenues from 30-plus percent to about 20 percent of GNP. However, this decline reflects a separate accounting for budgetary and nonbudgetary revenues; if the

Figure 11.1  Changes in China's Fiscal Balance and Fiscal Deficits
(1952 - 1992)

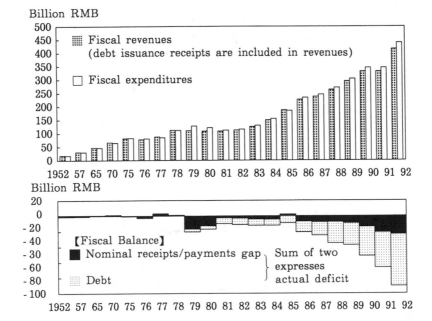

Billion RMB

Note: [Debt] comprises domestic and foreign borrowing and
domestic public bond issues.
Source: *Statistical Yearbook of China 1993*, pp. 215, 219.

Figure 11.2  Changes in Fiscal Revenues as Percentage of GNP
(1978 - 1992)

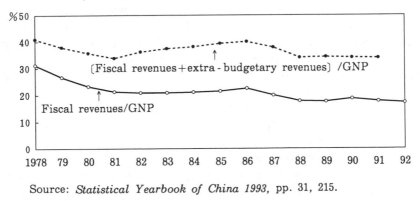

Source: *Statistical Yearbook of China 1993*, pp. 31, 215.

two are combined, the change is not so significant (see Figure 11.2). Nonbudgetary revenues are finances managed by units at the local and provincial levels that are not accounted for in the central government plan. Such finances include

- Surtaxes imposed by local fiscal departments on industrial and commercial taxes, and taxes on municipality-operated businesses
- Depreciation funds and worker welfare funds managed by state-owned enterprises and their main management departments
- Items not required to be included in the revenue budgets of central and regional enterprises
- Highway transit charges and port usage charges managed by business units or administrative units (Shu Yi and Shen Jingnong 1987, p. 230)

It is evident from the list that nonbudgetary revenues are a "second budget" of funds units hold that they may, within certain limits, use relatively freely. In the process of economic reform, the only effective way to elicit the initiative of the provincial, department, and enterprise levels has been to allow retention of a portion of funds. Use of these funds for equipment investment has been a factor in the tendency toward economic overheating.

## Effects on Tax Revenues of Fiscal and Enterprise Reforms

Fiscal revenues comprise (1) all types of tax receipts (including commodity taxes, value-added taxes, sales taxes, income taxes, customs duties, agricultural taxes,

Figure 11.3   Changes in State Revenues (1983 - 1992)

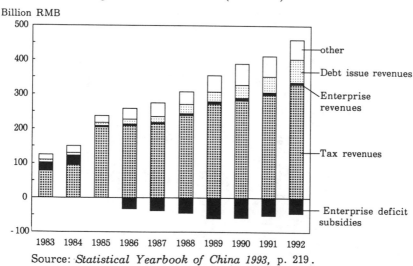

Source: *Statistical Yearbook of China 1993*, p. 219 .

Table 11.1  Financial Subsidies and Changes in Fiscal Revenues
Following Fiscal and Enterprise Reform (in billion RMB)

| Fiscal Year | Tax Revenues (a) | Enterprise Profit Remittances (b) | Taxes+ Profit Remittances (a)+(b) | Growth Rate % | Enterprise Deficit Subsidies (c) | (a)+(b)+(c) | Growth Rate % | Remarks |
|---|---|---|---|---|---|---|---|---|
| 1981 | 63 | 35 | 98 | | | 98 | | ⇨tightening |
| 1982 | 70 | 30 | 100 | 1.3 | | 100 | 1.3 | ⇨tightening |
| 1983 | 76 | 24 | 102 | 1.9 | | 102 | 1.9 | ⇨tightening |
| 1984 | 95 | 28 | 122 | 20.4 | | 122 | 20.4 | ⇨rapid reform |
| ⟨fiscal and enterprise reform begins⟩ | | | | | | | | |
| 1985 | 204 | 4 | 209 | 70.3 | | 209 | 70.3 | ⇨rapid reform |
| 1986 | 209 | 4 | 213 | 2.3 | -32 | 181 | -13.4 | ⇨tightening |
| 1987 | 214 | 4 | 218 | 2.4 | -38 | 181 | -0.1 | ⇨tightening |
| 1988 | 239 | 5 | 244 | 11.8 | -45 | 200 | 10.5 | ⇨rapid reform |
| 1989 | 273 | 6 | 279 | 14.3 | -60 | 219 | 9.9 | ⇨rapid reform |
| 1990 | 282 | 8 | 290 | 3.9 | -58 | 232 | 5.9 | ⇨tightening |
| 1991 | 299 | 7 | 306 | 5.7 | -51 | 255 | 10.1 | ⇨tightening |
| 1992 | 330 | 6 | 336 | 9.5 | -45 | 324 | 26.9 | ⇨open door policy fever |

Source: *Statistical Yearbook of China 1993*, p. 219.

cultivated land usage taxes, state-owned enterprise income taxes); (2) enterprise revenues (after 1985 a variety of reforms were introduced to replace the former system in which enterprises handed over all revenues to higher authorities—i.e., there was no distinction between profits and taxes—to one in which they remit only tax payments, except enterprises operating under the profit responsibility system still remit all enterprise revenues); (3) debt financing receipts (government bonds and foreign borrowing); and (4) other revenues (repayments of loans made for capital construction projects, energy and transport key construction project fund revenues, and the like). As shown in Figure 11.3, tax revenues have risen to make up fully 85 percent of total fiscal revenues; enterprise revenues, debt financing receipts, and other sources have declined to only 15 percent.

Let us look at the changes in the structure of enterprise profits and fiscal receipts after the enterprise and fiscal reforms initiated in 1985. Table 11.1 shows that as a result of the tax system changes, tax revenues increased dramatically, and, conversely, remittances of enterprises profits sharply declined. In the second half of the 1980s, the combination of tax receipts and payments to the central treasury in the form of enterprise profit remittances amounted to RMB 200 to 300 billion annually (Table 11.1, third column). In the period of economic overheating, 1988–1989, receipts increased by over 10 percent, but in the periods of tightening in 1986–1987 and 1990, growth was under 4 percent. There was a recovery to 9.5 percent in 1992.

Figure 11.3 conveys the impression that enterprise and fiscal system reform led to high growth in fiscal receipts. But there is another side to this. The apparent growth in fiscal revenues was much greater than the real growth. There was a large inflation element in the figures. Further, fiscal subsidies to money-losing state enterprises surged during this period. As can be seen from the chart, 1989–1990 fiscal subsidies rose to a peak of some RMB 60 billion. After this, the central government instituted tighter discipline, so that in 1992 the subsidy figure had declined to RMB 44.5 billion.

Thus, under a system that considers only "profits," enterprises incurring losses are not required to remit anything to higher authorities. However, for "taxes," apart from cumulative taxes payable on income, ad valorem taxes such as those on gross receipts are payable regardless of whether the enterprises are making or losing money.

In the 1980s China introduced the system of taxing profits to replace the previous system that made no distinction between profits and taxes (and indeed considered them the same because all enterprise earnings were handed back to higher authorities). The purpose of the new system was to force enterprises to pay taxes, to expose enterprise losses, and to clearly assign responsibility for performance to the enterprises. The policy toward money-losing enterprises had become one of the fiscal authorities attempting to aid the enterprises through fiscal subsidies. In other words, reforming the method of assessing taxes succeeded in exposing both enterprise deficits and fiscal subsidies.

In 1993 and early 1994 official policy became significantly more activist against deficit-operating companies, and concrete measures began to be taken against some of these enterprises. Measures included government-assisted "mergers" of deficit enterprises with profitable enterprises or groups and, in some special instances, closure. These actions and cases were well publicized, which gave the observer an impression of scope of activity that is probably greater than the reality. Nevertheless, test or demonstration cases have provided real impetus and models for more widespread actions. Restructurings of deficit enterprises can be expected to increase significantly. Of course, the major obstacle remains the large, usually greatly excessive, numbers of persons employed in the typical deficit state enterprise.

Figure 11.4   Changes in State Fiscal Outlays (1983 - 1992)

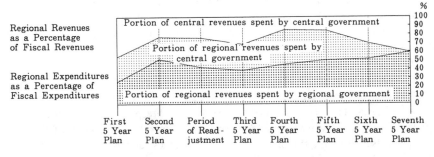

Source: *Statistical Yearbook of China 1993*, pp. 222 - 223.

Figure 11.5   Relationship of Central and Regional Finances
(first through seventh five year plans)

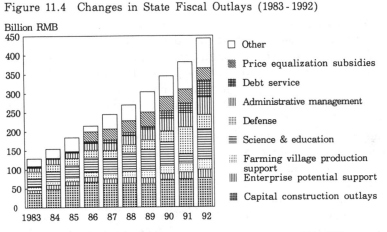

Source: *Statistical Yearbook of China 1991*, p. 221.

Table 11.2  Changes in the Growth Rates of Regional Finances
(Deng Xiaoping and Mao Zedong Eras)

| Ranking | | Annual Percentage Growth During Deng Xiaoping Era 1981 - 1989 | | Annual Percentage Growth During Mao Zedong Era 1953 - 1978 |
|---|---|---|---|---|
| 1 | Inner Mongolia | 24.0 | Shanghai | 17.5 |
| 2 | Yunnan | 20.7 | Qinghai | 13.8 |
| 3 | Hainan | 20.3 | Liaoning | 13.7 |
| 4 | Xinjiang | 19.1 | Beijing | 13.0 |
| 5 | Guizhou | 19.0 | Gansu | 11.8 |
| 6 | Heilongjiang | 17.4 | Heilongjiang | 10.9 |
| 7 | Qinghai | 16.8 | Ningxia | 9.8 |
| 8 | Guangdong | 16.0 | Shaanxi | 9.6 |
| 9 | Fujian | 14.8 | Shanxi | 9.6 |
| 10 | Jilin | 14.7 | Hebei | 9.3 |
| 11 | Guangxi | 14.4 | Xinjiang | 9.1 |
| 12 | Sichuan | 14.3 | Jiangsu | 8.8 |
| 13 | Zhejiang | 13.6 | Shandong | 8.5 |
| 14 | Ningxia | 13.4 | Anhui | 8.5 |
| 15 | Jiangxi | 13.0 | Henan | 8.2 |
| 16 | Henan | 10.9 | Zhejiang | 7.8 |
| 17 | Anhui | 10.8 | Fujian | 7.7 |
| 18 | Shaanxi | 10.5 | Hunan | 7.7 |
| 19 | Shanxi | 9.7 | Tianjin | 7.6 |
| 20 | Hunan | 9.7 | Guangxi | 7.5 |
| 21 | Hubei | 9.5 | Yunnan | 7.3 |
| 22 | Hebei | 9.0 | Guangdong | 6.8 |
| 23 | Gansu | 8.7 | Jiangxi | 6.7 |
| 24 | Shandong | 8.6 | Inner Mongolia | 6.6 |
| 25 | Jiangsu | 7.9 | Guizhou | 6.5 |
| 26 | Liaoning | 4.9 | Jilin | 6.0 |
| 27 | Beijing | 3.7 | Sichuan | 6.0 |
| 28 | Tianjin | 1.4 | Hubei | — |
| 29 | Shanghai | ▲5.3 | Hainan | — |
| 30 | Tibet | — | Tibet | — |
| | Nationally | 11.6 | Nationally | 7.2 |

Source: *Compendium of Historical Statistical Materials for All Provinces, Autonomous Regions, and Special Municipalities 1949 - 1989*, State Statistical Bureau (Beijing: Chinese Statistical Press, 1990), p. 51.

Table 11.3    Five Patterns of Payment to Central and
              Local Level Retention

(a) Case of 15 Provinces and    Municipalities Subject to Distribution of
    Total Value

| Name | Province/ Municipality Retention Ratio | Central Payment Ratio |
|------|---------------------------------------|-----------------------|
| Beijing | 49.55% | 50.45% |
| Tianjin | 39.45% | 60.55% |
| Shanghai | 23.54% | 76.46% |
| Hebei | 69.00% | 31.00% |
| Shanxi | 97.50% | 2.50% |
| Liaoning | 51.08% | 48.92% |
| Heilongjiang | (Fixed value of RMB 64.7 million paid) | |
| Jiangsu | 40.00% | 60.00% |
| Zhejiang | 55.00% | 45.00% |
| Anhui | 80.10% | 19.90% |
| Shandong | 59.00% | 41.00% |
| Henan | 81.00% | 19.00% |
| Hunan | 88.00% | 12.00% |
| Hubei | Retention ratio not calculated (see case of Wuhan) | |
| Sichuan | Retention ratio not calculated (see case of Chongqing) | |

Note: In calculating the retention ratio the denominator is the to tal
value of specified local revenue and central/local shared revenues; the n
umerator is the amount retained by each province.

(b) Four Provinces Receiving Fixed Subsidies from Central (Poor Provinces)

| Name | Subsidy from Central | Name | Subsidy from Central |
|------|----------------------|------|----------------------|
| Shaanxi | RMB 270 mil. | Jilin | RMB 397 mil. |
| Gansu | RMB 246 mil. | Jiangxi | RMB 239 mil. |

# Increasing Regional Financial Independence

Figure 11.4 shows China's principal fiscal outlays: (1) capital construction outlays (equipment investment in enterprises and public works investment); (2) enterprise working capital and enterprise modernization funds (presented in the graph as "potential support"); (3) assistance for agricultural production; (4) education, science, and health services expenditures; (5) national defense expenditures; (6) administrative management expenses; (7) debt-related payments; and (8) price equalization subsidies. These categories are based on "itemization of state fiscal outlays" (*Statistical Yearbook of China 1993*, pp. 222–223).

A different classification is used in "state fiscal outlays by cost category" (*Statistical Yearbook of China 1993*, p. 221), and the categories are somewhat different: economic construction expense, social education expense, national defense expense, administrative management expense, and debt payments. The statistics under this classification are lower than those in Figure 11.4.

(c) Five Autonomous Regions Receiving Gradually Increasing Subsidies from Central (Poorest Regions)

| Name | 1985 | Annually | 1986 | 1987 | 1988 | 1989 |
|---|---|---|---|---|---|---|
| Inner Mongolia | 17.83 | | 19.61 | 21.57 | 23.72 | 26.10 |
| Xinjiang | 14.50 | Planned to | 15.95 | 17.54 | 19.30 | 21.23 |
| Tibet | 7.50 | receive 10% | 8.25 | 9.07 | 9.98 | 10.98 |
| Guangxi | 7.16 | increase | 7.87 | 8.66 | 9.53 | 10.48 |
| Ningxia | 4.94 | annually | 5.43 | 5.98 | 6.57 | 7.23 |
| Yunnan | 6.37 | | 6.97 | 7.67 | 8.44 | 9.28 |
| Guizhou | 7.34 | | 8.17 | 8.99 | 9.89 | 10.88 |
| Qinghai | 6.11 | | 6.72 | 7.39 | 8.13 | 8.94 |

(d) Big Responsibility System (Decided in 1980 for Guandong and Fujian provinces. After fixed payment/receipt of subsidy, provinces had autonomy over provincial finances.)

| Fixed payment to Central | | Fixed subsidy from Central | |
|---|---|---|---|
| Guangdong | 0.8 | Fujian | 0.24 |

(e) Cities Included in the Plan

| Name | Retention ratio | Payment to Central | Payment to Province |
|---|---|---|---|
| Chongqing | 37.50% | 39.20% | 23.30% |
| Shenyang | 36.90% | 38.10% | 25.00% |
| Dalian | 34.14% | 40.86% | 25.00% |
| Wuhan | 20.00% | 66.10% | 13.90% |
| Harbin | 38.12% | 26.88% | 35.00% |
| Xian | Finances are included | in the provincial financial plan. | |
| Guangzhou | Finances are included | in the provincial financial plan. | |

Source: *Contemporary Chinese Finance* (Beijing: Chinese Social Sciences Press, 1988), Vol. 1, pp. 376-377.

Figure 11.5 presents the relationship between central finances and regional finances. Here one can see that central finances are in deficit, whereas regional finances are abundant. It follows that there is an unrelenting contest between the regions and the center as the center seeks to cover its deficits by obtaining fiscal remittances from the regions. In this context, the responsibility system method of distribution presents subtle problems, and it was no doubt inevitable that the attempt would be made to implement a tax separation system.

Table 11.2 illustrates the great change between the Mao Zedong and Deng Xiaoping eras in province-level rankings by growth rate of fiscal revenues. The growth rates of the leading provinces during the Mao era—Shanghai, Liaoning, and Beijing—plummeted during the Deng era. In contrast, the top provinces during the Deng era had very low growth rates during the Mao era. The stagnation of growth of Shanghai municipality and Liaoning province is attributable to the deficits of state-owned enterprises. The growth in agricultural regions is attributable to the development of township and village enterprises and agriculture.

# Distribution of Tax Revenues

In 1980 a new methodology was adopted for allocation of revenues between the central government and the regional governments (province-level) with a view to resolving existing problems. The phrase applied to this new methodology was "separate fiscal payments and assign work to specific administrative levels." This method aimed to identify revenues and expenditures specifically as either central or regional and on this differentiated basis to assign administrative responsibility to the provinces.

In this context, central government revenues were revenues of enterprises directly subordinate to principal departments and ministries of the State Council, customs revenues, and central industrial and commercial tax revenues. Regional revenues were revenues of regional enterprises, salt taxes, agricultural tax revenues, industrial and commercial income tax revenues, hog slaughter taxes, and market trade (free market trading) taxes.

Central expenditures were the central government's share of capital construction investment, cultural and educational activities expenditures, foreign assistance expenditures, and national defense expenditures. Regional expenditures were the region's assignments with respect to capital construction investment, cultural and educational activities expenses, municipal maintenance expenditures, and the like. The "separate payments, assign work" policy was revised several times in view of the cultural conditions in the regions. In March 1985 a new system was established: "differentiate taxes, check and ratify receipts and expenditures, assign work to specific administrative levels" (that is, differentiate between types of taxes, confirm fiscal receipts and payments, and assign administration to the regional governments).

Fiscal distribution in 1985 (Table 11.3) was accomplished by one of five methods. The government postponed implementation of the new system under which fiscal revenues were to be sharply differentiated for each expense item as appertaining to the central government or regional government. Table 11.4 presents findings of an investigation of Guangdong province and Shanghai municipality.

In the quickening mood of reform and liberalization following Deng Xiaoping's statements in 1992, it was decided to implement on an experimental basis in certain provinces the essential parts of the pending system. Thus, it was reported that Zhejiang province, Liaoning province, Xinjiang autonomous region, and Tianjin municipality (at the province level) and Wuhan, Qingdao, Dalian, Shengyang, and Chongqing (all plan unit municipalities, meaning municipalities at the same level as provinces in terms of being plan units) were to implement the tax separation system (*People's Daily*, June 20, 1992). [Translator's note: Vice Minister of Finance Xiang Huaicheng told a meeting of Western business executives in Beijing on September 28, 1993, that from January 1, 1994, a new system of revenues sharing would be implemented between the central government and the provinces. He said that part of the business tax would be kept by local governments, and the value-added

Table 11.4  Payments to Central and Local Retention: The Cases of Guangdong Province and Shanghai Municipality

| | 1980 Actual | 1985 Actual | 1987 Actual | 1989 Actual | 1990 Actual |
|---|---|---|---|---|---|
| **Guangdong Province** | | | | | |
| Fiscal revenues (bil. RMB) | 3.8 [a] | 6.9 [a] | 9.3 | 11.0 | 12.9 |
| Retained amount (bil. RMB) | 2.1 [a] | 4.4 [a] | 6.3 | 7.5 | 9.1 |
| Central payment ratio | 44.4 | 36.4 | 32.2 | 32.2 | 30.0 |
| Payment to Central(bil. RMB) | 1.7 [b] | 2.5 | 3.0 | 3.6 | 3.9 |
| **Shanghai Municipality** | | | | | |
| Fiscal revenues (bil. RMB) | 20 | 26 | 24 | 16 | 16 |
| Retained amount (bil. RMB) | 6 | 7 | 7 | 5 | 5 |
| Central payment ratio | 70 | 70 | 70 | 69 | 67 |
| Payment to Central(bil. RMB) | 14 [a] | 19 [c] | 17 [c] | 11 | 11 |

Notes:
[a] Includes Hainan.
[b] Of which 1 billion is a special remittance.
[c] Figure calculated from 70% entral payment ratio.
    Source: Taken from S. Yabuki, *Conservatives vs. Reformers — China Power Struggle* (Tokyo: Sososha Ltd., 1991), p. 149.

tax would be allocated on a 25:75 formula, with the central government receiving 75 percent of the revenue and the local government 25 percent. Ultimately 40 percent of all taxes collected will be retained and spent by the provinces. The central government will collect 60 percent of total revenues but account for 50 percent of total spending. Thus, in accordance with international practice, the central government will allocate some 10 percent of its collections to the provinces for local spending (The Economist Conferences 1993, p. 53).]

# 12
# Inflation: Threat to Reform and Social Stability

## Measuring Prices in China

There are several key price indices used in China that are pertinent to economic calculations. The *general index of retail prices* is defined as "average prices for all commodities in society." The meaning is (1) all products of labor—this includes both items already deemed "commodities" because production is completed and items that will become commodities (consumption goods) in the future; (2) service costs are not included (service costs are included in the general cost of living index discussed next). The general index of retail prices is produced in three series: the general index of urban retail prices, the general index of rural retail prices, and the general index of nationwide retail prices. Figures are available on the provincial level. In the case of the general index of retail prices, in 1987 "basic reporting units" comprised nationally 195 cities and 203 counties and towns. In the cities about 285 commodities and in the counties and towns some 377 commodities were selected, and weighted averages were calculated for the most representative of standard items. Included were not only controlled prices but also negotiated and free market prices.

The *general index of living costs* is also produced in three series by population category: staff and workers, farmers, and urban residents. Data are available at the provincial level. This index is equivalent to the index of consumer prices in Japan. The general index of living costs after 1957 has been calculated based on the retail price index for consumption goods and the service price index. As of 1987 it comprised 314 types of commodities and service items. Its calculation includes not only official mandated prices but also negotiated prices and market prices.

In addition, because of the traditional deep concern about relative disparities in prices between the cities and the countryside, or between agriculture and industry, the *general index of purchase prices of agricultural by-products* and the *gen-*

*eral index of retail prices for agricultural manufactures* are also compiled. The former presents payments from the cities to the countryside, and the latter shows payments from the countryside to the cities.

In recent years free markets have developed and now coexist with state-run trading. Indices developed in connection with this include the *index of retail prices for state-traded goods;* the *index of agricultural product market prices in cities;* and the *index of free market prices in the countryside.* In the inflationary tumult of 1988–1989, a particular problem was the explosion of free market prices. Further, because the same items were sold in state-owned shops as well as on the free market, diversion into the black market was rampant. Profiteers purchased goods at the official price through the state-run distribution system, then sold them at much higher prices in the free market, and this was practiced on a massive and organized scale. The result was that state stores soon ran out of stock, and consumers were compelled to purchase the goods at the higher free market prices.

## Inflation in the 1980s and 1990s

During the Mao Zedong era, China fundamentally froze prices within the economic plan, and apart from intentional increases in purchase prices for agricultural products, there was almost complete price stability (Figure 12.1). However, during the Deng Xiaoping era, prohibitions on the free market were gradually lifted, and supply and demand were given play in this area. What followed was a rise in the index of living costs (consumer prices) for workers (Table 12.1).

If we assign the index of retail prices nationwide in 1980 a value of 100, by 1992 the value was 208, a rise of over 100 percent in twelve years (Figure 12.2). For China this was an extremely rapid increase in prices. To illustrate, the index did not approach the level of 200 until 1987 (Figure 12.1). In other words, for nearly thirty years China severely controlled prices (at least as evidenced in statistics) and achieved remarkable economic stability. Price rises became noticeable in the 1980s, especially in the second half of the decade, and even more so in the early 1990s. The index (at 100 in base year 1950) was 306 in 1992. In other words, during the period 1980–1992, the index broke through both the 200 and 300 levels.

In 1980 prices rose 6 percent, an increase sufficiently large to create political problems. Hua Guofeng seized upon this as a pretext to criticize the "great leap overseas" and to institute a severe tightening, of which the symbolic incident was the cancellation of numerous foreign plant projects. Under this tightening, prices stabilized, but after 1985 they began to rise again because the "Decision on Reform of the Economic System" and the concept of the planned commodity economy (adopted at the Third Plenum of the Twelfth Party Congress in October 1984) accelerated economic reform. Until these decisions, economic reforms had been largely in agriculture and the countryside, but thereafter reforms began in industry and the cities.

Figure 12.1   Changes in Various Price Indices (1950 - 1992)

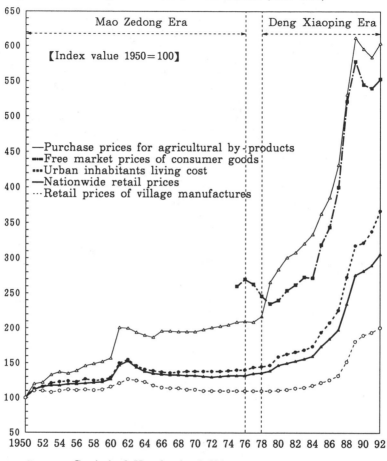

Source: *Statistical Yearbook of China 1993*, pp. 238, 256.

Almost immediately there were several incidents of reform being exploited to commit "economic crimes"—for example, the automobile smuggling centered around Hainan Island. In September 1986 the Sixth Plenum of the Twelfth Party Congress adopted the "Decision on Spiritual Civilization" in an effort to combat the corruption. However, this was opposed by students among others, and Hu Yaobang was purged (January 1987).

Zhao Ziyang put policy back on the economic reform track, and the decision at the Thirteenth Party Congress in October 1987 to accept the early-stage-of-socialism premise offered a great push to economic reform. The result in 1988 was double-digit inflation and a price panic. As this spread to include runs on banks, reform was temporarily halted, and there was no choice but to change to a policy of

Table 12.1  Gap Between Purchase Prices and Consumer Prices of
Agricultural Products (upper figures are purchase prices;
lower figures are consumer prices) (RMB)

| | Unit | 1952 | 1965 | 1978 | 1980 | 1985 | 1989 | 1990 | Note |
|---|---|---|---|---|---|---|---|---|---|
| Grain (traded grain) | ton | 138 | 229 | 263 | 360 | 416 | 750 | 716 | After 1980 purchase/ |
| | ton | 197 | 237 | 294 | 307 | 383 | 557 | 528 | sale produced a loss |
| Edible vegetable oil | ton | 605 | 1450 | 1746 | 2640 | 2701 | 4317 | 4424 | After 1978 purchase/ |
| | ton | 860 | 1639 | 1646 | 1713 | 2179 | 3364 | 3426 | sale produced a loss |
| Live hogs | 100 kg | 35 | 65 | 81 | 125 | 182 | 359 | 345 | |
| Pork | 100 kg | 92 | 162 | 162 | 202 | 274 | 540 | 529 | |
| Live cattle | 100 kg | 42 | 85 | 87 | 134 | 290 | 529 | 519 | |
| Beef | 100 kg | 83 | 116 | 119 | 176 | 319 | 641 | 637 | |
| Live sheep | 100 kg | 51 | 94 | 86 | 127 | 232 | 452 | 412 | |
| Mutton | 100 kg | 89 | 116 | 117 | 164 | 286 | 637 | 614 | |
| Eggs | 100 kg | 62 | 128 | 137 | 171 | 226 | 416 | 435 | |
| | 100 kg | 75 | 165 | 167 | 207 | 269 | 486 | 502 | |
| Fishery products | ton | 248 | 510 | 438 | 770 | 2045 | 4655 | 4305 | |
| (composite average) | ton | 465 | 751 | 953 | 1263 | 2624 | 6019 | 5523 | |
| Tea | 100 kg | 88 | 182 | 239 | 315 | 414 | 647 | 636 | |
| | 100 kg | 206 | 452 | 686 | 795 | 1021 | 1659 | 2021 | |

Source: *Statistical Yearbook of China 1991*, pp. 262-263.

Figure 12.2  Price Movements in the 1980s and 1990s

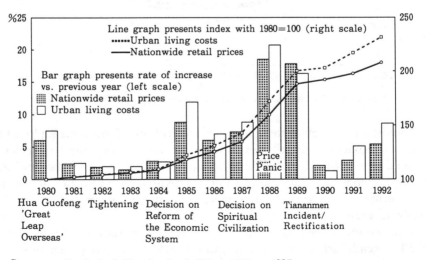

Source: *Statistical Yearbook of China 1993*, p. 237.

Figure 12.3   Situation of Price Management in 1990

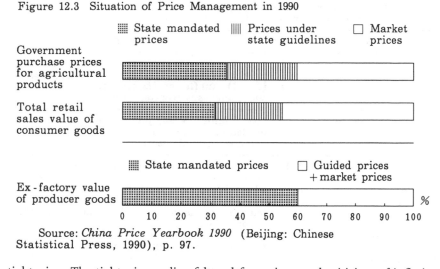

Source: *China Price Yearbook 1990* (Beijing: Chinese Statistical Press, 1990), p. 97.

tightening. The tightening policy faltered for a time, and criticism of inflation and of *guandao* erupted and led to the Tiananmen incident. Subsequently, under martial law and severe tightening, the rise in the index of retail prices in 1990 was held to 2.1 percent over the previous year. However, in 1992 and 1993 the momentum of activity following Deng Xiaoping's southern excursion caused the inflation problem to rise again (see Chapter 19).

## Adjusting for Distortions in the Price System

Figure 12.3 presents in broad terms the price management system in 1990. State management of prices of producer goods was rigorous. Market prices or nonbinding price guidelines prevailed for more than half of agricultural and consumer goods. Tables 12.2 and 12.3 list some key products for which the State Council directly controlled prices. The system of direct price control applied to 742 heavy industrial products; in most cases principal management departments under the State Council exercised control over "ex-factory" prices. ("Ex-factory" refers to products that have left the factory but are not yet in the distribution system; ex-factory prices thus do not include a wholesale markup.) Table 12.4 presents results of a survey of the number of products for which price control was carried out by respective principal management departments.

During the first half of the Deng Xiaoping era, price adjustment was carried out on a national scale five times. Each time the adjustment was of relative prices, and the effect was highly important in raising incomes and stimulating economic activity. Following is a synopsis:

Table 12.2   Agricultural Product Prices Controlled by
            the State Council

| Purchase Prices | No. of Items | Items |
| --- | --- | --- |
| Official prices set by the state | 17 | rice, wheat, corn, soybeans, peanuts (& oil), rapeseed (& oil), cottonseed (& oil), sesame (& oil), sunflower (& oil), cotton, tobacco, sugarcane, sugarbeets, cocoons, brick tea |
| Price guidelines set by the state | 11 | hogs, timber, wool, jute, bluish dogbane, tea leaves, rosin, musk, licorice, encommia, kalahoa (herbal medicine) |

| Sale Prices | No. of Items | Items |
| --- | --- | --- |
| Official prices established by the state | 14 | wheat flour, rice, corn, soybeans, soybean oil, peanut oil, rapeseed oil, sesame oil, tea seed oil, sunflower oil, cotton, lumber, soybean waste |
| Price guidelines established by the state | 4 | pork, tea leaves, lumber, musk |
| Ex-factory prices established by the state | 6 | logs, fir logs, lumber, plywood, rosin, turpentine |

Source: *China Price Yearbook 1990*, p. 98.

Table 12.3   Industrial Products Controlled by the State Council

| | No. of Items | Method of Control |
| --- | --- | --- |
| Ex-factory prices controlled by ministries under the State Council | 733 | Unified price set by the state Price guideline set by the state |
| Market sales prices controlled by ministries under the State Council | 9 | |

Source: *China Price Yearbook 1990*, p. 102.

1. In March 1979 purchase prices were raised for eighteen agricultural products, including grain and cotton. The index of purchase prices for agricultural products rose 20.1 percent.

2. In November 1979 retail prices for eight supplementary food products, including pork, beef, eggs, vegetables, and milk, were raised an average of 30 percent. At the same time, workers were given allowances to offset these price increases.

3. In 1979 ex-factory prices were raised for some heavy industrial products. For example, coal rose 30.5 percent, pig iron 33.0 percent, and rolled steel 20.0 percent.

4.  In 1981 synthetic fabric prices were lowered, and liquor and tobacco prices were raised. In 1983 prices for textile products were completely adjusted; synthetic prices were lowered, and cotton fabric prices were raised.
5.  In 1984 freight rates for railways and water transport were raised. Thereafter, freight charges for short-distance rail transport were raised again. (Ma Hong and Sun Shangqing 1993, p. 1005.)

Through this series of adjustments, the income level of farmers was raised, so that the gap between them and urban workers was narrowed from three to one to two and a half to one (*Statistical Yearbook of China 1988*, p. 800).

After the "Decision of the Communist Party Central on Reform of the Economic System" of October 1984, the problem reached new dimensions. The attempt to move beyond relative price adjustments and instead to reform the entire mechanism of price determination produced chaos. For example, for industrial goods used in the production process that were in short supply, 2 percent of production within the plan and total production outside the plan could be sold by the manufacturers at prices 20 percent above the official price. However, the 20 percent ceiling was immediately exceeded, and any attempt to limit prices was abandoned. Six months later this ceiling was abolished, and decisions on "prices outside the plan" were left to the market. Thus, in the production process a dual system of planned prices and market prices was established (Table 12.5 shows price disparities). What happens when two prices are established for the same good is common knowledge in economics: Profits can be made by procuring goods at official prices (planned prices) and selling them in the free market (market prices). More money can be made by diverting goods that are supposed to be supplied within the plan, labeling them nonplan goods, and selling them on the black market. Without question, the Chinese economy became a paradise for *guandao*—officials acting as brokers for personal gain.

## The Scourge of *Guandao*

*Guandao* is a verb or a noun, depending on the context, meaning official profiteers and profiteering. The phenomena and personages of *guandao* appear in various forms and are referred to in various ways.

The perpetrators seen in public are *si daoye* (private brokers). Supplying them by diverting goods from the distribution departments of state-owned enterprises are *guan daoye* (officials acting as brokers), abbreviated to *guandao*. The practice of using official authority to engage in profiteering also is referred to as *guandao* (power brokering).

The milieu of *guandao* includes variously labeled players and groups—from two or three "small brokers" to organized "big brokers," from openly active

Table 12.4  742 Industrial Products Controlled by Ministries under
the State Council

| Responsible State Council Ministry | Price - Controlled Items (742 Products) |
|---|---|
| Ministry of Energy | 34 types, such as coal, crude oil, and electric power |
| China Petrochemical Corp. | 34 types, such as gasoline |
| Ministry of Petrochemical Industry | 109 types, such as chemical fertilizer |
| Ministry of Agriculture | veterinary medicine |
| State Administration of Building Materials | 14 types, such as cement and flat glass |
| Ministry of Metallurgy | 41 types of steel |
| Jointly controlled by Materials Ministry, Commerce Ministry, Metallurgy Ministry | scrap iron |
| Jointly controlled by Ministry of Metallurgy and China Ferrous Metals Corp. | rare metal |
| China Ferrous Metals Corp. | 55 types, such as copper ore |
| Jointly controlled by Petrochemicals Industry Ministry and Metallurgy Ministry | coke by - product |
| Jointly controlled by People's Bank of China and Ministry of Metallurgy | gold |
| People's Bank of China and China Ferrous Metals Corp. | silver |
| Ministry of Construction | 9 types, such as excavator |
| Ministry of Electrical Machinery | 358 types, such as rock drill |
| Ministry of Light Industry | light industrial machinery |
| Ministry of Textile Industry | textile machinery |
| State Pharmaceutical Administration | pharmaceutical machinery |
| Ministry of Geology and Mineral Resources | 17 types, such as geological equipment |
| Ministry of Public Security | fire fighting equipment |
| Ministry of Commerce | edible oil equipment |
| Ministry of Transportation | 3 types, such as underwater equipment |
| Ministry of Railways | 22 types, such as railway engines |
| China Shipping Corp. | 16 types, such as passenger ships |
| Ministry of Aeronautics and Space | 3 types, such as civil aircraft |
| Ministry of Posts and Telecommunications | 13 types, such as communications equipment |

Source: *China Price Yearbook 1990*, pp. 103 - 118.

Table 12.5  Dual Price System and Price Panic
(Dec. 1988 Materials Ministry survey)

| | Unit | Plan price | Average market price nationwide | Highest price at peak | City of highest peak price |
|---|---|---|---|---|---|
| Wire rod | RMB/ton | 610 | 1,680 | 2,200 | Jingzhou, Wuxi, Zhengzhou |
| Steel | RMB/ton | 592 | 1,473 | 1,980 | Xiamen |
| Cold rolled steel sheets | RMB/ton | 870 | 4,602 | 6,670 | Nanchang |
| Hot rolled carbon steel | RMB/ton | 707 | 1,707 | 1,900 | Xiamen |
| Angle steel | RMB/ton | 593 | 1,665 | 1,960 | Xiamen |
| Medium sheets | RMB/ton | 570 | 1,804 | 3,850 | Guangzhou |
| Lead | RMB/ton | 4,000 | 16,077 | 19,000 | Wuhan |
| Pig iron | RMB/ton | 293 | 752 | 820 | Wuxi |
| Cement | RMB/ton | 90 | 193 | 279 | Shanghai |
| Soda | RMB/ton | 390 | 1,192 | 1,800 | Wuhan |
| Caustic soda | RMB/ton | 640 | 2,986 | 3,800 | Wuhan |
| Truck (Dongfang 140) | RMB/units | 25,800 | 46,538 | 63,800 | Shenyang |
| Truck (Jiefang 141) | RMB/units | 29,800 | 39,004 | 40,736 | Jinan |
| Larch logs | RMB/ m³ | 119 | 636 | 700 | Xining |

Source: Zhang Zhouyuan, *Theory and Practice in the Conversion of China's Price Model* (Beijing: Chinese Social Sciences Press, 1990), p. 75.

"bright brokers" to covert "dark brokers." Similarly, commodities are said to be turned over in the black market once (*yidao*), twice, or three times (*erdao*, *sandao*). All this constitutes an underground economy operating through a network of personal relationships.

There is a local coloring to the activities of the *daoye*. Two able reporters from the Xinhua agency observed the mode of living of the *daoye* who had come to Beijing:

> The *daoye* from the suburbs of Tianjin are mainly dealing in gasoline ration coupons.
>
> The *daoye* from Xinjiang traffic in foreign exchange and foreign exchange certificates.
>
> The *daoye* from Zhejiang and Fujian sell cheap clothes and eyeglasses.
>
> The *daoye* from Henan and Hebei traffic in grain ration coupons.
>
> The *daoye* from Guilin sell hanging scrolls. [Author's note: That these wind up in the hands of members of Japanese tourist groups is something that anyone who travels to China knows.]
>
> The *daoye* from the Northeast traffic in cigarettes. (Qiu Yongsheng and Ni Xiaolin 1988)

The fundamental problem in this milieu is not the black marketeers on the street but those persons engaged in official corruption, *guandao*. Retired cadres or incumbent senior cadres or their children are exploiting their positions and influence to divert goods from state-owned enterprises. The result is that the black market has assumed the name of "the market economy" and is devouring the planned economy. Severe criticism has been leveled against the huge profits being made through various kinds of illegal activity. One such case involved Deng Xiaoping's son, Deng Pufang, who exploited his position as the person responsible for welfare activities for physically handicapped persons to establish Kanghua Development Company, which engaged in smuggling color televisions into China and selling import licenses. No trial was held to determine the culpability of Deng Pufang or any other principals after activities of Kanghua Development Company became known. Officials nonetheless summarily ordered the company dissolved. This apparently forceful action can be seen as an attempt by authorities to assuage public outrage at corrupt behavior by persons with influence (especially relatives of high officials) in the case of a highly visible company and personage.

## The Relationship Between Prices and the Money Supply

From the 1950s through the 1970s, thinking in China was that it was desirable to hold the money supply to one-eighth of the gross value of retail transactions (Yang Peixin 1990). Officials postulated that the money supply would turn over eight times on average, and the money stock would be 12.5 percent of the gross

Figure 12.4    Relationship Between Gross Retail Sales Value and
                        Money in Circulation

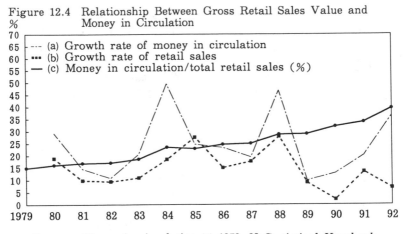

Sources: Money in circulation (a) 1979-83 *Statistical Yearbook of China 1984*, p. 422; 1984-91 *Statistical Yearbook of China 1993*, p. 664; Retail sales (b) *Statistical Yearbook of China 1993*, p. 611.

value of retail transactions, but that if it rose to 16.5 percent of this value, there would be a risk of inflation. However, in the midst of the 1980s economic reform, adherence to these standards was abandoned.

First, the "monetization of the economy" proceeded along with the development of the commodity economy. Second, the "cash settlement" component of commerce increased markedly along with the development of individual enterprises and township and village enterprises, whereas settlement by bank transfer among state-owned enterprises stagnated.

As these financial changes evolved, the previous 12.5 to 16.5 percent parameters were neglected. In the first half of the 1980s, the ratio of money supply to retail transactions was barely kept below 20 percent, and the inflation level reached about 25 percent in the rest of the decade (Figure 12.4). This adverse trend continued: The ratio had risen to an alarming 39.4 percent by the end of 1992.

To analyze why money increased, it is useful first to understand how money supply is calculated (component lettering corresponds to columns in upper section and lines and bars in lower section of Table 12.6): Increase in currency in circulation equals (a) fiscal deficit, plus (b) loans to the private sector minus increase in deposits, plus (c) increase in holdings of foreign exchange minus other factors.

Further, because a portion of deposits have the quality of money, we can classify them as money and adjust the equation as follows: Increase in money creation equals (a) fiscal deficit, plus (b) loans to the private sector minus increase in deposits not having the quality of money, plus (c) increase in holdings of foreign currency minus other factors.

Table 12.6 presents an analysis of the causes of increased money issuance during the 1980s using figures from the "balance sheet of loan funds of state banks" in each year's edition of *Statistical Yearbook of China*. In the first half of the 1980s, the annual increase in money issued was RMB 20 to 30 billion. However, in 1988 the figure surged to RMB 68.1 billion. Over 90 percent was loans in excess of deposits, and this overextension was the real culprit behind the surge in the money supply and prices that led to the Tiananmen incident. In the post-Tiananmen tightening, the increase in new money dropped by two-thirds to some RMB 21 billion, but subsequently soared to a new peak of RMB 115.8 billion in 1992 as liberalization and budget deficits combined to fuel economic overheating. After 1991 the increase in money resulted less from loans in excess of deposits and budgetary deficits (elements of overheating) than from RMB balances created in exchange for inflows of foreign capital. Table 12.6 shows increases in foreign currency holdings of RMB 61 billion in 1991 and RMB 144 billion in 1992. Thus, the increase in money in 1991–1992 (which has continued through 1994) should be considered a positive development that is promoting rather than threatening future growth.

According to statistics compiled by the International Monetary Fund (IMF), in 1990 the reported money supply measurement M1 was RMB 701 billion, reserve money was RMB 767.2 billion, and the two combined produced M2 of RMB 1,468.2 billion (far right column of Table 12.6).

# Banking System Reform and Creation of Securities Markets

After 1949 China established a financial system centering on the People's Bank of China. However, the bank's role in the Soviet-style planned economy was to do little more than issue currency and perform accounting and payment-receipts functions for the government's finances. The financial sector was limited to handling the flow of budgetary funds, and there were no financial activities in the usual sense of the term.

Reform of the financial sector was given high priority within the general economic reform in the 1980s. In 1984 the government announced a plan to convert the People's Bank into a central bank that would act principally as a "banker's bank" and only issue currency and provide liquidity to all types of financial institutions. A "reserve system" was established in which the People's Bank would receive a certain amount of funds from other types of financial institutions as "reserve deposits" and regulate lending by the specialized banks through adjustment of the "reserve ratio" (i.e., loosening or tightening credit).

A correlative step in this change in function of the People's Bank was to establish, revive, or revitalize a number of specialized banks. These included the Agricultural Bank of China, to support financial activities in the villages; the Bank of China, to handle foreign exchange; the People's Construction Bank of China, to manage investments in fixed assets; and the Industrial and Commercial Bank of China, to serve the industrial and commercial units in the cities. Added subsequently were the People's Insurance Company of China, to undertake insurance

Table 12.6   Reason for Money Issuance: Relationship Between
Government Deficits and Private Credit Creation
(in billions RMB)

| | Volume of money in circulation | Increase in money supply (a) + (b) + (c) | Fiscal deficits (a) | Increase in private lending in excess of increase in deposits (b) | Increase in holdings of foreign currency and other (c) | Money M₁ (d) | Near money (e) | M₂ (d) + (e) |
|---|---|---|---|---|---|---|---|---|
| 1981 | 40 | 5 | 0 | 0 | 5 | 134 | 63 | 198 |
| 1982 | 44 | 4 | 0 | -4 | 9 | 149 | 78 | 227 |
| 1983 | 53 | 9 | 3 | -2 | 8 | 175 | 96 | 271 |
| 1984 | 79 | 26 | 6 | 36 | -16 | 245 | 115 | 360 |
| 1985 | 99 | 20 | 1 | 64 | -45 | 302 | 185 | 488 |
| 1986 | 122 | 23 | 10 | 54 | -40 | 386 | 249 | 635 |
| 1987 | 145 | 24 | 15 | 25 | -16 | 457 | 338 | 796 |
| 1988 | 213 | 68 | 6 | 67 | -5 | 549 | 412 | 960 |
| 1989 | 234 | 21 | 11 | 27 | -17 | 583 | 556 | 1,139 |
| 1990 | 264 | 30 | 12 | 13 | 6 | 701 | 767 | 1,468 |
| 1991 | 318 | 53 | 37 | -34 | 61 | 583 | 556 | 1,139 |
| 1992 | 434 | 116 | 17 | -46 | 144 | 701 | 767 | 1,468 |

Note: Differences due to rounding.
Sources: Volume of money in circulation, increase in money, *Statistical Yearbook of China 1984*, p. 422; *Statistical Yearbook of China 1993*, p. 664. M₁ and M₂ IMF *International Financial Statistics.*

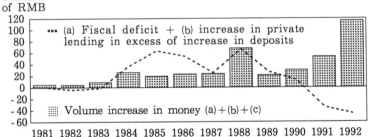

business; and the China International Trust Investment Company (CITIC), to act as an investment consultant and channel foreign investment funds to China. Postal deposits were also begun in 1986.

The conversion of banks to true enterprises has advanced through expansion of their management independence and approval of independent fund-raising and retention of profits. Accompanying the improvement of financial institutions was the establishment after 1986 of a short-term money market based principally on call money and bills discounting. Securities markets handling stocks and bonds also made an appearance, and initial steps were taken to establish a long-term capital market (Table 12.7).

However, conversion of specialized banks to real commercial banking enterprises remains at a superficial level. Bank branches are still inclined to look to head offices for funding, and head offices are inclined to seek credit from the central bank. Interference in a bank's management of funds from higher-level banks

Table 12.7 Overview of Principal Chinese Securities

| | | | | |
|---|---|---|---|---|
| Bonds | State Bonds | Treasury Certificates | Redemption and interest payment through lottery<br>Interest and principal paid at maturity | |
| | | Key state project construction bonds | | |
| | | Treasury notes | 2 Year notes<br>5 Year notes | |
| | | State construction bonds | | |
| | | Special government bonds | | |
| | | Inflation hedge bonds | | |
| | State Agency Bonds | Capital construction bonds | | |
| | | 1988,1989 key enterprise bonds | | |
| | Finan-cial Bonds | Regular financial debentures | | |
| | | Progressive interest financial debentures | | |
| | | Discount financial debentures | | |
| | Enter-prise Bonds | 1987 key enterprise bonds | | |
| | | Regional enterprise bonds | Enterprise bonds with interest coupons attached. Interest paid in advance.<br>Interest plus principal redemption-type enterprise debt certificates.<br>Enterprise debt with commodity dividends bonus awards | |
| | | Enterprise short-term loan paper | | |
| | Foreign currency bonds | | | |
| Stocks | Common stocks (e.g., Shanghai Feile Co., Ltd. shares, issued September 1987, listed April 1988) | | | |
| | Preferred stocks (e.g., Shenyang Jinbei Motors Co., Ltd., issued July 1988) | | | |
| | B Shares (RMB-denominated. However, may be purchased by FEC only.) | | | |
| Large-denomination negotiable fixed deposits | issued to individuals | registered form<br>bearer form | | |
| | issued to organization | registered form<br>bearer form | | |

Source: Wang Guangqian, ed., *China's Securities Market* (Beijing: Chinese Financial and Economic Press, 1991), p. 181.

and local governments is prevalent; real bank sovereignty is as yet unrealized. Moreover, the relationship of banks to fiscal administration is still ambiguous.

Chinese treasury bonds were first issued in 1981. The outstanding value in 1991 of all issued securities was RMB 280 billion. Stocks and bonds totaled RMB 200 billion, one-fourth of the total value of urban and rural savings. In 1988 the annual trading volume of securities was less than RMB 3 billion; in 1991 the figure was approaching RMB 20 billion. [Translator's note: Government bond sales and the secondary market in government bonds, centered in Shanghai, grew tremendously in 1993 and are slated to make greater leaps in 1994. In 1993 the Finance Ministry sold about RMB 40 billion of treasury bonds. In February 1994 the ministry announced that bond sales in 1994 would total RMB 100 billion. Reasons behind the huge flotation include the ministry's need to borrow from the public—because the People's Bank in January 1994 officially announced it would no longer allow the ministry to overdraw its account—and the government's intention to curb inflation by tapping money in circulation rather than by creating new money. One important by-product of the increase in government bonds outstanding is that it has now become possible for the central bank to conduct "open market operations" to adjust the supply and cost of money and credit in the economy, and the People's Bank has announced that it will begin these operations in 1994.] In 1991 administrative allocation of treasury bonds was ended in favor of sales in Shanghai and Shenzhen. Trading in these markets is connected to Beijing and other key cities nationwide through an automated securities trading price reporting system.

# 13

## The Energy Constraint

### Chronic Energy Insufficiency

Energy is one of the principal constraints in the Chinese economy. Figure 13.1 presents the relationship between the growth of energy production and the growth of real national income. The growth rate of the production of primary energy (converted to standard coal) over all of the five-year plans (exclusive of the 1963–1965 readjustment period, which was exceptional) shows a continuous downward trend. Further, again with the exception of the readjustment period, in all periods the growth rate of energy production has exceeded that of national income. However, the relatively rapid growth of national income in the sixth plan period (1981–1985) and the seventh plan period (1986–1990) was realized against a situation of low growth in energy supplies. At first glance, we might conclude from this that significant progress was realized in energy conservation; in fact, the chronic shortage of energy simply became more acute. China's net exports of energy constitute 5 percent of total production, which means that production and consumption are essentially equivalent.

Table 13.1 presents the correlation of a unit of growth in national income and production or consumption of primary energy and electric power (secondary energy)—technically, the production-consumption elasticity coefficients (growth in energy divided by growth in national income). For example, the 1989–1990 period was one of economic tightening and plummeting growth; however, the pattern observed in energy did not parallel the economy, so the elasticity coefficient declined, and volatility was high in relation to changes in the overall economy. Thus, the average elasticity coefficient of energy consumption of 0.55 percent in the earlier half of the 1980s increased slightly to 0.65 percent in the latter half. For electric power, the figure rose from 0.71 in the early half to 1.27 percent in the latter half. This indicates a deterioration in energy efficiency.

It is well known that energy utilization in China is highly inefficient. For example, per capita energy consumption in China is about 500 kilograms, approxi-

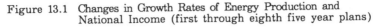

Figure 13.1   Changes in Growth Rates of Energy Production and
              National Income (first through eighth five year plans)

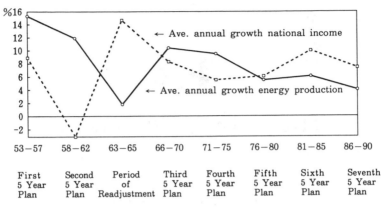

Source: National income: *Statistical Yearbook of China 1991*
p. 34; energy: p. 453.

mately one-fifth the level in Japan. However, China's GNP is only about one-fifti-
eth of Japan's. In other words, in order to produce the same income, China requires ten times as much energy as Japan. Table 13.2 presents the energy production targets of the eighth five-year plan (1991–1995) and for the year 2000; these
targets are quite conservative. Energy insufficiency is one of the greatest threats to
Chinese economic growth in the 1990s, and overcoming this problem is one of
China's greatest challenges.

# The Energy Mix

### Slow Growth of Crude Petroleum Production

As shown in Figure 13.2, petroleum's share of total energy production peaked at
23–24 percent in the second half of the 1970s, then dropped to some 21 percent in
the first half of the 1980s, and finally decreased below the 20 percent level by the
end of the decade. Although the Daqing oilfield of Heilongjiang province developed by leaps in the 1970s and has been a major contributor, it is reaching the limits of capacity as a result of excessive pumping, and production is stagnating. The
Shengli oilfield of Shandong province is trying to catch up with Daqing but is still
only about 60 percent the size of Daqing (see Figure 13.3).

Table 13.3 presents the supply-and-demand balance for crude petroleum. The
data reflect a stagnation of production: Export volume declined from 36.3 million
tons in 1985 to 19.3 million tons in 1991. Conversely, import volume increased
from less than 1 million tons to over 12 million tons. (Bunkerage of PRC-owned

Table 13.1 Changes in Elasticity Coefficients of Production and Consumption of Energy and Electric Power (1980 - 1990)

| | (a) Energy | | (b) Electric Power | | (c) National Income | (a)/(c) Energy | | (b)/(c) Electric Power | |
|---|---|---|---|---|---|---|---|---|---|
| | Growth of Production % | Growth of Consumption % | Growth of Production % | Growth of Consumption % | Growth Rate | Production Elasticity Coefficient | Consumption Elasticity Coefficient | Production Elasticity Coefficient | Consumption Elasticity Coefficient |
| 1980 | -1.3 | 2.9 | 6.6 | 6.6 | 6.4 | | 0.45 | 1.03 | 1.03 |
| 1981 | -0.8 | -1.4 | 2.9 | 3.0 | 4.9 | | | 0.59 | 0.61 |
| 1982 | 5.6 | 4.4 | 6.0 | 6.0 | 8.2 | 0.69 | 0.54 | 0.73 | 0.73 |
| 1983 | 6.7 | 6.4 | 7.3 | 7.3 | 10.0 | 0.67 | 0.64 | 0.73 | 0.73 |
| 1984 | 9.2 | 7.4 | 7.3 | 7.4 | 13.6 | 0.68 | 0.54 | 0.53 | 0.54 |
| 1985 | 9.9 | 8.1 | 8.9 | 9.0 | 13.5 | 0.73 | 0.60 | 0.66 | 0.67 |
| 1986 | 3.0 | 5.4 | 9.5 | 9.5 | 7.7 | 0.39 | 0.71 | 1.23 | 1.23 |
| 1987 | 3.6 | 7.2 | 10.6 | 10.6 | 10.2 | 0.35 | 0.70 | 1.04 | 1.04 |
| 1988 | 5.0 | 7.3 | 9.6 | 9.7 | 11.3 | 0.44 | 0.65 | 0.85 | 0.85 |
| 1989 | 6.1 | 4.2 | 7.3 | 7.3 | 3.7 | 1.65 | 1.14 | 1.96 | 1.97 |
| 1990 | 2.2 | 1.1 | 6.2 | 6.2 | 4.8 | 0.47 | 0.23 | 1.30 | 1.30 |

Source: *Statistical Yearbook of China 1991*, p. 468.

Table 13.2 Energy Production: Actual Performance and
Targets for 2000

| | Energy | Coal | Crude oil | Natural gas | Hydroelectric power |
|---|---|---|---|---|---|
| | Standard carbon million tons | Million tons | Million tons | Million cubic meters | (kWh) |
| 1980 | 637 (100) | 620 (69.5) | 105 (23.8) | 142 (3.0) | 582 (3.8) |
| 1985 | 855 (100) | 872 (72.8) | 124 (20.9) | 129 (2.0) | 924 (4.3) |
| 1989 | 1,016 (100) | 1,054 (74.1) | 137 (19.3) | 150 (2.0) | 1,184 (4.6) |
| 1990 | 1,040 (100) | 1,080 (74.9) | 138 (18.8) | 152 (1.5) | 1,260 (4.8) |
| 1995 | 1,140.0 | 1,230 | 145 | 200.0 | 8,100 (Generated power) |
| 2000 | | 1,400 | Maximum effort | | 11,000 (Generated power) |

Note: Figures in parentheses indicate conversion to standard
carbon in percent.
Source: *Statistical Yearbook of China 1991*, p. 435; for 1995,
2000 figures: "Recommendations on the Eighth Five Year Plan."

Figure 13.2 Composition of Energy Production

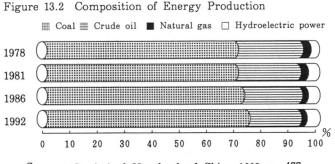

Source: *Statistical Yearbook of China 1993*, p. 477.

Figure 13.3 Proportion of the Daqing Oilfield
in China's Petroleum Production

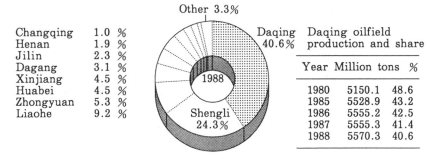

| Changqing | 1.0 % |
|---|---|
| Henan | 1.9 % |
| Jilin | 2.3 % |
| Dagang | 3.1 % |
| Xinjiang | 4.5 % |
| Huabei | 4.5 % |
| Zhongyuan | 5.3 % |
| Liaohe | 9.2 % |

Other 3.3%
Daqing 40.6%
Shengli 24.3%

Daqing oilfield
production and share

| Year | Million tons | % |
|---|---|---|
| 1980 | 5150.1 | 48.6 |
| 1985 | 5528.9 | 43.2 |
| 1986 | 5555.2 | 42.5 |
| 1987 | 5555.3 | 41.4 |
| 1988 | 5570.3 | 40.6 |

Source: *Statistical Yearbook of China 1991*, p. 127.

ships and aircraft in foreign ports is included in imports, and bunkerage of foreign-owned ships and aircraft in China is considered exports; the two essentially offset each other.) In 1992 and 1993 the trend seen in Table 13.2 continued, and China became a net oil importing country for the first time since the 1960s. Building new petroleum production bases is one of the urgent tasks of the 1990s. The key strategy in the eighth five-year plan is to develop the Tarim and Turfan areas under the policy of "stabilizing the east, while developing the west." [Translator's note: Prospects with regard to energy supply and development were communicated in an interview with Wang Tao, general manager of the China National Petroleum Corporation, published in *Nihon Keizai Shimbum,* March 20, 1994. Wang said that China would probably be a net importer of about 7 million tons of crude oil a year through the year 2000. He also said that in order to increase production of oil and gas, China was planning to bring in US$3–5 billion of foreign capital.]

A source of potential conflict is development of oilfields in the Nansha (Spratly) Islands area. In February 1992 the Chinese government promulgated a "territorial waters law" that clearly delineated the Nansha Islands and other areas as part of Chinese territory. In May contracts for oilfield development were signed with U.S. petroleum development companies. The Chinese navy's activity in the area is conspicuous, intended to leave no doubt about Chinese sovereign control. Against this, tensions have risen as Vietnam, Philippines, Malaysia, Brunei, and Taiwan, who also claim a part of the islands area, have dispatched military forces to the area.

## Coal Still King in Energy

Coal has traditionally been the most important form of energy in China, constituting three-fourths of total energy supply. The outline of the 1991–1995 five-year plan highlights development of fourteen coal-producing areas as key coal bases (see Map 13.1), distributed by province as follows: Inner Mongolia 4, Shanxi 2, Shaanxi 2, Liaoning 1, Heilongjiang 1, Shandong 1, Anhui 1, Henan 1, and Ningxia 1. The development of these bases is intended to raise coal output from 1.08 billion tons in 1990 to 1.23 billion in 1995, an increase of 150 million tons.

A glance at the map makes clear that all these coal bases are located north of the Yangtze River. This regional imbalance is the root of problems of coal transportation that have long plagued the economy. Indeed, it is said that half of all transport in China is transport of coal.

## Thermopower in the North, Hydropower in the South: Electric Power Generation

Map 13.2 identifies sites for the proposed construction of thirteen electric power generation plants (7 hydro, 5 thermal, and 1 nuclear) under the eighth five-year

Table 13.3   The Balance of Petroleum Supply and Consumption in China
             (in million tons)

|  | 1980 | 1985 | 1990 | 1991 |
|---|---|---|---|---|
| Possible supply volume | 87.95 | 91.94 | 114.35 | 123.65 |
| Production volume | 105.95 | 124.90 | 138.31 | 140.99 |
| Imports volume | 0.83 | 0.90 | 7.56 | 12.50 |
| Exports volume | - 18.06 | - 36.30 | - 31.10 | - 29.31 |
| Annual inventory change | - 0.77 | 2.45 | - 0.41 | - 0.53 |
| Consumption volume | 87.57 | 91.69 | 114.86 | 123.84 |
| Final consumption volume | 63.11 | 70.63 | 93.05 | 101.83 |
| Secondary energy conversion | 1.02 | 17.46 | 16.30 | 16.53 |
| Electricity generation | 20.65 | 14.26 | 12.34 | 12.71 |
| Heat supply |  | 2.86 | 3.56 | 3.37 |
| LPG | 0.37 | 0.35 | 0.40 | 0.45 |

Note: Production volume is production volume for crude petroleum.
Imports volume includes supplies of oil for Chinese ships and aircraft
received abroad. Export volume includes supplies of oil in China for
foreign aircraft and ships.
Source: *Statistical Yearbook of China 1993*, p. 480.

Map 13.1   Principal Coal Production Bases
           in the Eighth Five Year Plan

Map 13.2   Principal Electric Power
            Production Bases in the Eighth Five Year Plan

Table 13.4   The Balance of Electric Power Supply and Consumption
             in China (in billion kWh)

|                                     | 1980  | 1985  | 1990  | 1991  |
|-------------------------------------|-------|-------|-------|-------|
| Possible Supply Volume              | 300.6 | 411.8 | 623.0 | 680.4 |
| Production Volume                   | 300.6 | 410.7 | 621.2 | 677.6 |
| of which hydro power                | 58.2  | 92.4  | 126.7 | 125.1 |
| thermal power                       | 242.4 | 318.3 | 494.5 | 552.5 |
| Import volume                       | —     | 1.11  | 1.9   | 3.1   |
| Export volume                       | —     | 0.04  | -0.1  | -0.2  |
| Consumption volume                  | 300.6 | 411.8 | 623.0 | 680.4 |
| 5 sectors incl. industry and agriculture | 283.2 | 377.3 | 554.7 | 602.1 |
| Service sector                      | 6.88  | 12.2  | 20.2  | 23.9  |
| Daily living consumption            | 10.5  | 22.3  | 48.1  | 54.4  |

Source: *Statistical Yearbook of China 1993*, p. 481.

plan. The thermopower plants are concentrated north of the Yangtze River; hydropower plants dominate south of the Yangtze River. As a consequence of this planned expansion and building, electric power generation is projected to increase by 192 billion kilowatt-hours (kWh), from 618 billion kWh in 1990 to 810 billion kWh in 1995.

Table 13.4 presents the balance of electric power supply and consumption during the 1980s.

# 14

# Warnings of an Ecological Crisis

## The Myth That "Socialism Does Not Produce Pollution"

As unbelievable as it may be today, China at one time boasted of its success at treating the "three wastes"—industrial wastewater, gas, and materials. Photographs were published as evidence that fish were being nurtured in treated industrial wastewater. During my first trip to China in 1979, I was so troubled by the noxious smell coming from a factory in Shanghai that I inquired about pollution control policies. The factory director began waxing eloquent on the factory's great success in pollution control. From this painful experience it became clear to me that China's pollution control policies were in danger of falling greatly behind because the bureaucrats in charge did not differentiate between propaganda and scientific knowledge.

There are a number of major problem areas in China's environment that many people find alarming. One concern voiced is that "the Yangtze River is becoming the second Yellow River." It is well known that the waters of the Yellow River carry an enormous volume of silt, which accounts for the old saying "one must wait a hundred years for a clear Yellow River." However, ecological research has led one expert to warn that natural disasters also threaten the Yangtze because like the Yellow River, it is now being filled with huge amounts of soil erosion runoff (article by He Naiwei in *Guangming Daily* July 31, 1979). The primary cause of this is uncontrolled cutting of trees along the Yangtze's upper and middle reaches. Further, overgrazing by animals has reduced grasslands, and desertification is proceeding. In addition, in recent years fish catches have been declining because of uncontrolled fishing. In all of these instances, destruction of resources and the environment is resulting from overutilization of natural resources.

Apart from this are pollution problems attending the development of industry, which entails treatment of waste gases, wastewater, and waste materials. These problems include harmful gases such as fluorine, sulfur, and chlorine; harmful

Table 14.1   Environmental Pollutants and Environmental
             Recompensations and Fines in China (1981-1992)

| Year | Sulfuric gas(million tons | Coal dust (million tons) | Industrial waste water (million tons) | Pollution incidents (no.) | Pollution recompensation (million RMB) | Pollution fines (million RMB) |
|------|------|------|------|------|------|------|
| 1981 | 14.2 | 15.2 | 2379 | | | |
| 1982 | 13.3 | 14.1 | 2394 | | | |
| 1983 | 12.6 | 13.3 | 2388 | | | |
| 1984 | | | | | | |
| 1985 | 13.3 | 13.0 | 2574 | 2716 | 50.7 | 9.3 |
| 1986 | 12.5 | 13.8 | 2602 | 3207 | 52.7 | 12.7 |
| 1987 | 14.1 | 14.5 | 2637 | 3617 | 67.8 | 12.7 |
| 1988 | 15.2 | 14.5 | 2683 | 3699 | 82.6 | 35.7 |
| 1989 | 15.7 | 14.0 | 2521 | 3332 | 90.7 | 26.1 |
| 1990 | 14.9 | 13.2 | 2487 | 3462 | 97.4 | 16.0 |
| 1991 | 16.2 | 13.1 | 2357 | 3038 | 41.1 | 50.5 |
| 1992 | 16.9 | 14.1 | 2339 | 2667 | 51.9 | 33.6 |

Sources: 1981-83: *Chinese Social Statistical Materials* (Beijing: Chinese Statistical Press, August 1985), pp. 241-242. 1985-92: *Statistical Yearbook of China 1993*, p. 822.

wastewaters such as those containing mercury, phenol, cyanogen gas, cadmium, arsenic, and radioactive substances; and materials such as steel dregs, blast furnace dregs, sulfuric ore dregs, chrome dregs, and coal ash. To counter these problems, some environmental supervision has been undertaken. Earlier studies had investigated pollution of water, oceans, atmosphere, soil, agricultural products, and foodstuffs. Further, scientific research in environmental protection and training of specialists is in process.

As can be seen in Table 14.1, there were 3,462 pollution "incidents" reported in China in 1990 (statistics are compiled for instances of damage of RMB 1,000 or more), RMB 97.4 million was paid in compensation, and RMB 16 million was assessed as penalties. The figures for 1992 were 2,667, RMB 52 million, and RMB 34 million, respectively. The five worst provinces for sulfuric gas emissions are Shandong, Sichuan, Jiangsu, Liaoning, and Hebei. The five worst for coal dust emissions are Heilongjiang, Shandong, Liaoning, Jilin, and Shanxi (Table 14.2).

# The "External Diseconomies" of Environmental Destruction

China was originally blessed with an abundant ecological environment. In the early Qin period, the forest coverage ratio of the entire area of the loess plateau was over 50 percent and as much as 80 to 90 percent in the northeast, Sichuan, and Yunnan. However, centuries of waste and war damage under successive dynasties as well as excessive logging operations had extensively despoliated China's environment by 1949. For example, the Chinese Academy of Forestry Sciences estimated that the forest coverage ratio had declined to as low as 13 percent. The Nenjiang plateau in Heilongjiang province had been under cultivation less than 100 years, but soil erosion in half the area had resulted in loss of 70–80 centimeters of topsoil (*General Theory of China's Natural Geography,* 1985, p. 18).

Table 14.2   The Situation of Sulfuric Gas and Coal Dust
Emission at the Provincial Level (in thousand tons)

| Place | Sulfuric gas | Coal dust | Place | Sulfuric gas | Coal dust | Place | Sulfuric gas | Coal dust |
|---|---|---|---|---|---|---|---|---|
| Beijing | 340 | 250 | Zhejiang | 440 | 280 | Hainan | 10 | 10 |
| Tianjin | 220 | 180 | Anhui | 380 | 310 | Sichuan | 1480 | 800 |
| Hebei | 890 | 760 | Fujian | 120 | 100 | Guizhou | 500 | 250 |
| Shanxi | 780 | 810 | Jiangxi | 300 | 300 | Yunnan | 230 | 290 |
| Inner Mongolia | 530 | 660 | Shandong | 1930 | 1210 | Tibet | — | — |
| Liaoning | 970 | 1050 | Henan | 490 | 590 | Shaanxi | 590 | 490 |
| Jilin | 260 | 860 | Hubei | 560 | 470 | Gansu | 360 | 200 |
| Heilongjiang | 320 | 1280 | Hunan | 550 | 380 | Qinghai | 30 | 70 |
| Shanghai | 420 | 190 | Guangdong | 400 | 220 | Ningxia | 130 | 110 |
| Jiangsu | 1000 | 620 | Guangxi | 600 | 300 | Xinjiang | 160 | 190 |

Source: *Statistical Yearbook of China 1991*, p. 798.

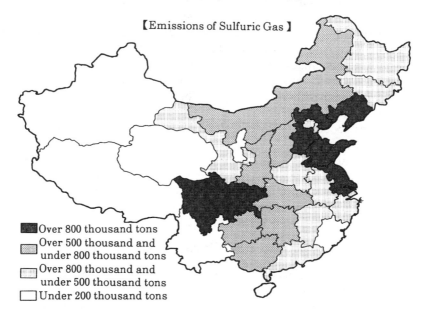

【Emissions of Sulfuric Gas 】

■ Over 800 thousand tons
▨ Over 500 thousand and under 800 thousand tons
▤ Over 800 thousand and under 500 thousand tons
□ Under 200 thousand tons

After the establishment of the PRC, efforts were made to ameliorate environmental degradation in order to improve conditions for agricultural production. However, damage was already extensive; further, knowledge of methods of protecting the environment was lacking. Environment deterioration was particularly severe later during the Great Leap Forward and Cultural Revolution. In recent years, under the production responsibility system in the countryside, peasants have engaged in "short-term behaviors" (careless handling of industrial wastes and other destructive land use practices) that have further damaged the environment. To exaggerate slightly, the Chinese environmental problem can be summarized as "a priori insufficiency and a posteriori disharmony—improvement in some areas, but further deterioration overall" (Hu Angang and Wang Yi 1989, p.

32). In short, environmental destruction continues through (1) expansion of areas of water erosion; (2) deforestation and retreat of grasslands; (3) expansion of desertification; (4) decrease in river and lake area; (5) neglect of maintenance and repair of waterworks; and (6) environmental pollution.

Hu Angang and Wang Yi pointed out that environmental pollution is spreading from the cities to the countryside. The situation is coming to resemble that of the advanced countries in the worst periods of the 1950s and 1960s. Pollution is causing not only great economic damage but also injurious health effects. Because over 80 percent of contaminated water is released without treatment, pollution is spread over wide areas. In certain areas in the south (especially in the southwestern provinces), severe acid rain has occurred. Thirty percent of all workers nationally work under noise levels that are injurious to health. Approximately 170 million people drink polluted water. Farmland polluted by industrial waste products and industrial and agricultural chemicals totals over 20 million hectares; over one-seventh of all cultivated land is polluted by agricultural chemicals. According to a study by the Chinese Academy of Environmental Sciences (cited in Hu Angang and Wang Yi 1989, p. 35), losses from "external diseconomies" engendered by environmental pollution and ecological destruction in China totaled RMB 86 billion, 7.8 percent of GNP.

Predictions about future environmental deterioration have sounded an ominous tone: "These projected results are delivering to us a warning. As scientists, we should not just have a normal degree of concern about environmental pollution. We should acknowledge that this is an extremely urgent and complex problem that is threatening the foundation of the future development and existence of the Chinese people" (Hu Angang and Wang Yi 1989, p. 35).

## Environmental Conditions in 1991

The Chinese Environmental Protection Bureau published the "1991 Report on Environmental Conditions in China" on May 29, 1992. The *People's Daily* on May 29, 1992, summarized the report after providing the following bureaucratic introduction:

> Taking an overall view, in the context of continuous economic development, the environmental situation in China in 1991 was relatively stable. Some environmental pollution and destruction has been seen, but this is not a big problem. In some areas the pollution is being controlled; in other areas the ecology is at the turning point for recovery.

The report, as summarized in the newspaper, provided the following analysis of China's environmental pollution:

> In the cities, atmospheric pollution continues to be of the coal smoke type, thus it is more severe in the winter and spring than in summer and fall. It is more severe in the North than in the South, and more severe in large cities than in small cities.
>
> The volume of arsenious acid gas emissions has increased, and more cities experienced acid rain than in 1990. Industrial waste water accounts for most waste water

emission; organic pollutants in waste water have been increasing. Pollution in the watersheds of the great rivers has become slightly greater. In some areas there has been an advance in land subsidence. Industrial pollution in the countryside has become greatly more serious in connection with the development of rural industries. In placing emphasis on developing such basic industries as energy and raw materials, pressure on the environment has dramatically increased, and the task of preventing industrial pollution is increasingly more difficult.

The report included details about ecological destruction.

In 1991 most areas experienced a mild winter, and in some areas there was major flooding. Particularly, Jiangsu and Anhui provinces suffered unusually great damage. Rock and mudslides, and collapse of cliffs and banks, were extensive.

Nationwide pollution of cultivated land from industrial pollutants and urban refuse has reached ten million hectares. Retreat of grasslands, rodent and insect damage, and water shortages, are all severe. There is as yet no alteration in the trend toward further ecological environmental deterioration.

The beginnings of China's environmental protection policy can be traced to China's attendance at the First United Nations Human Environmental Conference in Stockholm in 1972. In 1973 the National Environmental Protection Committee and the State Council Leading Group on Environmental Protection and Office for Environmental Protection (predecessor to the State Environmental Protection Bureau) were established. In 1979 the "Environmental Protection Law of the People's Republic of China (for Trial Implementation)" was enacted; this was amended in 1989 to become the "Environmental Protection Law of the People's Republic of China." In June 1991 the "Conference of Developing Countries on Environment and Development" was held in Beijing. China took the position at this meeting that the greatest global environmental issue was how to deal with the problem of global warming and that it was the responsibility of the developed countries; other more traditional environmental pollution questions were Chinese domestic matters. A law enacted in 1983 addressed marine environmental protection; another in 1984 dealt with water pollution.

Figures 14.1 and 14.2 provide international comparisons of carbon disulfide emissions and forested areas.

## Japan-China Cooperation in Environmental Protection

Japan and China began their cooperation in the environmental protection sphere under the impetus of their peace and friendship treaty of 1978. Activities related to Japan's official development assistance (ODA) program include several studies: Shanghai atmospheric pollution (1985 to 1988); Xian living waste products treatment (1988 to 1990); industrial wastewater treatment and reutilization (1988 to 1990); and Jiangxi province Poyang Lake pollution (fiscal year [FY] 1991). There has been a one-way dispatch of Japanese technical experts to teach and provide

Figure 14.1   The Share of Carbon Disulfide Emissions
by Major Country

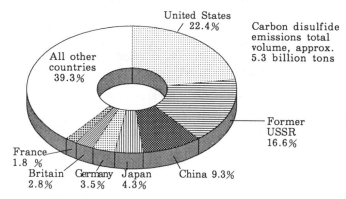

United States
22.4%

Carbon disulfide
emissions total
volume, approx.
5.3 billion tons

All other
countries
39.3%

Former
USSR
16.6%

France
1.8 %

Britain    Germany   Japan       China 9.3%
2.8%       3.5%       4.3%

Source: Japan Environmental Protection Agency,
*Environmental White Paper 1989.*

Figure 14.2   Global Country Ranking for Forested Area and
Forest Coverage Ratio

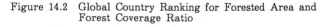

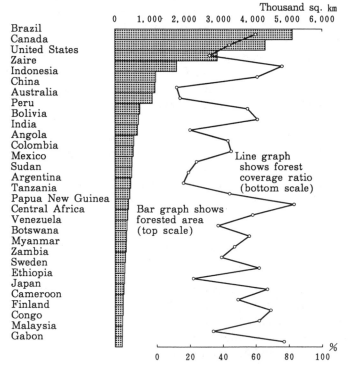

Thousand sq. km

0      1,000  2,000  3,000  4,000  5,000  6,000

Brazil
Canada
United States
Zaire
Indonesia
China
Australia
Peru
Bolivia
India
Angola
Colombia
Mexico
Sudan
Argentina
Tanzania
Papua New Guinea
Central Africa
Venezuela
Botswana
Myanmar
Zambia
Sweden
Ethiopia
Japan
Cameroon
Finland
Congo
Malaysia
Gabon

Line graph
shows forest
coverage ratio
(bottom scale)

Bar graph shows
forested area
(top scale)

0      20     40     60     80    100    %

Source: The World Bank, *World Development Report 1992,*
pp. 283 - 283.

assistance concerning environmental management for the steel industry (FY 1986); policy toward subsidence of Tianjin municipality (FY 1987); Poyang Lake water quality preservation (FY 1987); wastewater treatment for the Jilin province wool factory and starch factory (FY 1987); waste materials treatment for Beijing municipality (FY 1988); prevention and management of air pollution in Shanghai (FY 1989); and Taihu purification (FY 1989 to 1990). During his visit to China in late August 1988, Prime Minister Noboru Takeshita advanced the notion of cooperating in China's environmental protection policies via a Japanese grant to establish a joint environmental protection center. Japan is an "advanced" country in the negative sense of the term because it has suffered environmental despoliation, but it is now a truly advanced country because it is dealing effectively with pollution; thus there is doubtless much Japan can do to assist in China's environmental protection policies.

Acid rain from China is almost certainly reaching Japan and inexorably doing damage. In the context of Japan-China economic cooperation, it has been continually requested that neighboring countries implement effective environmental protection policies. Several measures have been taken in the field of nature preservation: A cultural grant in FY 1984 provided materials for observing and protecting the forest-area pandas. In July 1988 a three-year research cooperation agreement was concluded concerning protection and breeding of the Japanese crested ibis; experts were dispatched in FY 1989 and 1990. In FY 1990 experts visited China to do breeding research on the Yangtze River porpoise. Soil preservation was addressed in a FY 1990 agreement, and joint activities were begun under the Loess Plateau Mountain and Water Control Scientific and Technological Training Center project. As for non-ODA governmental cooperation, a Japan-China agreement on scientific and technological cooperation has led to research activities between Japan's National Pollution Research Institute and China's State Environmental Protection Bureau and the Academy of Environmental Sciences on such matters as prevention of atmospheric pollution and generation of photochemical smog and acid rain.

According to reports, in a meeting April 2, 1992 between Kozo Watanabe, head of Japan's Ministry of International Trade and Industry (MITI), and Chinese Vice Premier Zou Jiahua, the two sides approved a comprehensive program of Japanese technical assistance in the energy and environmental fields, such as technical assistance in atmospheric pollution prevention for Chinese thermoelectric power generating plants. Zou Jiahua was the first Chinese leader to admit that these Chinese plants were causing acid-rain damage as far as Japan. He actively called for the introduction of desulfurization technology from Japan. The Japanese proposal, one part of the "Green Aid Plan" drafted by MITI for the budget years 1992 and beyond, is to spend 7.3 billion yen in the following nine years to conduct tests of desulfurization technology in Chinese electric power generation facilities. Chinese sulfur dioxide emissions volume is some 15 million tons annually, about fourteen times more than Japan generates (*Yomiuri Shimbun,* April 19, 1992).

# 15
## Balance of Payments and Foreign Trade

### Emphasis on Foreign Trade Under the Liberalization Policy

The 1972 visit to China of Richard Nixon marked a major turning point in China's foreign relations. Until then China had pursued a fundamentally isolationist policy under the name of "self-reliance," and the volume of foreign trade was limited. Imports in the first half of the 1950s totaled $2–3 billion, increased in the second half to $3–4 billion, and remained at that level in the 1960s. In 1973, the year after normalization of Japan-China relations, the figure topped $10 billion, and in 1978, the start of the Deng Xiaoping era, it exceeded $20 billion. The next fourteen years brought an eightfold increase, to $165.6 billion in 1992. According to *World Development Report 1992* (World Bank 1992), the growth rate of China's exports in the 1980s was an annualized 11.0 percent and of imports 9.8 percent (p. 244), rates that put China at the top internationally.

During the Mao Zedong era the volume of imports was set according to projected receipts of foreign exchange, an approach that led to a pattern of small annual surpluses. The government enforced a firm policy of maintaining a balance by reducing imports following any year in which a deficit occurred.

This policy was maintained even after the Deng Xiaoping era began. Through 1984 there was a slight tendency toward deficits, but no large imbalances were recorded. However, deficits in 1985 and 1986 exceeded $10 billion because of the reform thrust initiated in the October 1984 "Decision on Reform of the Economic System," which mandated that reform begin in earnest in the urban sector. A large measure of authority over use of foreign exchange was given to the provinces and large-scale enterprises. As a consequence, controls over imports became ineffective, and deficits resulted; these continued, though at a reduced level, until 1989. Economic tightening, suspension of reform, and the export drive after the

154

Figure 15.1  Changes in Export-Import Values and the Balance
of Trade (1978-1992)

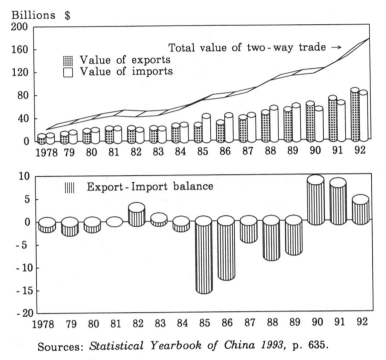

Sources: *Statistical Yearbook of China 1993*, p. 635.

Figure 15.2  Changes in the Export Dependency Ratio (1978-1992)

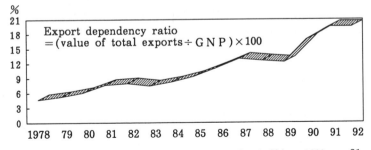

Source: For GNP, *Statistical Yearbook of China 1993*, p. 31;
for export value, p. 663.

Tiananmen incident finally brought a return to surpluses in the period 1990–1992 (see Figure 15.1).

The export dependency ratio (gross exports divided by GNP) increased from 4.6 percent in 1978 to 8–9 percent in the first half of the 1980s to 12–13 percent in the second half of the 1980s. As the export drive took effect in 1990 and 1991, the ratio; began to approach 20 percent (Figure 15.2). Because of the government's continued effort to balance exports and imports, the import dependency ratio followed the same pattern. By comparison, the 1990 export dependency ratio of Japan was 9.1 percent, the United States 7.2 percent, South Korea 28.0 percent, Thailand 29.1 percent, Hong Kong 43.9 percent, Malaysia 70.8 percent, and Singapore 157 percent (because of reexports).

# Composition of Foreign Trade Goods

## *Top Ten Traded Products*

The types of products China exported and imported varied in rank during the 1980s, as shown in Table 15.1. (Numbers in parentheses in the following discussion indicate ranking.) The leading export in 1980 was crude petroleum, with an overwhelming 15 percent share of total export value. This in combination with processed petroleum products (2) and coal (6) meant that energy was a major pillar of China's exports, over 20 percent. Textiles accounted for 10 percent; these included sewed goods (3), cotton cloth (4), and silk cloth (9). Other top ten exports were rice (5) and tea leaves (7).

In 1985 the top two products were still petroleum-related, and the relative share was greater than in 1980. (After this peak, petroleum exports stagnated, as indicated in Figure 15.3. Textiles remained at the 10 percent level based on sewed goods, cotton cloth, and cotton (3, 4, 5), mixed yarn (7), and silk goods (9). Other exports included canned goods (6) and tea leaves (10).

The top product in 1990 was sewed goods; in decline were crude petroleum (2) and processed petroleum products (6). As a result of the production slowdown of the Daqing oilfield and the decline in oil prices (Figure 15.3), petroleum-related products yielded their lead position as foreign exchange earners to textile-related goods. Textile products, including cotton cloth (3), cotton knitted goods (5), and silk cloth (7), constituted 13 percent of the total. This growth indicates the great advances made in manufacture of sewed goods including by the consignment method. These advances were the result of efforts to develop internationally competitive products made to order according to detailed design and style specifications from the West.

Table 15.1 also indicates the variation in imports. In 1980 the top-ranked import product was wheat, accounting for more than 10 percent of total imports. Rolled

Table 15.1   Changes in the Top Ten Export and Import Items
             (1980, 1985, 1990)

【Exports】

| Ranking | 1980 | | 1985 | | 1990 | |
|---|---|---|---|---|---|---|
| | Item | Percent of total | Item | Percent of total | Item | Percent of total |
| 1 | crude oil | 14.85 | crude oil | 19.19 | knitted goods | 6.36 |
| 2 | processed oil | 6.58 | processed oil | 5.30 | crude oil | 5.46 |
| 3 | knitted goods | 6.21 | knitted goods | 4.38 | cotton cloth | 2.58 |
| 4 | cotton cloth | 4.00 | cotton cloth | 3.63 | marine products | 2.12 |
| 5 | rice | 2.05 | cotton | 1.58 | cotton knitted goods | 1.55 |
| 6 | coal | 1.42 | canned goods | 1.44 | processed oil | 1.41 |
| 7 | tea leaves | 1.33 | mixed yarn | 1.30 | silk goods | 1.24 |
| 8 | slaughter hogs | 1.29 | coal | 1.15 | rolled steel | 1.10 |
| 9 | silk goods | 1.13 | silk goods | 1.14 | canned goods | 1.09 |
| 10 | rattan & wicker manufactures | 1.09 | tea leaves | 1.07 | coal | 1.05 |

【Imports】

| Ranking | 1980 | | 1985 | | 1990 | |
|---|---|---|---|---|---|---|
| | Item | Percent of total | Item | Percent of total | Item | Percent of total |
| 1 | wheat | 10.89 | rolled steel | 14.85 | rolled steel | 9.71 |
| 2 | rolled steel | 7.44 | television | 2.35 | wheat | 8.35 |
| 3 | raw cotton | 7.31 | trucks | 2.32 | urea | 4.47 |
| 4 | urea | 3.44 | wheat | 2.09 | automobiles | 2.91 |
| 5 | ethylene | 3.13 | logs | 1.91 | cotton | 2.76 |
| 6 | trucks | 2.35 | urea | 1.72 | paper,cardboard | 2.56 |
| 7 | synthetic fiber | 1.94 | synthetic fiber | 1.68 | synthetic fiber | 2.14 |
| 8 | natural gas | 1.67 | aluminum | 1.35 | edible vegetable oil | 2.02 |
| 9 | sugar | 1.67 | ships | 1.32 | machine tools | 1.90 |
| 10 | corn | 1.35 | copper alloys | 1.22 | ships | 1.79 |

Sources: *Statistical Yearbook of China 1991*, pp. 623-625.
1980, 1985 *China's Commercial and Foreign Economic Statistical Materials 1952-1988*, pp. 464-475.

Figure 15.3   Changes in the Overall Export Volume,
              Value, and Unit Price for Chinese Petroleum
              (1978-1990)

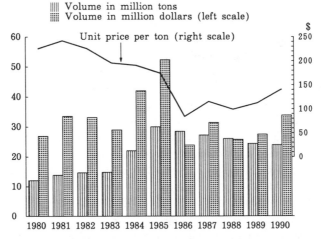

Sources: *China's Commercial and Foreign Economic
Statistical Materials*, pp. 448-151; *Statistical Yearbook
of China 1991*, p. 624.

steel (2) was not only a supplement to domestic production but also included some high-quality special steels. Cotton (3) and synthetic fibers (7) were imported as raw materials, processed into textile products, and exported. Urea (4) was related to the reforms taking place in the countryside. Trucks (6) were needed because of the constraints of China's transportation system.

The import mix shifted in 1985. Wheat dropped to fourth place after the bumper harvest in 1984. In first place was rolled steel, which was needed for construction that was accompanying advances in reform. Televisions (2) brought the people of China into contact with the Western world and gave them more information about the relatively advanced parts of China. The jump in imports of televisions was not planned; rather, it constituted an overrun of the foreign exchange control budget caused by irrepressible popular demand.

Rolled steel remained the top import in 1990. The elevated position of wheat (2) and urea (3) was an indication of a slowdown in agriculture. Automobiles (4) appeared among the top ten imports for the first time.

The extreme diversification of Chinese imports is a recent phenomenon. This is a reflection of the change in the Chinese economy from the previous perpendicular trade structure (through vertical specialized state trading corporations that served a vast number of end users across the country) to the present horizontal division of industry structure.

## Consignment-Processed Goods Become the Leading Export

Figure 15.4 presents the main categories by commodity of export and import goods during the 1980s. Exports of primary products (types 0, 1, and 2—i.e., foodstuffs, beverages, and nonfood raw materials) decreased from slightly under 30 percent to slightly under 20 percent. The most drastic drop was in the share of type 3 products (crude petroleum), which declined by almost half. Among secondary products, types 5 (chemical industry), 6 (products differentiated by raw materials), 7 (machinery, transport machinery), and 8 (miscellaneous manufactures) had some change in specific content but remained about the same in terms of share.

A remarkable shift was in type 9 products, which grew rapidly from almost nothing in 1980 to slightly less than 20 percent in 1990. Type 9 goods are difficult to break down into categories; also, they include some military weapons. A general description is "products processed on consignment." Table 15.2 presents the findings Hideo Ohashi (associate professor at Senshu University) made concerning these products based on the *Customs Statistics Yearbook of China 1990*. He calculated that of total exports of consignment manufactures, about 30 percent was apparel, followed by toys (10.3 percent) and machinery (9.0 percent). Consignment processing is carried out on imported goods, and goods imported are nearly equal to exports.

As shown in Figure 15.4, imports of raw materials for consignment processing (type 9) expanded, although type 7 (machinery and automobiles) commanded an

Figure 15.4  Changes in the Commodity Composition of Imports and
Exports (1980 - 1990)

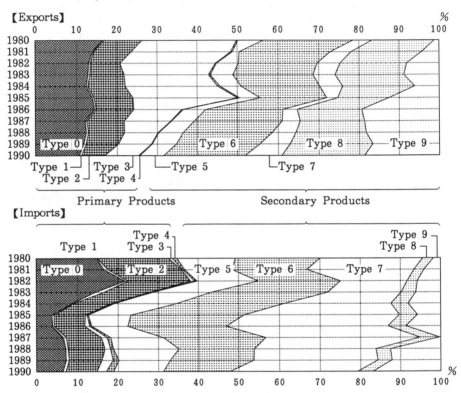

Note: Type 0 = foodstuffs, animals. Type 1 = beverages, tobacco.
Type 2 = non-food raw materials. Type 3 = mined fuels, lubricating
oil, and related raw materials. Type 4 = animal and vegetable
oils. Type 5 = petrochemical products. Type 6 = manufactures from
different raw materials. Type 7 = machinery, transport machinery.
Type 8 = miscellaneous manufactures. Type 9 = hard to classify
products.

Sources: *Statistical Yearbook of China 1991,* exports, p. 618;
imports, p. 619.  *Statistical Yearbook of China 1990,* exports,
p. 642; imports, p. 643.  Wang Huijiong, Li Boxi, eds., *China's
Long Term Industrial Policy* (Beijing: Chinese Financial and
Economic Press, 1991), pp. 45 - 46 .

Table 15.2   Export of Chinese Consignment Manufactures and
Imports of Raw Materials and Parts (1990)

| Item | Export | | Import | |
|---|---|---|---|---|
| | million dollars | % | million dollars | % |
| foodstuffs, animal feed | 126 | 1.2 | 122 | 1.4 |
| textiles | 220 | 2.1 | 135 | 1.6 |
| apparel | 3,172 | 30.3 | 2,542 | 29.2 |
| audio equipment | 848 | 8.1 | 626 | 7.2 |
| clocks & watches | 591 | 5.7 | 519 | 6.0 |
| toys | 1,080 | 10.3 | 697 | 8.0 |
| machinery | 944 | 9.0 | 936 | 10.7 |
| telephones | 193 | 1.8 | 188 | 2.2 |
| artificial flowers | 155 | 1.5 | 120 | 1.4 |
| travel goods, bags | 553 | 5.3 | 421 | 4.8 |
| jewelry | 198 | 1.9 | 187 | 2.1 |
| other | 2,374 | 22.8 | 2,214 | 25.4 |
| Total | 10,454 | 100.0 | 8,706 | 100.0 |

Original source: Compiled by 5 digit SITC code from *China's Customs Statistics Yearbook 1990.*
Source: Mitsubishi Research Institute, *MRI China Intelligence,* 1992 July edition, "Key Number" column by Hideo Ohashi.

even more prominent share. The great advances in types 7 and 9 are persuasive testimony to the metamorphosis of the Chinese economy.

# Trading Relationships by Country and Region

China's trade partners are ranked according to size of export market in the following list (see Figure 15.5 for details):

1. *Hong Kong.* In terms of China's exports, Hong Kong is the preeminent market. Exports to Hong Kong have literally skyrocketed. In the first half of the 1980s, Hong Kong took about 25 percent of exports; the share increased yearly in the second half of the 1980s and by 1992 had risen to 44 percent. Behind this growth is the multifaceted development of economic relations with the Shenzhen special economic zone and the Pearl River delta, notably the consignment-processing trade.

2. *Japan.* Exports to Japan made up 21 percent of total exports in 1980, peaked at 22.3 percent in 1985, then declined to 14–15 percent in the late 1980s. In 1992 the figure was 13.8 percent.

3. *The United States.* Exports to the United States were 5.5 percent of the total in 1980, increased to 8.6 percent in 1985, and maintained a level of 8–9 percent for the next five years. In 1992 the 10 percent level was breached, and a continuing increase is highly probable, notwithstanding the worsening PRC-U.S. trade friction over the widening U.S. deficit.

Figure 15.5   Changes in the Shares of China's Imports and
Exports with Japan, Hong Kong, U.S., and E.C.

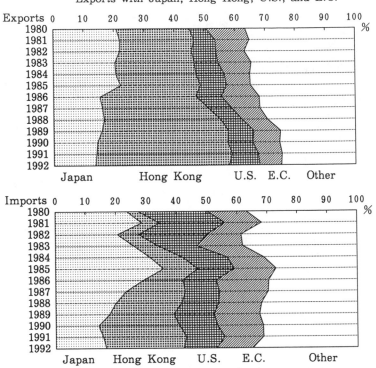

Note: E.C. comprises Germany, France, Italy, Great Britain,
The Netherlands, Belgium, and Spain, only.
    Sources: *Statistical Yearbook of China 1991*, pp. 620-622;
*China's Commercial and Foreign Economic Statistical Materials*,
pp. 478-501; *Statistical Yearbook of China 1993*, pp. 638-640.

4. *Seven European Community (EC) countries.* Of the EC countries, seven
   have relatively greater trade with China—Germany, France, Italy, the
   U.K., the Netherlands, Belgium, and Spain. Together these countries
   constitute a significant but relatively diminishing market for China of 8
   to 9 percent of total Chinese exports.

In summary, Chinese export markets are highly concentrated: Hong Kong takes
roughly 40 percent, Japan 15 percent, the United States 10 percent, and the EC
group slightly less than 10 percent.
    These trade partners also are sources of imports. Japan provided 24 percent of
Chinese imports in 1980. During the import boom attending the 1984–1985 reform leap, Japan's share increased to 35.6 percent. Yearly decreases thereafter,
along with the effects of the Tiananmen incident, resulted in 1990 in a drop to

about 14 percent. Considerable recovery was recorded in 1991, and in 1992 the figure was 17 percent.

Imports from Hong Kong were less than 10 percent of the total in the first half of the 1980s and increased yearly in the second half. By 1992 Hong Kong provided 25.5 percent of imports and was China's largest source.

In the early 1980s the United States supplied large quantities of wheat imports and consequently provided over 20 percent of China's imports. The figure remained around 12 percent in the second half of the decade. In 1992 the figure was 11 percent. The seven EC countries have consistently provided 13–14 percent.

An interesting relationship exists between Chinese exports to Hong Kong and the goods reexported by Hong Kong. Market destinations for Hong Kong's reexports in 1990 were China 26.8 percent, the United States 21.2 percent, Japan 5.9 percent, Germany 5.7 percent, Taiwan 5.1 percent, South Korea 3.1 percent, and other areas 32.2 percent. Hong Kong's "reexports to China" are in fact raw materials for consignment processing, and the finished products are exported to the United States, Japan, and the EC or to Taiwan, Korea, and the other NIEs (*Foreign Economic and Trade Yearbook 1991–1992*, p. 295). For 1993 and thereafter, Chinese statistics will present a substantially changed picture from that in Figure 15.5. This is because prior to 1993 a substantial portion of goods shipped to Hong Kong for reexport were classified as exports to Hong Kong. From 1993 Chinese statistics will be based on final destinations. The result will be a drop in exports to Hong Kong and an increase in exports to other countries. Japan will emerge as China's largest export market. (U.S. import statistics are based on country of first origin, so reexports from Hong Kong to the United States are classified as imports from China.)

Prior to 1992 no official Chinese statistics were available for PRC–South Korea and PRC-Taiwan trade. The first published statistics (*Statistical Yearbook of China 1993*, p. 638) were some $5 billion for two-way trade with South Korea and $6.6 billion for two-way trade with Taiwan.

# Foreign Borrowing and Acceptance of Direct Investment

Figure 15.6 presents trends in the introduction of foreign capital to China. Figures for the early period of the liberalization policy, 1978 to 1982, were small and consequently have been aggregated for presentation.

Introduction of foreign capital can be divided into two categories: borrowing from abroad and accepting direct investment from abroad. Since the introduction of foreign capital, there have been three peak periods: 1985–1986, 1988, and 1991 to the present. The first peak was in response to the fall 1984 decision to reform the cities and industry in line with reform of the economic system. The second peak was related to the strategic direction of developing the coastal region, a policy

Figure 15.6   Changes in China's Introduction of Foreign Capital
(1978 - 1992, contract base)

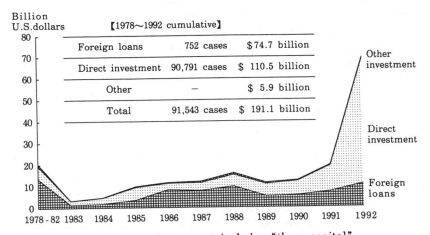

Billion
U.S.dollars 　　　【1978~1992 cumulative】

| | | |
|---|---|---|
| Foreign loans | 752 cases | $ 74.7 billion |
| Direct investment | 90,791 cases | $ 110.5 billion |
| Other | — | $ 5.9 billion |
| Total | 91,543 cases | $ 191.1 billion |

Note: Direct foreign investment includes "three capital"
investment: joint ventures, foreign - assisted, and wholly
foreign - owned; and joint undersea petroleum exploration and
development. "Other" investment includes international leases,
compensation trade, and processing and assembly.
Source: *Statistical Yearbook of China 1993*, p. 647.

Figure 15.7   Breakdown by Country of Loans, Direct Investment, and
Other Investment (contract base)

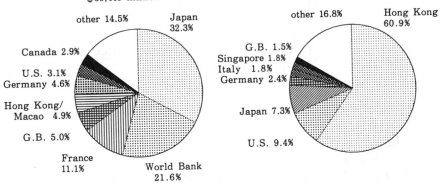

【Cumulative loans 1983 - 1991】

$ 50,446 million

other 14.5%
Japan 32.3%
Canada 2.9%
U.S. 3.1%
Germany 4.6%
Hong Kong/
Macao 4.9%
G.B. 5.0%
France 11.1%
World Bank 21.6%

【Cumulative direct investment
and other investment 1983 - 1991】

$ 50,667 million

other 16.8%
Hong Kong 60.9%
G.B. 1.5%
Singapore 1.8%
Italy 1.8%
Germany 2.4%
Japan 7.3%
U.S. 9.4%

Source: *China's Foreign Trade and Economic Relations Yearbook.*

communicated at the Thirteenth Party Congress in fall 1987. The third peak was in connection with the switch to accelerating reform and liberalization after Deng Xiaoping's southern tour in spring 1992.

Aggregate figures for 1979 to 1992 in Figure 15.6 show 752 loans valued at $74.7 billion (39 percent of total value) and 91,000 cases of investment valued at $110.5 billion (57.8 percent of the total). Until 1991, aggregate value of loans was greater than aggregate investment, but the trend thereafter was to place primary emphasis on accepting direct investment. In 1992 investment surged to become the predominant source of external capital.

Figure 15.7 presents the breakdown by source country for Chinese borrowing and receipt of direct investment during the period 1983–1991. Japan was the leading source of loans (left side) with 32.3 percent of the total, followed by the World Bank. Japan's position is attributable to Japan's governmental yen loans to China. These have been extended since 1979 based on Japan's sense that it should assist in China's development in consideration of China's forgiveness of war reparations from Japan (see Chapter 16 for further details).

The right-hand side of Figure 15.7 depicts nonborrowed foreign capital—foreign capital introduced in connection with direct investment and cooperative ventures. Hong Kong's position is overwhelming with 60.9 percent of the total. The United States is next with 9.4 percent, followed by Japan with 7.3 percent.

Included in "Hong Kong" capital is capital from Hong Kong subsidiaries of Japanese, U.S., German, and other foreign firms as well as capital from Taiwanese- and Korean-affiliated companies in Hong Kong. Hong Kong was previously a critical export base from which to earn precious foreign exchange. Now, however, it is also playing a key role as a source for raising foreign capital. In one sense, China's liberalization policy is being underwritten by Hong Kong.

Debt repayment is an issue because there is a great difference between borrowing and direct investment. The former may have grace periods and high or low interest rates, but in any event the money must be repaid. In contrast, direct investment is made at the risk of the investor; there is no repayment obligation. However, if profits are not realized, capital cannot be attracted; it can also flee quickly.

## The Balance of Payments and Foreign Debt Repayment

China's entry into the IMF in April 1979 was one of the events that symbolized the start of the liberalization policy. As a member, China had to report statistics on international payments and financial matters, and when such data became public knowledge, a number of areas that had been like "black holes" acquired a spectacularly higher level of transparency.

Financial reporting entails several carefully defined concepts. The trade balance is the difference in the value of commodity imports and exports. The nontrade balance is the difference in imports and exports of services; main items are transport, receipts and payments in tourism, and receipts and payments of profits on investments. The transfer payments balance is nongovernmental unilateral transfers such as taxes, pensions and gifts (remittances from overseas Chinese), and governmental economic assistance such as grants and reparations. These three accounts (or balances) together constitute the current account, which is the principal account of the balance of international payments (current account = trade balance + nontrade balance + transfers balance).

The long-term capital balance accounts for increases or decreases in foreign assets or foreign liabilities having maturities of over one year or of unspecified duration. Principal components are direct investment, securities investment, foreign debt issuance, and deferred payment credits. The combination of the long-term capital balance and the current account is called the basic balance (basic balance = current account + long-term capital balance). The basic balance is considered useful in ascertaining trends in the balance of payments because it excludes the short-term capital account that tends to have irregular movements.

The short-term capital balance accounts for increases or decreases in foreign assets or foreign liabilities having maturities of less than one year, excluding financial accounts. These are short-term trade credits. Adding the short-term capital balance and errors and omissions to the basic balance produces the overall balance (overall balance = basic balance + short-term capital account + errors and omissions).

Financial accounts are the posted increases or decreases in liquid foreign assets and liabilities of public organs (the government and the People's Bank of China) and the foreign exchange bank (the Bank of China). The financial accounts in aggregate equate to the overall balance.

Many of these concepts are used in Table 15.3, which shows that in the second half of the 1980s China had a general surplus of imports and a trade balance deficit. Because of the vibrant economic activity accompanying economic reform, demand for imports increased dramatically. At this time, the basic balance (which includes the long-term capital balance) registered a deficit. In other words, deficits occurred because of the booming imports in 1985 and 1986. Deficits also followed the tumult accompanying the Tiananmen incident in 1989.

Figure 15.8 shows how China's foreign indebtedness skyrocketed in the 1980s and early 1990s. At year-end 1991 it was approaching $61 billion according to IMF statistics. Over 90 percent was long-term debt; short-term debt and IMF credits constituted less than 10 percent. The World Bank and other observers were predicting in 1990 that China's debt service ratio in the first half of the 1990s would be in the 10–11 percent range (debt service ratio = value of current year's debt repayments divided by value of current year's exports). In 1991 the ratio was already at 12 percent.

[Translator's note: Managing debt service could prove difficult or relatively easy, depending on China's trade balance, access to international capital markets

Table 15.3   China's Statement of International Payments 1984-1992
(in million U.S. dollars.)

|  | 1986 | 1987 | 1988 | 1989 | 1990 | 1991 | 1992 |
|---|---|---|---|---|---|---|---|
| Current account | -7,034 | 300 | -3,802 | -4,317 | 11,997 | 13,272 | 6,401 |
| Trade account | -9,140 | -1,661 | -5,315 | -5,620 | 9,165 | 8,743 | 5,183 |
| Non-trade account | 1,551 | 1,901 | 1,120 | 640 | 1,451 | 2,784 | -225 |
| Transfer payments | 555 | 60 | 293 | 663 | 1,381 | 1,745 | 1,443 |
| Basic account | 5,944 | 6,001 | 7,133 | 3,723 | 3,255 | 8,032 | -250 |
| Direct investment | 1,425 | 1,669 | 2,344 | 2,613 | 2,657 | 3,453 | 7,156 |
| Portfolio investment | 1,568 | 1,051 | 876 | -180 | -241 | 235 | -57 |
| Other capital | 2,951 | 3,281 | 3,913 | 1,290 | 839 | 4,344 | -7,349 |
| Errors & omissions | -958 | -1,518 | -957 | 115 | -3,205 | -6,767 | -8,211 |
| Overall account | 2,048 | 4,783 | 2,374 | -479 | 12,047 | -14,537 | -2,060 |
| Public sector foreign debt outstanding | 23,746 | 35,296 | 42,362 | 44,791 | 52,519 | 60,802 | |
| Debt service ratio | 9.6 | 9.5 | 9.7 | 11.4 | 11.6 | 12.0 | |

Source: International accounts: IMF, *International Financial
Statistics*. Debt outstanding: World Bank, *World Debt Tables.*

Figure 15.8   China's Foreign Debts

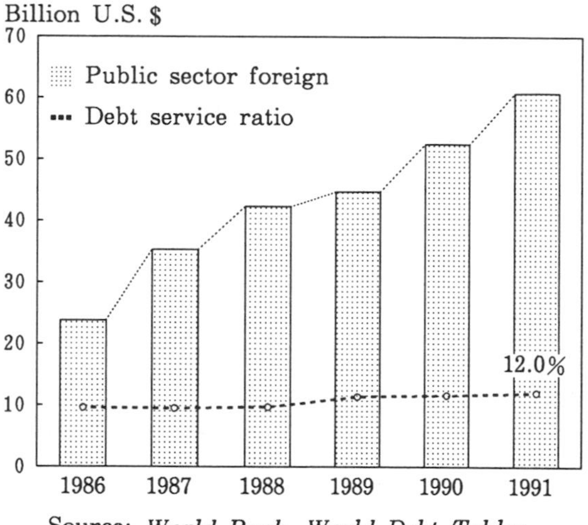

Source: *World Bank, World Debt Tables.*

for refinancing, and, particularly, magnitude of inflows of direct investments. The surge in direct foreign investment into China in 1992 and 1993 has helped to finance a trade deficit and debt service. Direct investment will continue and may increase, but so will requirements for foreign capital. Besides using foreign currency for debt service and payment for imports, China has recently made some significant investments abroad, especially in Hong Kong. After a post-Tiananmen pause, China returned to the international capital markets in 1992 and 1993 with both large debt and equity issues. The latter largely constitute partial privatizations of state-owned companies. The largest Chinese company to issue stock abroad has been Shanghai Petrochemical Company, whose 1993 listing on the Hong Kong Stock Exchange and New York Stock Exchange [in the form of American Depository Receipts] was lead-underwritten by Merrill Lynch. Chinese sovereign debt is rated by Moody's Investors Service as A3, which is seven ranks under the top grade. An interesting new development in November 1993 was China's tapping of the Asian capital market with the issuance of a $300 million "Dragon bond." Apparently China felt it was likely to get equivalent or better terms for borrowing in Asian markets than in European and U.S. markets, an assumption that was probably justified.]

# 16

# Japan-China Economic Relations Post-1972

## Twenty-Year Record of Japan-China Trade

From the normalization of diplomatic relations in 1972 through 1978, Japan-China two-way trade remained at a low level of less than $5 billion (Figure 16.1). China held firmly to the objective of balancing the trade and thus tried to keep imports from Japan within the range of export earnings. Notwithstanding this, China sought many Japanese products, so that there were frequent Chinese deficits (Japanese surpluses) that were financed with foreign exchange earned from exporting to Hong Kong.

In the context of China's conversion in the 1980s to a liberalized, open policy, Japan-China trade began a great advance. In 1981 the $10 billion level was surpassed. However, in 1982 Japanese industry was shocked when China abruptly canceled a number of major plant import contracts. Japanese exports to China dropped sharply, and trade became politicized. The cause became clear only after the fact and was linked with the power struggle between the coalition of pragmatists such as Deng Xiaoping and Chen Yun and the supporters of Hua Guofeng's "great leap to the outside world." As Hua Guofeng, the handpicked successor of Mao Zedong, was eased out of office, the problem was summarily resolved, and the reform move brought the 1984–1985 import boom. In the midst of "sweet deal" sales of consumer electronics and automobiles, optimism that China had indeed reached a takeoff stage began to take hold in some parts of Japan. In 1985 Japanese exports topped $12 billion. In 1986 and 1987 efforts were made to moderate the overheated economy, but before adjustment measures took firm hold, people continued to behave in conformity with the expansive line adopted at the Thirteenth Party Congress in 1987, and China's import boom continued into 1988. After the 1988 price panic, China shifted to a tightening policy, but it proved difficult to cool an overheated economy, and it was only after the 1989 Tiananmen incident that it became possible to hold imports to the $6–7 billion level.

Figure 16.1  Trends in Japan's Trade with China (1975-1992)

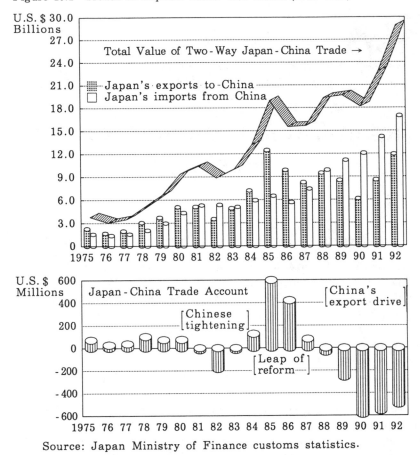

Source: Japan Ministry of Finance customs statistics.

Thus, Chinese imports have been subject to great variations in relation to political shifts. In contrast, Japanese imports began to develop strongly in the second half of the 1980s. As Japan developed into a highly advanced economy, China became an integral supplier of raw materials and consumer goods, especially in agricultural products and textiles. Simultaneously with its 1990–1991 economic tightening, China launched its export drive, which resulted in large export surpluses.

Table 16.1 presents China's trade position in the context of Japan's overall trade. In 1991 the value of Japan's total exports was $314.5 billion. Exports to China were only $8.6 billion, or 2.7 percent of the total, putting China in ninth place (down from second place in 1985). Of Japan's 1991 imports of $236.7 billion, China accounted for 6 percent, in second place (up from sixth in 1985); the United States led the list at 22.5 percent.

Table 16.1   The Position of Trade with China in Japan's Overall Trade
(1985, 1991)

| | Exports | | | | | Imports | | | |
|---|---|---|---|---|---|---|---|---|---|
| | 1985 | | 1991 | | | 1985 | | 1991 | |
| | Country | % Share | Country | % Share | | Country | % Share | Country | % Share |
| (1) | U.S. | 37.2 | U.S. | 29.1 | (1) | U.S. | 19.9 | U.S. | 22.5 |
| (2) | China | 7.1 | Germany | 6.6 | (2) | Saudi Arabia | 7.9 | China | 6.0 |
| (3) | South Korea | 4.0 | South Korea | 6.4 | (3) | Indonesia | 7.8 | Australia | 5.5 |
| (4) | West Germany | 4.0 | Taiwan | 5.8 | (4) | U.A.E. | 6.9 | Indonesia | 5.4 |
| (5) | Hong Kong | 3.7 | Hong Kong | 5.2 | (5) | Australia | 5.8 | South Korea | 5.2 |
| (6) | Australia | 3.1 | Singapore | 3.9 | (6) | China | 5.0 | Germany | 4.5 |
| (7) | Taiwan | 2.9 | U.K. | 3.5 | (7) | Canada | 3.7 | U.A.E. | 4.4 |
| (8) | U.K. | 2.7 | Thailand | 3.0 | (8) | Malaysia | 3.3 | Saudi Arabia | 4.3 |
| (9) | Canada | 2.6 | China | 2.7 | (9) | South Korea | 3.2 | Taiwan | 4.0 |
| (10) | Saudi Arabia | 2.2 | Malaysia | 2.4 | (10) | Taiwan | 2.6 | Canada | 3.3 |

Source: *Japan Ministry of Finance Customs Statistics.*

Figure 16.2   Changes in Commodity Composition of Japan's Trade
with China (1980 - 1992)

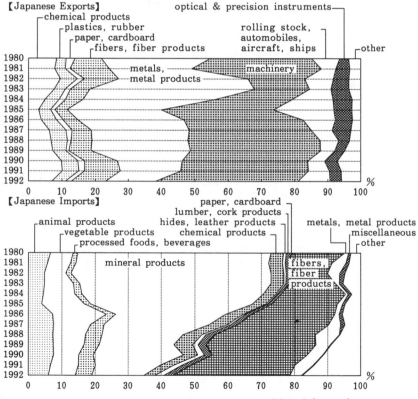

Source: Japan - China Economic Association, *Materials on the
Japan - China Economy,* annual editions.

# The Commodity Composition
# of Japan-China Trade

In terms of the commodity composition of Japan-China trade after 1980 (Figure 16.2), the major Japanese exports to China were metals and machinery. In 1980 these two categories accounted for over 60 percent, with metals at 33 percent and machinery at 31 percent. The bulk of metals is regular steel; there are also small quantities of pipe and special steels. Machinery comprises generally regular machinery. Because of 1983 plant cancellations, the share of machinery abruptly fell by half, but steel was not targeted in this move and the share of steel increased to 46 percent, 40 percent of which was regular steel.

In 1985 automobile exports more than doubled; this surge had much to do with the Hainan Island auto-smuggling scandal and so was not long lasting. In the second half of the 1980s the category of machinery exports was stable, but the composition changed. Formerly, because of industrialization needs, heavy machinery had predominated, but gradually there was a shift to electronics and high-technology goods. Thus, there were simultaneous increases in the shares of televisions, home electric appliances, semiconductors, and electronic products (these products are included in the machinery category in Figure 16.2). The 1990–1992 drop by half in the share of steel reflected structural factors.

The lower section of Figure 16.2 presents Chinese exports to Japan. In the first half of the 1980s mineral products (crude petroleum and its processed derivatives) made up 50–60 percent of the total. However, in 1985 this category dropped to below 50 percent. By 1989 it had fallen to 22.6 percent, and in 1992 to 15.8 percent. Although the volume of petroleum imports increased to some degree during this period, the dollar value decreased by two-thirds because of a decline in the price of oil. This was a painful blow to China.

China overcame the petroleum-related downturn in foreign exchange earnings by turning to textiles and textile products. In the first half of the 1980s, the category of textiles comprised mainly cotton cloth and raw silk thread, but the composition shifted in the second half of the 1980s to sewed goods. This category increased from 11 percent in 1987 to 14.3 percent in 1988 to 19.2 percent in 1989; at this point textiles surpassed crude oil as the leading export. (Figure 16.2 does not clearly reflect this timing because of a difference in the data series used.) In 1991 this category reached 22 percent.

There are no doubt a number of reasons that Chinese sewed goods achieved competitiveness in the Japanese market. Certainly, it was due in part to the technological base of the existing textile industry and the ability to employ cheap labor. However, the main reason was probably the advent of the consignment-processing method of business. The secret of success was to manufacture according to designs provided by the Japanese that paralleled their fashion trends and then to sell them the entire output.

# Momentum Builds for Japanese Direct Investment

Japanese yen loans have followed from governmental commitments, and in many aspects the decisions have been informed by a high degree of political calculation. But the opposite approach exists in the record of direct investment: When all is said and done, pursuit of profit is the basic motive, and activity is quickly adapted to circumstances with a view to augmenting profits. When China shifted to the liberalization policy in the early 1980s and enacted the foreign joint venture enterprise law as an initial step, little interest was evidenced by large Japanese enterprises, which at the time were shifting investment from the NIEs to the members of the Association of Southeast Asian Nations (ASEAN).

Expansion of direct investment began as confidence in the likely continuity of China's reform line grew among Japanese who observed the mood evidenced at the 1987 Thirteenth Party Congress. However, China soon implemented economic readjustment policies against overheating, and then the world was shocked by the Tiananmen incident. In summary, in the 1980s, Japanese investment targeted first Europe and the United States, second the NIEs, and subsequently the ASEAN countries (especially Thailand, Malaysia, and Indonesia). Investment in China was small (Figure 16.3).

However, in the early 1990s China became a source of interest primarily because of the substantial improvement in the environment for investment stemming from China's overall liberalization. Further, the previous advantage of low-

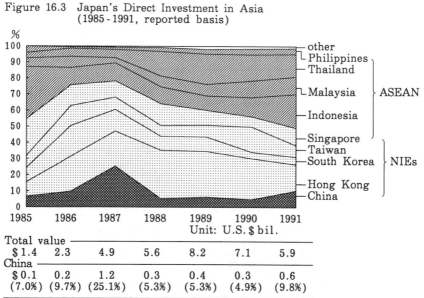

Figure 16.3　Japan's Direct Investment in Asia
(1985 - 1991, reported basis)

| Total value | | | | | | |
|---|---|---|---|---|---|---|
| $1.4 | 2.3 | 4.9 | 5.6 | 8.2 | 7.1 | 5.9 |

China

| $0.1 | 0.2 | 1.2 | 0.3 | 0.4 | 0.3 | 0.6 |
|---|---|---|---|---|---|---|
| (7.0%) | (9.7%) | (25.1%) | (5.3%) | (5.3%) | (4.9%) | (9.8%) |

Source: Japan Ministry of Finance, reported actual foreign direct investment.

cost labor in the NIEs and certain of the ASEAN countries was being lost due to wage increases attending the high rates of growth in these economies. At one time China had mistakenly considered the NIEs rivals; however, with respect to introduction of foreign capital through direct investment, the ASEAN countries were the true rivals.

Table 16.2 presents a comparison of Japanese and U.S. direct investment in China. Aggregate investment from 1979 to 1992 was $5.7 billion from Japan and $6.2 billion from the United States. It is interesting to note that the figures (both for number of cases and aggregate volume) are relatively close for both countries, even though the United States traditionally has been a large capital-exporting nation and Japan only recently began to emphasize investment abroad. Investment

Table 16.2  Comparison of U.S. and Japanese Direct Investment in China (1979 - 1992) (in cases, U.S. $ millions)

| Year | Japan | | U.S. | | World | |
|------|-------|--------|-------|--------|-------|--------|
| | Cases | Amount | Cases | Amount | Cases | Amount |
| 1979~83 cumulative | 52 | 955 | 46 | 781 | 1,392 | 7,926 |
| 1984 | 138 | 203 | 55 | 165 | 1,856 | 2,874 |
| 1985 | 127 | 471 | 101 | 1,152 | 3,073 | 6,332 |
| 1986 | 94 | 210 | 102 | 526 | 1,498 | 3,330 |
| 1987 | 113 | 301 | 103 | 361 | 2,392 | 4,391 |
| 1988 | 237 | 276 | 269 | 384 | 5,945 | 6,191 |
| 1989 | 294 | 440 | 276 | 645 | 5,779 | 6,293 |
| 1990 | 341 | 457 | 357 | 366 | 7,273 | 6,986 |
| 1991 | 599 | 812 | 694 | 548 | 12,978 | 12,430 |
| 1992 | 1,116 | 1,614 | 1,600 | 1,380 | 48,764 | 57,506 |
| 1979~92 cumulative | 3,111 | 5,739 | 3,603 | 6,230 | 90,950 | 114,259 |
| | (3.4%) | (5.0%) | (4.0%) | (5.5%) | (100%) | (100%) |

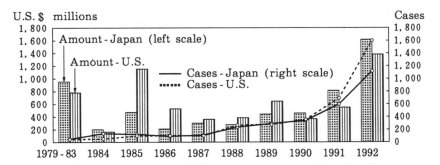

Note: Direct investment includes consignment processing and compensation trade. World means investment in China from all countries, including Japan and the U.S.
Source: Mitsubishi Research Institute, ed., *Overview of Companies Investing in China (Chugoku Shinshutsu Kigyo Ichiran)*, 1993 edition, p. 39. Original source: Chinese Ministry of Foreign Economic Relations and Trade.

in China by the two countries seems to be roughly equal, as if they were running neck and neck and exchanging lead position in a competitive race. However, within this competition the cooperative aspect conceivably is greater.

As discussed in Chapter 17 and the accompanying tables, there are clear differences in investments from Japan and the United States in terms of regional location; the same is true for investments from Hong Kong, Taiwan, Korea, and other countries. Currently, China's most economically active regions are in the south, the Shanghai area, and the Pohai rim (Liaodong peninsula and Shandong peninsula). In light of the various geographic distances and time differences and other factors, it remains to be seen what forms of cross-border economic zones will develop in the future. In any event, the previous concept of ocean and continent may very well be reversed. The East Asian ocean is the "center of the world." Surrounding the ocean are ports, customs-free zones, and special economic zones, and the future may bring a renaissance of the pattern of the ancient Phoenician trading state.

## Behind the First to Third Yen Loans to China

Japan made three yen loans to China during the period 1979–1988 (see Table 16.3). The first commitment for a loan was made during Prime Minister Ohira's visit to China in December 1979. Its terms were for 330 billion yen to be disbursed over five years starting in 1979, an annual interest rate of 3 percent, and repayment over thirty years with a ten-year grace period. It was to be used for railway and port projects.

The second loan, promised during the Nakasone visit in March 1984, provided 470 billion yen for seven projects in the transport, telecommunications, and energy sectors. The original disbursement period of seven years (1984–1990) was subsequently shortened by one year, and disbursement was completed in 1989.

The third loan was directed at forty-two projects; Prime Minister Takeshita committed the sum of 800 billion yen during his visit to China in summer 1988. The provision period was advanced one year from its initial schedule to six years, from 1990 to 1995.

Yen loans are "compensated capital cooperation," but "uncompensated capital cooperation" and "technical cooperation" are also being carried out. Representative examples of uncompensated capital cooperation (figures are in yen) include the China-Japan Friendship Hospital (total construction cost 16 billion), the China Meat Foodstuffs Center (2.7 billion), provision of equipment for the Beijing Post and Telecommunications Training Center (2.2 billion), Crippled Persons Rehabilitation Center (1.4 billion), provision of equipment for the Minerals Investigation and Research Center (1.1 billion), the Japan-China Youth Exchange Center (10.1 billion), and the Japan-China Friendship Environmental Protection Center. Technical cooperation includes activities sponsored by both the govern-

Table 16.3    Japanese Yen Loans to China (First to Third)
              Combined Table

|  | First Yen Loan | Second Yen Loan | Third Yen Loan |
|---|---|---|---|
| When requested | August 1979 | January 1983 | August 1987 |
| When agreed | December 1979 | March 1984 | August 1988 |
|  | Prime Minister | Prime Minister | Prime Minister |
|  | Ohira | Nakasone | Takeshita |
| No.of projects requested | 8 projects | 13 projects | 31 projects |
| No.of projects approved | 6 projects | 7 projects | 42 projects |
| Amount requested (initial) | ¥785 billion | ¥1,430 billion | ¥1,187 billion |
|  | $3.6 billion |  | 2.5 times ¥470 billion |
| Amount disbursed (actual) | ¥330 billion | ¥470 billion | Approx. ¥800 billion |
| % of requested amt. disbursed | 42.15% | 32.86% |  |
| Reference period | FY1979~83  5 Years | FY1984~89  6 Years | FY1990~95  6 Years |

Source: Japanese Ministry of Foreign Affairs, *Japan's Official
Development Assistance 1991.*

Table 16.4    Changes in the Top Five Recipient Countries of Japanese
              Government Development Assistance (1985-1992)
              (in hundred million $ )

| Fiscal Year | First | | Second | | Third | | Fourth | | Fifth | |
|---|---|---|---|---|---|---|---|---|---|---|
| 1985 | China | 3.9 | Thailand | 2.6 | Philippines | 2.4 | Indonesia | 1.6 | Myanmar | 1.5 |
| 1986 | China | 5.0 | Philippines | 4.4 | Thailand | 2.6 | Bangladesh | 2.5 | Myanmar | 2.4 |
| 1987 | Indonesia | 7.1 | China | 5.5 | Philippines | 2.7 | Bangladesh | 2.0 | India | 2.7 |
| 1988 | Indonesia | 9.8 | China | 6.7 | Philippines | 5.3 | Thailand | 3.6 | Bangladesh | 3.4 |
| 1989 | Indonesia | 11.5 | China | 8.3 | Thailand | 4.9 | Philippines | 4.0 | Bangladesh | 3.7 |
| 1990 | Indonesia | 8.7 | China | 7.2 | Philippines | 6.5 | Thailand | 4.2 | Bangladesh | 3.7 |
| 1991 | Indonesia | 12.0 | India | 10.0 | Egypt | 7.0 | China | 6.6 | Philippines | 5.2 |
| 1992 | Indonesia | 16.0 | China | 12.4 | Philippines | 12.1 | India | 5.0 | Thailand | 4.9 |

Source: Japanese Ministry of Foreign Affairs, *The Situation of Japan's
Foreign Policy 1993.*

Table 16.5    Geographic Distribution of Japan's Bilateral ODA
              (in U.S. $ millions, disbursement basis)

|  | 1975 | 1980 | 1985 | 1990 | 1992 |
|---|---|---|---|---|---|
| Asia | 638 (75.0) | 1,383 (70.5) | 1,732 (67.8) | 4,117 (59.3) | 5,524 (65.1) |
| Northeast Asia | 76 ( 8.9) | 82 ( 4.2) | 392 (15.3) | 835 (12.0) | 1,166 (13.7) |
| Southeast Asia | 426 (50.1) | 861 (44.0) | 962 (37.6) | 2,379 (34.3) | 3,361 (39.6) |
| ASEAN | 380 (44.7) | 703 (35.9) | 800 (31.3) | 2,299 (33.1) | 2,978 (35.1) |
| Southwest Asia | 133 (15.6) | 435 (22.2) | 375 (14.7) | 898 (12.9) | 989 (11.7) |
| other | 3 ( 3.9) | 5 ( 0.3) | 3 ( 0.1) | 4 ( 1.1) | 9 ( 0.1) |
| Middle East | 90 (10.6) | 204 (10.6) | 201 ( 7.9) | 7 (10.2) | 364 ( 4.3) |
| Africa | 59 ( 6.9) | 223 (11.4) | 252 ( 9.9) | 792 (11.4) | 859 (10.1) |
| South & Central America | 47 ( 5.6) | 118 ( 6.0) | 225 ( 8.8) | 561 ( 8.1) | 772 ( 9.1) |
| Oceania | 5 ( 0.6) | 12 ( 0.6) | 24 ( 0.9) | 114 ( 1.6) | 166 ( 2.0) |
| Europe | 0 ( 0.0) | -1.5 ( - ) | 1 ( 0.0) | 158 ( 2.6) | 103 ( 1.2) |
| East Europe |  |  |  | 153 ( 2.2) | 99  0.1 |
| indivisible | 11 ( 1.3) | 23 ( 1.2) | 122 ( 4.8) | 494 ( 7.1) | 696 ( 8.2) |
| Total Bilateral | 850(100.0) | 1,961(100.0) | 2,557(100.0) | 6,940(100.0) | 8,484(100.0) |

Note: Figure in parentheses is indicated share in percent. East Europe
figures complete from 1990.
Source: Japanese Ministry of Foreign Affairs, *The Situation of Japan's
Foreign Policy 1993,* p. 118.

ment and the private sector. Government-sponsored efforts include exchange of Chinese researchers and Japanese experts in the areas of agriculture, industry, business management, and public health; various kinds of technical cooperation also have been carried out. There are over twenty such cases, including the Enterprise Management Center and the Sanjiang Plateau Comprehensive Agricultural Experimentation Station.

Japan's basic philosophy and approach toward aid to China were defined first in 1979, at the time of the first yen loans, in the "Ohira three principles": (1) coordination with Europe and the United States; (2) balance with ASEAN; and (3) no cooperation in the military field. In 1991 a study group chaired by Saburo Okita was established by Japan's aid agency to formulate new guidelines for aid to China. The group offered four principles that continue to guide policy: (1) to promote Japan-China friendship and world peace; (2) to support China's economic reform and opening to the outside world; (3) to militate to correct imbalances resulting from economic development; and (4) to take into consideration China's geographic scale and large population (Japan International Cooperation Agency 1992). Also in 1991, the Japanese government announced four principles to govern Japan's granting of official development assistance on a worldwide basis, including to China. In considering whether to provide assistance, the Japanese government will take account of the recipient country's actions with regard to military expenditures, development and production of weapons of mass destruction, export and import of military weapons, and conditions with respect to a market economy and respect for human rights. Table 16.4 presents changes in the top five recipients of Japanese ODA in the late 1980s. Table 16.5 presents the geographic distribution of Japan's bilateral foreign aid. Not surprisingly, Asia is the most favored region.

# 17

## Opening the Coastal Region: Achievements and Regional Disparities

### Comparative Power of China's Economic Zones

Figure 17.1 presents an overview on a national basis of proportionate economic power at the province and region levels. The source data for the figure appear in Table 17.1.

There has been diverse terminology used to delineate regions. For example, China has identified "seven great joint industrial regions," "ten great economic regions," and "six central regions." Behind these divisions have been a variety of unspoken motives, such as the imperatives of political control and systems for the mobilization of military personnel. For purposes of this discussion, regions are divided into "market economic zones." This is the perspective used in Table 17.1.

Let us first take the three most obvious economic zones. They are (1) the Bohai rim (comprising Beijing and Tianjin municipalities and Hebei, Shandong, and Liaoning provinces), a zone that includes 18.0 percent of China's population and produces 22.8 percent of GNP; (2) the Yangtze delta (one municipality, Shanghai, and two provinces, Jiangsu and Zhejiang) with 10.8 percent of the population and GNP of 16.9 percent; and (3) south China (Guangdong, Fujian, and Hainan provinces and Guangxi autonomous region) with 12.6 percent of the population and GNP of 14.1 percent.

All three of these economic zones lie in the coastal region. Together they constitute 41.4 percent of population and 53.8 percent of GNP. Although China overall is a vast and materially abundant country, these figures evidence an overwhelming bias toward the coastal region in terms of population and material wealth.

The interior regions are less significant economically; they can be divided into four economic zones (bottom portion of Table 17.1): (4) the Yangtze River basin (Anhui, Jiangxi, Hubei, Hunan, and Sichuan provinces); (5) the northeast (Jilin

Figure 17.1 Proportionate Economic Power of Provinces,
Municipalities, and Autonomous Regions

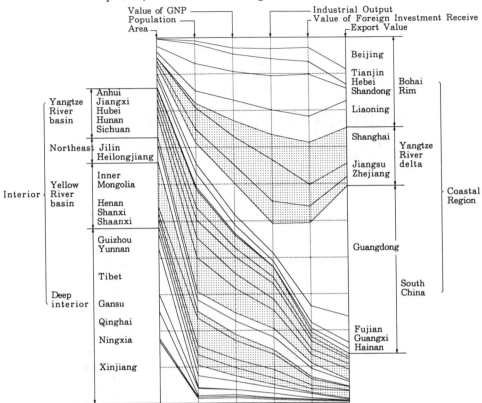

Note: The vertical axis presents 100% of China; divisions are 10%.
Source: Graphic presentation of Table 17.1.

and Heilongjiang provinces); (6) the Yellow River basin (Inner Mongolia autonomous region and Henan, Shanxi, and Shaanxi provinces); and (7) the deep interior (Guizhou, Yunnan, Gansu, and Qinhai provinces and Tibet, Ningxia, and
Xinjiang autonomous regions).

If we consider GNP per capita as an indicator of wealth, Table 17.1 shows the
coastal economic zones clearly in the lead: the Yangtze delta at RMB 2,360, the
Bohai rim at RMB 1,903, and south China at RMB 1,695, all far higher than the
deep interior economic zone at RMB 1,081. Similarly, the three coastal economic
zones lead in total value of industrial output: the Bohai rim at 26.5 percent, the
Yangtze delta at 24.4 percent, and south China at 11.8 percent, for a combined
total of 62.7 percent.

In value of exports, there is an even more pronounced bias toward the coastal
economic zones, which together account for 80.5 percent of the total: the Bohai

rim at 28.8 percent, the Yangtze delta at 21.8 percent, and south China at 29.9 percent. The increase in value of exports of the coastal region is of course partly the result of success in production of internationally competitive products, but more important has been the buildup of a production structure tied into overseas markets through the introduction of foreign capital (see Table 17.2).

The left-hand column of Figure 17.1 shows that the coastal regions occupy only 15 percent of China's total land area; the interior is overwhelmingly larger at 85 percent. However, population density in the coastal region is extremely high; the region has more than 40 percent of total population. The following list shows the coastal area's share data (ranged from low to high) for various socioeconomic indicators:

- Land area, 15 percent of total
- Population, over 40 percent of total
- GNP, over 50 percent of total
- Value of industrial production, over 60 percent of total
- Export value, approximately 80 percent of total
- Value of foreign capital received, over 85 percent of total

Thus, compared to the interior, the coastal region is clearly the economic giant, notwithstanding its small size (15 percent versus the interior's 85 percent). The disparity is obvious when each statistic in the list is subtracted from 100 percent to determine the interior's share—for example, only 20 percent of export value and less than 15 percent of foreign capital. Map 17.1 is a stylized representation that clearly evidences the disproportionate power of the coastal regions in value of exports.

These disparities have engendered a variety of economic and political contradictions. Currently, the policy is that the coastal regions should be allowed to pursue economic development freely, and efforts to rein in development in the name of correcting the imbalance should not be pursued. Rather, the view is that after the coastal region has achieved a high level of development toward the end of the 1990s, it will be able to underwrite economic assistance to the interior and thereby at that time correct disparities. Until then, the government intends to tolerate the economic gap and to oppose leftist egalitarianism.

## Formation of Transnational Market Areas

Table 17.3 lists overseas export markets of the coastal economic zones. The top three markets for exports from the Bohai rim are Japan with 31 percent, Hong Kong with 15 percent, and the United States with 12 percent. For the Yangtze delta, the top two positions are the reverse: Hong Kong leads at 22 percent, followed by Japan at 16 percent and the United States at 13 percent. For the south China zone,

Table 17.1  Proportionate Economic Power of Provinces, Municipalities, and Autonomous Regions

| Area | Population | | | G N P | | | Per Capita GNP | |
|---|---|---|---|---|---|---|---|---|
| | 1990 Population (millions) | Percent of national total (%) | 1980-90 Average growth rate (‰) | 1990 (RMB billions) | Percent of national total (%) | 1980-90 Average growth rate (%) | 1990 (RMB) | 1980-90 Average growth rate (%) |
| Beijing | 10.9 | 0.9 | 20.6 | 50.1 | 2.9 | 9.0 | 4,611 | 6.8 |
| Tianjin | 8.8 | 0.8 | 16.7 | 30.0 | 1.7 | 7.0 | 3,397 | 5.2 |
| Hebei | 61.6 | 5.4 | 17.7 | 82.0 | 4.8 | 8.9 | 1,331 | 7.0 |
| Shandong | 84.9 | 7.5 | 15.3 | 133.2 | 7.8 | 10.0 | 1,569 | 8.3 |
| Liaoning | 39.7 | 3.4 | 13.0 | 96.5 | 5.6 | 8.5 | 2,432 | 7.1 |
| Bohai Rim | 205.9 | 18.0 | 15.9 | 391.8 | 22.8 | | 1,903 | |
| Shanghai | 13.3 | 1.2 | 15.5 | 74.5 | 4.3 | 7.4 | 5,570 | 5.7 |
| Jiangsu | 67.7 | 5.9 | 13.2 | 131.4 | 7.7 | 10.5 | 1,942 | 9.1 |
| Zhejiang | 41.7 | 3.7 | 8.6 | 83.7 | 4.9 | 11.2 | 2,008 | 10.2 |
| Yangtze River Delta | 122.7 | 10.8 | 11.8 | 289.6 | 16.9 | | 2,360 | |
| Guangdong | 63.5 | 5.6 | 19.6 | 147.2 | 8.6 | 12.3 | 2,319 | 10.2 |
| Fujian | 30.4 | 2.7 | 18.9 | 46.6 | 2.7 | 10.4 | 1,554 | 8.4 |
| Guangxi | 42.6 | 3.7 | 18.8 | 39.3 | 2.3 | 7.2 | 922 | 5.2 |
| Hainan | 6.6 | 0.6 | 18.5 | 9.5 | 0.5 | n.a. | 1,433 | n.a. |
| South China | 143.1 | 12.6 | 19.1 | 242.6 | 14.1 | | 1,695 | |
| Coastal Region | 471.7 | 41.4 | 15.8 | 923.9 | 53.8 | | 1,959 | |
| Anhui | 56.8 | 5.0 | 14.9 | 60.7 | 3.5 | 9.7 | 1,069 | 8.1 |
| Jiangxi | 38.1 | 3.3 | 15.4 | 41.7 | 2.4 | 8.9 | 1,095 | 7.2 |
| Hubei | 54.4 | 4.8 | 15.0 | 79.3 | 4.6 | 8.1 | 1,457 | 7.1 |
| Hunan | 61.3 | 5.4 | 15.0 | 70.3 | 4.1 | 7.8 | 1,147 | 6.3 |
| Sichuan | 108.0 | 9.4 | 9.6 | 114.7 | 6.7 | 8.4 | 1,061 | 7.4 |
| Yangtze River Basin | 318.6 | 27.9 | 15.2 | 366.6 | 21.3 | | 1,151 | |
| Jilin | 24.8 | 2.2 | 11.7 | 39.4 | 2.3 | 8.7 | 1,586 | 7.4 |
| Heilongjiang | 35.4 | 3.1 | 10.1 | 63.5 | 3.7 | 10.9 | 1,792 | 9.8 |
| Northeast | 60.3 | 5.3 | 10.7 | 102.9 | 6.0 | | 1,707 | |
| Inner Mongolia | 21.6 | 1.9 | 14.3 | 28.7 | 1.7 | 9.7 | 1,325 | 8.2 |
| Henan | 86.5 | 7.6 | 17.3 | 89.6 | 5.2 | 9.6 | 1,036 | 7.8 |
| Shanxi | 29.0 | 2.5 | 15.9 | 39.8 | 2.3 | 8.2 | 1,374 | 6.5 |
| Shaanxi | 33.2 | 2.9 | 15.9 | 37.5 | 2.2 | 9.2 | 1,130 | 7.5 |
| Yellow River Basin | 170.2 | 14.9 | 16.4 | 195.6 | 11.4 | | 1,148 | |
| Guizhou | 32.7 | 2.9 | 16.4 | 25.5 | 1.5 | 9.5 | 779 | 7.7 |
| Yunnan | 37.3 | 3.3 | 16.9 | 39.6 | 2.3 | 10.6 | 1,061 | 8.8 |
| Tibet | 2.2 | 0.2 | 18.4 | 2.4 | 0.0 | n.a. | 1,101 | n.a. |
| Gansu | 22.6 | 2.0 | 16.3 | 23.4 | 1.4 | 8.8 | 919 | 7.1 |
| Qinghai | 4.5 | 0.4 | 17.4 | 6.6 | 0.4 | 7.1 | 1,480 | 5.3 |
| Ningxia | 4.7 | 0.4 | 23.1 | 6.1 | 0.4 | 9.7 | 1,299 | 7.3 |
| Xinjiang | 15.3 | 1.3 | 17.7 | 25.2 | 1.5 | 10.9 | 1,647 | 8.9 |
| Deep Interior Region | 119.2 | 10.5 | 16.9 | 128.9 | 7.5 | | 1,081 | |
| Interior | 668.3 | 58.6 | 15.4 | 793.8 | 46.2 | | 1,181 | |
| Total Country | 114,000 | 100.0 | 15.5 | 1,717.8 | 100.0 | 8.9 | 1,507 | 7.3 |

| Value of Industrial Output | | | Export Value | | | | Value of Foreign Investment Received (Actual usage) | |
|---|---|---|---|---|---|---|---|---|
| 1990 (RMB billions) | Percent of national total (%) | 1980-90 Average growth rate (‰) | 1990 (U.S. $ millions) | Percent of national total (%) | % of GNP | 1980-90 Average growth rate (‰) | 1983-90 Aggregate (U.S. $ millions) | Percent of national total (%) |
| 73.5 | 3.1 | 8.6 | 1,344 | 2.8 | 12.8 | 17.3 | 2,039 | 8.8 |
| 68.0 | 2.8 | 10.4 | 1,909 | 3.9 | 30.4 | 11.6 | 966 | 4.2 |
| 112.3 | 4.7 | 12.3 | 1,678 | 3.5 | 9.8 | 5.5 | 266 | 1.1 |
| 220.2 | 9.2 | 16.7 | 5,588 | 11.5 | 27.7 | 5.1 | 807 | 3.4 |
| 160.7 | 6.7 | 10.0 | 3,417 | 7.1 | 12.3 | 2.2 | 1,695 | 7.3 |
| 634.6 | 26.5 | | 13,937 | 28.8 | 17.0 | 5.5 | 5,773 | 24.8 |
| 163.3 | 6.8 | 7.1 | 5,524 | 11.4 | 35.5 | 10.8 | 2,248 | 9.7 |
| 276.4 | 11.6 | 17.1 | 2,873 | 5.9 | 10.5 | 13.7 | 847 | 3.7 |
| 143.3 | 6.0 | 20.1 | 2,211 | 4.5 | 12.6 | 18.8 | 596 | 2.5 |
| 583.0 | 24.4 | | 10,608 | 21.8 | 17.5 | 13.0 | 3,692 | 15.9 |
| 190.2 | 8.0 | 20.0 | 11,015 | 22.7 | 35.8 | 29.2 | 8,289 | 35.6 |
| 53.2 | 2.2 | 17.8 | 2,224 | 4.6 | 22.8 | 35.7 | 1,675 | 7.2 |
| 35.3 | 1.5 | 11.3 | 731 | 1.5 | 8.9 | 14.6 | 399 | 1.7 |
| 4.4 | 0.1 | 15.1 | 501 | 1.1 | 25.2 | n.a. | 329 | 1.4 |
| 283.1 | 11.8 | | 14,471 | 29.9 | 28.5 | 29.9 | 10,693 | 45.9 |
| 1,500.7 | 62.7 | | 39,016 | 80.5 | 20.2 | 13.9 | 20,157 | 86.6 |
| 67.0 | 2.8 | 14.7 | 637 | 1.3 | 5.0 | 15.9 | 232 | 1.0 |
| 42.6 | 1.8 | 13.6 | 562 | 1.2 | 6.4 | 16.8 | 133 | 0.6 |
| 100.8 | 4.2 | 13.8 | 1,045 | 2.2 | 6.3 | 15.3 | 312 | 1.3 |
| 71.3 | 3.0 | 11.4 | 791 | 1.6 | 5.4 | 14.7 | 352 | 1.5 |
| 122.3 | 5.1 | 12.2 | 1,127 | 2.3 | 4.7 | 26.8 | 667 | 2.9 |
| 404.0 | 16.9 | | 4,161 | 8.6 | 5.4 | 18.0 | 1,696 | 7.3 |
| 55.2 | 2.3 | 11.5 | 732 | 1.5 | 8.9 | 11.7 | 127 | 0.5 |
| 86.3 | 3.6 | 8.3 | 1,114 | 2.3 | 8.4 | 21.8 | 273 | 1.2 |
| 141.6 | 5.9 | | 1,846 | 3.8 | 8.6 | 17.2 | 401 | 1.7 |
| 26.0 | 1.1 | 10.9 | 323 | 0.6 | 5.4 | 19.3 | 48 | 0.2 |
| 103.7 | 4.3 | 13.4 | 831 | 1.7 | 4.4 | 17.9 | 206 | 0.9 |
| 53.8 | 2.3 | 11.6 | 455 | 1.0 | 5.5 | 15.0 | 36 | 0.2 |
| 44.3 | 1.8 | 12.2 | 462 | 1.0 | 5.9 | 35.0 | 490 | 2.1 |
| 227.7 | 9.5 | | 2,071 | 4.3 | 5.1 | 20.1 | 780 | 3.4 |
| 21.8 | 0.9 | 12.5 | 153 | 0.3 | 2.9 | 31.0 | 62 | 0.3 |
| 34.5 | 1.5 | 12.5 | 563 | 1.2 | 6.8 | 30.4 | 47 | 0.2 |
| 0.3 | 0.0 | 3.2 | 10 | 0.0 | 1.9 | 45.1 | 0.03 | 0.0 |
| 27.8 | 1.2 | 8.8 | 182 | 0.4 | 3.7 | 22.4 | 35 | 0.2 |
| 5.5 | 0.2 | 9.8 | 68 | 0.1 | 4.9 | 29.6 | 4 | 0.0 |
| 6.5 | 0.3 | 11.5 | 75 | 0.2 | 5.8 | 18.9 | 6 | 0.0 |
| 22.0 | 0.9 | 12.8 | 312 | 0.6 | 5.9 | 11.7 | 100 | 0.4 |
| 118.4 | 5.0 | | 1,362 | 2.8 | 5.1 | 22.9 | 254 | 1.1 |
| 891.7 | 37.3 | | 9,440 | 19.5 | 5.7 | 18.9 | 3,131 | 13.4 |
| 2,392.4 | 100.0 | 13.2 | 48,455 | 100.0 | 13.5 | 14.8 | 23,288 | 100.0 |

Note: Prices are historical prices. Increase rates are real rates (however, exports are nominal). Aggregation of provincial figures at the national level produces slight discrepancies with national figures. Therefore percent of national total calculations for provinces are calculated against the provincial figures aggregate.

Sources: *Statistical Yearbook of China 1991*, pp. 36, 81, 397. *Compendium of Historical Statistical Materials for All Provinces, Autonomous Regions, and Special Municipalities, 1949-89,* Provincial statistics: *Foreign Trade Yearbook of China 1991 pp.* 336, 582. *China's Commercial and Foreign Economic Statistical Materials,* p. 501.

Table 17.2   Direct Investment in Coastal Cities and Provinces from
Hong Kong, Japan, U.S., Taiwan, and South Korea
(contract base. currency unit U.S. $ millions)

|  | | Liaoning Province | Beijing Municipal | Shandong Province | Guangdong Province |
|---|---|---|---|---|---|
| Hong Kong | (cases) | 181 (49.6%) | 106 (44.0%) | 194 (53.0%) [a] | 2,635 (86.6%) [a] |
|  | (amt.) | 314 (67.3%) | 35 (30.0%) | 88 (37.2%) [a] | 2,109 (81.8%) [a] |
| Japan | (cases) | 68 (18.6%) | 29 (12.0%) | 31 ( 8.5%) | 15 ( 0.5%) |
|  | (amt.) | 28 ( 6.0%) | 9 ( 7.6%) | 26 (11.0%) | 31 ( 1.2%) |
| U.S. | (cases) | 28 ( 7.7%) | 45 (18.7%) | 47 (10.0%) | 45 ( 1.5%) |
|  | (amt.) | 22 ( 4.7%) | 11 ( 9.7%) | 23 (10.0%) | 62 ( 2.3%) |
| Taiwan | (cases) | 36 ( 9.9%) | 32 (13.3%) | 48 (13.1%) | 267 ( 8.8%) |
|  | (amt.) | 11 ( 2.4%) | 25 (21.6%) | 32 (13.6%) | 257 ( 9.6%) |
| South | (cases) | 21 ( 5.8%) | 3 ( 1.2%) | 12 ( 3.3%) | 1 ( 0.0%) |
| Korea | (amt.) | 15 ( 3.3%) | 0.5 ( 0.4%) | 22 ( 9.5%) | 0.8 ( 0.0%) |
| Other | (cases) | 31 ( 8.5%) | 26 (10.8%) | 34 ( 9.3%) | 79 ( 2.6%) |
|  | (amt.) | 76 (16.3%) | 36 (30.7%) | 43 (18.5%) | 229 ( 8.5%) |
| Total | (cases) | 365 (100.0 %) | 241 (100.0 %) | 366 (100.0 %) | 3,042 (100.0 %) |
|  | (amt.) | 467 (100.0 %) | 117 (100.0 %) | 233 (100.0 %) | 2,690 (100.0 %) |

Note : Direct investment from Taiwan and South Korea indicated
for coastal cities only. [a]Hong Kong figure includes Macao.
Sources: *Economic Statistical Yearbook of Liaoning 1991*, p. 591;
*Social Economic Statistical Yearbook of Beijing 1991*, p. 506;
*Statistical Yearbook of Shandong 1991*, p. 458; *Statistical Yearbook
of Guangdong 1991*, p. 319-320.

Hong Kong holds an overwhelming lead at 71 percent, followed by the United
States and Japan, both at 5 percent. In the aggregate for the three coastal economic zones, Hong Kong is the first market at 37 percent, Japan second at 17 percent, and the United States third at 10 percent.

A close relationship is manifest in Table 17.3 between export markets and direct
investment. In ranked order of direct investment, Hong Kong holds fast to the
first position in every area. Regional spheres of relative power are evident in second position: Japan in the northeast, Taiwan in south China, and the United
States along the Yangtze River. In third place, depending on region, we can also
find Singapore, which along with Taiwan has become an important new investment source in the 1990s.

Taiwanese and South Korean interests have been especially aggressive investors
in China in recent years. However, whereas Taiwan is expanding in all of the provinces and cities, South Korea is focusing on the geographically closer provinces of
Liaoning and Shandong.

It is immediately evident that the strategy of coastal region development truly
opened the doors not only to China's Pacific rim neighbors (Hong Kong, Taiwan,
South Korea, Japan) but also to the United States. Thus, the market area formed
thereby, rather than being a local regional one, in fact constitutes a transnational
or even a supranational market area.

Map 17.1 The Chinese Map Redrawn in Proportion to Value of Exports

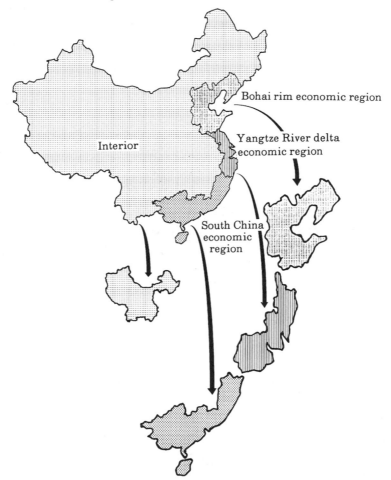

# The Nonstate Sector: Driving Force of Coastal Development

Table 17.4 shows in terms of value of industrial production how six coastal areas (Jiangsu, Shandong, Guangdong, Liaoning, and Zhejiang provinces and Shanghai municipality) have developed under the liberalization policy. From 1975 to 1990 in national province-level comparisons, Jiangsu province jumped from third place to first, Shandong province from fourth place to second, Guangdong province from sixth place to third, and Zhejiang province from sixteenth place to sixth. However, Shanghai dropped from first place to fourth, and Liaoning province fell from second to fifth place. Notwithstanding that they are part of the same

Table 17.3 Export Markets of the Coastal Cities and Provinces and Direct Investment in These Areas by Country and Region (1990)

| Region | Province /City | Principal Export Market | | | Principal Sources of Direct Investment Country / Region | | |
|---|---|---|---|---|---|---|---|
| | | First place | Second place | Third place | First place | Second place | Third place |
| Bohai Rim | Liaoning | Japan (40%) | U.S. (19%) | Singapore (9%) | Hong Kong | Japan | U.S. |
| | Beijing | Hong Kong (22%) | Japan (14%) | U.S. (12%) | Hong Kong 108 cases $38 mil. | Taiwan 32 cases $25 mil. | U.S. 44 cases $10 mil. |
| | Tianjin | Hong Kong (20%) | Japan (14%) | U.S. (13%) | Hong Kong 67 cases | Japan 12 cases | U.S. 13 cases |
| | Hebei | Japan (40%) | Hong Kong (20%) | U.S. (7%) | Hong Kong 71 cases $51 mil. | Taiwan 15 cases $14 mil. | Panama 1 cases $10 mil. |
| | Shandong | Japan (26%) | Hong Kong (17%) | E.C. (11%) | Hong Kong 99 cases $120 mil. | Taiwan 48 cases $32 mil. | Japan 31 cases $26 mil. |
| | Subtotal | Japan (31%) | Hong Kong (15%) | U.S. (12%) | | | |
| Yangtze River Delta | Jiangsu | Hong Kong (22%) | Japan (20%) | E.C. (16%) | Hong Kong ᵃ 233 cases $159 mil. | U.S. 31 cases $57 mil. | Taiwan 60 cases $28 mil. |
| | Shanghai | Hong Kong (19.4) | Hong Kong (14%) | U.S. (14%) | Hong Kong ᵇ 444 cases $773 mil. | U.S.ᵇ 122 cases $715 mil. | Japanᵇ 128 cases $407 mil. |
| | Zhejiang | Hong Kong (29%) | Japan (15%) | U.S. (10%) | Hong Kong 169 cases $70 mil. | Taiwan 60 cases $30 mil. | Singapore 5 cases $12 mil. |
| | Subtotal | Hong Kong (22%) | Japan (16%) | U.S. (13%) | | | |
| South China | Fujian | Hong Kong (47%) | Japan (13%) | U.S. (12%) | Hong Kong 607 cases $565 mil. | Taiwan 380 cases $462 mil. | Japan 24 cases $24 mil. |
| | Guang-dong | Hong Kong (81%) | U.S. (4%) | Japan (3%) | Hong Kong 2432 cases $2109 mil. | Macao | Taiwan |
| | Guanxi | Hong Kong ᵃ (52%) | U.S. (8%) | Japan (6%) | Hong Kong 82 cases | Taiwan 19 cases | U.S. 7 cases |
| | Hainan | Hong Kong (80%) | Japan (7%) | Sri Lanka (2%) | Hong Kong 159 cases $109 mil. | Taiwan 50 cases $23 mil. | Singapore 4 cases $20 mil. |
| | Subtotal | Hong Kong (71%) | U.S. (5%) | Japan (5%) | | | |
| 12 Provinces & Cities | Total | Hong Kong (37%) | Japan (17%) | U.S. (10%) | | | |

Note: The data above are taken from *Foreign Economic Relations and Trade Yearbook of China 1991/92*, which is compiled from reports of regional foreign economic relations and trade committees and is slightly different from the summary data produced by The State Council Committee on Foreign Economic Relations and Trade. ᵃ Hong Kong includes Macao. ᵇ Country source of investment in Shanghai is year-end aggregate figure.

Sources: *Statistical Yearbook of China 1991. Foreign Economic Relations and Trade Yearbook of China 1991/92*. Direct investment figures in *Foreign Economic Relations and Trade Yearbook 1991/92*, pp. 583-585. Country source of investment from foreign economic relations and trade committees of each province.

Table 17.4  Value of Industrial Production of Six Leading Coastal Cities and Provinces (in RMB billions)

| | 1975 Amount | As percentage of national total | 1980 Amount | As percentage of national total | 1985 Amount | As percentage of national total | 1990 Amount | As percentage of national total |
|---|---|---|---|---|---|---|---|---|
| Jiangsu | 23.5 | 7.3 ③ | 46.8 | 9.1 ② | 103.7 | 10.7 ① | 276.4 | 11.6 |
| Shandong | 19.0 | 5.9 ④ | 34.0 | 6.6 ④ | 68.3 | 7.0 ④ | 220.2 | 9.2 |
| Guangdong | 15.4 | 4.8 ⑥ | 22.3 | 4.3 ⑨ | 53.3 | 5.5 ⑥ | 190.2 | 8.0 |
| Shanghai | 42.0 | 13.1 ① | 59.9 | 11.6 ① | 86.3 | 8.9 ② | 163.3 | 6.8 |
| Liaoning | 32.6 | 10.1 ② | 45.3 | 8.8 ③ | 77.5 | 8.0 ③ | 160.7 | 6.7 |
| Zhejiang | 7.8 | 2.4 ⑯ | 20.2 | 3.9 ⑫ | 55.1 | 5.7 ⑤ | 143.3 | 6.0 |
| Subtotal | 140.3 | 43.7 | 228.4 | 44.3 | 414.0 | 42.6 | 1154.0 | 48.2 |
| National Total | 320.7 | 100.0 | 515.4 | 100.0 | 971.7 | 100.0 | 2392.4 | 100.0 |

Note: Value of industrial output is in historical prices.
Figure within circle is national ranking.
Sources: *Compendium of Historical Statistical Materials for All Provinces, Autonomous Regions, and Special Municipalities,* and *Statistical Yearbook of China 1991*, p. 397.

Table 17.5  Ownership Structure of Industrial Production in Six Leading Coastal Cities and Provinces (%)

| | Ownership by All of the People Employees | Amount | Collective Ownership Employees | Amount | Other Forms Employees | Amount | (of which, Three Capital Enterprises) Employees | Amount |
|---|---|---|---|---|---|---|---|---|
| Jiangsu | 55.9 | 34.3 | 40.0 | 58.0 | 4.1 | 7.7 | | |
| Shandong | 67.6 | 41.4 | 31.3 | 50.7 | 1.1 | 7.9 | | |
| Guangdong | 54.9 | 40.2 | 32.9 | 34.7 | 12.2 | 25.1 | | |
| Shanghai | 76.4 | 68.2 | 20.6 | 19.9 | 2.9 | 11.8 | | 5.7 |
| Liaoning | 60.2 | 61.2 | 36.4 | 28.2 | 3.4 | 10.6 | | 0.8 |
| Zhejiang | 50.2 | 31.2 | 47.7 | 60.1 | 2.1 | 8.7 | | |
| National Total | 68.4 | 54.6 | 29.4 | 35.6 | 2.2 | 9.8 | | |

Note: Employees include staff and workers. Amount is value of industrial output at historical prices.
Source: *Statistical Yearbook of China 1991*, pp. 393, 398. Three capital enterprises are from *Statistical Yearbook* of each province.

coastal region, Shanghai and Liaoning province failed to make the leap. We can glean the reason from Table 17.5, which shows the valued of industrial production for each area according to form of ownership. In terms of value of industrial production in both Shanghai municipality and Liaoning province, the state-owned sector is over 60 percent. Put another way, sectors under collective or other ownership systems are small. In short, overall economic activity in Shanghai and Liaoning has been controlled by state-owned enterprises enjoying "total state-guaranteed security," and the dullness of this sector has caused them to stagnate. In contrast, because the collectively owned sector is large in Jiangsu and Shandong and other ownership types form a significant sector in Guangdong province, these areas have succeeded in realizing rapid growth.

Table 17.6 presents data about heavy industry, light industry, and enterprise scale. No simple conclusion suggests itself with respect to the structure of heavy and light industry, but there is a significant factor for enterprise scale: With the exception of Zhejiang province, provinces with a high value of industrial production coming from large-scale enterprises have performed poorly. Because large-scale enterprises generally are state-owned, this corresponds to the performance by different form of ownership shown in Table 17.5. In sum, although the six coastal areas developed extensively, domination of Shanghai and Liaoning by state-owned enterprises kept these areas from participating equally in growth. This slower growth is a consequence of economic reform not yet extending to state-owned enterprises.

Table 17.7 presents a comparison of the export structure of Guangdong province in 1985 and 1990. In 1985 normal exports accounted for over 80 percent of total, but by 1990 these had declined to under 60 percent. Conversely, there was dramatic growth in exports from "three capital enterprises" (foreign-invested enterprises). The major portion of this growth was in consignment processing.

## Direct Foreign Investment in Open Cities

The provinces of China each possess a population in the tens of millions; indeed, an analyst taking a worldview could consider them countries. Consequently, when statistics are aggregated to the province level, much information is obscured by the vastness of territory and sheer numbers of people. To avoid this drawback, it is desirable to study the figures at the municipal level.

Table 17.8 presents the so-called three capital enterprises—foreign-invested enterprises—for the advance guard of the liberalization policy: the four special economic zones and the fourteen opened coastal cities. (Actually, there are five special economic zones. Omitted in this discussion is Hainan Island, which was opened too recently to produce significant results or data.)

The top portion of the table lists the four special economic zones. From 1984 to 1990 Shenzhen made an aggregate of 2,944 contracts with a total value of $3.5 billion. This is the contracted amount committed. The actual amount of capital paid

Table 17.6   Scale Structure of Industrial Production in Six Leading Coastal Cities and Provinces (%)

| | Light Industry | | Heavy Industry | | Large Scale Enterprises | | Medium Scale Enterprises | | Small Scale Enterprises | |
|---|---|---|---|---|---|---|---|---|---|---|
| | Employ- ment | Value | Employ- ment | Value | No. | Value | No. | Value | No. | Value |
| Jiangsu | 50.7 | 54.7 | 49.3 | 45.3 | 0.7 | 21.3 | 2.6 | 21.0 | 96.7 | 57.7 |
| Shandong | 47.8 | 50.8 | 52.2 | 49.2 | 1.0 | 31.1 | 4.0 | 21.1 | 95.1 | 49.6 |
| Guangdong | 65.5 | 67.5 | 34.5 | 32.5 | 1.2 | 28.0 | 2.9 | 21.1 | 95.9 | 50.9 |
| Shanghai | 47.9 | 51.9 | 52.1 | 48.1 | 3.2 | 46.3 | 5.9 | 20.3 | 90.9 | 33.4 |
| Liaoning | 31.0 | 32.6 | 69.0 | 67.4 | 1.6 | 52.0 | 3.0 | 17.3 | 95.4 | 30.7 |
| Zhejiang | 57.5 | 65.1 | 42.5 | 34.8 | 0.3 | 12.8 | 1.0 | 17.0 | 98.7 | 70.2 |
| National Total | 41.6 | 49.4 | 58.4 | 50.6 | 1.0 | 34.8 | 2.3 | 19.8 | 96.8 | 45.4 |

Note: Large, medium and small enterprise refers to independent industrial enterprises (historical prices).
Source: *Statistical Yearbook of China 1991*, pp. 393, 398, 405.

Table 17.7   Composition of Exports from Guangdong Province (1985, 1990) in U.S. $ millions

| | Export volume | (of which to Hong Kong) | Trade exports | Export of processed materials | Compen- sation trade | Three capital co. exports |
|---|---|---|---|---|---|---|
| 1985 | 2,953 (100.0%) | 2,168 (73.4%) | 2,450 (83.0%) | 273 (9.2%) | 9 (0.3%) | 221 (7.5%) |
| 1990 | 10,560 (100.0%) | 8,709 (82.5%) | 6,175 (58.5%) | 583 (5.5%) | 78 ( 0.8%) | 3,724 (35.3%) |

Note:   Three capital companies include Chinese-foreign joint venures, cooperative enterprises, and 100% foreign owned companies.
Source:   *Statistical Yearbook of Guangdong 1991*, p. 304.

in (actual utilization) of this sum was some $1.9 billion, or slightly over 50 percent of commitments. The Zhuhai special zone had 1,105 cases for a total of $758 million, Xiamen had 944 cases for $1.9 billion, and Shantou had 636 cases for $479 million. In the aggregate, the special economic zones from 1984 to 1990 accounted for about 20 percent of the nation's total contracts—a major achievement given that these zones are little more than pinpoints within the great expanse of Chinese territory. It can thus be understood that the special economic zones have truly played the role of advance guard in China's liberalization policy.

Over the years, there have been three surges of economic activity. The first was the 1984–1985 reform period that resulted from the decision to transfer emphasis from agricultural reform to reform of the cities and industry. The second peak, 1987 to 1989, ensued after the Thirteenth Party Congress adopted the theory of the initial stage of socialism, a decision that gave a great boost to the liberalization policy. Momentum was especially high in 1988. The 1989 Tiananmen incident did

Table 17.8  Situation of Receipt of Direct Investment of Four Special
Economic Zones and Fourteen Opened Coastal Cities
(1984 to 1990) (in  U.S. $  millions,  %)

| | | 1984 | 1985 | 1986 | 1987 | 1988 | 1989 | 1990 | 1984 -90 | Actual investment |
|---|---|---|---|---|---|---|---|---|---|---|
| Shenzhen | (cases) | 331 | 253 | 190 | 310 | 591 | 706 | 563 | 2,944 | |
| | (amt.) | 533 | 763 | 227 | 557 | 430 | 483 | 502 | 3,495 | 1,924 |
| Zhuhai | (cases) | 70 | 71 | 45 | 95 | 252 | 225 | 347 | 1,105 | |
| | (amt.) | 97 | 60 | 52 | 42 | 140 | 128 | 238 | 758 | 361 |
| Shantou | (cases) | 24 | 23 | 16 | 21 | 76 | 285 | 191 | 636 | |
| | (amt.) | 21 | 13 | 12 | 8 | 56 | 198 | 171 | 479 | 242 |
| Xiamen | (cases) | 86 | 107 | 34 | 50 | 180 | 225 | 262 | 944 | |
| | (amt.) | 150 | 236 | 28 | 57 | 156 | 769 | 486 | 1,880 | 495 |
| Special Zones (a) (cases) | | 511 | 454 | 285 | 476 | 1,099 | 1,441 | 1,363 | 5,629 | |
| Total (b) | (amt.) | 800 | 1,073 | 319 | 664 | 782 | 1,579 | 1,396 | 6,612 | 3,024 |
| (a)/(g)% | | 27.5 | 14.8 | 19.0 | 21.3 | 18.5 | 24.9 | 18.7 | 20.4 | |
| (b)/(h)% | | 30.2 | 18.1 | 11.2 | 17.9 | 14.8 | 28.2 | 21.2 | 20.3 | 17.6 |
| Dalian | (cases) | 19 | 50 | 26 | 31 | 27 | 144 | 173 | 570 | |
| | (amt.) | 26 | 142 | 56 | 87 | 88 | 209 | 564 | 1,173 | 444 |
| Qinhuangdao | (cases) | 1 | 11 | 7 | 6 | 18 | 23 | 15 | 81 | |
| | (amt.) | 0.03 | 26 | 12 | 22 | 9 | 20 | 163 | 95 | 39 |
| Tianjin | (cases) | 46 | 88 | 49 | 50 | 94 | 97 | 129 | 553 | |
| | (amt.) | 133 | 68 | 94 | 14 | 92 | 85 | 164 | 650 | 375 |
| Yantai | (cases) | 4 | 8 | 15 | 15 | 63 | 63 | 23 | 191 | |
| | (amt.) | 61 | 8 | 9 | 8 | 50 | 32 | 6 | 174 | 37 |
| Qingdao | (cases) | 3 | 10 | 12 | 14 | 29 | 44 | 38 | 150 | |
| | (amt.) | 2 | 35 | 36 | 19 | 106 | 32 | 54 | 283 | 125 |
| Lianyungang | (cases) | 3 | 5 | 3 | 4 | 10 | 6 | 5 | 36 | |
| | (amt.) | 7 | 2 | 2 | 3 | 3 | 6 | 2 | 25 | 21 |
| Nantong | (cases) | 4 | 13 | 11 | 12 | 21 | 21 | 16 | 98 | |
| | (amt.) | 2 | 29 | 6 | 20 | 11 | 19 | 42 | 129 | 46 |
| Shanghai | (cases) | 43 | 96 | 62 | 76 | 19 | 199 | 119 | 814 | |
| | (amt.) | 337 | 762 | 303 | 338 | 333 | 360 | 291 | 2,724 | 1,455 |
| Ningbo | (cases) | 8 | 12 | 7 | 13 | 62 | 64 | 46 | 212 | |
| | (amt.) | 4 | 5 | 4 | 42 | 40 | 63 | 45 | 203 | 56 |
| Wenzhou | (cases) | | 5 | 3 | 4 | 14 | 28 | 20 | 74 | |
| | (amt.) | | 0.7 | 1 | 0.7 | 4 | 9 | 4 | 20 | 10 |
| Fuzhou | (cases) | 62 | 70 | 29 | 56 | 68 | 214 | 168 | 767 | |
| | (amt.) | 54 | 44 | 9 | 31 | 118 | 152 | 205 | 612 | 201 |
| Guangzhou | (cases) | 141 | 297 | 109 | 137 | 89 | 292 | 241 | 1,506 | |
| | (amt.) | 214 | 482 | 315 | 209 | 393 | 401 | 364 | 2,379 | 762 |
| Zhanjiang | (cases) | 72 | 89 | 23 | 33 | 80 | 49 | 44 | 390 | |
| | (amt.) | 70 | 109 | 19 | 31 | 62 | 26 | 31 | 348 | 120 |
| Beihai | (cases) | 20 | 15 | 3 | 13 | 23 | 7 | 17 | 98 | |
| | (amt.) | 8 | 5 | 2 | 6 | 22 | 1 | 34 | 78 | 16 |
| 14 Cities (c) (cases) | | 426 | 769 | 359 | 464 | 1,217 | 1,251 | 1,054 | 5,540 | |
| Total (d) | (amt.) | 919 | 1,717 | 868 | 830 | 1,332 | 1,414 | 1,811 | 8,892 | 3,707 |
| (c)/(g)% | | 23.0 | 25.0 | 24.0 | 20.8 | 20.5 | 21.6 | 14.5 | 20.0 | |
| (d)/(h)% | | 34.7 | 29.0 | 30.6 | 22.4 | 25.2 | 25.3 | 27.5 | 27.3 | 21.6 |
| Total (e) | (cases) | 937 | 1,223 | 644 | 940 | 2,316 | 2,692 | 2,417 | 11,169 | |
| (f) | (amt.) | 1,719 | 2,790 | 1,187 | 1,494 | 2,115 | 2,993 | 3,207 | 15,505 | 6,731 |
| Nationally (g) (cases) | | 1,856 | 3,073 | 1,498 | 2,233 | 5,945 | 5,779 | 7,273 | 27,657 | |
| (h) | (amt.) | 2,651 | 5,931 | 2,834 | 3,709 | 5,297 | 5,600 | 6,596 | 32,618 | 17,193 |
| (e)/(g)% | | 50.5 | 40.0 | 43.0 | 42.1 | 39.0 | 46.6 | 33.2 | 40.4 | |
| (f)/(h)% | | 64.9 | 47.0 | 41.9 | 40.3 | 39.9 | 53.4 | 48.6 | 47.5 | 39.1 |

Sources: *China's Commercial and Foreign Economic Statistical
Materials 1952-1988* (Beijing: China Statistical Press, 1990),
pp. 556-557. 1989, 1990 and national figures, *Statistical Yearbook
of China*, pp. 71-76 (1990), pp. 629, 659-666 (1991).

not particularly influence the conclusion of contracts because most of the contracts signed in 1989 had been negotiated in 1988 or at the latest in the first half of 1989. The third boom, from 1991 to 1993, reached the greatest heights of all according to preliminary figures; these are discussed in Chapter 19.

For the fourteen cities listed in Table 17.8, the aggregate statistics are 5,540 cases for a total contracted value of $8.9 billion. In terms of national share, this constitutes 20 percent for cases and 27 percent for value. On an actual utilization basis the share is 21 percent. Over the years, the same pattern of three peaks has obtained as for the special economic zones.

The four special economic zones and the fourteen coastal cities in aggregate account for 40.4 percent of cases and 47.5 percent of contracted value. In essence, only eighteen cities are the engines pulling China forward.

# 18

# The Surge in Regional Liberalization

## Documents No. 2 and No. 4 (1992) of the Chinese Communist Party Central

Deng Xiaoping, whose visit to Shenzhen in 1984 served to boost the development of special economic zones, paid a second visit to Shenzhen and Zhuhai just before the 1992 Spring Festival. In his remarks during this southern inspection, which were published as "Chinese Communist Party Central Document No. 2 (1992)," he called for acceleration of reform and liberalization (see Appendix 1). After receiving this document, the Party Central on May 16, 1992, convened an expanded meeting of the Politburo, adopted "Party Central Document No. 4," and disseminated it within the party (see Appendix 2.). This statement (see summary in Box 18.1) translated Deng Xiaoping's remarks into concrete policies for furthering the liberalization policy.

Newspapers in Hong Kong reported what transpired behind the scenes. The person responsible for drafting the document was actually Vice Premier Zhu Rongji. The document is divided into four sections, the second of which contained the concept of "a new multidirectional liberalization." This catchphrase was first introduced by Vice Premier Tian Jiyun in a lecture at the Central Party Academy (April 25, 1992). In his talk, Tian first pointed approvingly to the opening of the coastal region—the special economic zones and open cities. Then he advocated several measures: opening border regions; building special economic zones in the provinces and autonomous regions in the border regions of the northeast, northwest, and southwest; diversifying trade; opening riparian areas and developing Pudong as the "dragon head" to drive the opening to the outside of the entire Yangtze River; and establishing experimental special economic zones in the interior regions. Tian Jiyun severely criticized the attitude of leftists (con-

## Document Summary: CPC Document No. 4 (1992): Regional Policy for Promoting Reform and Liberalization

"Party Central Opinion Concerning Accelerating Reform, Expanding Liberalization, and Endeavoring to More Quickly and More Boldly Raise the Economy to a New Level"

*Series of New Measures to Reach a New Level of Opening to the Outside*

1. With development of the Pudong area of Shanghai as the "dragon head," reach a new level of expansion of the Yangtze River riparian cities of Wuhu, Jiujiang, Wuhan, Yueyang, and Chongqing; implement in these cities the same policies as in the open coastal cities.
2. Gradually open border cities and build a structure of openness to the outside in their vicinities. Slated for opening are four cities in Heihe (Heihe, Manzhouli, Suifenhe, Huichun), nine cities and counties in the Southwest and Northwest (namely, Pingxiangshi and Dongxingzhen in Guangxi; Hekouxian, Wandingshi, and Ruilixian in Yunnan; Yiningshi, Tachengshi, and Boleshi in Xinjiang; and Erenhot in Inner Mongolia).
3. In order to aggressively develop border trade with neighboring countries, open city policies shall be implemented in such cities as Harbin, Changchun, Huhehot, Urumchi, Kunming, and Nanning.
4. It is necessary to continue to realize the potential of special economic zones, open coastal cities, and development zones, boldly utilize foreign capital, and introduce technology.
5. Select one port city in each of the special economic zones, and in Shandong, Jiangsu, Zhejiang, and Fujian provinces, for building of a customs-free zone.
6. Strengthen the connections and influence of the coastal regions toward the interior. Fully realize the potential of the road transportation link to the southwestern region of Guangxi province. Speed up the pace of liberalization of the interior regions. Capitals of interior provinces and autonomous areas should undertake foreign capital projects and implement policies like those in the open coastal cities.
7. Carry out the policy of uniting preferential regional policies with preferential industrial policies, and expand the territory opened to the outside. In order to broaden the scope for utilization of foreign capital, utilize flexible methods to absorb more foreign capital from Hong Kong, Macao, and other sources. Major projects and high technology projects that have received basic State approval and are in line with industrial policies shall enjoy the preferential policies of the development zones, regardless of where the project is located. After appropriate testing, regions that can make direct use of foreign capital should gradually expand into such tertiary industries as finance, trade, commerce, transport, and tourism. A certain number of cities that have been specifically designated, are each authorized to approve one or two retail commercial enterprises invested by foreign banks and foreign capitalists. Shanghai can approve the operation of one foreign capital invested insurance company on an experimental basis.

Box 18.1

*Areas Where China Must Exert Efforts Now*

1. Develop Yangpu on Hainan Island.
2. Construct water conservancy, energy, transport, post and telecommunications, and raw materials projects.
3. Manage population relocation in the Three Gorges Dam region; expand experimental relocation. Complete the preparatory stages of the Three Gorges project. Establish a Three Gorges project commission under the State Council.
4. Accelerate the pace of development of Guangdong. Catch up to the level of Asia's four "little dragons" within 20 years. Establish in Guangdong province a strong, internationally competitive social economic system and externally-oriented economic marketplace. Make fuller use in international exchanges of relationship networks and spin-offs from other activities.

Source: Hong Kong *Ta Kong Pao*, June 19, 1992.

servatives): "The greatest task for the leading departments is to free themselves from the spell of leftist thinking. If this is not grasped, then reform and liberalization will be just empty talk. If this problem is not thoroughly resolved, it is to be doubted that reform and liberalization can continue" ("Red Leaders in Beijing in a Document Fever," Hong Kong's *Ta Kong Pao*, June 13, 1992).

Descriptive labels for the comments of different officials—Deng Xiaoping's remarks, Jiang Zemin's directives, Zhu Rongji's plans, Tian Jiyun's exhortations—give an indication of the varied lineup of people behind the policies. Along with the dissemination of the Party Central documents, the *People's Daily* launched an extensive publicity campaign. On June 9 General Secretary Jiang Zemin delivered a criticism of leftism at the Central Party Academy (*People's Daily*, June 15). The June 9 editorial discussed policy and described the key points: extension of the scope of liberalization "from the coastal regions to the (Yangtze) riparian and border regions" and explanation of the "multi-directional, multi-strata structure of opening to the outside world." The editorial noted that "the growing gap in development between the eastern regions and the western regions is affecting the overall unity of the nation, and having an influence on the strengthening of defenses along the borders." Thus, the positive evaluation of the liberalization policy in the coastal regions led to the campaign to expand in multiple directions (see Table 18.1 and Map 18.1).

## The Development of Shanghai's Pudong District

Excitement is rising concerning the development of the Pudong district of Shanghai municipality (population 1.1 million, area approximately 350 square kilome-

Table 18.1  Overview of Key Designated Cities in the Reform and Liberalization Program

| Region · Province / City Area | | ■ 4 Special economic zones (plus Hainan province) ● 14 Open coastal cities □ 14 Plan unit municipalities ◇ Interior provincial capitals | 25 open interior cities (along rivers, along borders) | Customs areas (Duty free in principle. 13, of which 9 were designated in 1992.) |
|---|---|---|---|---|
| Bohai Rim | Beijing | ◇ Beijing | | |
| | Tianjin | ● Tianjin | | Tianjin |
| | Hebei | ◇ Shijiazhuang  ● Qinhuangdao | | |
| | Shandong | □● Qingdao  ● Yantai | | Qingdao |
| | Liaoning | □ Shenyang  □● Dalian | Shenyang | Dalian |
| Yangtze River Delta | Shanghai | ● Shanghai | | Waigaoqiao |
| | Jiangsu | □ Nanjing ● Nantong ● Lianyungang | | Zhangjiagang |
| | Zhejiang | □● Ningbo  ● Wenzhou | | Ningbo |
| South China | Guang -dong | □● Guangzhou ● Zhanjiang | | Futian |
| | | □■ Shenzhen  ■ Zhuhai  ■ Shantou | | Shafoujiao |
| | Fujian | ● Fuzhou  □■ Xiamen | | Guangzhou |
| | Guangxi | ◇ Nanning  ● Beihai | Pingxiang | Shantou |
| | | | Dongxing | Xiamen, Fuzhou |
| | | | Nanning | |
| | Hainan | ■ Haikou | | Haikou |
| Yangtze River Basin | Anhui | ◇ Hefei | Wuhu | |
| | Jiangxi | ◇ Nanchang | Jiujiang | |
| | | | Nanchang | |
| | Hubai | ◇□ Wuhan | Wuhan, Yueyang | |
| | Hunan | ◇ Changsha | | |
| | Sichuan | ◇□ Chengdu □ Chongqing | | |
| North -east | Jilin | ◇□ Changchun | Hunchun | |
| | Heilong -jiang | ◇□ Harbin | Harbin, Heihe | |
| | | | Manzhouli | |
| | | | Suifenhe | |
| Yellow River Basin | Inner Mongolia | ◇ Huhehot | Erenhot | |
| | | | Huhehot | |
| | Henan | ◇ Zhengzhou | | |
| | Shanxi | ◇ Taiyuan | | |
| | Shaanxi | ◇□ Xian | | |
| Other | Guizhou | ◇ Guiyang | | |
| | Yunnan | ◇ Kunming | Ruili, Wanding | |
| | | | Kunming | |
| | | | Hekou | |
| | Gansu | ◇ Lanzhou | | |
| | Qinghai | ◇ Xining | Xining | |
| | Ningxia | ◇ Yinchuan | | |
| | Xinjiang | ◇ Urumchi | Yining, Bole | |
| | | | Tacheng | |
| | | | Urumchi | |

Sources: *China's Cities*, p. 5. Interior open cities listed in *People's Daily*, June 16, 19, 1992: customs zones, *People's Daily*, June 17, 1992.

Map 18.1 Map of Key Designated Cities in the Reform and Liberalization Program

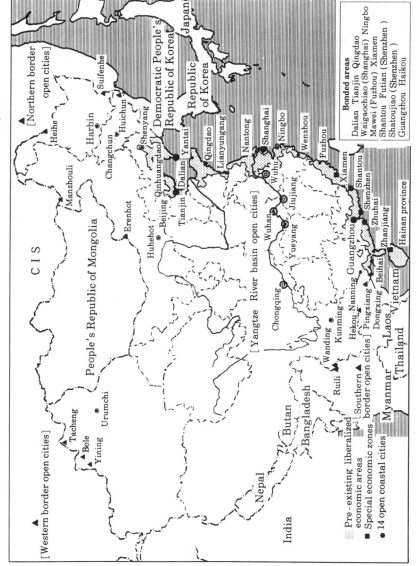

[Northern border open cities]

[Western border open cities]

C I S

People's Republic of Mongolia

Democratic People's Republic of Korea

Republic of Korea

Japan

Suifenhe
Heihe
Harbin
Manzhouli
Huichun
Changchun
Shenyang
Erenhot
Qinhuangdao
Yantai
Huhehot
Beijing
Tianjin
Dalian
Qingdao
Lianyungang
Nantong
Shanghai
Ningbo
Wenzhou
Fuzhou
Xiamen
Shantou
Shenzhen
Zhuhai
Beihai
Zhanjiang
Hainan province

[Yangtze River basin open cities]

Chongqing
Wuhan
Yueyang
Jiujiang
Wuhu
Guangzhou
Nanning
Hekou
Kunming
Pingxiang
Dongxing
Wanding
Ruili

[Southern border open cities]

Nepal
Butan
Bangladesh
India
Myanmar
Laos
Thailand
Vietnam

Tacheng
Bole
Yining
Urumchi

**Bonded areas**
Dalian  Tianjin  Qingdao
Waigaochiao (Shanghai)  Ningbo
Mawei (Fuzhou)  Xiamen
Shantou  Futian (Shenzhen )
Shatoujiao (Shenzhen )
Guangzhou  Haikou

▲ Pre-existing liberalized
    economic areas
■ Special economic zones
● 14 open coastal cities

ters) (Map 18.2). On July 18, 1992, Shanghai municipality unveiled a newly constructed 88-story office building; it displaced the recently completed Guangdong International Building (63 stories) as the tallest building in China. This construction activity symbolizes the yearning of Shanghai municipality to catch up with Guangdong province.

Foreign investment in the Pudong development area in 1991 is illustrated in Figure 18.1. Investment from domestic and foreign sources boomed in Pudong and greater Shanghai in 1992, and the momentum quickened in 1993. As for foreign investment, the most significant, from January to August 1993 Shanghai approved 2,606 new foreign-invested ventures and absorbed some $5.5 billion in foreign investment; this burst of activity brought the totals for 1992 through August 1993 to 5,895 cases and $12.2 billion. Some 702 or 12.4 percent of the ventures involved U.S. concerns (*Liberation Daily,* September 14, 1993).

The new Pudong development district comprises Waigaoqiao (75 square kilometers, 260,000 residents); Qingningsi (21 square kilometers, 340,000 residents); Lujiazui (28 square kilometers, 350,000 residents); Zhoujiadu (34 square kilometers, 400,000 residents); and Beicai (19 square kilometers, 350,000 residents). Waigaoqiao has planned to introduce high-technology and processing industries centered around its port and harbor facilities and to establish a customs-free zone, the first stage of which is already completed. Expansion of the zone is under way, as is accelerated development of the Lujiazui financial and trade zone.

Officials have decided to advance work on development of both sides of the Yanggao Road and construction of Pudong central thoroughfare and Pudong section of the Shanghai perimeter road. Preparations have begun on a subway line connecting Pudong and Puxi (the older developed part of the city on the western side of the Huangpu River), a second airport, a rail line within the new district, and new port construction. In addition, reform is proceeding apace in "soft sectors"—for example, development of a real estate market, conversion of enterprises to limited stock companies on an experimental basis, development of tertiary industries, and improvement in the financial securities market (*Liberation Daily,* June 14, 1992).

The Pudong development financial plan initially called for expenditure of RMB 50 billion by 1995, but recently this was raised to RMB 70 billion. This sum is supposed to be raised through debt issues by Shanghai municipality, stock issues by enterprises, borrowing from abroad, and direct investment from abroad. Shanghai municipality authorities have stated that the target has already been reached but that the total funds needed through the year 2000 will be RMB 200 billion.

To some extent Shanghai is still in the stranglehold of huge state-owned enterprises and has continued to evidence lukewarm enthusiasm for reform and liberalization and instead to defend the core tenets of the socialist planned economy. Against this background former mayor Zhu Rongji, who took the lead, Party Secretary Wu Bangguo, Mayor Huang Ju, and others have sought to advance development by playing both the "China card" (infusion of domestic capital) and the "world card" (infusion of foreign capital) (*Liberation Daily*, June 15, 1992).

# The Grand Project: Construction of the Three Gorges Dam

Constructing a dam in the Three Gorges of the Yangtze River is one of the long-cherished hopes of some Chinese people. Sun Yat-sen wrote of this vision in his *Strategy for National Construction* in 1918. The Kuomintang government reached the point of undertaking to select the location for the dam after completing geological studies in 1932. In 1944 a U.S. expert on dams, Dr. John L. Savage, carried out an on-site investigation and produced the famous "Savage Plan."

The Party Central met in Chengdu in 1958 to assess Three Gorges water conservancy and the Yangtze River long-term plan. Construction began on the Gezhouba dam downstream from the Three Gorges in the 1970s. As it was being completed in the 1980s, officials placed planning for the Three Gorges dam on the agenda. In March 1984 the State Council convened a briefing on feasibility of the project. The resulting report was adopted, and on this basis State Council Vice Premier Li Peng announced November 15, 1984, that foreign cooperation in the dam project would be "welcomed," and this stimulated active discussion inside and outside of China.

In spring 1985 at a meeting of the All-China Political Consultative Congress, a group of delegates voiced strong opposition to the dam project. Thereafter, the economic construction group of the Political Consultative Congress (PCC) carried out a thirty-eight-day on-site investigation and issued a report on problems with the Three Gorges project (July 1985). The group reported that the dam construction would "produce more damage than benefit," a conclusion that delivered a great shock.

In response, advocates of the dam project (members of the Construction Preparation Advisory Group of the China Three Gorges Project Development Corporation) frontally refuted the PCC's report by releasing their views against it (October 1985). As the debate burst into the open, the project became a great topic of discussion during meetings of the PCC and the National People's Congress in March 1986.

This stalemate was broken in one stroke with the great flood damage experienced in summer 1991 (Illustration 18.1). On March 21, 1992, Vice Premier Zou Jiahua (also director of the State Planning Commission) in his economic report officially proposed construction of the Three Gorges dam and offered a summary explanation. The plan envisages construction of the world's largest dam, some 2 kilometers wide and 185 meters high (the lower section of Illustration 18.1 is an

198

Map 18.2  Shanghai's Development Zones

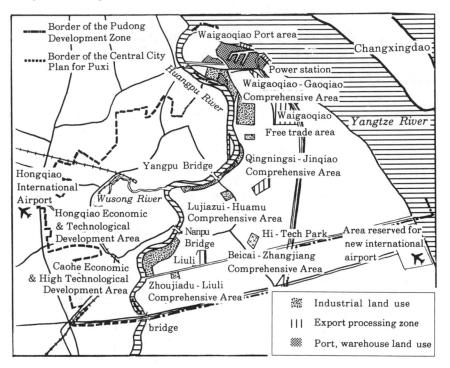

Figure 18.1  Situation of Foreign Investment in the Pudong Area (end 1991)

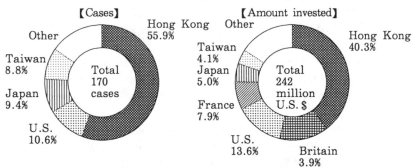

Source: Shanghai Government Office for Pudong Development
and Shanghai Municipality Government Foreign Affairs Office.

artist's conception of the completed dam). Water storage capacity would be 120 times greater than that of Japan's largest dam, Okutadami dam. The intention seemed to be to include the Three Gorges dam in the ten-year plan through 2000, but no mention was made of a concrete date for start of construction.

Proponents of the dam argue that the project technically is possible, and such benefits as flood control and power generation render it economically justifiable. Opponents claim the dam will be buried in silt, and water will back up all the way to Chongqing. Because of the reduction of water, seawater will flow upriver to Shanghai and the port of Shanghai will become unusable. Consequently, construction must be delayed until the problem of silt accumulation can be solved. The opponents raise the examples of the Gongzui dam on the Daduhe, the Huanglongtan dam on the Duhe of Hubei, and the Sanmenxia and Qingtongxia dams on the Yellow River to illustrate the severity of the silting problem. The obvious solution for the problem of flooding would be efforts to reforest the hills, but the pragmatic argument has prevailed that if construction on the dam is not undertaken quickly, further flooding of the Yangtze River will be unavoidable.

[Translator's note: China's openness to foreign assistance in the Three Gorges project can be explained by its enormous cost. On October 29, 1993, in Beijing, Guo Shuyuan, deputy director of the State Council Three Gorges Project construction commission, told journalists that the cost of the seventeen-year project is estimated at RMB 95.4 billion ($16.6 billion) at May 1993 constant prices. The project has three phases: Phase one, before the Yangtze River is actually contained, will take five years and cost RMB 19.5 billion. Phase two, to be completed when the first power station begins producing electricity, will take six years and cost RMB 34 billion. Phase three, ending with full project completion, will take six years and cost RMB 35 billion. In addition, RMB 6.9 billion will be needed to relocate people and enterprises from the area. The project will begin to earn substantial revenues from sales of electricity when the power plants come on stream. The problem is financing during the eleven years until then (*Nihon Keizai Shimbun*, October 30, 1993).]

# Opening of the Port Cities on the Yangtze River

Many Chinese who support liberalization and modernization embrace the concept of "T-shaped strategy." The concept is that the coastal regions are the horizontal line of the T, and the Yangtze River is the stem of the letter. This concept is actually rooted in China's history after the Opium War. The second half of the nineteenth century saw the same pattern of opening and commercial development beginning from coastal ports and then extending into China's interior via Yangtze River communications. Of course, unlike the case today, the driving forces behind the earlier development were Western powers.

To delineate the Yangtze River riparian area in terms of provinces, Shanghai, Jiangsu, and Zhejiang form the entrance that leads past Anhui and Jiangxi to Hubei and Hunan, then through the Three Gorges into Sichuan. Because the Yangtze River riparian area economic zone would include only about half of the Anhui, Jiangxi, Hubei, and Hunan provinces that border on the Yangtze banks, provincial-level statistics are not as useful as data at the region and county levels. Such data undoubtedly will be compiled in response to actual economic development.

The Shanghai delta region comprises fourteen cities (Shanghai, Nanjing, Suzhou, Wuxi, Changzhou, Nantong, Yangzhou, Zhenjiang, Hangzhou, Ningbo, Jiaxing, Huzhou, Shaoxing, and Zhoushan); the riparian region comprises twenty-two cities and regions (Maanshan, Wuhu, Tongling, Anqing, Chaohu, Chizhou, Jiujiang, Wuhan, Huangshi, Ezhou, Shashi, Jingmen, Yichang, Huanggang, Weining, Jingzhou, Yueyang, Changde, Yiyang, Chongqing, Wanxian, and Peiling) (Map 18.3). The two regions combined encompass 329,000 square kilometers, or 3.4 percent of China's total area, and have 14.7 percent of the total population, or 168 million persons (Xinhua News Agency Wire, June 28, 1992).

The Yangtze River is a natural transport artery. Shipping upriver requires substantial energy, and although it cannot compete with coastal transport, it is more economical than train or truck transport. In the early 1980s China's transport costs per kilometer were as follows: coastal transport RMB 3.6 per ton; Yangtze River main line transport RMB 7.5 per ton; railway transport RMB 8.9 per ton; and truck transport RMB 100–157 per ton (Wang Derong 1986, p. 14). (Costs of truck transport have declined substantially from this level as a result of improvements in roads.) In 1990 total transport volume was 2.6 trillion ton-kilometers. Of this, waterborne transport was 1.16 trillion ton-kilometers, or 44 percent of the total. The Yangtze River carried about one-third of total waterborne transport. Simply in terms of cost, it is easy to see the rationale for a strategy of advancing from the coastal region to the Yangtze River. There is some historical irony in this strategy: After the Opium War when the Western powers sought to open China, they advanced from the coastal region up the Yangtze River.

The five most active ports in the Yangtze River basin in order of volume of cargo handled are Nanjing, Wuhan, Nantong, Anqing, and Wuhu (Table 18.2). Next are Zhenjiang, Jiujiang, Chongqing, Zhangjiagang, and Huangshi. Also shown in the table are the number and length of berths, warehouse area, and units of handling equipment.

These ports all possess their own historical legacies. For example, since the Qing dynasty, Wuxi, Wuhu, Jiujiang, and Changsha have boasted the name of the "four great rice cities." Ningbo, Nanjing, Wuhan, and Chongqing are all "plan unit municipalities," a designation that gives them province-level status in terms of the plan and degree of autonomy. These principal ports have grown prosperous as the collection and distribution centers for materials produced in their respective regions. The expansion of market economic zones around these cities will fundamentally be determined by the transportation and shipping methods available.

Illustration 18.1   Flood Area of the Southern Bank of the Jingjiang
River in the Middle Reaches of the Yangtze River
and the Envisaged Completed Three Gorges Dam Area

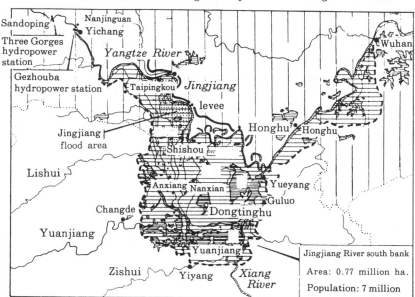

Map from *People's Daily,* January 4, 1992.
Envisaged completed dam sketch from *China Pictorial* April 4,
1992 issue.

# Dalian: Preferred Entry Point for Japanese Firms

Dalian city is situated on the southern tip of the Liaodong peninsula. It faces the Yellow Sea on the east and the Bohai gulf to the west, views Shandong province across the sea to the south, and connects to the northeast region to the north. Dalian is first and foremost the gateway to the northeast. At the same time it is an entry point to the north China region and also can provide access to east China via sea transportation (Map 18.4).

Dalian's opening to the outside started with the April 1984 decision on coastal cities. The following July Dalian was designated a plan unit municipality. Its pace of economic and technical development has been the fastest of all the fourteen coastal cities, and it has had great success in attracting enterprises. As of September 1991 there were 705 cases of foreign capital enterprise investment (387 of them in operation), of which 217 were Japanese firms (125 in operation) (Table 18.3).

Japanese firms have been particularly attracted to Dalian for several reasons:

1. The way of thinking of the Dalian municipal authorities, which was well represented by former mayor Wei Fuhai (later deputy general manager of China International Investment Trust Company), has been extremely progressive and farsighted.
2. Infrastructural arrangements such as ports and roads are advanced.
3. Machinery assembly processes are refined.
4. Japanese hold a certain kind of nostalgia toward Dalian (Mitsubishi Research Institute 1992, p. 228).

The northeast region of China, led by Dalian, has deep historical significance for the Japanese. A business group with particular interest in this region has been organized under the name Japan-China Northeast Development Association. It has published over eighty issues of its monthly magazine, *Japan-China Northeast.* This publication is something unseen in connection with any other region.

Companies recently entering the area include Ononda Cement, Nisshin Petroleum, and Canon in the equipment, materials, and electronic equipment industries, and the number of large-scale investments over $10 million is increasing. That these newly invested enterprises will be producing internationally competitive products is not to be doubted. Of Dalian's imports and exports, one-third are with Japan; such interaction suggests that Dalian will in the future become an increasingly critical base of a Japan Sea rim economic zone.

In the environs of Dalian are the industrial cities of Shenyang, Yingkou, Dandong, Anshan, and Jinzhou. These areas and cities together form the Liaodong economic development district, which constitutes a powerful component of the Bohai rim economic zone. Needless to say, the three economic zones of the Bohai rim, Shanghai (east China), and south China are the leading troika of China's modernization.

Map 18.3   Open Cities and Development Zones Along the Banks of
the Yangtze River

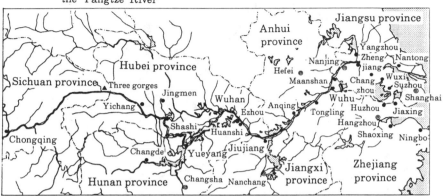

Table 18.2   Principal Ports on the Yangtze River (1985)

| Port name | Freight handing volume (million tons) | | | No. of berths | Length of berths (m) | Total warehouse area (m²) | Unloading equipment (units) |
|---|---|---|---|---|---|---|---|
| | Total volume | Exports | Imports | | | | |
| Nanjing | 36.6 | 26.1 | 10.5 | 30 | 2,274 | 150,404 | 353 |
| Wuhan | 14.8 | 6.4 | 8.4 | 32 | 1,930 | 401,096 | 452 |
| Nantong | 10.2 | 3.8 | 6.4 | 13 | 1,268 | 153,277 | 334 |
| Anqing | 5.9 | 2.8 | 3.2 | 22 | 1,015 | 24,751 | 101 |
| Wuhu | 5.6 | 4.1 | 1.6 | 41 | 1,552 | 106,564 | 121 |
| Zhenjiang | 5.9 | 1.1 | 4.8 | 20 | 1,702 | 80,167 | 372 |
| Jiujiang | 5.2 | 2.0 | 3.2 | 11 | 707 | 64,161 | 143 |
| Chongqing | 4.1 | 1.1 | 2.4 | 43 | 2,068 | 104,116 | 218 |
| Zhangjiagang | 3.4 | 1.7 | 1.7 | 7 | 968 | 121,482 | 227 |
| Huangshi | 3.1 | 2.3 | 0.8 | 26 | 1,094 | 33,890 | 118 |
| Chenglingji | 3.2 | 0.6 | 2.6 | 9 | 375 | 61,965 | 44 |
| Maanshan | 2.6 | 0.4 | 2.2 | 29 | 999 | 252,121 | 168 |
| Wuxue | 2.2 | 2.1 | 0.07 | 9 | 565 | 16,637 | 24 |
| Zhicheng | 1.7 | 1.4 | 0.4 | 24 | 1,566 | 62,173 | 64 |
| Wanxian | 1.5 | 0.9 | 0.6 | 17 | 948 | 41,981 | 36 |
| Shashi | 1.5 | 0.6 | 0.9 | 30 | 981 | 68,726 | 81 |
| Tongling | 1.4 | 0.6 | 0.8 | 12 | 606 | 40,770 | 65 |
| Chizhou | 1.4 | 0.8 | 0.6 | 17 | 851 | 102,800 | 36 |
| Yichang | 1.3 | 0.7 | 0.6 | 20 | 1,227 | 67,752 | 87 |
| Yangluo | 1.1 | 0.8 | 0.3 | 12 | 348 | 8,100 | 2 |
| Tongling | 0.6 | 0.4 | 0.2 | 11 | 493 | 10,526 | 12 |
| Honghu | 0.4 | 0.2 | 0.2 | 21 | 740 | 15,600 | 3 |
| Jianli | 0.3 | 0.1 | 0.2 | 8 | 313 | 6,023 | 6 |
| Badong | 0.3 | 0.2 | 0.1 | 7 | 352 | 6,900 | 18 |
| Total | 114.3 | 61.2 | 52.8 | 471 | 24,942 | 2,001,982 | 3,085 |

Note: Chenglingji includes Yueyang municipality.
Source: *Contemporary China's Water Transport Industry* (Beijing:
Chinese Social Sciences Press, 1989), p. 91.

204

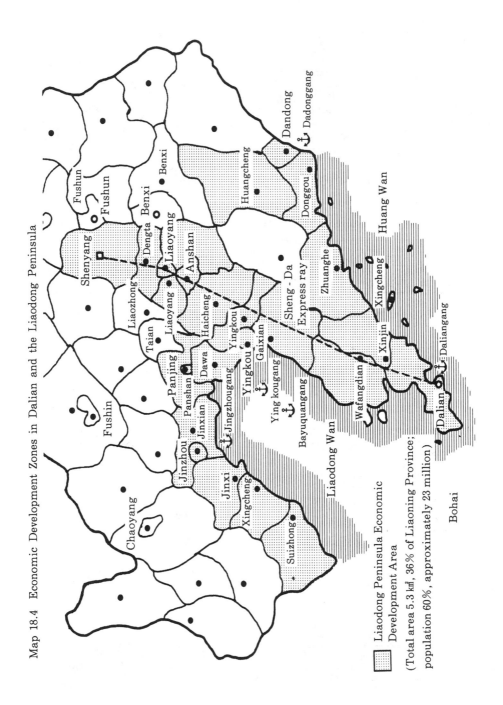

Map 18.4  Economic Development Zones in Dalian and the Liaodong Peninsula

Liaodong Peninsula Economic Development Area

(Total area 5.3 k㎡, 36% of Liaoning Province; population 60%, approximately 23 million)

# The UN's Transnational Plan for the Tumen River

On July 6 and 7, 1991, the United Nations Development Program (UNDP) held its Asia region planning conference in Ulam Bator, Mongolia. Attending this conference were China, South Korea, North Korea, and Mongolia. The principal topic of discussion was the development plan for the Tumen River region (Map 18.5). The event marked a milestone of the countries of East Asia—where the Cold War geopolitical structure was in the process of being dismantled—coming together for a common purpose through the initiative of the United Nations.

Three months later (October 16–18, 1991) another conference of countries concerned with development of the Tumen River basin was held under UNDP sponsorship in Pyongyang and was attended by China, North Korea, and the former Soviet Union, among others. The outlines of the Tumen River basin development initiative, based on the advance investigative mission report presented at the conference, are generally as follows:

- The Tumen River delta area occupies an important strategic position in international trade. Its position provides access to the labor and natural resources of China's Jilin and Heilongjiang provinces, Russian Siberia, North Korea, and Mongolia. It is near Japan and South Korea, and access to Europe is not difficult.
- For the resources of the northeast Asian region and their supplementation, the Tumen River delta area will in the future become a materials collection and distribution port like Hong Kong, Singapore, or Rotterdam.
- The UNDP has received the official request of the four countries of the area (China, North Korea, Russia, and Mongolia) to perform the role of facilitator to realize these objectives through regional cooperation.
- The views presented by the participants were preliminary, and there were major differences among them. Consequently, all the participants are reconsidering the objectives they wish to pursue. An approach that tries to maximize the interests of all parties is desirable.
- The issues for the time being are to secure the approximately $30 billion required for long-term development (social infrastructure in the area $13 billion, transport infrastructure $11 billion, education $1 billion, preparation expenses $5 billion); to avoid unnecessary or costly redundant facilities; and to avoid unprofitable or harmful competition.

The report proposed as the next step starting a regional project with the backing of the UNDP. This regional project should be placed under management of a committee made up of senior representatives of five or six nations (the above-mentioned four countries plus Japan and South Korea) and the UNDP. Under this committee would be four subcommittees: (1) trade and interior assistance

Table 18.3 Situation of Direct Investment in Dalian and Other Key Coastal Cities by Country or Region of Origin (1990 year end aggregate figure contract base in U.S. $ million, %)

| | Dalian | | Tianjin | | Shanghai | | Xiamen special zone | | Shenzhen special zone | |
|---|---|---|---|---|---|---|---|---|---|---|
| | Cases | Amount | Cases | Amount | Cases | Amount | Cases | Amount | Cases | Amount |
| Japan | 159 (29.9) | 555 (35.2) | 93 (16.8) | 157 (13.7) | 128 (14.1) | 407 (14.4) | 26 ( 2.8) | 62 ( 2.5) | 154 ( 2.0) | 440 ( 7.1) |
| Hong Kong Macao | 241 (45.3) | 419 (26.6) | 289 (51.8) | 526 (45.9) | 450 (49.5) | 781 (27.6) | 468 (50.6) | 1552 (62.9) | 7181 (93.4) | 4557 (73.7) |
| U.S. | 41 ( 7.7) | 190 (12.0) | 64 (11.6) | 168 (14.6) | 122 (13.4) | 715 (25.2) | 30 ( 3.2) | 92 ( 3.7) | 118 ( 1.5) | 216 ( 3.5) |
| E.C. | 12 ( 2.3) | 52 ( 3.3) | 32 ( 5.8) | 93 ( 8.1) | 51 ( 5.6) | 392 (13.8) | 4 ( 0.4) | 30 ( 1.2) | 63 ( 0.8) | 248 ( 4.0) |
| Taiwan | 53 (10.0) | 52 ( 3.3) | 31 ( 5.6) | 24 ( 2.1) | n.a. | n.a. | 322 (34.8) | 519 (21.0) | 78 ( 1.0) | 72 ( 1.2) |
| South Korea | 8 ( 1.5) | 10 ( 0.6) | 6 ( 1.1) | 13 ( 1.1) | n.a. | n.a. | n.a. | n.a. | n.a. | n.a. |
| Others | 18 ( 3.4) | 299 (19.0) | 40 ( 7.2) | 166 (14.5) | 159 (17.5) | 537 (19.0) | 74 ( 8.0) | 211 ( 8.6) | 92 ( 1.2) | 650 (10.5) |
| Total | 532 (100.0) | 1577 (100.0) | 552 (100.0) | 1147 (100.0) | 950 (100.0) | 2832 (100.0) | 924 (100.0) | 2466 (100.0) | 7686 (100.0) | 6183 (100.0) |

Source: *Economic Development of Dalian and the Liaodong Peninsula* (Tokyo: Japan - China Northeastern Development Association, 1991), p. 129.

Map 18.5 Map of the Tumen River Basin

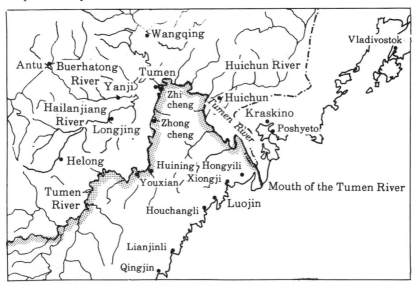

Table 18.4  Complementarity of Interests for Northeast Asian Countries Concerned in Development of the Tumen River Basin Area

| Country or Area | Endowments | Deficiencies |
|---|---|---|
| Japan | Capital savings, advanced technology. Large volume of high tech equipment could be immediately transferred quickly. Experience in management and pioneering manufacturing. | Severe shortages of energy and industrial resources. Shortage of grain for animal feed and some agricultural products, relative shortage of labor. |
| Russian Far East Region | Abundance of forests, non-ferrous metal ores, crude oil, gas, coal, certain heavy chemical and industrial products (including steel and fertilizer). | Severe shortage of agricultural products and light industrial products. Shortages of capital. Backward industrial equipment and management technology. |
| Chinese Northeast Region | Advantageous agricultural conditions. Sufficient and varied agricultural products (including corn, soybeans, meat, and fruit); certain textile products; crude oil, coal, building materials, herbal medicine, excess labor resources. | Shortages of capital, advanced equipment and technology and management experience. Relative inadequacy of certain mineral resources and developed infrastructure. |
| North Korea | Abundant mineral resources, metal ores, crude manufactures, aquatic products, and certain manufactured goods. Abundant labor resources. | Shortage of capital. Shortages of secondary light manufactures in connection with shortage of agricultural products. Backward equipment and technology. |
| South Korea | Excess capital, advanced technology, transferable equipment, pioneering industrial products. | Shortages of energy and industrial resources. Shortages of animal feed. Shortages of labor resources. |
| Mongolia | Abundant animal products and minerals, ores, especially fluorspar. | No convenient method of directly communicating with other countries in Northeast Asia. Shortages of capital, technology, equipment, agricultural products, and light industrial products. |

Original source: Chen Cal, Yuan Shuren, Wang Li, Ding Sibao, "*Regional Cooperation in Development of Northeast Asia and the Lower Tumen River Delta Area,*" Second Northeast Asian Economic and Technological Geographical Research Institute, Jilin Provincial Northeast Normal University.

Source: JETRO, *The Chinese Economy,* November 1991 (translation from the original source).

services, (2) electrical equipment, (3) banking services, and (4) industrial and infrastructure investment strategy.

Notwithstanding that the pros and cons are still rather nebulous, this project obviously symbolizes the transformation from Cold War confrontation to an age of dialogue and understanding (Table 18.4).

# 19

# Managing Growth and Reform in 1993: Transition to the Post-Deng Era

## Deng Xiaoping Unleashes Faster Growth, Then Overheating, in 1992 and 1993

### Deng Counterattacks Conservative "Leftists"

From January 18 to February 21, 1992, Deng Xiaoping, accompanied by his family, went on an inspection tour of southern China. He visited Wuchang in Hubei province, the Shenzhen and Zhuhai special economic zones in Guangdong province, and Shanghai. Wherever he went, in a way reminiscent of the gestures and style of Mao Zedong, he appealed for acceleration of reform and liberalization (see Appendix 1). In his calls to "boldly advance with giant strides" and "not proceed like a bound-footed woman," and in the use of terms like "adventurous spirit" and "courage of making breakthroughs and conducting experiments," Deng's presentations were very much like those of Mao Zedong.

Deng Xiaoping's southern tour and attendant talks were essentially the manifestations and means of mounting a frontal counterattack against conservatives who were assaulting him and his line. We can organize his main points as follows.

First, Deng specifically rejected the "peaceful evolution" shibboleth being used by the conservatives. "Peaceful evolution" was the term used by U.S. Secretary of State John Foster Dulles to describe the strategic objective of "containment" against China. The strategic concept was that the socialist system would eventually be subverted by peaceful—that is, economic—means. Mao Zedong repeatedly emphasized this danger, and Mao's mantle was assumed by the conservative faction whose members wanted to debate the issue of "capitalism or socialism in name." Specifically, they wanted to examine thoroughly which ideology the reform and liberalization line represented. In the unusually threatening circumstances of the dismantling of the former Soviet Union, the conservatives elevated the visibility of their concerns about the direction China was taking. Against this barrage Deng Xiaoping countered that there would be no survival for the Communist Party as a leading party unless it could garner the support of the masses through achieving economic development via the reform and liberalization policy. He stressed that the standard against which to judge the correctness of a policy was whether it was beneficial in developing productive forces, whether it was advantageous in strengthening overall national power, and whether it was efficacious in raising the people's living standards. This was a repackaging of the former "White Cat, Black Cat" doctrine into a so-called New Cat theory.

Second, Deng attempted to reject the concept of stable growth embraced by the conservatives and to substitute his own belief in high growth. During the more than ten years of the Deng Xiaoping era, the period of greatest advancement in reform and liberalization was the second half of the 1980s when Hu Yaobang and Zhao Ziyang were carrying out the struggle on the front line. Notwithstanding this, Deng Xiaoping congratulated himself on the economic growth achievement of the period 1984–1988, stating that agricultural production and the income of peasants recorded great increases, and the township and village enterprises appeared out of nowhere. The "four sacred treasures"—bicycles, sewing machines, radios, and wristwatches—appeared in peasant households. Deng noted that industry was growing at over 20 percent a year. The production of color televisions, electric refrigerators, and washing machines was growing by wide margins, and the production of such goods as steel and cement was also growing dramatically. At the same time, he berated as "merely achieving stability" the record of the three-year period of economic readjustment (1988–1991) after the Tiananmen incident under the Jiang Zemin and Li Peng regime.

Deng's third point was the handling of the problem of disparities in economic development. Deng Xiaoping encouraged people to "get rich ahead of others" and thus was tolerant of regional and income disparities. He was criticized for this by conservatives who held fast to a line of egalitarianism, but he had a pragmatic response: "We must not kill the vitality of the regions that have already developed. It will be enough to turn our attention to resolving this problem when we have reached a level of being well off by the end of this century. When we reach that point, the developed areas can support the backward regions with a lot of profits, taxes and transfers of technology." Implied in these remarks is that for the time being—until the end of the twentieth century—development can only be expected for the coastal regions. Deng's point was that there is no effective policy for dealing with the problem of regional disparities. In this kind of debate, Deng is frank.

In sum, Deng's position in this debate essentially was that in China only "leftism" must be guarded against. To those who were attacking his line as "rightist," Deng attached the label "leftist."

Deng's 1992 southern excursion was brilliantly successful in reviving his reform and liberalization line after it was inevitably set back by the shock of the dismemberment of the Soviet Union. It was in this heady mood that the Fourteenth Party Congress met in October 1992 and the leadership that would take China into the post-Deng era was selected. Indeed, the theme, centering on the concept of the "socialist market economy," of the political report given by the elected general secretary, Jiang Zemin, was similar in its section on economic reform to the report delivered by Zhao Ziyang to the Thirteenth Party Congress. Now the renaissance of economic reform was clear to all.

## Economic Performance in 1993

After the Tiananmen incident, with the exception of certain areas of Guangdong and Shandong provinces, reform and liberalization had stagnated nationwide. Against this background, publication of Deng's talks caused a great stir both inside and outside China, emboldening local interests to resume economic expansion. In the summer of 1992 a great swell arose in the Chinese economy, and its momentum carried over through 1993.

Table 19.1 presents statistics for 1993, as well as updated revised statistics for previous years to 1984, from the State Statistical Bureau (*People's Daily*, March 1, 1994). China's GNP grew at a spectacular real rate of 13.4 percent in 1993; this followed the equally outstanding performance of 13.0 percent in 1992. Even if we assume a measure of padding in these figures, in the context of a global economic recession, China's economic vitality was remarkable.

Particularly noteworthy was the dramatic increase in the introduction of foreign capital. Foreign confidence in China's continued reform and liberalization was such in 1992 that some $69.4 billion was committed to China under contracts (both investments and loans), more than three times the figure in 1991. For 1993 the foreign capital commitments totaled $122 billion, more than double the previous year. This level of capital commitment (which was mostly for direct investment) established China as the most attractive new market in the world for investment. Actual capital inflows were $36.4 billion in 1993, up from $19.2 billion in 1992.

Economic growth in the second half of 1992 and all of 1993 was generated in large part from the pull of exceedingly rapid growth of fixed capital investment (public works investment and nonstate equipment investment). Fixed asset investment grew by 42.6 percent in 1992 and by 50.6 in 1993. Principal contributors were construction of development zones established in 1992 and investments in real estate and housing. Much of this investment was wasteful and unplanned and constituted speculation in an increasingly overheated economy. This situation called for the government's efforts to reassert macro control in July 1993 (discussed later in this chapter). As further evidence that the overheating resulted from investment, not consumer demand, the index of consumer goods sales

Table 19.1  China's High Economic Growth (1984 - 1993)

| Year | GNP & Population | | | Supply | Demand | |
|---|---|---|---|---|---|---|
| | GNP growth | Per capita GNP growth | Growth in population | Growth in industrial output | Growth in fixed assets investment | Growth in consumer goods sales (index) |
| | % | % | % | % | % | % |
| 1984 | 14.7 | 13.4 | 1.30 | 16.3 | 28.1 | 18.5 |
| 1985 | 12.8 | 11.4 | 1.42 | 21.4 | 38.8 | 27.5 |
| 1986 | 8.1 | 6.6 | 1.55 | 11.7 | 18.7 | 15.0 |
| 1987 | 10.9 | 9.2 | 1.66 | 17.7 | 20.6 | 17.6 |
| 1988 | 11.3 | 9.7 | 1.57 | 20.8 | 23.5 | 27.8 |
| 1989 | 4.4 | 2.9 | 1.50 | 8.5 | -8.0 | 8.9 |
| 1990 | 4.1 | 2.7 | 1.43 | 7.8 | 7.5 | 2.5 |
| 1991 | 8.2 | 6.9 | 1.29 | 14.8 | 23.8 | 13.4 |
| 1992 | 13.0 | 11.8 | 1.16 | 27.5 | 42.6 | 16.8 |
| 1993 | 13.4 | 12.4 | 1.14 | 21.1 | ·50.6 | 11.3 |
| Average | 10.0 | 8.6 | 1.14 | 16.8 | 24.6 | 15.9 |

| | Prices | | External Accounts | | | |
|---|---|---|---|---|---|---|
| | Wholesale - Overall retail prices (index) | Consumer - Urban residents living cost | Growth in exports | Growth in imports | Foreign capital imports | |
| | | | | | contract base | actual base |
| | % | % | % | % | (in US$ billions) | |
| 1984 | 2.8 | 2.7 | 17.6 | 28.1 | 4.8 | 2.7 |
| 1985 | 8.8 | 11.9 | 4.6 | 54.1 | 9.8 | 4.6 |
| 1986 | 6.0 | 7.0 | 13.1 | 1.5 | 11.7 | 7.3 |
| 1987 | 7.3 | 8.8 | 27.5 | 0.7 | 12.1 | 8.4 |
| 1988 | 18.5 | 20.7 | 20.5 | 27.9 | 16.0 | 10.2 |
| 1989 | 17.8 | 16.3 | 10.6 | 7.0 | 11.5 | 10.1 |
| 1990 | 2.1 | 1.3 | 18.2 | -9.8 | 12.1 | 10.3 |
| 1991 | 2.9 | 5.1 | 15.7 | 19.6 | 19.6 | 11.6 |
| 1992 | 5.4 | 8.6 | 18.3 | 26.4 | 69.4 | 19.2 |
| 1993 | 13.0 | 14.7 | 8.0 | 29.0 | 122.0 | 36.4 |
| Average | 8.5 | 9.7 | 16.2 | 18.5 | 289.0 | 120.8 |

Note: Chinese "overall retail price index" is used as most proximate indicator of wholesale prices, as prices to producers are included. Foreign capital includes loans and direct investment. Final capital figures are aggregate totals.

Sources: 1993: announcement of the State Statistical Bureau, *People's Daily*, March 1, 1994. 1984 - 1992: *Statistical Year Book of China 1993*, p. 413 for industry, p. 145 for fixed assets, p. 611 for retail sales of consumer goods, p. 237 for national retail price index, p. 633 for imports and exports, p. 647 for foreign capital imports.

showed an increase of 16.8 percent (high, but far lower than investment) in 1992 and a slightly lower 11.3 percent in 1993.

As for external relations, in 1993 imports increased 29.0 percent after an increase of 26.4 percent in 1992. Against this strong growth there was a problematic decline in the growth rate for exports. In 1993 exports grew a disappointing 8.0 percent, down from 18.3 percent in 1992. Some of this decline is attributable to strong internal demand for goods, which decreased availability for export.

Rapid growth has been dramatically shaking the society of "China, the sleeping giant," but the greatest problems, as previously noted, are inflation induced by overheating and official corruption. From mid-1992 through most of 1993, shortages of raw materials and energy and choked transportation became more evident, and inflation intensified, reaching double-digit levels in the cities. During the first half of 1993 the Chinese economy began to acquire the character of a dangerously expanding bubble.

## The Great Wall Electrical Equipment Technology Company Fraud Incident

One highly publicized fraud case involved Shen Taifu of the Great Wall Electrical Equipment Technology Company of Beijing (the Great Wall Company), who formed this shell company and proceeded to illegally accumulate RMB 800 million from 200,000 investors in seventeen cities around the country. Shen Taifu was originally a cadre in Siping municipality in Jilin province. He tried to form a company there but only accumulated debts. He moved to Beijing, and in May 1992 he enticed many investors by ostensibly offering "technical development" and promising a rate of return of 24 percent a year. As funds came in, he became wealthy and adopted a life-style to match: high-class apartment, expensive foreign cars, bodyguards, and so on.

In March 1993 the People's Bank of China charged that the purpose of the Great Wall Company's collections of funds was unclear and froze the company's deposit account. Shen Taifu responded by suing the People's Bank and even held a press conference charging that its actions were impeding his company's business operations. While pursuing this diversionary operation in court, Shen planned to flee the country under a false name. He was arrested at the airport, and the bubble burst. There was additional fallout in this case: The deputy chairman of the State Science and Technology Commission, Li Xiaoshi, and the *People's Daily* economics department director were arrested on the charge of taking bribes for arranging for the swindler to meet with the chairman of the State Science and Technology Commission, Song Jian. In revealing the defects and pitfalls of a financial system that has not adapted to the needs of a market economy, this case is an excellent lesson by counterexample of acute contradictions in the Chinese economy (*People's Daily*, July 31, 1993, report).

Perhaps the final words on this case will be from the spokesman for the Beijing Municipal Middle Court, who announced on March 8, 1994, that the court had meted out the death sentence for Shen Taifu. The court sentenced Li Xiaoshi to twenty years in prison (*Mainichi Shimbun*, March 4, 1994).

# Zhu Rongji Grasps for Macro Control of the Economy

## Shakeup at the People's Bank

On July 2, 1993, it was announced that the second session of the Standing Committee of the Eighth National People's Congress had decided to dismiss Li Guixian as governor of the People's Bank and to place Vice Premier Zhu Rongji concurrently in the position. In the same action, Zhou Zhengqing was promoted to first deputy governor (while concurrently party committee secretary) to assist Zhu Rongji in the task of bringing financial disruption under control. Two deputy governors, Guo Zhenqian and Tong Zengyin, were charged with responsibility for the financial turmoil and were dismissed. They were reassigned, respectively, to positions of deputy auditor general of the State Audit Administration and deputy director of the State Securities Commission (Table 19.2).

Selected to replace the dismissed bankers were Dai Xianglong (former general manager of the Bank of Communications), Wang Qishan (former deputy head of the People's Construction Bank of China and son-in-law of the conservative leader Yao Yilin), and Zhu Xiaohua (previously from the economics department of the Hong Kong branch of the Xinhua News Agency). Among these, the selection of Zhu Xiaohua received the most attention. Zhu Rongji had become acquainted with Zhu Xiaohua when the former was mayor of Shanghai and the latter was deputy head of the Shanghai branch of the People's Bank. With Zhu Rongji's sponsorship, Zhu Xiaohua spent a year studying at the IMF in New York and subsequently returned to Hong Kong to get practical experience in international finance. Zhu Xiaohua serves as Zhu Rongji's right hand in implementing international financial policies. Two other deputy governors, Chen Yuan and Bai Wenqing, were retained because it was concluded that in their positions they could not have shared in the responsibility for the financial chaos.

## Party Central Document No. 6

After the major changes in the leadership ranks of the People's Bank, Zhu Rongji convened a national work conference July 5–7, 1993. The conference's deliberations were summarized in the "Three Simple Rules."

1. All illegal lending must be stopped immediately and this practice must be strictly rooted out. Illegally lent funds must be recovered through loan callbacks within specified time periods.

Table 19.2   Leadership Changes at the People's Bank of China (July 1993)

| | Old Leadership | New Leadership |
|---|---|---|
| Governor | Li Guixian (dismissed; retained membership in State Council) | Zhu Rongji (concurrently vice premier) |
| Deputy governor | Guo Zhenqian (dismissed; appointed deputy auditor general of the State Auditing Administration) | Zhou Zhengqing (first deputy governor, secretary of Party Committee) |
| | Tong Zengyin (dismissed; appointed deputy director of State Securities Commission) | Dai Xianglong (former general manager of Bank of Communications) |
| | Zhou Zhengqing | Wang Qishan (former deputy head of the People's Construction Bank of China) |
| | Chen Yuan | Zhu Xiaohua (former general manager of economics department of Xinhua News Agency, Hong Kong Branch) |
| | Bai Wenqing | Chen Yuan (retained, eldest son of Chen Yun) |
| | | Bai Wenqing (retained) |

Table 19.3   Positive Market Reaction to Financial Rectification Breaks RMB's Decline

| Locality | July 1 | July 2 | July 5 | RMB appreciation July 1-5 |
|---|---|---|---|---|
| Shenzhen | 10.650 | 10.355 | 8.500 | 20.1% |
| Zhejiang | 10.740 | 10.150 | 9.500 | 9.2% |
| Shanghai | 10.398 | 10.344 | 9.557 | 8.0% |
| Beijing | 10.744 | 10.520 | 10.300 | 4.1% |
| Fujian | 10.300 | 10.300 | 9.890 | 3.9% |
| Chengdu | 10.755 | 10.735 | 10.726 | 0.2% |

Note: RMB per U.S. dollar.
Source: Hong Kong *Ming Po,* July 6, 1993.

2. No financial institution of any kind will be permitted to covertly raise loan interest rates, nor will raising deposit rates in order to compete for deposits be permitted. Acceptance of commissions from borrowers is prohibited.

3. Banks must immediately desist from lending to economic organizations of whatever kind that have been set up by the banks. Banks should completely sever ties to such economic organizations (*People's Daily,* July 10, 1993).

We can infer much about the state of turmoil in China's financial system from Zhu Rongji's three rules. The first rule called for cessation and recall of illegal loans. This measure took aim at the incidents increasingly evident since 1992 of persons obtaining short-term bank loans through personal connections and using the proceeds to speculate in stocks and real estate and to trade commodity futures.

The purpose of the second rule was to stabilize deposit and loan interest rates and stop inappropriate competition. At the same time, interest rates were raised again July 10 (they had been raised the previous May 15) in order to attract deposits broadly and to restrain lending. The new rates announced were 3.15 percent for regular savings deposits (up from 2.16 percent in May), 10.98 percent for one-year time deposits (up from 9.18 percent), and 10.98 percent for loans (up from 9.36 percent).

The third rule aimed to shut down speculative nonbanking enterprises set up by banks and aggressively funded (incidentally lining the pockets of many people) after liberalization resumed in 1992. "Economic organizations of whatever kind" refers to a range of structures, from shell companies to speculative investment companies. Many individuals took advantage of the pace of organizational change to establish bogus companies in order to receive bank funds.

Participants in the "grey" market for foreign exchange in China responded positively to Zhu Rongji's decisive personnel actions and his three rules, and the theretofore depreciating RMB began to stabilize. Changes in the rates in the main national foreign exchange adjustment centers in early July are indicated in Table 19.3.

Before Zhu Rongji undertook his financial rectification program, the rate of exchange between U.S. dollars and RMB in the major foreign exchange adjustment centers nationwide was 10.755 RMB/dollar at the lowest and 10.398 RMB/dollar at the highest. After the new policies were communicated July 5, the RMB appreciated as much as 20 percent in Shenzhen and about 10 percent in such places as Shanghai and Zhejiang. At the end of August, the rate was at about 8.8 RMB/dollar. By the end of 1993 the floating RMB rate had been so firmly established in the 8.6–8.8 range that no significant change was seen when the "official rate" was abolished and all transactions were unified versus the floating rate from January 1, 1994.

On July 10 Zhu Rongji convened the second meeting of the State Council and disseminated the new policy of "macro control" to all the leading departments and organs under the State Council. The policy, quickly termed "The Sixteen Points," was disseminated as Chinese Communist Party Central Committee Document No. 6 (1993) (see summary in Box 19.1). At the same time, he dispatched Central Investigation Teams to all twenty province-level units nationwide, thus establishing a system to ensure that necessary tasks would be thoroughly carried out (*People's Daily,* July 11, 1993). Next he convened several conferences. On July 11 at the National Conference on Agricultural Financial Work he delivered an important speech calling for rectification of agricultural finance (*People's Daily,* July 12, 1993). Subsequently, July 20–23, he addressed the National Conference on Gov-

# Summary of CPC Document No. 6 (1993)
## Rectification of Financial Policy

1.    All specialized bank must call in unauthorized loans by the deadline set. They must not exceed the ceiling on loans stipulated by the People's Bank of China.

2.    All localities should fulfill their tasks for purchasing treasury bonds before July 15.

3.    Interest rates of savings deposits will be raised beginning July to resolve the problem of funds circulating outside the system. (Implemented July 11.)

4.    Financial institutions should liquidate loans made to non-bank institutions within the time limit set.

5.    Government organs should cut administrative expenses by 20 percent and restrict group purchasing power. Importation of automobiles during the second half of 1993 will be basically prohibited.

6.    Apart from those directives already issued, new price reform measures will be suspended during the second half of the year.

7.    Funds for summer grain purchase and spring farming should be ensured; it is forbidden to issue new IOUs to peasants.

8.    All social fund-raising schemes not standardized since 1992 should be weeded out.

9.    Development zones in all areas should be rationalized. Laws, regulations, and control over real estate should be completed and perfected. Real estate development companies in all places must sell 20 percent of their homes to residents at low prices.

10.    Investment scales of capital construction projects should be reduced.

11.    Enterprises that have implemented a joint stock company system and are scheduled to sell stock on the market should do so step by step according to state rules. They must not come onto the market at one time.

12.    The system of the state collecting a portion of foreign exchange and foreign exchange settlements for exporting enterprises are to be improved.

13.    Specialized banks should differentiate commercial lending and loans made according to state plans. Funds for agricultural lending and priority state construction projects must be ensured.

14.    The People's Bank of China must strengthen its functions as the Central Bank, and effectively carry out macro control.

15.    Bottlenecks in the transportation system should be realistically resolved.

16.    The central government will dispatch work teams to all areas to carry out inspections.

Sources:    Newspaper reports, especially *Ming Po*, Hong Kong, July 1993.

Box 19.1

ernment Financial Work and the National Conference on Taxation Work in Beijing. At these meetings, which brought together finance and taxation bureau chiefs from all province-level units and planning-unit municipalities and responsible persons from all related organs under the State Council, Zhu Rongji pointed out that in the first half of 1993 the growth of government revenues had fallen far below the growth of GNP. The reasons for this decline were (1) unauthorized reductions or exemptions of taxes; (2) collection of circulation taxes; and (3) lack of diligence in tax collection. In addition, while asserting that the basic policy must be financial and taxation reform, Zhu Rongji called for a "great investigation of tax collection and financial work" in financial and taxation departments at all levels, meeting sales targets for national bonds, and ensuring sufficiency of funds for priority national projects. Specifically, Zhu attached the label "antiquated method incompatible with the market economy" to the existing taxation system of "consolidating everything and dividing the whole" (the contract-based system for dividing total revenues according to a predetermined ratio between the central and provincial governments). He called for government financial system reform according to four principles:

1.  Establish a new government financial and taxation system after duly considering the successful methods of market economy countries.
2.  Carry out a "divided taxation system" for the central and regional governments—separately collect and manage central government taxes and regional government taxes. (See Chapter 11 for comments of Vice Minister of Finance Xiang Huaicheng on the new system that was implemented January 1, 1994.)
3.  Clarify the functions of government finance. Make devolution of authority for government expenditures the basic concept, clearly differentiate types of taxes, and guarantee necessary expenditures by the central government.
4.  Delimit the distributional relationships between the government and enterprises on the basis of the "enterprise accounting standards" and the "enterprise financial conventions."

Zhu stated that until reform of the financial system could be implemented under these four principles, government financial and taxation organs would be subject to emergency measures in accordance with the following dictates:

1.  Strictly control reductions of or exemptions from taxes. Both the recipient and the perpetrator of unauthorized tax reductions or exemptions will be held accountable for their actions.
2.  Strictly control government expenditures. Cease the practice of "putting it on the bank's account." Government deficits should be met by the issuance of government bonds; resort must not be taken to the method of receiving subsidies from banks.

3.  Henceforth, government financial and taxation departments will not be permitted to engage in commercial financial operations without receiving permission from the People's Bank of China. Government financial departments must, within the time period set, sever ties with all types of companies engaged in financial activities (*People's Daily*, July 24, 1993).

Under the program of macro control personally directed by Zhu Rongji, the growth rate of industrial production in July 1993 compared with the previous July was held to 25.1 percent, down 5.1 percentage points from June. The number of fixed capital investment projects also declined, and the real estate and development zone booms appeared to be cooling (*People's Daily*, August 20, 1993, report of the State Statistical Bureau). The plan was to achieve a change in the overheated economy by the end of the year and thus to celebrate a victory for the Deng Xiaoping line on the fifteenth anniversary of the decision of the Third Plenum of the Eleventh Party Congress on reform and liberalization.

## The Future of Zhu Rongji's Macro Control

Zhu Rongji was elevated to the position of vice premier in spring 1991. In that year he immersed himself in resolving the problem of "triangle debt." At the Fourteenth Party Congress in fall 1992 he became a member of the Politburo's Standing Committee, and at the Eighth National People's Congress in March 1993 he was reelected vice premier. However, in the context of the political structure of "supporting the regime of (general secretary) Jiang Zemin and (premier) Li Peng," Zhu Rongji's position in the State Council was ambiguous. Li Peng made assignments of responsibility at a plenary session of the State Council on April 10, 1993, but Zhu Rongji's position was still not clarified. Indeed, on the one hand, Li Peng was exercising principal control over overall government administration, including economic work; on the other hand, Jiang Zemin at the Party Central level was chairman of the Central Leading Group on Finances; Zhu Rongji's ability to exercise actual leadership thus was circumscribed.

However, at the end of April Li Peng collapsed from sickness and was forced to convalesce for several months. At the same time, economic overheating and loss of economic order, particularly chaos in the financial system, reached a stage where action could no longer be postponed. In late June, after approval of the Politburo based on the sanction of Deng Xiaoping, Zhu Rongji was sent out to reconstruct the economic order. As in the past, Zhu issued bold, clear policies. Moreover, using the method of strengthening the levers of macro control by deepening reform, he sought to avoid the experience of undirected, destructive administrative edicts seen in previous economic readjustments and instead tried to find instrumentalities of macro control within the market economy. In this approach he has gained the support of most members of the economic community, and as previously noted, his policies had some effect. Consequently, we can posit that if macro control is continued, the double-digit growth rate will decrease substantially, the chaos in the financial system will recede, and some form of stability will emerge.

There is a major difference between the current overheating and that in 1988 and 1989. Previously there was severe imbalance between the demand and supply of consumer goods, and excess demand led to inflation. In the current case, on the contrary, consumer goods are plentiful. Rather, because of huge investment demand, the problems of constricted conditions in raw materials, energy, and transportation have grown critical, but funds that should be going into these sectors have been streaming into securities and real estate speculation, causing a bubble phenomenon that inevitably must burst.

Zhu Rongji, acutely mindful of this situation, undertook to deal with it by macro control, knowing that results would not be as immediate as with adjustments in a planned economy but hopeful that high growth could be maintained, reform could be deepened, and the tools for indirectly controlling the economy could be successfully developed.

## Jiang Zemin Cracks the Whip on Corruption

As Zhu Rongji took responsibility for economic policy, Jiang Zemin organized an all-out attack on another critical problem for the Communist Party—corruption. At its August 20–25 plenary session in Beijing, the Chinese Communist Party Central Disciplinary Investigation Committee adopted rules prohibiting party and government cadres above the county level from engaging in activities in five areas:

1. Cadres are prohibited from engaging in commercial or enterprise activities and from accepting money for intermediary activities. Partiality must not be shown for commercial or enterprise activities involving relatives, friends, or children.
2. All concurrent positions, including honorary positions, are prohibited. If a position is assumed after due approval, no compensation may be received.
3. Trading in stocks is prohibited.
4. No gifts of any kind, including money and securities, may be accepted.
5. Public funds may not be used to purchase memberships in clubs or for other such purposes (*People's Daily,* August 26, 1993).

Corruption is an inevitable weakness of a Communist Party dictatorship—indeed, of any single-party dictatorship. Because of the absence of checks and balances on power in a system of unitary leadership, effectively controlling corruption is extremely difficult.

However, officials are clearly mindful of the danger that corruption causes the people to lose trust in authority, and as long as there remains the desire to continue the struggle, a certain measure of restraint on corruption will be enforced. Nevertheless, it has always been understood in Chinese society that under-the-table payments are part of dealings with officials; thus, the people do not expect officials to be totally pure.

The outrage of the people against *guandao* at the time of the Tiananmen incident taught officials a lesson. So long as the Chinese Communist Party adopts the stance of sternly dealing with egregious cases of corruption, the people should be mollified even if corruption is not rooted out completely. These efforts to defuse the corruption time bomb, along with the economic leadership of Zhu Rongji, increase the possibility of comparatively stable development of China's politics and economics.

# 20

## China's Prospects and U.S.-China Relations

### China's Economic Fundamentals

*Three Reasons for Continued High Growth*

The first reason China is capable of such high rates of economic growth is that as indicated by international comparisons of per capita GNP, the living standard of the Chinese people is low. The people are hungry in spirit and ready to work tirelessly to achieve a more prosperous existence.

Second, the Chinese mainland is integrated with the international environment of East Asia. As a developing country, China is joining with and being stimulated by certain ASEAN countries like Thailand and Malaysia to emulate and catch up with the four little dragons (Taiwan, Korea, Hong Kong, and Singapore) and Japan. China not only is receiving stimulation of a spiritual kind but also is acting as a partner as a market for goods or as a supplier or buyer of raw materials and technology in the course of economic intercourse. As long as East Asia remains the center of growth of the world economy, the Chinese economy will be able to enjoy the ripple effects of this activity and at the same time to add locomotive force of its own.

Third, China is a huge country with large regional disparities that will serve to keep labor costs low for a long time. In the past, this situation was the cause of a vicious cycle of poverty. However, now that a certain development dynamism has taken root within the Chinese economy, the interior regions have started functioning as a great hinterland for the coastal regions, and conditions have been changing so as to support long-term economic growth.

*Obstacles to Growth*

Thus, a China that has awakened to economic stimulation can be expected to take off economically by the twenty-first century. However, it will have to face some major problems.

The first is the contradiction between economic development and the political system. China is rapidly advancing down the road toward a market economy, but the type of society that ultimately develops under a market system can be expected to fundamentally shake the political system of Communist Party dictatorship. If a new political system adapted to economic development can be successfully structured, then even greater economic strides are likely. However, if the country descends into political chaos, there could be a deadlock in economic development.

Second, there are the problems of the global environment. Coal makes up three-fourths of the energy supply of China. Desulfurization is more troublesome for coal than for petroleum. As industry contributes to China's high economic growth, acid rain and atmospheric pollution will grow more severe. This could create danger for people not only in China but worldwide.

The third problem is that of disparities between regions and incomes. The coastal regions are already taking off. However, the interior regions not only are unable to take off by themselves but are also holding back the coastal regions. The solution to this problem of disparities can be found within economic growth; in this sense, much can be expected from high growth. At the same time, it is likely that along with economic growth will come development of market fragmentation, and the Chinese economy will take the form of several regional economic areas. Indeed, there is a strong probability that in the twenty-first century a "developed China" will not be one People's Republic of China but rather a "China federation" of regional economic areas with loose ties. "Chinese nationalism" was first and foremost a slogan, the purpose of which was to unite a weakened China after the Opium War. For a developed, stronger China, Chinese nationalism would be unnecessary.

## Why Soviet Reforms Failed and Deng's Reforms Succeeded

Western observers have cast a keen eye on the high growth of the Chinese economy. The Western mass media and intelligentsia probably began to notice and focus on China's high growth rate when they began to make comparisons with the former Soviet Union. Previously the Western media had viewed positively the "shock therapy" of Gorbachev's perestroika policy and had accepted the position that political democratization was a precondition for a market economy. They had of course censured Deng Xiaoping's military suppression. However, the chaos that ensued in the former Soviet Union's politics and economics forced a major rethinking of previous views, and it became clear that in the Soviet case "shock therapy" was a failure.

Another mistake in perception was the deficient analysis of the situation in China after the Tiananmen incident. The West portrayed the former Soviet Union under perestroika in rosy terms and viewed China after Tiananmen darkly. Even if perceptions of the two have not been totally reversed, there has been a great deal of revision. Examples of this new analysis are reports about China in major magazines and some other studies:

1. *The Economist* China Survey, November 11, 1992. "China: The Titan Stirs." This article noted that the World Bank calculated China's 1991 GNP at the RMB/U.S. dollar exchange rate to produce a figure of approximately $420 billion (tenth in the world), but that if it had been calculated on a purchasing-power parity basis, the figure would have been three times greater to place China in third or fourth place globally (behind the United States and Japan and near Germany). If China continued to develop at the real rate of 9 percent seen in the previous fourteen years, in twenty years it would rank with the United States and Japan as a top economic power.

2. *Newsweek,* February 18, 1993, special issue "Red Capitalism." According to this article, in terms of combined GNP the "Greater China" region (China, Taiwan, and Hong Kong) by 2020 would surpass Japan and the United States to become the world's leading economic power.

3. *United States and China: Relations at a Crossroads* (Washington, D.C.: The Atlantic Council, February 1993). This study was commissioned by the Atlantic Council of the United States and the National Committee on United States–China Relations and written under the supervision of Barber Conable and David Lampton. The study described China's rapid growth and advanced the notion of an "Asian path of development." Exemplified by South Korea and Taiwan, the model is of a market economy nurtured under a one-party dictatorship and of a gradual democratization after a certain level of economic well-being has been reached.

4. "China: The Coming Power," *Foreign Affairs,* Winter 1992–93, by Barber Conable and David Lampton. This article, in an issue of *Foreign Affairs* designed as a policy briefing book for the Clinton administration, was the authors' summary of the arguments of the Atlantic Council study.

5. The World Bank, *Global Economic Prospects and the Developing Countries 1993.* This report noted the possibility that by 2002, the Greater China economic region would in economic scale exceed the United States and leap to first position in the world.

6. "China: The Next Superpower," *Time,* May 10, 1993. This article expanded the analysis of the rapid growth of China's economic power with discussion of its similarly increasing military strength and reach. The possibility was advanced that China could become a destabilizing force in the Asian region security system.

In common in these six reports on China was, first, an optimistic view of a possible continuance of the high growth realized during the fourteen years of the Deng Xiaoping era (1979–1993), which would lead to a bounding expansion of Chinese GNP. Second was that in place of an exchange rate conversion of Chinese GNP, calculations were made based on purchasing-power parity, which produced a figure three to four times greater than the converted GNP value. The third prominent feature was the positive view that economic development was producing a change deep in Chinese society and hence was promoting the process of democratization.

The article that most clearly made the third point was *United States and China: Relations at a Crossroads*. It delivered an extremely positive and accurate appraisal, noting that the policy of first undertaking economic reform paves the way for germination of conditions for political democratization—that this is the "Asian path of development."

It is apparent that behind these glowing descriptions of China's future is a reappraisal of the previous excessively pessimistic view. However, it is probably also true that these reports were trying to convey to the new Clinton administration some advice on policy toward China.

## Japanese and U.S. Approaches to China: Political or Economic Reform First?

In contrast with China, a country possessing an ancient history, the United States is a young country with a short history. However, both countries are composites comprising vast expanses of territory and multiple races. Relations between China and the United States have swung from war to coexistence, from competition to cooperation.

If the Korean War had not occurred and China had not entered that conflict, the post–World War II Cold War structure would have probably changed more quickly to a structure of cooperation and coexistence. The Korean War provided the context for the United States to lock in a "containment policy" toward China. This policy was tightened as the United States deepened its involvement in the Vietnam War. Perhaps as a result, Mao Zedong firmly believed in the real danger of a third world war with the "imperialist powers" and devoted much thought to China's strategic defenses. The enormous commitment of resources to strategic defense, of which the third-front initiative (Chapter 4) was but one example, demonstrably impaired China's overall economic development and thus was a great tragedy. The mistrust and fear between the United States and China fueled an arms race that exacerbated antagonisms in a vicious cycle.

Relations between the two countries were normalized in the 1970s in the context of mutual opposition to the Soviet Union. For China, relations with the United States provided an important component of security as China's confrontation with the Soviet Union grew more intense; a secondary but also important factor was U.S. economic cooperation. However, for the United States, the only real significance of friendly relations with China was the strategic value of the "China card."

From the mid-1980s the perestroika line of Mikhail Gorbachev pursued by the former Soviet Union led not only to the dismantling of the Soviet Communist Party but also to the dismemberment of the former Soviet Union itself. In stark contrast, China's response to the democratization movement, symbolized by the Tiananmen Square incident, was suppression.

After these events the world began to enter the post–Cold War era. In this new international setting, the United States is adopting contradictory approaches as it edges closer to a China that is the last socialist power but that is also advancing rapidly toward a market economy.

The United States continues to exert pressure on the Chinese government to free the Chinese people as quickly as possible from the oppression of communist dictatorship. The thinking behind this is that, apart from the human rights issue, only a democratized China will really be successful in developing its economy. Economic cooperation with China before it is democratized thus constitutes aiding and abetting a "reactionary government" and is inimical to the interests of the people. Consequently such aid is unconscionable.

But an opposing approach takes the perspective provided by the histories of "developmental dictatorship" in South Korea and Taiwan: Political stability is essential for economic development. This was Japan's approach before and after World War II, and it was adopted with even greater efficiency in the four Asian dragons. China's adoption of this course would provide the highest likelihood of success. A U.S. policy that pursues excessive democratization and emphasis on human rights is likely to undermine China's stability and in the long run set back economic development. In summary, if there is no underpinning of economic development, it is futile to attempt frontally to ameliorate human rights in China. Only by taking the slightly circuitous route to democracy via economic development can the problem of the human rights of the Chinese people truly be resolved.

Of these two approaches, Japan is effectively adopting the latter. Neither the Japanese government nor the business community has been vociferous in advocating this way of thinking, but it clearly informs their views. Two events in the late 1980s and the early 1990s have confirmed the correctness of the view that economic development must come first.

The first is the Tiananmen incident of June 1989. The Chinese government used military force to suppress demands for democracy and government reform from students and citizens. Although such a reaction cannot be condoned, we should nevertheless acknowledge that through this dictatorial recourse to suppression, political stability was maintained, and the framework supporting economic development was sustained.

Second are the lessons of the failure of perestroika. The strategy adopted by Mikhail Gorbachev of proceeding from political reform to economic reform produced very uneven and troubled progress. In Russia today economic chaos continues, and people are living in severe economic hardship. The difficulties of perestroika versus the success of the Deng Xiaoping line of separating politics and economics are indirect proof of the correctness of the strategy of proceeding from economic reform to political reform and the futility of attempting the reverse.

Thus, China should move in the economic sphere from a planned economy to a market economy, thus providing the material conditions for a transformation from one-party dictatorship to a multiparty system in the political sphere. This approach would provide the firmest foundation for the subsequent breaking out of the socialist system, building of a democratized society, and smooth entry into the world market economy. It should be hoped that the United States would come to appreciate and support this course.

China strongly hopes by virtue of joining the General Agreement on Tariffs and Trade (GATT) and other international institutions to achieve a soft landing in the world market economy. As a participant in the world economy, China can continue its high growth and on that basis develop a middle class; in this way it is likely to achieve economic takeoff toward the end of the twentieth century and into the twenty-first. At that time, there will have to be progress in democratization of the political system in adaptation to the market economy. The practicalities of advancing along this road are likely to involve difficulties and setbacks, but it should not be doubted that a Chinese economy under a market system will lead to democratization of the political system (in the past there was the possibility that a rigid political system would put a brake on transformation to a market economy, but that possibility no longer exists).

Deng Xiaoping cleared the way to throwing off socialism and put the Chinese economy on track toward a soft landing in the global market economy. For these great achievements his name will find an indelible place in modern history.

# 21

# Charting China's Development to the Year 2000

## China's Standard for "Being Well-Off" in the Year 2000

China has announced the goal of "completing the initial stage of establishing a socialist market economic structure" and rising to a new level of "economic construction, living standards, and overall national strength" by the end of the twentieth century. These words taken together express the previously announced target of achieving a level of "being well-off." The elements of and concrete path toward this standard appear as twelve indicators in three categories established in *The Standard for China's Being Well-Off* (1992), the work of a project team of the State Statistical Bureau (see Table 21.1).

### Progress Toward Standard by 1990

The Chinese standard offers for international comparison eight of its twelve indicators (omitted are poor population, Gini coefficient, per capita income, and share of culture and education in income). Year 2000 targets for the eight indicators, if achieved, would place China in the year 2000 at a level comparable to the 1988 international standard for a "lower-middle-income country." This standard was applied to countries with per capita GNP in the range of US$600–2,000 (on average $1,380) and included in Asia the Philippines ($630), Thailand ($1,000), and Malaysia ($1,940). In 1988 China, with a per capita GNP of $330, was classified as a low-income country (World Bank 1990).

The Chinese effort to reach a level of being well-off is a twenty-year process that began in 1980. The 1990 level of attainment of the final targets—that is, halfway into the process—is presented in Figure 21.1 and Table 21.2. If the year 2000 targets are indexed as 100, in 1990 China's attainment level stood at 57.4 points.

We can get a good sense of China's 1990 situation and characteristics by looking more closely at specific indicators. On the one hand, average lifespan had already

Table 21.1    Components of the Level of Being Well-Off

|  |  |  |
|---|---|---|
| Indicators of the Level of Being Well-Off | 1. Objective economic conditions | 1. GNP per capita of RMB 2400 (1990 prices)<br>2. tertiary industry at 36% of total production<br>3. poor population under 58% (1990 was 88%)<br>4. Gini coefficient at 0.3-0.35 |
|  | 2. Quality of life | 5. income per capita of RMB 1400 (RMB 2380 in the cities, RMB 110 in the villages)<br>6. calorie consumption per capita of 2600 kcal<br>7. protein consumption per capita of 75 grams<br>8. living space per capita of 15.5 square meters<br>9. Engel coefficient at 47-49% (44-46% in the cities, 50% in the villages)<br>10. share of culture and education in total consumption of 16% |
|  | 3. Effectiveness of life | 11. average lifespan of 70 years<br>12. middle school attendance at 55-60% |

Source: *Standard for China's Being Well-Off* (Beijing: Chinese Statistical Press, 1992), p. 9.

Figure 21.1    China's (National) Level of Being Well-Off in the Year 2000 (Graph of attainment index in 1990. With year 2000 level equal to 100, 1990 overall attainment index is 57.4.)

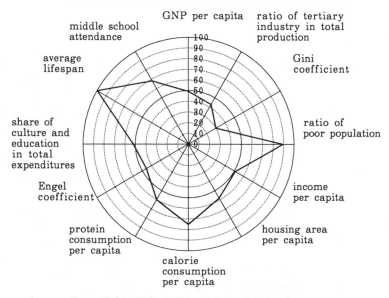

Source: From Table 21.2, "1990 attainment index."

reached the target, reduction of poverty had attained 89.3 percent of the objective, and per capita caloric intake was at 75 percent of the target. On the other hand were areas where attainment was still low: a Gini coefficient at 30.0 points, per capita GNP at 49.4, and per capita income at 51.1.

### Comparison of Cities and Villages

It is well known that the gap between China's cities and villages is immense. Thus averaged figures often obscure the reality of the situation. Because of this, in coming up with indicators for *The Standard of China's Being Well-Off,* analysts separated the cities and villages and attempted to formulate differentiated approaches and measures.

For China's cities, the indicators were set from an international perspective at the level of a middle-income country. At this level countries had average GNP per capita of $1,930 in 1988; included at the top of the range was South Korea with GNP per capita of $3,600.

Chinese cities by 1990 had an overall attainment level toward the targets of 65.2 points (see Figure 21.2 and Table 21.3), 7.8 points better than the national average. Especially high were attainments in middle school attendance, average lifespan, and per capita fat consumption; particularly low were protein consumption, Engel coefficient, and ratio of tertiary industry in total production.

Compared with the situation in cities, it is more problematic to describe statistically the lives of village residents. As seen in Figure 21.3 and Table 21.4, by 1990 the overall attainment level of China's village areas was 50.6 points, almost exactly halfway along the progression charted from 1980 to the year 2000. The Gini coefficient and average lifespan had already reached 100 percent of the target. Still relatively lagging were some measures of material well-being (protein intake and clothing expenditures), elements of living environment such as safety and availability of pure water, and public security.

# The November 1993 Third Plenum Decision to Establish a Socialist Market Economy

The Chinese Communist Party convened the Third Plenum of the Fourteenth Central Committee in Beijing November 11–14, 1993, and adopted "Decisions of the Chinese Communist Party Central on Some Issues Concerning Establishment of a Socialist Market Economic Structure" (the Fifty Articles). The occasion was a full fifteen years after the Third Plenum of the Eleventh CPC Central Committee in December 1978, at which the Deng Xiaoping line was officially adopted; thus, Deng's tactic of "smuggling" the market economy incrementally into the planned economy was finally completed. The Fifty Articles represent a constitutionaliza-

Table 21.2  Progress Toward China's Level of Being Well-Off

| Indicator | Unit | 1980 (A) | 1990 (B) | Well-off level in 2000 (C) | Points (a) | 1990 attainment index (b) |
|---|---|---|---|---|---|---|
| GNP per capita | RMB | 735 | 1,558 | 2,400 | 15 | 49.4 |
| ratio of tertiary industry | % | 20.5 | 27.2 | 36 | 8 | 42.9 |
| Gini coefficient | – | 0.28 | 0.36 | 0.325 | 9 | 30.0 |
| ratio of poor population | | 33 | 8 | 5 | 5 | 89.3 |
| income per capita | % | 320 | 970 | 1,400 | 14 | 51.1 |
| housing area per capita | RMB | 4.7 | 11.0 | 15.5 | 10 | 58.3 |
| calorie consumption per capita | kcal/day | 2,400 | 2,550 | 2,600 | 4 | 75.0 |
| protein consumption per capita | g/day | 50 | 35 | 75 | 5 | 60.0 |
| Engel coefficient | % | 60 | 54.5 | 48 | 8 | 45.8 |
| share of culture and education | % | 6 | 11.2 | 16 | 5 | 52.0 |
| average lifespan | years | 67 | 70 | 70 | 10 | 100.0 |
| middle school attendance | % | 35 | 50 | 57 | 6 | 68.2 |
| Overall index | | – | – | | 100 | 57.4* |

Notes: Prices are 1990 prices. 1990 attainment figure is derived as
(B-A)+(C-A)×100. *Cumulative index derived as (a)×(b)/100.
The Gini coefficient is a measure of dispersion of income distributions
derived from the Lorenze Curve. The closer the coefficient is to 1
the more unequal is income distribution. The Engel coefficient is
an expression of the relationship between income and food consumption.
It is generally taken that the lower the figure, the higher the general
living standard.
Source: *Standard for China's Being Well-Off*, p. 17.

Figure 21.2  Level of Being Well-Off in Chinese Cities in the Year 2000
(Graph of attainment index in 1990. With year 2000 level
equal to 100, 1990 overall attainment index is 65.2.)

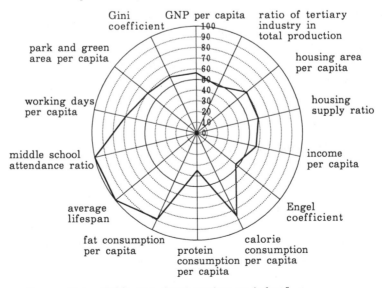

Source: From Table 21.3, "1990 attainment index."

Table 21.3    Progress Toward the Level of Being Well-Off of
Chinese Cities (1980, 1990, 2000)

| Indicator | Unit | 1980 (A) | 1990 (B) | Well-off level in 2000 (C) | Points (a) | 1990 attainment index (b) |
|---|---|---|---|---|---|---|
| GNP per capita | RMB | 1,750 | 3,580 | 5,000 | 15 | 56.3 |
| ratio of tertiary industry | % | 20.6 | 30 | 40 | 9 | 48.5 |
| housing area per capita | m² | 3.9 | 7.1 | 9 | 9 | 60.7 |
| housing supply ratio | % | 25 | 46 | 60 | 6 | 60.0 |
| real income per capita | RMB | 974 | 1,783 | 2,380 | 10 | 57.5 |
| Engel coefficient | % | 62 | 54 | 45 | 7 | 47.1 |
| calorie consumption per capita | kcal/day | 2,200 | 2,544 | 2,600 | 4 | 86.0 |
| protein consumption per capita | g/day | 60 | 67 | 80 | 4 | 35.0 |
| fat consumption per capita | g/day | 66 | 74 | 75 | 4 | 88.9 |
| average lifespan | year | 67.5 | 70 | 70 | 11 | 100.0 |
| middle school attendance ratio | % | 70 | 91.7 | 90 | 5 | 100.0 |
| working days per capita | days | 6 | 6 | 5.5 | 4 | 70.0 |
| park and green area per capita | m² | 3 | 6.6 | 9.0 | 5 | 60.0 |
| Gini coefficient | | 0.16 | 0.23 | 0.28 | 10 | 58.3 |
| Overall index | | — | — | — | 100 | 65.2[a] |

Notes: Prices are 1990 prices. 1990 attainment figure is derived
as (B-A)+(C-A)×100.   [a] Cumulative index derived as (a) ×(b)/100.
Source: *Standard for China's Being Well-Off, p. 46.*

Figure 21.3    Level of Being Well-Off in Chinese Villages in the Year 2000
(Graph of attainment index in 1990. With year 2000 level
equal to 100, 1990 overall attainment index is 50.6.)

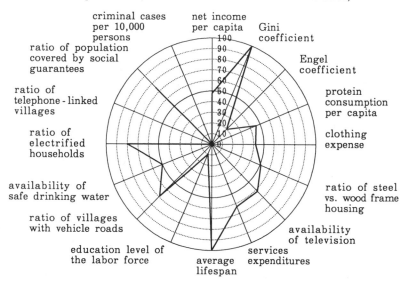

Source: From Table 21.4, "1990 attainment index."

Table 21.4     Progress Toward the Level of Being Well-Off
of Chinese Villages (1980, 1990, 2000)

| Indicator | Unit | Minimum standard level (A) | 1990 (B) | Well-off level in 2000 (C) | Points in 2000 | 1990 attain-ment index |
|---|---|---|---|---|---|---|
| 1. Income distribution | | | | 35 | 55 | 19 |
| net income per capita | RMB | 300 | 686 | >1,100 | 30 | 48 |
| Gini coefficient | % | 20 | 31 | >30-40 | 5 | 100 |
| 2. Material life | | | | | 25 | 41 |
| Engel coefficient | % | 60 | 58 | < 50 | 6 | 20 |
| protein consumption per capita | g/day | 47 | 60 | > 75 | 9 | 46 |
| clothing expense | RMB | 27 | 45 | > 70 | 3 | 42 |
| ratio of steel vs. wood frame housing | % | 43 | 62 | > 80 | 7 | 51 |
| 3. Intellectual life | | | | | 12 | 63 |
| availability of television | sets/100 households | 1 | 44 | > 70 | 6 | 62 |
| services expenditures ratio | % | 2 | 7 | > 10 | 6 | 63 |
| 4. Population | | | | | 9 | 50 |
| average lifespan | year | 68 | 70 | > 70 | 4 | 100 |
| education level of the labor force | year | 6 | 6.2 | > 8 | 5 | 10 |
| 5. Living environment | | | | | 11 | 55 |
| ratio of villages with vehicle roads | % | 50 | 74 | > 85 | 3 | 69 |
| availability of safe drinking water | % | 50 | 70 | > 90 | 3 | 50 |
| ratio of electrified households | % | 50 | 86 | > 95 | 3 | 80 |
| ratio of telephone-linked villages | % | 50 | 43 | > 70 | 2 | 0 |
| 6. Social security and safety | | | | | 8 | 38 |
| ratio of population covered by social guarantees | % | 50 | 80 | > 90 | 4 | 75 |
| criminal cases per 10,000 persons | cases | 5 | 20 | < 5 | 4 | 0 |
| Overall index | | — | — | — | 100 | 50.6 |

Notes: > means more than, < means less than. Prices are 1990 prices.
1990 attainment index derived as $(B-A)+(C-A) \times 100$.
*Source: Standard for China's Being Well-Off*, p. 82.

tion of the Deng Xiaoping line and for the first time offer a complete view of this agenda.

The drafting committee for the Fifty Articles was organized in May 1993 under the Politburo's Central Leading Group on Finance and Economics. Over thirty persons worked on them under the direction of Wen Jiabao, secretary of the Central Secretariat. From May to September, the articles were revised and redrafted five times. On September 18 the fifth draft was distributed "for comments" to thirty provincial units, ninety central organs, and three general departments, as well as to sixteen "elders" (including Deng Xiaoping, Chen Yun, Bo Yipo, Yang Shangkun, and Wan Li). The committee received 138 proposed revisions that were incorporated into subsequent drafts. Finally the eighth draft was adopted by the Standing Committee of the Politburo in early November and was presented to the Third Plenum on November 11 (Hong Kong, *Wen Wei Po,* November 24).

The document, structured in ten sections with fifty articles, broadly and in typically flowery language describes the Chinese road to a market economy. There are five principal areas of reform.

*Conversion of state-owned enterprises to joint stock companies.* The idea of converting state-owned enterprises to limited corporations is explained as follows. A company that is a legal corporate person can effectively realize the ownership rights of investor-shareholders and can clearly apportion ownership rights over corporate assets. Such a company is advantageous for separating government functions from corporate functions and effecting the transition to professional management. Such companies make it possible to remove government administrative organs from the corporations and to end unlimited state liability toward the enterprise. The form is also beneficial for raising capital and diversifying risk.

The types of companies envisaged are wholly owned companies with a single ownership structure and limited liability or joint stock companies with a multiple ownership structure. The document describes the mixture: "Limited liability stock companies listed on exchanges will be limited in number, and will be subject to rigorous audit requirements. What proportion of the shares will be held by the state will depend on the industry, and also on how widely shares are held. Companies producing certain special products and military industrial enterprises will be wholly owned by the state." The last sentence is significant: The state will be able to control the shares of the key enterprises in the basic and strategic industries. Thus the objective of the transformation to the company system is to introduce modern enterprise management.

National-scale Chinese companies now existing will be reorganized into stock holding companies. Thereafter, with ownership still mainly in the hands of the state, ownership and management rights will be brought together, and large industrial groups spanning regions and industries will be nurtured in order to promote new technology, new product development, and international competitiveness. Small state-owned enterprises can be contracted out or rented, converted to cooperative stock ownership, or sold to collectives or individuals.

*Reform of the financial system.* Conversion of the People's Bank of China into a central bank is a long-standing policy, one supposedly implemented. This time the concrete central banking tools for controlling the money supply of reserve requirements, a central bank lending rate (discount rate), and open market operations were specified as the means by which the PBOC would stabilize the value of the currency. A monetary policy committee is to be established to set and appropriately adjust monetary and financial policy.

The document calls for separation of "policy banks" (banks whose lending activities are dictated by government development priorities and programs) and commercial banks (banks operating under the profit motive). A State Development Bank and an Export-Import Bank are to be established as new policy banks, and the existing Agricultural Bank of China is to be reorganized into a policy bank. The existing specialized banks (including Industrial and Commercial Bank of China, China Investment Bank, Bank of Communications, and People's Construction Bank of China) are gradually to become exclusively commercial banks. Agricultural cooperative banks and urban cooperative banks are to be established. Commercial banks will manage both the asset and liability sides of their balance sheets, control risk, and become the standard for nonbanks.

The central bank will adjust its discount rate according to supply-and-demand conditions, and commercial banks will be permitted to adjust their lending rates within certain policy ranges. The foreign exchange management system will be improved with the establishment of a market-based floating rate system. The foreign exchange market will be unified nationwide, and the RMB will gradually be made convertible. Banks will be brought on-line to computerized systems; at the same time credit card settlement systems will be actively introduced and cash settlement minimized.

*Reform of the investment system.* Article 20 elborates the principle and practice that investment risk will be primarily borne by companies, which will also reap the benefits of profits. Banks (i.e., commercial banks) will lend capital funds and will be responsible for managing the risks and garnering the profits of lending. This is a reform of the previous central planning economic system in which state banks funded state-owned enterprises but took no responsibility for the use of funds or quality of the loans. The new policy is an effort to establish clearly both the rights and responsibilities of commercial banks to pursue profits but also to underscore the banks' role as supporters of corporate enterprises whose main function is to pursue profits.

*Issues in fiscal reform.* There are three main elements in fiscal and taxation reform.

1.  Separation of taxation systems. The proposal is to convert the current regional fiscal contractual responsibility system to a separate taxation system. Central and regional authorities will each have fiscal administrative duties, and central taxes and local taxes will be differentiated. "Central taxes" will be taxes needed to maintain the ability to exercise macro control on a national scale for the national benefit. "Regional taxes" will be taxes required to meet regional needs. "Shared taxes" will be taxes directly supporting economic development at the central and local levels. Fiscal receipts as a percentage of GNP should be raised, with a more rational balance established between central and regional revenues. A system of returning central revenues to the regions and arranging transfer payments should be established, especially for undeveloped regions and to support transformation of old industrial bases.

2. Introduction of a value-added tax. A turnover tax based primarily on a value-added tax will be introduced. For certain commodities a sales tax will be imposed. For most noncommodity activities a gross receipts tax will be imposed. The relationship between the state and enterprises in terms of sharing profits will be rationalized largely through lowering the income tax for state-owned enterprises and abolishing the key energy and communications project construction funds and budgetary adjustment funds. Enterprise income taxes and individual income taxes will be unified, and the tax rates will be made standard.

3. Establishment of a double-entry budgetary system. Separate budgets for government activities and for the management of state assets will be established, as will social security program budgets and other budgets. State deficits will not be financed by overdrafts from the banking system but rather by the issuance of long- and short-term government bonds. The government's domestic and external debt will be brought under unified management.

*Reform of the trade system.* The new policy advances the basic concept that modern enterprises have the right to manage foreign trade themselves. At the same time there is discussion of the development of general trading companies. Henceforth the state will exercise levers of control over enterprises through policies on the exchange rate, taxation, and bank credit. Clearly indicated is a reduction in direct administrative intervention of the kind practiced heretofore in export and import control administration and indicative planning.

## Central-Regional Fiscal Conflict: Quick Resolution Unlikely

Of the three main elements of fiscal reform, the most important is the attempt to resolve the problem of the weak central government and strong regional governments by introducing a separate tax system. In retrospect, the Deng Xiaoping system nurtured economic development by tolerating the emergence of "little empire economies"—by allowing such provinces as Guangdong and Shandong and then Zhejiang and Jiangsu to establish financial policies independently. For the provinces, this freedom was akin to surreptitiously receiving an award of independence from the central government.

The new term "separate tax systems" is gaining currency, but in fact the initiative to separate central and regional taxes dates from the mid-1980s. Table 21.5 shows that the initiative of separating central and regional taxes was taken and a differentiation made between types of taxes. However, although this initiative was adopted in 1985, implementation was postponed on the ground that arrangements were not in place. The separation of tax systems set for implementation in the future can be expected generally to parallel this scheme.

Table 21.5   Central and Regional Taxes

| Central Taxes | Taxes Divided Between Central and Regions | Regional Taxes |
|---|---|---|
| 1. income tax, adjustment tax (in case of Central state-owned enterprises)<br>2. gross receipts tax (Railways Ministry, and bank head offices and insurance company headquarters)<br>3. revenues of military industrial enterprises<br>4. subsidy on purchase price paid for food grain, cotton, and edible oils (negative number)<br>5. special fuel oil tax<br>6. customs duties (and commodity and value added taxes collected by customs as agent)<br>7. specific adjustment tax<br>8. unified industrial and commercial tax, income tax, mineral area use tax (in case of foreign companies and off-shore oil development)<br>9. proceeds of government debt issues<br>10. key energy and communication construction fund<br>11. other revenues | 1. commodity tax, gross receipts tax, value added tax<br>2. resource tax<br>3. construction tax<br>4. salt tax<br>5. personal income tax<br>6. state-owned enterprises bonus tax<br>7. unified industrial and commercial tax, income tax (in case of foreign invested companies and JV companies) | 1. income tax, adjustment tax, contract fees (in case of regional state-owned enterprises)<br>2. collective-owned enterprise income tax<br>3. agriculture and animal husbandry tax<br>4. land use tax<br>5. automobile, ship use tax<br>6. urban real estate tax<br>7. slaughter tax<br>8. livestock transaction tax<br>9. open market transaction tax<br>10. stamp tax<br>11. contract revenues of regional enterprises<br>12. food grain, supply and marketing enterprises losses (region-owned, negative number)<br>13. tax delinquencies, penalties revenues<br>14. city maintenance tax<br>15. other revenues |

| Items Financed From Central Taxes | Special Items of Central Financing | Items Financed From Regional Taxes |
|---|---|---|
| 1. capital construction investment (Central projects)<br>2. enterprise transformation funds, new product development costs, simple construction expenditures (Central enterprises)<br>3. geological exploration expenditures<br>4. defense expenditures<br>5. costs of armed police units<br>6. people's air defense expenditures<br>7. foreign assistance outlays<br>8. foreign affairs expenditures<br>9. state materials reserve costs<br>10. agriculture, forestry, and water conservancy utility expenditures (Central level projects)<br>11. industry, transport, and commerce department undertakings costs<br>12. culture, education, science, and health activities costs<br>13. administration and management expenses<br>14. other outlays | 1. extraordinary national disaster relief expenditures<br>2. extraordinary drought and flood counter-measures subsidies<br>3. development funds for assisting economically undeveloped regions<br>4. subsidies for border construction projects | 1. capital construction investment (regional projects)<br>2. enterprise transformation funds, new product development costs, simple construction expenditures (regional enterprises)<br>3. agricultural assistance expenditures<br>4. city maintenance construction expenditures<br>5. agriculture, forestry, and water conservancy utility expenditures (regional projects)<br>6. industry, transport, commerce department undertakings costs<br>7. culture, education, science, and health activities costs<br>8. administration and management expenses (public security, safety, judicial, and investigative expenditures) |

Source: *Contemporary Chinese Finance* (Beijing: Chinese Social Sciences Press, September 1988), p. 74.

The critical issue that has caused and will cause tension between the center and the regions is the tax receipts allocation ratio assigned to each province. The 1985 proposal for tax separation used as its basis 1983 actual provincial fiscal data (State Council Notice, March 3, 1985). Table 21.6 (column A) presents 1983 actual data in order from the highest fiscal revenues to the lowest (the figure is for total tax collections at the province level, excluding the "central taxes" portion; i.e., the total of "regional taxes" plus "shared taxes"). Column B lists the amount of payments to the central government in 1985 calculated on publicly announced payment rates against this fiscal revenue; the result is about the same as the net revenues in 1983. Further, there is almost equal value both in terms of total payments for sixteen provinces and municipalities (RMB 31.4 billion versus RMB 31.5 billion) and for each individual province. The table shows that over RMB 1 billion was paid to the center from eight provinces and municipalities—Shanghai, Jiangsu, Liaoning, Shandong, Zhejiang, Beijing, Tianjin, and Hebei.

The main regions receiving fiscal subsidies in 1985 (bottom portion of Table 21.6) were the five minority autonomous regions—Guangxi (Zhuang minority), Xinjiang (Uigur), Inner Mongolia, Ningxia (Hui), and Tibet—and three provinces that are not autonomous regions but that have large minority populations—Yunnan, Guizhou, and Qinghai. These regions' subsidies were increasing by 10 percent a year. The interior regions of Gansu and Shaanxi provinces, the mountainous and poor Jiangxi and Fujian provinces, and Jilin province in the northeast were receiving fixed subsidies.

These fourteen provinces and regions received subsidies in the total amount of RMB 8.6 billion. Not surprisingly, this was roughly equivalent to their combined fiscal deficit. In other words, it was clearly decided to scale fiscal subsidies in 1985 on the basis of deficit figures in 1983. The initiative that changed this 1985 system to allow greater retention of taxes at the regional level was a 1988 tax system reform (*People's Daily*, August 10, 1988). This reform led to the current situation of strong regions and a weak center and brought this status into stark relief.

The limits of the fiscal contract responsibility system are clearly evident. However, as the history of stalled reform efforts indicates, a quick resolution of the conflict between the center and the regions over local tax revenues is unlikely. Also, there can be no doubt that increased financial autonomy was one of the most important stimuli to provincial development in the last decade. The danger is a dampening of the spirit.

## The Record of New Taxes During the Deng Xiaoping Era

Table 21.7 presents an overview of the new types of taxes introduced during the Deng Xiaoping era. In general, industrial and commercial taxes comprise distribution taxes, resource taxes, income taxes, special purpose taxes, and property and activity taxes. In addition, there are customs duties at the central level and agricultural and animal husbandry taxes at the regional level.

Table 21.6    Payments to Central in 1985 Based on 1983 Fiscal Record
(in RMB billions)

Payments to Central of  16 provinces & municipalities

| | | (A) 1983 Actuals | | | (B)Payments to Central in 1985 | | (C)1991 Fiscal receipts |
|---|---|---|---|---|---|---|---|
| | | Revenue | Expenditure | Balance | percentage | value | |
| 1 | Shanghai | 15.4 | 1.9 | 13.5 | 76.5% | 11.8 | 19.2 |
| 2 | Jiangsu | 7.5 | 3.2 | 4.2 | 6.0% | 4.5 | 14.3 |
| 3 | Liaoning | 6.8 | 3.4 | 3.4 | 48.9% | 3.3 | 16.2 |
| 4 | Shandong | 5.1 | 3.2 | 1.9 | 41.0% | 2.1 | 14.3 |
| 5 | Zhejiang | 4.2 | 2.1 | 2.0 | 45.0% | 1.9 | 12.1 |
| 6 | Sichuan | 4.1 | 3.7 | 0.5 | a) | | 14.8 |
| 7 | Hubei | 4.0 | 2.8 | 1.2 | b) | | 9.5 |
| 8 | Beijing | 4.0 | 2.0 | 2.0 | 50.5% | 2.0 | 9.0 |
| 9 | Tianjin | 3.9 | 2.1 | 1.8 | 60.6% | 2.4 | 5.8 |
| 10 | Henan | 3.7 | 3.0 | 0.6 | 19.0% | 0.7 | 10.5 |
| 11 | Hebei | 3.6 | 2.8 | 0.8 | 31.0% | 1.1 | 9.9 |
| 12 | Guangdong | 3.6 | 3.8 | -0.1 | fixed amt. | 0.8 | 19.2 |
| 13 | Hunan | 2.9 | 2.5 | 0.4 | 12.0% | 0.4 | 9.6 |
| 14 | Shanxi | 2.4 | 2.4 | 0.0 | 2.5% | 0.1 | 7.3 |
| 15 | Anhui | 2.2 | 2.0 | 0.2 | 19.0% | 0.4 | 5.4 |
| 16 | Heilongjiang | 2.1 | 3.1 | -0.9 | fixed amt. | 0.1 | 9.5 |
| | Total | 75.6 | 44.1 | 31.5 | Total | 31.4 | 186.6 |

14 Provinces/regions receiving subsidies from Central

| | | (A) 1983 Actuals | | | (B)Fiscal subsidies in 1985 | | (C)1991 Fiscal receipts |
|---|---|---|---|---|---|---|---|
| | | Revenue | Expenditure | Balance | Method | Subsidy amount | |
| 17 | Yunnan | 1.7 | 2.4 | -0.7 | gradual increase | 0.6 | 100.0 |
| 18 | Shaanxi | 1.5 | 1.9 | 0.4 | fixed amount | 0.3 | 5.4 |
| 19 | Jilin | 1.4 | 1.9 | 0.5 | fixed amount | 0.4 | 6.3 |
| 20 | Guangxi | 1.4 | 1.9 | 0.5 | gradual increase | 0.7 | 6.2 |
| 21 | Jiangxi | 1.4 | 1.7 | 0.4 | fixed amount | 0.3 | 5.1 |
| 22 | Fujian | 1.2 | 1.8 | 0.5 | fixed amount | 0.2 | 7.0 |
| 23 | Gansu | 1.1 | 1.6 | 0.5 | fixed amount | 0.2 | 4.0 |
| 24 | Guizhou | 0.9 | 1.6 | 0.7 | gradual increase | 0.7 | 4.6 |
| 25 | Inner Mongolia | 0.7 | 2.3 | 1.6 | gradual increase | 1.8 | 3.9 |
| 26 | Xinjiang | 0.6 | 1.9 | 1.3 | gradual increase | 1.5 | 2.7 |
| 27 | Ningxia | 0.2 | 0.7 | 0.5 | gradual increase | 0.5 | 0.8 |
| 28 | Qinghai | 0.2 | 0.7 | 0.6 | gradual increase | 0.6 | 0.9 |
| 29 | Hainan | | unspecified | | | | 1.0 |
| 30 | Tibet | 0.1 | 0.6 | 0.6 | gradual increase | 0.8 | 0.1 |
| | Total | 12.1 | 20.8 | 8.8 | — | 8.6 | 57.7 |
| | National total | 87.7 | 65.0 | 22.7 | — | — | 244.4 |

Note 1: Fiscal revenue does not include Central taxes collected at the regional level; it is the aggregate of regional taxes and common Central and regional taxes.

Note 2: In the interest of simplicity, plan unit municipalities have been omitted. a) Payments from Chongqing. b) Payments from Wuhan. The fiscal scale of Wuhan and Chongqing municipalilties in 1986 was some RMB 2.4 billion and RMB 1.7 billion, respectively.

Sources: (A): Data for 1983 fiscal receipts and expenditures; *National Fiscal Statistics 1950-1985* (Beijing: Chinese Financial and Economic Press, October 1987), pp. 54, 92. (B): Data for payments to Central percentages and subsidies, *Contemporary Chinese Finance* (Beijing: Chinese Social Sciences Press, September 1988), pp. 376-377. (C): Data for 1991 financial receipts and expenditures, *Chinese Financial Statistics 1950-1991* (Beijing: Scientific Press, October 1992), pp. 59, 138.

Table 21.7   New Taxes During the Deng Xiaoping Era (1980-1993)

| 1980 | 1981 | 1982 | 1983 | 1984 | 1985 | 1986 | 1987 | 1988 | Currently in effect |
|------|------|------|------|------|------|------|------|------|---------------------|

《1. Distribution taxes》
industrial and
commercial tax<sup>a)</sup> ────────── ┌1984 commodity tax 1 ──→
                        └1984 gross receipts tax 2 ──→
          1982 value added tax 3──→

《2. Resource taxes》
salt tax 4 ──→
                     1984 resource tax 5 ──→

《3. Income taxes》
                     1984 state-owned enterprise income tax 6 ──→
industrial and             1984 state-owned enterprise adjustment tax 7 ──→
commercial income tax ─────────── 1985 group enterprise income tax 8 ──→
                                 1986 individual industrial and
                                 commercial operator income tax 9→
1980 personal income tax 10 ──→
               1982 foreign enterprise income tax 11 ──→
1980 joint venture enterprise income tax 12 ──→
                               1986 individual revenue
                               adjustment tax 13 ──→
                                        1988 individually
                                        operated enterprise
                                        income tax 14 ──→

《4. Specific item taxes》
          1982 special fuel oil tax 15 ──→
               1983 construction tax 16 ──→
                        1985 state-owned enterprise bonus tax 17→
                        1985 collective-owned enterprise
                        bonus tax 18 ──→
                        1985 business unit bonus tax 19 ──→
                        1985 state-owned enterprise bonus
                        adjustment tax 20 ──→

《5. Property, activity taxes 》
urban real estate tax 21 ───────────── <sup>b)</sup> ──→
automobile, ship inspection tax 22 ─────── <sup>c)</sup> ──→
                       1985 city maintenance building tax 23 →
slaughter tax 24 ──→
livestock transaction tax 25 ──→
open market transaction tax 26 ──→
                                        1988 land use tax 27→
                                        1988 stamp tax 28 →
                                        1988 banquet tax 29→

《6.Other》
customs duties 30 ──→
agriculture and animal husbandry tax 31 ──→

Sources: Ministry of Finance, Tax Affairs Bureau, eds., *Industrial and Commercial Tax Statistical Materials 1950-1985* (Beijing: Chinese Financial and Economic Press, October 1988), and State Taxation Administration, eds., *Complete Collection of Tax Legislation* (Beijing: Chinese Financial and Economic Press, November 1989).

Note: <sup>a)</sup> The industrial and commercial tax was renamed in 1984 the commodity tax and the gross receipts tax. However the broad notion of an industrial and commercial tax is seen to be applied in many of the taxes in this table. <sup>b)</sup> The urban real estate tax was renamed in 1986 the housing tax. <sup>c)</sup> The automobile, ship inspection tax was renamed in 1986 the automobile, ship use tax.

Table 21.8    Structure of Fiscal Revenues 1992 (in RMB billions, %)

| | | |
|---|---|---|
| Fiscal revenues | 415.3 | 100.00 |
| of which, taxes | 329.7 | 79.38 |
| debt proceeds | 67.0 | 16.13 |
| other receipts | 41.4 | 9.98 |
| key construction fund revenues | 15.7 | 3.78 |
| enterprise revenues | 6.0 | 1.44 |
| enterprise loss subsidies | -44.5 | -10.71 |

Note: Debt proceeds includes proceeds from external and domestic borrowing. Enterprise revenues means remittances of profits from those state-owned enterprises that have not converted to a tax payment method. Other receipts includes such items as repayment of capital construction loans.
Source: *Statistical Yearbook of China 1993*, pp. 215, 219.

Table 21.9    Structure of Tax Receipts 1992 (in RMB billions, %)

| | | | | |
|---|---|---|---|---|
| Government revenues | 415.3 | 100.00 | | |
| Tax receipts | 329.7 | 79.38 | 100.00 | |
| of which, | | | | |
| industrial & commercial tax | 227.7 | 54.83 | 69.07 | shared |
| customs duties | 21.3 | 5.12 | 6.45 | Central tax |
| agriculture & animal husbandry tax | 11.9 | 2.87 | 3.62 | regional tax |
| construction tax | 3.2 | 0.78 | 0.98 | shared |
| salt tax | 0.8 | 0.20 | 0.25 | shared |
| special fuel oil tax | 0.7 | 0.18 | 0.22 | Central tax |
| other | 64.0 | 15.41 | 19.41 | |

Source: *Statistical Yearbook of China 1993*, pp. 215, 220.

Tables 21.8 and 21.9 provide data on the structure of tax revenues in 1992. Roughly 80 percent of revenues were from the combination of industrial and commercial taxes (about 70 percent of total), customs duties (6.5 percent), and agricultural and animal husbandry taxes (3.6 percent).

# 22

# Chronology: Evolution of the Reform and Liberalization Policy (1978–1993)

China's internal and external policies during the Deng Xiaoping era are distinguished by the policy of "economic revitalization" on the domestic front and "economic liberalization" vis-à-vis the outside world. The following discussion summarizes the evolution of the economic liberalization policy.

## Establishment of Special Economic Zones

On February 15, 1979, the State Council of the Chinese government decided to develop Baoan county (now Shenzhen municipality) of Guangdong province as an "export commodities production base" and to invest from the state budget RMB 150 million for this purpose. After this decision, planning for concrete implementation began immediately in Guangdong province.

Five months later, on July 15, results of investigations concerning the initiative of export commodity production bases were reported by both Guangdong province and Fujian province, and these reports were "approved in principle" by the Party Central and the State Council. This action gave the two provinces authority to adopt "special policies" and "flexible measures" in economic relationships with the outside world. On July 30 the tenth meeting of the Standing Committee of the Fifth National People's Congress established the Foreign Investment Management Committee of the PRC (chairman, Gu Mu), formally signaling the policy of actively introducing foreign investment. On October 4 the China International Trust and Investment Corporation (CITIC) was established with Rong Yiren as its chairman.

In May 1980 the Party Central adopted the term "special economic zones" to refer to the export commodity production bases. On August 26 the fifteenth meeting of the Standing Committee of the Fifth National People's Congress approved a proposal from the State Council to establish four special economic zones—Shenzhen (formerly Baoan county), Zhuhai, and Shantou in Guangdong province and Xiamen (Amoy) in Fujian province. Simultaneous approval of "Regulations Governing the Special Economic Zones of Guangdong Province" officially brought the zones into existence.

Establishing the economic zones was like launching a ship into a stormy sea. This was first and foremost because internal objections to "capitalist methods" were still profound, as indicated in an August 1981 article: "Some comrades harbor concerns and doubts; they raise such objections as whether there is a theoretical basis for special economic zones, and whether it is consistent with the principles of Marxism-Leninism" (*Road to Development of the Shenzhen Special Economic Zone*, 1984, p. 16).

On December 22, 1981, veteran conservative Chen Yun sought to put a brake on the special zones:

> Some areas in parts of the cities of Shenzhen, Zhuhai, Shantou, and Xiamen in Guangdong and Fujian provinces are experimentally implementing special economic zones (the whole province of Guangdong is not a special zone, and the whole province of Fujian is not a special zone). This is good for now, and should not be increased. Of course, consignment processing and joint ventures are being undertaken in numerous localities; special zones are not permitted to go beyond these forms. In the case of consignment processing there must be no incidences of such production crushing our own products. ("A Few Important Policies for Economic Construction," Chen Yun 1986, pp. 276–277)

In fall 1983 the Party Central launched the campaign against "spiritual pollution." Doubtless this was intimidating to the persons concerned with the special economic zones because if capitalism was deemed the source of spiritual pollution, the special economic zones would be expected to have been most influenced by it. It appeared that the just-born special economic zones would suffer death by ideological strangulation.

Shortly thereafter (January 24–29, 1984) Deng Xiaoping visited the Shenzhen and Zhuhai special economic zones in Guangdong province and wrote approvingly about Shenzhen: "The development and experience of Shenzhen is confirmation of the correctness of our policy of establishing special economic zones." Next (February 7–10) he visited the Xiamen special economic zone of Fujian province and wrote, "let us build special economic zones faster and better," thereby greatly encouraging the local leadership. After returning to Beijing, Deng Xiaoping on February 24, 1984, addressed the leading cadres of the Party Central.

> I have just visited Shenzhen, and the impression I received was of development proceeding with good momentum. The pace of construction is rather rapid. Particularly, Shekou is fast. The reason is that the local people have been accorded a certain amount of authority. It is now possible for them to approve expenditures under $5

million. Their slogan is "time is money and efficiency is life." … The special economic zones are windows. They are windows for technology, windows for management, windows for capital, and windows for our foreign policy. ("Concerning the Problem of Increasing Special Economic Zones and Open Cities," Deng Xiaoping 1987, p. 40)

Deng Xiaoping's comments, especially the concept of "four windows," served to clarify and elevate the importance of the special economic zones.

Contemporaneous developments in the liberalization policy were enactment of a law governing joint venture enterprises and entry into the IMF and other international institutions. Specifically, on July 1, 1979, the second session of the Fifth National People's Congress adopted the "Law of the People's Republic of China on Joint Ventures Using Chinese and Foreign Investment," the so-called joint venture law (promulgated and effective July 8), and opened the door to direct foreign capital investment. In April 1980 the IMF restored China's representative rights, and the next month the executive board of the World Bank likewise restored China's rights in the World Bank, the International Development Association, and the International Finance Corporation. (Membership in the Asian Development Bank was delayed because of the Taiwan question but was finally realized in February 1986. At the general meeting in April 1987 China was elected a member of the board and thus regained membership in all international institutions.)

## Opening of Fourteen Coastal Cities

In his talk of February 24, 1984, Deng Xiaoping also mentioned opening up to the outside world "a number of port cities, such as Dalian and Qingdao," in addition to the special economic zones. On the basis of this instruction, the Party Central Secretariat and the State Council convened a symposium on coastal cities (March 26 to April 6). On the last day of discussions, a proposal was made to open fourteen coastal cities to foreign participation. These cities were, from north to south, Dalian, Qinhuangdao, Tianjin, Yantai, Qingdao, Lianyungang, Nantong, Shanghai, Ningbo, Wenzhou, Fuzhou, Guangzhou, Zhanjiang, and Beihai.

The main issues under consideration at this symposium were the process of opening the coastal cities and policy questions regarding introduction of foreign capital and technology. It was proposed that within these fourteen cities, except for the old-town sections in some of them, "economic development areas" would be established, and efforts would be made to provide infrastructure and to attract joint venture enterprises (*People's Daily,* April 7, 1984). With these decisions a second surge of opening to the outside world began.

There were three reasons for Deng Xiaoping's urgency in promoting the opening policy, according to a July 1986 article by Li Qingping in *Party History Research,* a Beijing bimonthly journal. First Deng recognized trends in the development of the global economy. He was quoted as saying, "Today's world is an open world" (June 30, 1984). (Unless otherwise noted, Li Qingping cited to Deng

Xiaoping 1984.) On another occasion Deng said, "Every kind of country must develop. Autarchy is impossible" (October 24, 1984, talk to the Central Advisory Committee).

Second, Deng had an appreciation of Chinese history. According to him, China had pursued a long history of autarchy. Even after the establishment of the PRC in 1949, "we in fact continued to pursue a degree of autarchy, and this caused some difficulties. In addition, slightly 'leftist' policies gave rise to some calamities. Certainly this is true of the 'Great Cultural Revolution.' ... It is impossible to build the country behind a closed door. [It is] Impossible to develop" (June 30, 1984).

The third reason was Deng's recognition of the actual situation of the Chinese economy. He knew China faced a number of obstacles to modernization but the greatest were lack of capital and backwardness of technology and management. Deng Xiaoping said, "The absorption of capital from abroad is an important supplement in our country's social construction. Looking forward from today it is an indispensable supplement" (June 30, 1984).

The three reasons offered by Li Qingping are persuasive. In addition, it is likely that considerations of the 1997 reversion of Hong Kong to China were also involved. This can be understood from Deng Xiaoping's statements about "one country, two systems" (June 22–23, 1984, included in Deng Xiaoping 1984).

In any event, the decision to open fourteen coastal cities after the four special economic zones gave a tremendous boost to the liberalization boom. In the second half of 1984 the special economic zones, particularly Shenzhen, developed rapidly. However, at the same time several problems became evident.

## The Contradiction of Special Economic Zones

In November 1984 State Council Premier Zhao Ziyang toured Shenzhen and Zhuhai and raised the issue of foreign exchange balance. The special economic zones were importing machinery, equipment, and raw materials and carrying out processing, but only part of their output of goods was being exported. Thus, Zhao pointed out, the original objective of the economic zones of garnering foreign exchange was not being achieved. At the beginning of 1985, State Council Vice Premier Yao Yilin made an inspection tour of the Shenzhen economic zone. He reportedly put a damper on the project, but nothing was announced publicly. It was a surprise inspection. In an interview with a Hong Kong journalist on March 28, 1985, Yao Yilin pointed out that "of the output of the special economic zones, the ratio of goods being exported is no more than one-third. ... This level of exports is inadequate." Hong Kong newspapers reported that Yao Yilin subsequently compiled a detailed report on the special zones, and that there were indications that the report prompted some people to reconsider the policy. Reportedly, he asserted that "the special zones are dependent upon blood transfusions from the state."

Around this time, Deng Xiaoping again warned that "the liberalization policy must not be mistaken." On June 25, 1985, he delivered a shock internally and externally by saying "the Shenzhen special economic zone is one experiment. We hope it is a success, but if it is a failure we will still have received a lesson" (quoted in all Hong Kong newspapers June 26). One reason Deng Xiaoping used the word "failure" was the rampant incidence of economic crimes—for example, black market trading and import and export smuggling. The official rate of the RMB to the U.S. dollar was then about RMB 2.8 to $1.00. However, the black market rate was two to two and one-half times more than the official rate—some RMB 6 to 7 to $1.00. Foreign currency accumulated in the black market was used to import all types of consumer goods, from automobiles to radio cassette players to color televisions and even to ballpoint pens.

## Hainan Island's Illegal Automobile Import Scheme

A classic example of the corruption was the smuggling scheme involving automobiles and other goods on Hainan Island, a quasi–special economic zone (it was elevated to province and full special economic zone status in 1988). On Hainan Island, the Party Committee secretary, Lei Yu, among many others, operated an illegal automobile import scheme. Finally, unable to ignore complaints and secret reports from all corners that "Hainan Island is making tremendous profits smuggling automobiles," the Party Central dispatched a team and resolved the problem. The "Report Concerning Cases of Serious Violations of Law and Discipline Such as Importation and Reselling of Large Volumes of Automobiles by Hainan Island" by the Central Disciplinary Investigative Committee (*People's Daily*, August 1, 1985) disclosed that for more than a year, from January 1, 1984, to March 5, 1985, authorities on Hainan Island had imported with black market foreign currency and later resold on the mainland 89,000 automobiles, televisions, videos, and motorcycles.

Hong Kong newspapers reported that Hainan Island dock workers committed acts of sabotage in protest of the seizure of some automobiles, and it was necessary for the government to mobilize troops to move the vehicles. Most of them were Japanese makes. There were some bankruptcies among the Hong Kong traders who handled the exports.

## Externally Directed Model or "Two Fans"

The widespread incidence of import smuggling that attended the liberalization policy became a political problem and was taken up in the debate over the special economic zones. Liu Guoguang, an economist serving as deputy director of the Chinese Academy of Social Sciences (and at the time concurrently acting as director of the Economics Research Institute of the Chinese Academy of Social Sciences), in speaking of the development strategy of the Shenzhen special economic zone, articulated the views of the "passive openers."

Liu Guoguang proffered three indicators of adherence to the "externally directed model," pursuit of which was essential in the conversion from the current internally directed economy to one externally directed. The first was giving foreign capital the principal role in financing, achieving a sourcing ratio of 50 to 60 percent for foreign capital for major financings. The second was giving product exporting the principal role, with the export ratio over 70 percent. The third was maintaining a surplus in foreign exchange receipts and payments. In emphasizing the externally directed model, Liu Guoguang was implicitly contrasting and criticizing the notion of the "two fans" approach.

The "two fans" idea was that the special economic zones would figuratively be like the rivet of a fan with respect to both export trade and the domestic market. The zones not only would be a place where domestic goods would undergo "consignment processing" before being distributed worldwide as exports, but they also would be permitted to accept semifinished products from abroad for assembly before selling to the domestic market. In terms of categories, the "two fans" advocates could be called the "aggressive openers," whereas those like Liu Guoguang who criticized them were the "passive openers."

According to Wang Zhuo, theorist in the Guangdong province Office of System Reform, the person who advanced the idea of the "two fans" was actually Zhao Ziyang ("An Investigation into Some Questions of the Special Economic Zones," *People's Daily,* October 7, 1985). Liu Guoguang actually seemed to be directing his criticism at Zhao Ziyang. (Zhao Ziyang's aggressive ideas were later seen again in the strategy of developing the coastal region economies.)

In December 1985 Shenzhen Party Committee Secretary Liang Xiang delivered a comprehensive report on the Shenzhen special economic zone at the "Conference of Cadres of Central Organs" (reported in *Economic Daily,* December 11, 1985; excerpts carried in *People's Daily,* December 13). The most interesting aspect of this report was the statement that at the end of 1984 Zhao Ziyang had made an inspection visit to Shenzhen and advanced the notion of "a rivet of two fans, one directed externally, one directed internally." This was the principle against which Liu Guoguang was directing criticism.

The "All-China Special Economic Zone Work Conference" (December 25, 1985, to January 5, 1986) ended in a compromise between the two sides. In its report about the conference on January 7, 1986, the *People's Daily* noted both positions: On the one hand, it appealed for a struggle "toward the objective of establishing an externally directed type economy" as advocated by Liu Guoguang; on the other hand, it supported the notion of the zones "playing an even greater role as rivet of the two fans of the domestic and overseas markets." In other words, the summary conclusion gave equal place to these two opposed viewpoints.

## Position of the Open Zones in the Seventh Five-Year Plan

On April 12, 1986, the fourth meeting of the Sixth National People's Congress adopted the seventh five-year plan. Chapter 35 set forth proposals for the special zones and open cities and regions (*Seventh Five-Year Plan,* 1986).

*Special Economic Zones*

The Shenzhen, Zhuhai, Shantou, and Xiamen special economic zones will complete current infrastructure, place emphasis on engineering relating to projects utilizing foreign capital, and concentrate efforts on construction in areas that are already under development. [They will] aggressively absorb foreign capital, develop productive projects, particularly those involving intensive knowledge and technology; and create as soon as possible export products with competitive power in international markets. With industry in the leading role, and advanced technology, [they will] gradually fashion an externally directed type economy capable of garnering foreign exchange; and further play their potential role as a window for technology, window for management, and window for policy toward the outside world.

*Open Coastal Cities*

The 14 open coastal cities and Hainan Island, will, based on their respective conditions and special characteristics, give full play to their own initiative to actively carry out "introducing from abroad, connecting domestically" [bringing in foreign capital and tying up with domestic enterprises], and implement a program emphasizing foreign economics and trade and technical exchange. Those cities possessing a relatively well-developed industrial base will build on this base to more rapidly introduce advanced technology and undertake technological reform and expansion for existing enterprises. At the same time, [they will] construct some new projects and actively develop leading-edge industries, and gradually establish bases on a slightly different model mainly as export product production bases. Cities with a comparatively weak industrial base will place emphasis on building infrastructure and creating an optimal investment environment for establishing enterprises, capable of attracting foreign capital. In order to build economic and technological development areas in the coastal cities, efforts must be calculated, with strict adherence to the principle of gradual implementation, with building following development, leading to quick garnering of profits. [They will] make technological development the main focus, promote joint venture enterprises, foreign-Chinese cooperative enterprises, and 100 percent foreign capital enterprises; and bring in the advanced technology needed by our country.

*Coastal Development Areas*

Such development areas as the Yangtze River delta, Zhujiang delta, and Minnan triangle area will gradually acquire a trading-industrial-agricultural type production structure. Processing industries necessary to support exporting will be developed, and agricultural and other raw materials production necessary to support processing industries will be developed. Introduction of technology and technological reform will be carried out first. Upgrading of products will be pursued relentlessly. Exports will be increased in an effort to capture foreign exchange, and open economic areas will be bases for foreign trade. Economic ties with the interior will be greatly strengthened, entraining the development of the interior economy.

# New Regulations Governing Foreign Investment

The January 27, 1986, *People's Daily* reported that the State Council had amended article 100 of the "Implementing Regulations of the Chinese-Foreign Joint Venture

Enterprise Law" to extend the joint venture period to fifty years. It was reported that the State Council had also promulgated "Regulations of the State Council Concerning the Question of the Balance of the Foreign Exchange Receipts and Expenditures for Joint Ventures Using Chinese and Foreign Investment."

In March the fourth meeting of the National People's Congress adopted the "Foreign Capital Enterprise Law," which set as conditions for establishing enterprises "utilizing advanced technology or equipment, or exporting all or a portion of production" and specified that "foreign capital enterprises will not be nationalized or expropriated." In this connection, China was rigidly focusing on the introduction of advanced technology, but the countries providing it were suggesting that China should not be concentrating exclusively on high technology but on technology appropriate to China's actual needs.

On August 7, 1986, Premier Zhao Ziyang met in Beidaihe, Hebei province, with Japanese, U.S., West German, and British executives in the petrochemical and financial industries and encouraged foreign investment, as reported in Hong Kong's *Wen Wei Po* August 11:

> Proceeding further toward accomplishing China's four modernizations, capital will remain a major constraining element. For this reason, China is welcoming all forms of foreign loans, and is actively pursuing foreign enterprise investment in China. I encourage you to establish joint venture enterprises, cooperative enterprises, and 100 percent foreign owned enterprises. ...
>
> Financial leaders from abroad are thinking that China possesses an enormous potential market, and, further, that it should be possible to lower wages, land costs, and other service costs . ... Having said that, some foreign enterprises are being disappointed as they realize that the cost of investment in China is rather high. ... In view of this situation, the Chinese government is now preparing to make the Chinese investment market more attractive to foreign investors. By this means, it is expected that the cost of finished products of foreign invested enterprises will drop, and that this will enhance the international competitiveness of these enterprises.

Soon after this statement, the State Council established the Leading Group on Foreign Investment (*Wen Wei Po*, August 11, 1986), which subsequently drafted the "Foreign Investment Incentives Regulations."

On September 25 to 28, the Party Central convened the Sixth Plenum of the Twelfth Congress. At this meeting Hu Yaobang tried to bring up the "Political System Reform Initiative," but it was tabled; on the contrary, conservatives gained control and the "Decision on Spiritual Civilization" was adopted. Students sensed in this reversal a crisis and began street demonstrations to support the reformers. As a result, Hu Yaobang was quickly purged. On January 16, 1987, the Party Central convened an expanded Politburo meeting and accepted his resignation as general secretary. Hu Yaobang's crimes were listed as "violating the principle of collective leadership" and "tolerating bourgeois liberalism."

On October 11, 1986, the State Council promulgated the "Regulations Concerning Incentives for Foreign Investment." These regulations described preferential treatment in a variety of areas, such as lower costs for labor and land use and reduction or elimination of income taxes, for enterprises manufacturing for export and for enterprises with advanced technology (*People's Daily,* October 12, 1986). These preferences were proposed as necessary supplements to the inadequate incentives in the existing investment incentive policy; however, one senses that the effectiveness of the new provisions was dissipated in the context of the resignation of Hu Yaobang.

On November 27 the *People's Daily* reported that the State Council Ministry of Labor had promulgated the "Regulations on Sovereignty in Hiring Staff, and in Staff Wages, Insurance Premiums and Welfare Expenses of Foreign Capital–Affiliated Enterprises." These regulations guaranteed that such enterprises would have sovereignty in hiring. Similar control was granted for imported components; on November 29 the *People's Daily* carried the "Regulations of the People's Republic of China with Respect to Control of Materials and Parts Imported by Foreign Capital–Affiliated Enterprises for the Purpose of Fulfilling Export Production Contracts."

On March 1, 1987, the *People's Daily* published "Provisional Regulations Governing the Ratios of Total Investment Capital Investment in Joint Venture Enterprises." A few months later (August 27), it published the "Provisional Regulations Governing Accounting and Supervision of Foreign Liabilities." This was the first time that China openly disclosed its foreign indebtedness.

# Wavering on Liberalization After the Purge of Hu Yaobang

After the purge of Hu Yaobang in January 1987, the political tide in China shifted to move the conservatives into a dominant position. As a consequence, in February to April of that year the reform policy seemed to be suspended, alive in name but dead in fact.

Amid this shift to the left, Zhao Ziyang in a May 13 address to a Party Central propaganda work meeting called for a revival of the reform policy. Afterward, seizing this opportunity, the reformers began their counterattack (a record of the address was carried in the July 10, 1987, *People's Daily*).

The July 1 *People's Daily* sought to revive the reformist mood by reissuing Deng Xiaoping's "On Reform of the Leadership System of the Party and the State" (originally announced August 18, 1980). In that document (see Deng Xiaoping 1983, pp. 208–302), Deng Xiaoping employed the device of referring to the words of Mao Zedong—who once criticized Stalin for trampling on the socialist legal system and said that such abuses could not have occurred in the advanced democracies of Britain, France, and the United States—to criticize indirectly the mistakes of Mao Zedong himself in the Great Leap Forward and the Cultural Revolution, to point out the defects in the current Chinese political system, and to call for reform. However, Deng Xiaoping's platform entailed reform at the administrative level. When later there were demands from below for democratization and students and workers began to demonstrate, there was quick resort to military repression.

## Thirteenth Party Congress Reconfirms Liberalization Policy

At the Thirteenth Party Congress October 25 to November 1, 1987, Zhao Ziyang incorporated in his political report the "theory of the early stage of socialism" and succeeded in obtaining confirmation of the reform and liberalization line. Late in November 1987 Zhao made an inspection tour of coastal regions and cities, including Shanghai, Zhejiang, Jiangsu, and Fujian, and announced his "important views" regarding "the development strategy for the coastal region economy." (These were carried later in the January 23, 1988, *People's Daily.*) Zhao Ziyang declared that "in determining whether an investment environment is good or not, the most important point is whether or not the investors can make money." He further clarified that the key is "permitting foreign capital to directly manage the enterprise, respecting their management authority." Zhao berated as "an incorrect point of view" the idea that "permitting foreign capital to manage their enterprises is a loss of sovereignty."

Zhao's remarks were a bold concession to foreign capital, which had often been dissatisfied with the Chinese investment environment and had been hesitating. The intention was probably to promote further introduction of foreign capital. In this sense, his development strategy for the coastal region propelled China's liberalization policy into its second stage.

Initially, because the party's internal leadership structure was controlled by oppositionists (especially the "totalist faction") representing the conservatives, there were limits to the implementation of a bold liberalization policy. However, after the Thirteenth Party Congress, reformers gained control of personnel matters in the leadership, and implementation of the policy became easier. The significant points of Zhao Ziyang's speeches were (1) to recognize expressly that it was necessary to create an investment system in which foreign investors could make money; and (2) to reflect on the limitations of the initial "passive" liberalization policy, acknowledging that the investment incentives contained in the joint venture enterprise law were largely window dressing and that the investment environment was deficient. This internal assessment led China to embark on a more substantive policy, but it was ambushed by inflation.

In January 1989 there was a shuffle in membership of the State Council's Leading Group for Foreign Investment: Tian Jiyun became head (replacing Gu Mu); Gan Ziyu, deputy director of the State Planning Commission, became deputy head (replacing Zhou Jiannan, who became adviser); other members were Shen

Jueren, vice minister of the Ministry of Foreign Economic Relations and Trade, and He Chunlin, deputy secretary of the State Council. This group had been established in July 1986 principally (1) to investigate foreign capital utilization policies and plans, as well as important measures with regard to foreign capital, and to present its findings to the State Council; (2) to supervise and investigate activities of all regions and organs with respect to utilization of foreign capital, and to resolve, arbitrate, and settle major problems; and (3) to organize concerned departments, strengthen investigations and research, and provide macro guidance on the use of foreign capital.

# China Acknowledges Net Aid Recipient Status

Not until the beginning of 1989 did China frankly acknowledge the reality that it was a "net aid receiving country" and note that such status was fitting given China's world economic position. *People's Daily* reporter Zhang Yi gave this analysis:

> From 1986 until today, the aid that our country has provided to other countries has been less than the bilateral and multilateral aid that we have received. In fact, our country has long been a net aid receiving country. This is appropriate for our country given its position as a developing country.
>
> Since the implementation of the liberalization policy, our country's multilateral cooperation with the United Nations Development Program as well as other bilateral cooperation has been carried out under the policy of reciprocal "giving as well as receiving"—appropriately administering aid while receiving aid. According to statistics, from 1972 through 1987 our country contributed to the UNDP RMB 29,110,000 and foreign currency totalling $23,410,000. From 1979 through 1987 the amount of actual aid received from the United Nations in the areas under control of the Ministry of External Economic Relations and Trade alone exceeded $300 million. If we take account also of aid from the World Food Program and FAO, the number will be much larger.
>
> Since 1981 our country has been receiving economic and technical assistance grants provided by friendly country governments. The main countries are as follows. The Japanese government is providing some Yen 6–7 billion of grant assistance annually. West Germany in general provides DM 70–80 million. Canada is providing annually some C$40 million. Australia is contributing annually some A$20 million. The total amount is over $100 million. Using this bilateral and multilateral aid, our country is undertaking over 600 projects, bringing in a substantial quantity of advanced technology and equipment, and training a group of expert personnel. Development of certain areas of our country's economy and society is being promoted, and certain difficult technical problems have been solved. (Zhang Yi, "Our Country Has Become a Net Aid Receiving Country," *People's Daily,* January 4, 1989, p. 1)

The full text of this article ran twenty-six lines. Perhaps in anticipation of a negative reaction to this frank analysis, the *People's Daily* three days later carried an article on the subject of China's foreign economic assistance that was 80 percent longer (forty-seven lines).

In the ten years since 1979, China—on the basis of seeking truth from facts and adhering to the principle of proceeding by measured efforts—has been rationally adjusting the scale, scope, and structure of foreign economic and technical assistance, and concentrating efforts on garnering the fruits of completed projects. Currently over 80 countries are receiving assistance from China. China's foreign assistance work is contributing to the development of people's economies of friendly countries of the Third World, and playing a positive role in international affairs.

In the last ten years, new dimensions in foreign assistance work have been seen in four areas:

1.  In line with the development of China's external relations, at the same time that we have continued to provide assistance to 64 previous aid receiving countries, we have provided aid to 24 new countries, and further increased assistance to the least developed countries. From 1984 through 1988 new aid authorized and new aid actually disbursed to the 34 least developed countries increased 63 percent and 46 percent respectively compared with the period 1979 through 1983. At the same time the structure of aid was adjusted to raise the ratio of complete plants, technical assistance, and knowledge assistance. Over ten years expenditures on this aspect of assistance have accounted for 74 percent of total spending for economic and technical assistance, twice the ratio during the previous eight years of the 1970s (1970–77).

2.  In the last few years, while continuing to carry out traditional forms of assistance, we have adopted the approach of combining bilateral and United Nations multilateral assistance. The two parties jointly contribute funds, while implementation is organized by experts dispatched from China. Aid is combined with arrangement of engineering sub-contracts to assist aid receiving countries to implement development projects. In some cases, after complete construction of a plant provided through aid, rather than the previous simple technical cooperation, Chinese experts are remaining to participate in operational management.

3.  In the last ten years, China assisted in construction of 335 plants in 67 countries. These included some large and medium sized projects that had demonstrable economic and social effects. Small projects involving small investments and producing rapid results are also having excellent effects.

4.  In the 1960s and 1970s China helped the Third World through the construction of a great many large plants. Included were many productive projects achieving substantial economic results. *However, after Chinese experts returned home, for reasons such as lack of management personnel in the aid receiving countries and poor management, production at some of the enterprises became abnormal and some fell into chronic loss situations.* After 1982 we took full account of experience and gave the work of garnering of the fruits of projects priority equivalent to that for construction of new projects. Hence, various kinds of technical cooperation and management cooperation were undertaken with respect to 275 finished projects. Most of the projects have performed to their full economic

and social potential. Some projects were quickly returned to profitability and placed on a sound basis. (Ye Rugen, "New Aspects Seen in Our Country's Foreign Economic Assistance," *People's Daily*, January 7, 1989, emphasis added)

This article is also of great interest. If we read the article from the perspective not of China but of countries providing aid to China, we can understand how China is seeking to receive aid. In particular, we can read the italicized sentence as self-criticism.

# The Tiananmen Incident (June 4, 1989): Liberalization Suspended

From the outset, Zhao Ziyang's economic development strategy for the coastal region was linked with debate on inflation. In the interior, the issue of growing regional disparities aroused great controversy. Against these criticisms the *People's Daily* carried a series of articles by its "Commentator" explaining the aims of the strategy, but criticism continued (*People's Daily* Commentator articles, May 19, 21, 23, 25, 27, June 3, 25, 1988).

Subsequently, it appeared the strategy would be suspended after an adjustment policy was launched at the Third Plenum of the Thirteenth Party Congress (September 26–30, 1988). However, Deng Xiaoping, Zhao Ziyang, and others emphasized that the coastal region strategy would be continued even in the context of economic adjustment. For example, there were statements affirming the coastal development strategy from Deng Xiaoping to the president of Kenya on October 5, 1988, from Tian Jiyun in Qingdao on October 23, from Zhao Ziyang to foreign business executives on November 2, from Zhao Ziyang to participants at a *Nihon Keizai Shimbun* symposium on November 4, from Zhao Ziyang to the National Planning Meeting on December 2, and from Zhao Ziyang to the Seminar on Coastal Region External Liberalization Work on December 3. However, repeatedly propounded in these statements were many nuances that differentiated the strategy from the concept advanced by Zhao Ziyang at the beginning of the year. It became apparent that, quite apart from economic adjustment measures, "reform and liberalization" had become linked in people's minds with and had come to symbolize inflation. Consequently it seemed hard to conceive of success in adjustment without effectively suspending the liberalization policy.

It was in this delicate political context that the democracy movement arose in spring 1989, to be met by the government with military suppression June 3–4. Martial law was enforced in Beijing for eight months from May 20 to January 10, 1990. In reality, the liberalization policy existed in name only and was dead. The communiqué of the Fourth Plenary Session of the Thirteenth Party Congress (*People's Daily*, June 25, 1989) emphasized that there would be "no change in policy" even after the military suppression and reiterated "firm support for the liberalization policy." These themes were repeated in the communiqué of the Fifth Plenary Session (November 6–9, 1989). Against this, the West was exerting pressure on the Chinese government by insisting that it lift martial law as a precondition for resumption of economic cooperation. The Chinese government, which found itself in crisis after economic retrenchment and subject to what were in reality economic sanctions by the West, soon lifted martial law.

The communiqué of the Fourth Plenary Session, in dealing summarily with the Tiananmen incident, asserted the "two pillars" doctrine (which had been advanced as a slogan of the Thirteenth Party Congress): (1) upholding the "four basic principles" (the socialist road; dictatorship of the people's democracy; leadership of the Communist Party; and Marxism, Leninism, and Mao Zedong thought, as the "basis of the nation") and (2) "firmly adhering to the reform and liberalization" as the "road to national strength." However, this "two pillars" concept was riven by fundamental contradictions. Hu Yaobang and Zhao Ziyang were successively purged from the position of general secretary and charged with the crime of trying to undermine "support for the four basic principles." Their ouster showed how treacherous it was to try to balance government policy and party politics between the two pillars.

## Resurrection of the Liberalization Policy

The Shanghai Communist Party organ *Liberation Daily* carried a series of articles by commentator Huang Puping based on Deng Xiaoping's 1991 Lunar New Year instructions. (Huang Puping was the pen name adopted by a group of the paper's editors that included Zhou Ruijin, an intimate of Zhang Zemin and Zhu Rongji, who has become deputy editor of the *People's Daily* in Beijing.) These were (1) "Be a 'Lead Sheep' of Reform and Liberalization" on February 15; (2) "New Thinking Required for Reform and Liberalization" on March 2; (3) "Further Strengthen the Mentality of Expanding Liberalization" on March 22; and (4) "Cadres Possessing Both Morality and Skills Needed in Reform and Liberalization" on April 12.

The first article argued that Shanghai should assume its historical role as the leading force in China's development, a role that had been assumed in the 1980s by Guangdong province. The second asserted that thinking that posited a conflict between adjustment under the plan and adjustment in the market was a "new mental roadblock." Pointedly it said that "placing utilization of foreign capital in conflict with self reliance, and excessive timidity on the question of using foreign capital, are unacceptable." The third item was a systematic criticism of the thinking of conservatives. "Comrade Deng Xiaoping is warmly hoping that Shanghai in the 1990s will raise high the banner of reform and liberalization, and more rapidly, splendidly, and boldly develop Pudong. ... The development of Pudong may be called an attempt to create a 'socialist Hong Kong' by implementing special free port type policies such as establishment of a customs free zone, free importing and exporting, and abolition of export taxes. ... Asking the complicated question of whether the name is socialism or capitalism will only cause us to lose the immediate opportunity of development." The fourth article discussed policy regarding cadres. "Some comrades are critical, saying capitalist society is bad; however in terms of tapping potential and utilizing human resources, it is extremely bold. It must be considered normal to utilize people who are equal to the task regardless of qualifications and seniority."

The *Liberation Daily*'s continuous campaign in the two months after the 1991 Spring Festival presumably was a fillip to the National People's Congress in March and April. Observers believed that Deng Xiaoping's basic strategy was to achieve a full revival of the reform and liberalization line by June 1991, two full years after the Tiananmen incident. Symbolic of this spirit was the "New Cat theory": "Whether our policies and actual work are correct or not, good or not, is a matter of whether or not they are favorable for the development of production. In general what benefits the development of production is correct and good. What does not benefit it is incorrect and bad" (*Jingbao*, Hong Kong, July 1991, article by Zhang Mu).

After the Huang Puping campaign, Deng Xiaoping sought to revive reform and liberalization; he delivered three basic directives to the reformist leadership group of Jiang Zemin, Li Ruihuan, and others. First, in future references to the Tiananmen incident, the words "insurrection and riot" should not be used; only "political storm" should be used. Second, with a view toward freeing people's minds, the four basic principles should be downgraded to "Party principles." Third, the question of rehabilitating Zhao Ziyang should be discussed in the Politburo. (The report on Zhao by the special group of Wang Renzhong, among others, concluded that Zhao's mistakes were "violations of party organization discipline" and that charges of "splitting the party" and "supporting insurrection" were groundless. [*Jingbao*, October 1991, article by Liu Bi.])

## Soviet Disintegration Sets Back Deng's Initiatives

However, the unpredictable can always disrupt plans. The Chinese Communist Party suffered a direct blow from the failure of the coup d'état attempt of the conservatives in the former Soviet Union and the resulting breakup of the Soviet Communist Party in August 1991. Mao Zedong said that "the cannon's roar of the October revolution delivered Marxism-Leninism to China." The failure of the August 1991 revolution evidenced for China the failure of the Soviet Communist Party and the defeat of Marxism-Leninism.

The conservatives in Beijing went on a fierce counterattack. One element was an article in the September 1 *People's Daily* by Chen Yeping ("Possessing Both Morality and Skills, Assuming Leadership on the Basis of Morality—Discussing Standards for Selecting and Promoting Cadres"), who stated: "Our Party has settled the series of mistakes made by comrade Zhao Ziyang; among the mistakes was selecting and promoting cadres based on a standard of productivity, emphasizing skills and deemphasizing morals." What was generally thought to be the "production standard" was Deng Xiaoping's Black Cat, White Cat theory and the New Cat theory advanced in summer 1991. In other words, the important aspect of the article was that by criticizing Zhao Ziyang, Chen Yeping implicitly also was criticizing Deng's production theory that Zhao had adopted.

The Party Central work conference was held September 23–27, 1991. Ostensibly the only accomplishment was a decision on reviving state-owned enterprises that were troubled by losses. But during the conference session, Deng Xiaoping criticized as a "leftist retrogression" what he saw as a failure to implement seriously the concepts of (1) making economic construction (not class struggle) the focus of the party's basic line and (2) firmly upholding the productivity theory that science and technology are most important. After hearing this, Yang Shangkun (state chairman) in an October 9 speech commemorating the eightieth anniversary of the Xinhai revolution ("The Current Situation and Our Tasks," *People's Daily,* October 10, 1991) reiterated the priority of economic construction and completely avoided mentioning opposition to the conservative theme of "peaceful evolution."

A meeting of all province-level Party Committee Organization Department heads was convened December 9–13, 1991, in Beijing. Central Organization Department head Lu Feng delivered an opening address in which he stipulated the standard for selecting and promoting cadres: those "possessing both morality and skills, with morality of first importance, [i.e.,] ... political attitude at key moments—for example, the Tiananmen Incident." A similar address was delivered by Politburo Standing Committee member Song Ping (former Central Organization Department head). Articulation of this conservative platform was significant because delegates for the Fourteenth Party Congress and Central Committee members would be selected at this meeting and instructions would be received for personnel decisions for all levels of positions within the party. Thus, just as with the commentary by Chen Yeping, for the conservatives to define the terms of the debate was a major challenge to the reformers that could not be ignored.

At the end of November at the Eighth Plenum of the Thirteenth Congress, Deng Xiaoping's theory of production (New Cat theory) managed to obtain approval, but conservatives attained a dominant position in the party organization structure. It seemed that the massive blow of their fellow conservatives' failed coup in the Soviet Union had brought together in one stroke the conservative forces in the Chinese Communist Party.

## Deng Xiaoping's 1992 Spring Festival Performance Speeds Up Liberalization

From January 18 to February 21, 1992 (Spring Festival fell on February 4), Deng Xiaoping conducted an inspection tour of Wuchang, Shenzhen, Zhuhai, and Shanghai. Manifesting that he was in good health, he issued "important talks" at each location advocating a speedup of reform and liberalization: "Reform and liberalization is the only viable road for China. Those who will not undertake reform, no matter who they are, have no course but to resign. ... Some persons are saying that securities trading is capitalism, but the result of the experiments in Shanghai and Shenzhen have proven that it is a success. Even if something is capitalist there is nothing wrong with incorporating it in the socialist system" (translated from Communist Party Central Document No. 2 [1992], see Appendix 1).

Deng's theme was nothing more than a reiteration of his previous Black Cat, White Cat theory. Indeed, his actions resembled the stance he took during his visit to Shenzhen in February 1984. Deng's 1992 tour was significant first as a frontal counteroffensive to growing conservative criticism of his line (expressed in conservative jargon as "opposing peaceful evolution") after the shock of the breakup of the former Soviet Union. In touting the success of reform and liberalization, he thrust back in criticism at the conservatives' perversity.

The second meaning of Deng Xiaoping's performance was a signal that shifts in China's political structures had started in advance of the Fourteenth Party Congress the previous fall—a meeting that had obvious importance because it would commence the establishment of a post–Deng Xiaoping system that would determine the future course of China. Whether the leadership group would primarily include persons who would actively pursue reform and liberalization or, on the contrary, stand-patters and conservatives had enormous significance not only for China, but for the political and economic system of East Asia as a whole.

Deng Xiaoping later (May 22) visited the Beijing Capital Steel Company. Saying that reform of state-owned enterprises would "begin with liberating our minds," he praised the economic management ability of Zhu Rongji. On June 12 the Production Office of the State Council was abolished and the State Council Office of Economic Trade was reorganized with Vice Premier Zhu Rongji placed in concurrent charge. This was a significant expansion of his authority.

In June the Party Central and State Council, drawing from Deng Xiaoping's statements, produced and disseminated Communist Party Central Document No. 4 (1992) (Appendix 2). This document noted the success of the coastal opening strategy and was an instruction to accelerate reform according to the guideline of "multidirectional, multistrata liberalization." Next came Document No. 5 (1992) (Appendix 3), which ordered "development of tertiary industries." By virtue of Documents No. 4 and No. 5, Deng Xiaoping's initiative to speed up reform and liberalization began to infiltrate the entire party.

Document No. 4 (1992) designated new localities as opened areas: The first group included five Yangtze River riparian cities—in order moving upriver, Wuhu (Anhui province), Jiujiang (Jiangxi), Wuhan (Hubei), Yueyang (Hunan), and Chongqing (Sichuan). In March 1993 Huangshi (Hubei) was added for a total of six opened Yangtze River riparian cities.

The second group included border cities in three regions: (1) the northern border with Russia—the four cities of Manzhouli, Heihe, Suifenhe (Heilongjiang province), and Hunchun (Jilin); (2) the northwestern border with Kazakhstan and Mongolia—the four cities and counties of Yining, Bole, Tacheng (Xinjiang), and Erenhot (Inner Mongolia); and (3) the southwestern border area with Myanmar and Vietnam—the five cities and counties of Ruili, Tianwanding, Hekou (Yunnan), Pingxiang, and Dongxingzhen (Guangxi).

Third were the provincial capitals that are the essential links to the hinterland for the border cities. These include for the cities listed in (1) in the preceding paragraph, the provincial capitals of Harbin (Heilongjiang) and Changchun (Jilin); for (2) the autonomous region capitals of Huhehot (Inner Mongolia) and Urumchi (Xinjiang); and for (3) the provincial and autonomous region capitals, respectively, of Kunming (Yunnan) and Nanning (Guangxi).

The fourth group included interior provincial capitals without any connections with the coastal regions, the border regions, or the Yangtze River riparian area: Shijiazhuang (Hebei), Taiyuan (Shanxi), Hefei (Anhui), Nanchang (Jiangxi), Zhengzhou (Henan), Changsha (Hunan), Chengdu (Sichuan), Guiyang (Guizhou), Xian (Shaanxi), Lanzhou (Gansu), Xining (Qinghai), and Yinchuan (Ningxia).

Thus the "multi-directional, multi-strata" liberalization structure took form. It became referred to as the structure of opening to the outside world in the context of "multi-directional, multi-strata, multi-channeled integration of coastal, border, riparian, and interior areas."

Deng Xiaoping, in the fifteen years after the establishment of the Shenzhen special economic zone, finally opened to the outside all the principal cities and regions of China. Notwithstanding that the degree of liberalization and preferential treatment for foreign capital vary from region to region, it remains that Deng Xiaoping's approach of opening cities by increments succeeded in reversing the isolationist policy of the Mao Zedong era. In the whole country only Tibet is without an open city.

After the designation of three customs-free zones in 1991—Waigaoqiao (Shanghai), Futian (Shenzhen), and Shatoujiao (Shenzhen)—an additional ten zones were designated in 1992. These were Tianjingang (Tianjin), Dalian (Liaoning), Guangzhou (Guangdong), Xiamen (Fujian), Zhangjiagang (Jiangsu), Haikou (Hainan), Shantou (Guangdong), Ningbo (Zhejiang), Fuzhou (Fujian), and Qingdao (Shandong).

In the grip of this mood of accelerating reform and liberalization, elections of delegates to the Fourteenth Party Congress were carried out in the central organs and at the provincial level. As a consequence, at the congress held October 12–18, the concept of the "socialist market economy" was adopted, and the reformist faction headed by Jiang Zemin and Li Peng consolidated their hold on the leadership position of the party.

In March 1993 selections for leadership positions in the state and government reflected how the post-Deng structure would take shape: Jiang Zemin assumed the state chairmanship, Qiao Shi assumed chairmanship of the Standing Committee of the National People's Congress, Li Ruihuan became chairman of the Political Consultative Conference, and Li Peng remained as premier.

The rapid economic growth in 1992 had by early summer 1993 reached a condition of economic overheating. In July, Vice Premier Zhu Rongji assumed command of a financial rectification and austerity campaign. The next month General Secretary Jiang Zemin announced a campaign to combat corruption and abuse of power among Communist Party cadres.

If the problem of overheating can be successfully resolved, and if constraints can be placed on corruption and abuses of authority, then a continuation of the high level of growth of the Chinese economy will be possible, and the emergence of China as the center of growth for the world economy in the twenty-first century is highly probable.

# Annotated Chronology

## 1978

| | |
|---|---|
| **August 12** | Signing of the Japan-China Treaty on Peace and Friendship. |
| **December 16** | Resumption of U.S.-China diplomatic relations (January 1, 1979) announced. |
| **December 18–22** | Third Plenum of the Eleventh Party Congress. The Deng Xiaoping faction achieves dominance. |

## 1979

| | |
|---|---|
| **January 23** | The Guangdong Provincial Communist Party Committee decides to reorganize Baoan county as Shenzhen municipality under direct provincial control and to establish the Shenzhen Communist Party Committee. |
| **January 31** | The Party Central and the State Council decide to establish Shekou in Shenzhen as an industrial zone. |
| **February 15** | The State Council decides that Shenzhen municipality in Guangdong province should be built up as an "export products production base." |
| **July 1** | The "Law of the People's Republic of China on Joint Ventures Using Chinese and Foreign Investment" (Joint Venture Law) is enacted at the second session of the Fifth National People's Congress. Law is effective from July 8. |

*Source: New China Monthly,* various issues.

| July 15 | After reports from Guangdong and Fujian provinces of investigations into issues concerning export bases, the Party Central and State Council approve in principle the creation of "special export zones" in Shenzhen, Zhuhai, and Shantou. |
| July 30 | The Foreign Investment Control Committee (director, Gu Mu) is established at the tenth session of the Fifth National People's Congress. |
| October 4 | The China International Trust and Investment Company is established (chairman, Rong Yiren). |
| December 5–9 | Premier Ohira Masayoshi makes a state visit to China and commits to provide the first yen loan. |

# 1980

| May 27–June 1 | Chairman Hua Guofeng makes a state visit to Japan. |
| May | The Party Central changes the name of the initiative called "export products production bases" to "special economic zones." |
| June 30–July 1 | The State Council convenes a meeting in Beijing to discuss the Hainan Island smuggling problem. |
| July 30 | The State Council promulgates the "Measures for the Registration of Joint Ventures Using Chinese and Foreign Investment." |
| August 26 | The fifteenth meeting of the Standing Committee of the Fifth National People's Congress approves "Regulations on the Special Economic Zones of the Guangdong Province" and promulgates them the same day. On the same day it is announced that special economic zones would be established within the province at Shenzhen, Zhuhai, and Shantou. |
| September 10 | The third session of the Fifth National People's Congress adopts and announces to take immediate effect the "Income Tax Law of the People's Republic of China Concerning Joint Ventures Using Chinese and Foreign Investment" and the "Individual Income Tax Law of the People's Republic of China." |
| November 28 | The Shenzhen Communist Party Committee promulgates "Twelve Provisional Regulations Concern- |

|  | ing Problems Related to Implementation of Special Policies and Flexible Measures in the Agricultural Village of Shenzhen." |
|---|---|
| December 14 | The Ministry of Finance promulgates "Detailed Rules and Regulations for the Implementation of the Individual Income Tax Law of the People's Republic of China" and "Detailed Rules and Regulations for the Implementation of the Income Tax Law of the People's Republic of China Concerning Joint Ventures Using Chinese and Foreign Investment." |
| December 18 | The State Council promulgates "Provisional Regulations Governing Foreign Exchange Control." |

# 1981

| Spring | Japanese plant cancellation incidents occur. |
|---|---|
| March 13 | The Bank of China announces "Provisional Measures for Providing Loans to Joint Ventures Using Chinese and Foreign Investment by the Bank of China," which have previously been approved by the State Council. |
| May 27–June 1 | The State Council convenes in Beijing the "Work Conference on Guangdong Province, Fujian Province, and Special Economic Zones." |
| October 15 | Construction begins on the 2.5-square-kilometer Huli export processing zone of the Xiamen special economic zone. |
| November 24 | The State Council approves the private placement in the Japanese market of a 10-billion-yen bond issue by the China International Trust and Investment Company (CITIC). |
| November 26 | The twenty-first meeting of the Standing Committee of the Fifth National People's Congress grants authority to the standing committees of the People's Congresses of Guangdong and Fujian provinces to make economic regulations concerning special economic zones under their jurisdiction. |
| December 22 | Veteran leader of the conservative faction Chen Yun issues statements designed to put a brake on the special economic zones ("A Few Important Directives for Eco- |

nomic Construction," included in Chen Yun 1986, p.
276).

December 24    The Standing Committee of the People's Congress of
               Guangdong province promulgates "Provisional Regula-
               tions of the Special Economic Zones in Guangdong
               Province Governing Entry and Exit of Personnel"; "Pro-
               visional Regulations of the Special Economic Zones of
               Guangdong Province Governing Registration of Busi-
               ness Enterprises"; "Provisional Regulations Governing
               Labor Wages of Enterprises in the Guangdong Province
               Special Economic Zones"; and "Provisional Regulations
               Governing Land in the Shenzhen Special Economic
               Zone." All are to be effective from January 1, 1982.

# 1982

January 1      The State Administration of Exchange Control promul-
               gates "Implementing Rules for Audits of Foreign Ex-
               change Applications from Individuals" and "Imple-
               menting Rules for Control of Foreign Exchange with
               Individuals."

January 15     Xinhua News Agency reports that the State Council had
               convened a symposium on external economic work of
               nine coastal provinces, cities, and autonomous areas,
               including Beijing, Tianjin, Shanghai, Liaoning, Hebei,
               Shandong, Zhejiang, and Guangxi.

February 21    The Ministry of Finance promulgates "Detailed Rules
               and Regulations for the Implementation of the Income
               Tax Law of the People's Republic of China Concerning
               Foreign Enterprises."

March 13       The State Council approves "Provisional Regulations of
               the General Administration for Industry and Com-
               merce of the People's Republic of China on Standards
               for the Payment of Registration Fees by Joint Ventures
               Using Chinese and Foreign Investment."

April 1–8      The Shenzhen municipal government convenes an audit
               meeting on the "Outline of the Social and Economic
               Development Plan for the Shenzhen Special Economic
               Zone."

| | |
|---|---|
| May 26 | The Shenzhen municipal government announces the "Outline of the Near-Term Industrial Development Plan for the Shenzhen Special Economic Zone (1982–1985)." |
| May 28 | The State Council approves creation of limited stock companies and development of Chiwan harbor in the Shenzhen special economic zone. |
| September 16–October 1 | Japanese Prime Minister Suzuki Zenko makes a state visit to China. The textbook problem is smoothed over. |
| September 21 | The State Council issues "Notice of the State Council Regarding the Question of the Levy of Taxation on Chinese-Foreign Joint Venture and Co-operative Projects." |

# 1983

| | |
|---|---|
| May 1 | The State Council decides to provide preferences to Taiwanese compatriots investing in the special economic zones. |
| May 16 | The State Council issues its "Decision on Expanding the Autonomy of Shanghai Municipality in Foreign Trade." |
| June 26 | Publication of Deng Xiaoping's "Initiative on Peaceful Unification of Taiwan and the Chinese Mainland" (in Deng Xiaoping 1987). |
| July 8 | Publication of Deng Xiaoping's "Let Us Learn from Foreign Knowledge" (Deng Xiaoping 1987). |
| July 11 | The Party Central and the State Council decide to accelerate development of Hainan Island (the previous April the "Minutes of Discussions on Issues Relating to Acceleration of Development and Construction of Hainan Island" had been approved and circulated). |
| July 27 | The State Council approves the proposal of Guangdong province to expand the area of the Zhuhai special economic zone from 6.81 square kilometers to 14.1 square kilometers. |
| August 1 | The State Council approves, effective immediately, "Detailed Rules for the Implementation of Regulations Relating to Overseas Chinese Enterprises, Foreign Enter- |

prises, and Chinese-Foreign Joint Ventures" of the State Administration of Exchange Control.

September 20    The State Council promulgates the "Implementing Act for the Law of the People's Republic of China on Joint Ventures Using Chinese and Foreign Investment" (this was a supplementary explanation of the joint venture law promulgated in 1979).

October 11–12   After the Second Plenum of the Twelfth Party Congress the Party Central launched the campaign against "spiritual pollution." Persons involved in the special economic zones began to fear a reversal of policy that would place them in political danger.

November 23–30  General Secretary Hu Yaobang visits Japan.

November 27     The State Council approves expanded authority for Dalian municipality to manage introduction of technology (Dalian obtained the same authority as Liaoning province to directly utilize foreign capital to modernize technology).

November        Shenzhen municipality establishes the Labor Services Corporation.

# 1984

January 24–29   Deng Xiaoping, Wang Zhen, Yang Shangkun, and other officials make inspection visits to the Shenzhen and Zhuhai special economic zones of Guangdong province. On January 26 Deng Xiaoping writes, "Shenzhen's development and experience are proof of the correctness of our policy of establishing special economic zones."

February 1      The General Administration of Customs establishes "Regulations of the General Administration of Customs, the Ministry of Finance, the Ministry of Foreign Economic Relations and Trade of the People's Republic of China Concerning the Supervision and Control over, and the Imposition of or Exemption from Tax on, Imports and Exports by Chinese-Foreign Co-operative Ventures."

February 7–10   Deng Xiaoping makes an inspection visit to the Xiamen special economic zone and advocates that China "develop special economic zones more quickly and splendidly."

February 7   The Guangdong provincial people's government promulgates "Regulations on Foreign Economic Contracts of the Shenzhen Special Economic Zone" and "Provisional Regulations on the Importation of Technology in the Special Zones."

February 24   Publication of Deng Xiaoping's "On the Question of Increasing the Number of Open Cities and Special Economic Zones" (Deng Xiaoping 1987).

March 3   National Foreign Trade Work Conference decides to centralize trade management authority in the Ministry of Foreign Economic Relations and Trade and to carry out a unified trade policy.

March 23–26   Prime Minister Nakasone Yasuhiro makes a state visit to China, commits to provide the second yen loan, and launches the Japan-China Twenty-first Century Friendship Committee.

March 26–April 6   The Party Central Secretariat and the State Council convene the "Symposium on Selected Coastal Cities" (decision to open fourteen coastal cities).

April 10   The *People's Daily* reports that the Guangdong provincial government had decided to apply province-wide the personnel and wage systems of the Shenzhen special economic zone.

June 22–23   Publication of Deng Xiaoping's "One Country, Two Systems" (Deng Xiaoping 1987).

July 11   The Xinhua News Agency wire carries comments of the responsible persons of the fourteen open coastal cities.

July 12   The responsible person of the State Council answers questions posed by the Xinhua News Agency about certain policies for the fourteen open coastal cities.

July 14   The eighth meeting of the Standing Committee of the Sixth Fujian Provincial People's Congress adopts "Regulations of the Xiamen Special Economic Zone Governing the Entry and Exit of Personnel"; "Regulations of Xiamen Special Economic Zone on the Registration of Enterprises"; "Regulations of Xiamen Special Economic Zone on Labor Management"; and "Regulations of

Xiamen Special Economic Zone on Land Use." It also approved "Regulations of Xiamen Special Economic Zone on the Import of Technology" and "Regulations of Xiamen Special Economic Zone on Economic Association with Inland Areas."

| | |
|---|---|
| July 17 | It is decided that the Shenzhen special economic zone branch of the People's Bank of China will assume central bank functions for the zone. |
| July 24 | The Economic and Technical Development Corporation for the Open Coastal Cities is established in Beijing. |
| August 12–16 | Wan Li, Gu Mu, and Li Peng make an inspection visit to Dalian. |
| August 16 | At Dalian, Wan Li calls for an acceleration of importation of technology and technology transformation in the open coastal cities. |
| August 17 | The State Council approves expanded devolution of authority to register foreign capital enterprises from the State Administration for Industry and Commerce to the special economic zones, fourteen open coastal cities, and Hainan administrative region (until this time, authority had devolved only to Guangdong and Fujian provinces, Guangzhou, and Shenzhen). |
| September 3–15 | Gu Mu (Central Secretariat secretary and member of the State Council) makes an inspection visit to Yantai and Qingdao. |
| September 25 | The State Council approves and circulates "Minutes of the Meeting on Questions Concerning Developing Energy and Transportation and Greatly Expanding Openness to the Outside World of Dalian Municipality." |
| September 26 | China and Britain initial an agreement on the question of Hong Kong (officially signed December 19). |
| October 3 | Publication of Deng Xiaoping's "Let Us Preserve the Stability and Prosperity of Hong Kong" (Deng Xiaoping 1987). |
| November 6 | The *People's Daily* reports that Shenzhen has decided to reorganize its management system for transportation and post and telecommunications by "making local management primary, and making vertical lines of au- |

thority secondary." In this connection the Ministry of Posts and Telecommunications took four types of measures to support the open cities and special economic zones.

November 15  The State Council promulgates "Provisional Regulations of the State Council of the People's Republic of China Regarding the Reduction of and Exemption from Enterprise Income Tax and Consolidated Industrial and Commercial Tax in the Special Economic Zones and the Fourteen Coastal Port Cities."

Late November– early December  Premier Zhao Ziyang makes an inspection visit to Guangzhou, Foshan, Shunde, Xinhui, Jiangmen, Zhongshan, Zhuhai, Shenzhen, Dongwan, Shanghai, Jiading, Wuxi, and Shazhou (reported by the Xinhua News Agency wire December 25).

# 1985

January 19  The journal *Economic Reference* reports that the per capita national income in the Shenzhen special zone has surpassed $1,000.

January 25–31  The State Council convenes the "Symposium on the Yangtze River, Zhujiang Delta, and Minnan Delta Regions."

Early 1985  State Council Vice Premier Yao Yilin's report on the situation of the Shenzhen special economic zone creates a chill.

March 4  Publication of Deng Xiaoping's "Peace and Development Are the Two Greatest Problems of the Modern World" (Deng Xiaoping 1987).

March 21  The tenth meeting of the Standing Committee of the Sixth National People's Congress adopts "The Foreign Economic Contracts Law of the People's Republic of China."

March 28  Yao Yilin, speaking with a Hong Kong journalist, complains that "less than one-third of the products produced in the special economic zones is exported. ... Exports are insufficient."

| April 1 | The director of the State Council Special Economic Zone Office, He Chunlin, reveals the performance of the special economic zones as of year-end 1984 to a Hong Kong journalist. |
| April 2 | The State Council promulgates "Provisions Governing Management of Foreign Banks and Joint Venture Banks in the Special Economic Zones." |
| June 25 | Deng Xiaoping warns that "the liberalization policy must not be mistaken" and adds "the Shenzhen special economic zone is one experiment. We hope it is a success, but if it is a failure we will still have received a lesson." |
| August 1 | Publication of Deng Xiaoping's "Let Us Convert from the Internally Directed Model to the Externally Directed Model Within the Special Economic Zones" (Deng Xiaoping 1987). |
| August 1 | The *People's Daily* reports approval by the Party Central and the State Council of "The Report on the Investigation of the Material Issues of Automobile Importation and Reselling on Hainan Island." |
| August 10, 12 | The *People's Daily* publishes the theses of Liu Guoguang, "Strategic Development Objectives of the Shenzhen Special Economic Zone" and "The Development of Shenzhen Special Economic Zone Is Facing a New Strategic Stage" (originally in an academic report delivered in Shenzhen April 23). |
| September 18 | A student demonstration in Beijing protests the attendance of Japanese Prime Minister Nakasone Yasuhiro at a ceremony for war dead at the Yasukuni Shrine. |
| September | The problem of "defects" in Japanese goods is raised. |
| October 7 | The *People's Daily* carries an article by Wang Zhuo, "A Discussion of Certain Questions About the Special Economic Zones" (a critical response to the theses of Liu Guoguang). |
| December 25 | A conference on work of the special economic zones is convened in Shenzhen. The Communist Party Committee secretary of Shenzhen municipality, Liang Xiang, delivers a summary report on the Shenzhen special economic zone at the "Conference of Cadres of Organs Directly Under the Party Central" (*Economic Daily*, December 11, 1985, excerpts carried in *People's Daily*, December 13). |

# 1986

| | |
|---|---|
| January 15 | The State Council promulgates the "Regulations of the State Council Concerning the Question of the Balance of the Foreign Exchange Receipts and Expenditures for Joint Ventures Using Chinese and Foreign Investment." |
| February 17 | The *People's Daily* reports that the Zhujiang delta is developing with great momentum. |
| March 28 | The People's Bank of China and the Japanese Ministry of Finance agree on the establishment of branches in Shenzhen for Tokai, Sanwa, and Takugin banks (branches opened May 16). |
| March 25–April 12 | The fourth session of the Sixth National People's Congress adopts the "Law of the People's Republic of China on Wholly Foreign-Owned Enterprises." |
| April 10 | Gu Mu, member of the State Council, remarks that the question of issuing a special economic zone currency had been tabled (the debate over a special zone currency quiets down). |
| April 12 | The fourth session of the National People's Congress adopts the "Wholly Foreign-Owned Enterprise Law." |
| July | The State Council Leading Group for Foreign Investment (group head, Gu Mu) is established. |
| August 20 | The Beijing newspaper *Economic Daily* reports that Dalian has enacted eleven preferential measures toward horizontal economic integration. |
| November 21 | The Japan-Shenzhen Cooperation Council is established in Tokyo. |
| December 30 | Publication of Deng Xiaoping's "Raise High the Banner of Opposing Bourgeois Liberalism" (Deng Xiaoping 1987). |

# 1987

| | |
|---|---|
| January 13 | Publication of Deng Xiaoping's "Overcome Obstacles and Earnestly Implement the Reform and Liberalization Policy" (Deng Xiaoping 1987). |

| January 16 | General Secretary Hu Yaobang resigns. One criticism against him is his policy toward Japan. |
| February 6–10 | Special economic zone work meeting held in Shenzhen. |
| February 7 | The *People's Daily* reports the performance of the four special economic zones in 1986. |
| March 1 | The State Administration for Industry and Commerce promulgates "Temporary Provisions on Registered Capital and Ratios of Total Investment Value of Chinese-Foreign Joint Ventures." |
| September 15 | The *People's Daily* carries "The Window of Hope: An Account of Reform and Liberalization in the Shekou Industrial Zone" by Chen Yushan and Lei Wei. |
| October 19 | The State Council approves the State Planning Commission's "Method of Import Substitution for the Products of Chinese-Foreign Joint Ventures and Contractual Joint Ventures." |
| December 30 | The State Council approves the Ministry of Foreign Economic Relations and Trade's "Certain Regulations Governing Capitalization by Each Partner of Chinese-Foreign Joint Venture Enterprises." |

# 1988

| January 5 | The *Economic Daily* publishes "A New Great Choice: The Economic Development Strategy in the Context of International Cycles" by Li Delai (*Economic Daily* reporter). |
| January 13 | *Red Flag,* No. 20, 1987, carries "The Shenzhen Special Zone Is Advancing in the Context of Reform and Liberalization" by Li Hao (Shenzhen Party Committee secretary and mayor). |
| January 16 | *Red Flag,* No. 2, 1988, carries "A Retrospective and Prospective View of Guangdong's Reform and Liberalization" by Lin Ruo (Guangdong Party Committee secretary). |
| January 23 | The *People's Daily* carries Zhao Ziyang's "Comments on the Economic Development Strategy of the Coastal Region." |

| | |
|---|---|
| **February 1** | *Red Flag,* No. 3, 1988, carries "Let Us Splendidly Build the Xiamen Special Economic Zone" by Qu Erzhun (Xiamen mayor). |
| **March 4–8** | The State Council convenes a conference on coastal region external opening work. Gu Mu and Tian Jiyun speak. |
| **April 13** | The first session of the Seventh National People's Congress elevates Hainan Island to provincial level and establishes the island as Hainan special economic zone. |
| **April 13** | The first session of the Seventh National People's Congress adopts and promulgates "The Chinese-Foreign Joint Venture Law of the PRC." |
| **April 18** | *Economic Work News,* No. 11, 1988, and *Xinhua Monthly,* No. 7, 1988, carry "Questions on Several Relationships in the Implementation of the Coastal Region Development Strategy" by Gan Ziyu (deputy director of the State Planning Commission). |
| **May 19, 21, 23, 25, 27, June 3, 25** | The *People's Daily* carries on seven occasions Commentator discourses on "The Coastal Region Economic Development Strategy." |
| **July 6** | The State Council promulgates "Provisions Concerning Encouragement of Investment from Taiwan." |
| **August 12** | The Guangdong People's Congress adopts "Regulations Governing Labor in the Special Economic Zones." |
| **August 25–30** | Prime Minister Takeshita Noboru pays a state visit to China and commits to providing the third yen loan. |
| **October 5** | Deng Xiaoping, in a meeting with the president of Kenya, emphasizes the coastal region development strategy. |
| **October 23** | Tian Jiyun underscores the coastal region development strategy while in Qingdao. |
| **November 2** | Zhao Ziyang makes a point of the coastal region development strategy in remarks to foreign executives. |
| **November 4** | Zhao Ziyang emphasizes the coastal region development strategy to participants in a *Nihon Keizai Shimbun* symposium. |
| **December 2** | Zhao Ziyang underscores the coastal region development strategy at the state planning meeting. |

| December 3 | Zhao Ziyang stresses the coastal region development strategy at a symposium on coastal region external opening work. |

# 1989

| January 3 | The *People's Daily* carries an analytical article, "Our Country Has Already Become a Net Aid Receiving Country." |
| January 7 | The *People's Daily* carries an article "New Aspects Seen in Our Country's Foreign Economic Assistance" (the real meaning of this article becomes clear when it is read in contrast to the previous article). |
| January | The membership of the State Council Leading Group on Foreign Investment is shuffled (new head is Tian Jiyun; deputy head Gan Ziyu, deputy director of the State Planning Commission; other members are Shen Jueren, vice minister of the Ministry of Foreign Economic Relations and Trade, and He Chunlin, deputy secretary of the State Council; Zhou Jiannan, former deputy group head, is named adviser). |
| January 28 | Zhao Ziyang addresses the Party Construction Research Group (carried in the March 17, 1989, *People's Daily*). |
| Late February | Persons from other provinces flood into Guangdong province seeking residence, and 30,000 wander around Shenzhen. |
| February 3–20 | Second session of the Seventh National People's Congress is held. Li Peng delivers a report. |
| April 15 | Hu Yaobang dies. The democratization movement begins. |
| May 4 | The seventienth anniversary of the May the Fourth Movement is observed in official ceremonies and by nonofficial student demonstrations. |
| May 15–18 | Gorbachev visits China. Sino-Soviet leadership discussions are held. |
| May 20 | Martial law is declared in some sections of Beijing municipality. |

| June 3–4 | Military force is used to suppress the democratization movement. |
| June 23–24 | At the Fourth Plenum of the Thirteenth Communist Party Congress, Zhao Ziyang is removed from office. Jiang Zemin assumes position of general secretary. |
| October 1 | Celebration of the fortieth anniversary of the founding of the PRC takes place under martial law. |
| November 6–9 | At the Fifth Plenum of the Thirteenth Party Congress, Deng Xiaoping retires from the position of chairman of the Party Central Military Affairs Commission. His successor is Jiang Zemin. |
| December | The Communist regime in Romania collapses. |

# 1990

| January 11 | Martial law is lifted. |
| March 9–12 | The Sixth Plenum of the Thirteenth Party Congress adopts the "Decision on the Mass Line." |
| March 20–April 4 | At the National People's Congress Deng Xiaoping retires from the chairmanship of the government Military Affairs Commission. Jiang Zemin assumes the chairmanship. |
| May 1 | Martial law is lifted in Lhasa city. |
| June 25 | Fang Lizhi and his wife leave China. |
| July 1 | The fourth population census is taken. |
| September 22–October 7 | The Asian athletic games are held in Beijing. |
| October 20 | Agreement reached to establish the Chinese-Korean Trade Office. |
| December 25–30 | The Seventh Plenum of the Thirteenth Party Congress adopts the "Outline of the Eighth Five-Year Plan." |

# 1991

| February 4 | Deng Xiaoping issues his Spring Festival instructions. Huang Puping's campaign begins in Shanghai's *Liberation Daily*. |

| | |
|---|---|
| February 15 | Publication of Huang Puping's "Be a 'Lead Sheep' of Reform and Liberalization." |
| March 2 | Publication of Huang Puping's "New Thinking Required for Reform and Liberalization." |
| March 22 | Publication of Huang Puping's "Further Strengthen the Mentality of Expanding Liberalization." |
| April 12 | Publication of Huang Puping's "Cadres Possessing Both Morality and Skills Needed in Reform and Liberalization." |
| March–April | The National People's Congress elevates Zhu Rongji from mayor of Shanghai to State Council deputy premier. |
| April 24 | General Secretary Jiang Zemin articulates the concept that "science and technology is the number one productive force" (*People's Daily,* April 24, 1991). |
| May 24 | The "number one productive force theory" is reiterated at the National Conference of the China Science and Technology Council. This is an acknowledgment of the result of the Gulf war. |
| June 1 | Rehabilitation of persons purged after the Tiananmen incident: Hu Qili (Politburo Standing Committee member), Yan Mingfu (Communist Party Central United Front Department head), and Rui Xingwen (Communist Party Central Secretariat secretary). |
| July | Deng Xiaoping advances his "New Cat theory." "Is our policy and actual work correct or not?" |
| May–July | Major flood damage in Anhui and Jiangsu provinces. |
| August | The conservative coup d'état attempt fails in the former Soviet Union. The Soviet Communist Party is to be disbanded. |
| August 31 | An article from the Commentator of *Liberation Daily* in Shanghai insists that it will be impossible to overcome difficulties by "sticking to old conventions" and calls for courage and determination in pursuing reform and liberalization. |
| September 1 | Chen Yeping's commentary "Possessing Both Morals and Skills, While Putting Morals First: A Discussion of Standards for Selecting and Promoting Cadres" noted that "our Party cleared away a series of mistakes of com- |

rade Zhao Ziyang. Among them was making productivity the standard for selecting and promoting cadres, the error of a bias of giving too much weight to skills and too little to morals." This was actually a criticism of Deng Xiaoping's White Cat, Black Cat doctrine and New Cat theory.

**September 2**      The *People's Daily* editorial "Cut Out Disturbances" rehashes the discussion of "socialist in name, or capitalist in name" (rebuttal to the March 22 commentary by Huang Puping).

**September 23–27**      The Party Central Work Conference is convened. A resolution on reviving loss-ridden state-owned enterprises is adopted.

**October 9**      Yang Shangkun delivers a commemorative address "The Current Situation and Our Tasks" on the eightieth anniversary of the Xinhai revolution (*People's Daily,* October 10). He is totally silent on the issue of opposition to "peaceful evolution."

**October 23**      Deng Lichun's article "Correctly Recognize the Contradictions in Socialism" (*People's Daily*) emphasizes the intensity of the class struggle against the bourgeois liberalist mentality.

**November 20**      At a forum on theoretical works on party history and construction organized by the Central Propaganda Department, Deng Lichun asserts that "there is nothing more important than opposing bourgeois liberalism. The struggle with the mentality of bourgeois liberalism cannot be abandoned for one second or one minute. Now liberalization within the Party and in the media is apparent everyday; it is receiving the support of leading comrades in the Party. Is this not extremely dangerous?"

**November 26**      The *Liberation Daily* carries an article by Liu Ji (Shanghai Party Committee Propaganda Department, deputy department head), "How Should We View the Current Situation?"

**November 25–29**      At the Eighth Plenum of the Thirteenth Party Congress, Deng Xiaoping's productive forces theory (New Cat theory) barely achieves acceptance, and it appears that the conservative faction achieves a dominant position in the party organization.

December 9–13   A national conference of province-level Party Committee Organization Department heads is convened in Beijing. Central Organization Department Head Lu Feng says in an opening address that the standard for selecting and promoting cadres should be "possessing both morality and skills, with morality of first importance." Morality means correct "political attitude at key moments—for example, the Tiananmen Incident." Song Ping, Politburo Standing Committee member (former Central Organization Department head), makes similar statements in his opening remarks.

# 1992

January 20      Deng Xiaoping visits Shenzhen. Later he visits the Zhuhai special zone and on the afternoon of January 29 enters Guangzhou. He calls for an acceleration of reform and liberalization. "Reform and liberalization is the only road viable for China. Those who will not undertake reform, no matter who they are, have no choice but to resign. ... Some persons are saying that securities trading is capitalism, but the results of the experiments in Shanghai and Shenzhen have proven that it is a success. ... Even if something is capitalist there is nothing wrong with incorporating it in the socialism system" (reported January 28 in Hong Kong's *Wen Wei Po* and *Ta Kong Pao*).

January 18–25   Jiang Zemin visits Jiangsu province and pronounces "Stand on solid ground and deal with reality. Guard against formalism" (*People's Daily*, January 26, 1992, which the same day carries an editorial entitled "Change Our Workstyle").

February 5      All newspapers carry photos and reports of Deng Xiaoping's celebration of Spring Festival in Shanghai.

February 21     The *People's Daily* carries a Commentator article criticizing "Formalism and Bureaucratism."

February 22     The *People's Daily* editorial appeals "Firmly Uphold Making Economic Construction the Focus."

February 23     The *People's Daily* carries an article by Fang Sheng, "Utilizing External Opening and Capitalism."

| | |
|---|---|
| March 1 | Communist Party Central Document No. 2 (1992) is disseminated (Deng Xiaoping's remarks during his southern tour). |
| March 9–12 | A plenary session of the Chinese Communist Party Political Bureau (Politburo) is convened in Beijing. A number of important questions regarding reform and development are discussed. The spirit of Deng Xiaoping's "important talks" is reaffirmed. |
| March 20 | The National People's Congress is convened. Li Peng's report is true to the directives of Deng Xiaoping. |
| March 31 | The article by reporter Chen Xitian, "The East Wind Blowing Has Brought Spring: Comrade Deng Xiaoping's Shenzhen Travelogue," is carried in the *Shenzhen Special Zone Bulletin*. |
| March | Opening and border trade is approved for thirteen border cities and areas, including Heihe and Suifanghe in Heilongjiang province; Hunchun in Jilin province; Manzhouli and Erenhot in Inner Mongolia; Yining, Tacheng, and Bole in Xinjiang autonomous region; Ruili, Tianwanding, and Hekouxian in Yunnan province; and Pinpxiang and Dongxingzhen in Guangxi autonomous region. |
| April 7 | The *People's Daily* editorializes "Celebrate the Inclusion of the Three Gorges Dam in the Ten-Year Plan." |
| April 16 | The *Liberation Daily* carries "Reader's Notes to the Works of Deng Xiaoping" by Gong Yuzhi. |
| April 28 | The *People's Daily* editorial "Firmly Strive to Achieve a New Level" calls for an acceleration of reform and liberalization. |
| May 2 | The *People's Daily* reports that Chen Yun (chairman of the Chinese Communist Party Central Advisory Committee) on the eve of May Day in Shanghai listened to a report of municipal government activities to the Shanghai Party Committee and at the same time expressed support for development of Pudong. |
| May 22 | Deng Xiaoping makes a visit to the Capital Steel Company in Beijing and encourages reform of state-owned enterprises (*Guangjiaojing*, Hong Kong, 1992, No. 7). |

| | |
|---|---|
| **End May** | Communist Party Central Document No. 4 (1992) is issued. "Multi-directional, multi-strata" liberalization is announced. |
| **June 8** | Li Peng, Yao Yilin, Zou Jiahua, and Zhu Rongji conduct a discussion meeting on June 6 concerning reform and liberalization in the northwestern regions with the responsible persons of these regions and confirm opening of some of the cities. |
| **June 12** | The Production Office of the State Council is abolished and reorganized into the State Council Office of Economic Trade with Vice Premier Zhu Rongji in concurrent charge. This is an expansion of Zhu's authority. |
| **June 15** | General Secretary Jiang Zemin delivers an important speech at the Party Central Academy School and emphasizes thoroughly implementing the Deng Xiaoping line. |
| **June 23** | Li Xiannian, chairman of the All-China Political Consultative Conference, dies. |
| **June 30** | Communist Party Central Document No. 5 (1992) is issued. The "Decision Concerning Speeding Up the Development of Tertiary Industries" of the Party Central and State Council is announced in the *People's Daily* (decision taken June 16). |
| **June–July** | Five Yangtze River riparian cities (Chongqing, Yueyang, Wuhan, Jiujiang, and Wuhu); and seven border cities (Kunming, Nanning, Urumchi, Harbin, Changchun, Huhehot, and Shijiazhuang) are opened to the outside. Eleven interior cities (Taiyuan, Hefei, Nanchang, Zhengzhou, Changsha, Chengdu, Guiyang, Xian, Xining, and Yinchuan) are opened to the outside. |
| **July 4** | The *People's Daily* "Liberating Thinking" roundly criticizes the conservatives' ideology. |
| **July 11** | Deng Yinqiao, widow of Zhou Enlai, dies. |
| **July 25** | The *People's Daily* publishes "Rules and Regulations Concerning Transformation of the Management System of Industrial Enterprises Under Ownership of the Whole People" (previously enacted on June 30). |
| **August 4–6** | The Second Scholarly Research Meeting on Relations Across the Taiwan Straits is convened in Beijing. |

| | |
|---|---|
| **August 5** | The State Council approves the "Report Concerning Significantly Expanding the Sovereignty of Capital Steel Works," after which Capital Steel Works gains authority to conduct foreign trade directly. |
| **August 10** | The State Council grants significantly greater independent authority to Hainan province in the areas of import and export, fixed capital investment, and introduction of foreign capital. |
| **August 10–12** | The China Institute of International Affairs convenes "Symposium on the Asia-Pacific Region in the 1990s." |
| **August 18** | The Yangpu economic development zone of Hainan province signs a contract in Beijing to lease 300,000 square kilometers to Kumagai Gumi (a Japanese construction firm now registered as a Hong Kong company). (The contract is approved by the State Council on November 30.) |
| **August 24** | China and the Republic of Korea establish diplomatic relations. |
| **September 2** | The "1992 Urumchi Border and Regional Economic and Trade Fair" is convened in Urumchi. Premier Li Peng attends and exhorts officials to make Urumchi a "base for opening of the northwest." |
| **September 14** | The "Northwest Regional International Economic and Technical Cooperation Commercial Fair" is convened in Xian (sponsored by five northwestern provinces and autonomous areas, the Xinjiang production construction corps, and the UNDP). |
| **September 15** | The State Industrial and Commercial Bureau reaches the decision to "promote development and liberalization of coastal, riparian, and border cities under the principle of 'first open up, later establish regulations.'" |
| **September 25** | The State Council approves the establishment of the Shanghai Pudong Customs. |
| **September 27–30** | President Roh Tae Woo of South Korea makes a state visit to China. |
| **September 28** | Twentieth anniversary of normalization of Japan-China relations. |
| **October 9–10** | The second meeting of the Management Committee of the Tumen River Development Project is convened in |

|  | Beijing. The conference report is signed by five countries: China, Mongolia, North Korea, South Korea, and Russia. |
|---|---|
| October 12–18 | The Fourteenth Congress of the Chinese Communist Party is convened. The concept of the "socialist market economy" is endorsed, and Jiang Zemin is reelected general secretary (on October 19 Deng Xiaoping meets with the congress delegates). |
| October 15 | The Party Central and the State Council jointly disseminate the "Rules on Conversion of the Management System of State-Owned Enterprises," commencing reform of these enterprises. |
| October 20–23 | Hong Kong governor Chris Patten makes an official visit to Beijing and meets with Lu Ping (director of the State Council Office of Hong Kong and Macao Affairs) and Jiang Enzhu (vice minister of foreign affairs). |
| December 2 | The China Telecommunications and Broadcasting Satellite Corporation signs a contract with the U.S. CTE Space Network Corporation to import telecommunications satellite technology. |
| December 4–9 | Li Peng visits the Guangxi autonomous region and exhorts Guangxi to open as quickly as possible a transportation route from the greater southwest (Guangxi) to the sea (i.e., the rail link to Beihaigang). |
| December 15 | In order to export two freighters, the China Machinery Export-Import Corporation arranges with the Bank of China for a credit to the buyer of $20 million. This is China's first export credit. |
| December 29 | It is announced that in the first nine months of 1992 China netted $790 million in foreign capital from the issuance of stocks and bonds (*People's Daily*). |

## Also in 1992

- Shenzhen municipality abolishes Baoan county and establishes the Baoan and Longgang districts.
- Seven localities are approved for establishing economic and technological development areas—Wenzhou in Zhejiang province, Yingkou in Liaoning province, Kunshan in Jiangsu province, Weihai in Shandong province, Fuqing municipality, and Rongqiao and Dongshan in Fujian province.

- Shaoguan, Heyuan, and Meizhou in Guangdong province are designated coastal economic development zones.
- In the Pudong new district of Shanghai, construction gets well under way on Yanggao Road, the Yangpu great bridge, Waigaoqiao port area, the Waigaoqiao power plant, and telecommunications facilities. The Lujiazui finance and trade area, the Jinqiao export processing zone, and the Waigaoqiao customs-free zone are constructed.
- Customs-free zones are established in Tianjin port, Dalian, Guangzhou, Xiamen, Zhangjiagang, Haikou, Shantou, Ningbo, Fuzhou, and Qingdao. These join the group of zones established in 1991: Shanghai's Waigaoqiao, Shenzhen's Futian, and Shenzhen's Shatoujiao.

# 1993

| | |
|---|---|
| January 1 | The State Council approves establishment of a development zone for Taiwanese commercial investment in Xiamen's Jimei district. |
| January 7 | The State Council approves establishment in Guiyang of a state-level high-technology technical development district. |
| January 20 | Promulgation of "Management Procedures of the PRC Government for the Import or Export of Currency." (Effective date is March 1.) |
| January 22 | Deng Xiaoping celebrates the eve of the lunar New Year with persons from various circles in Shanghai. He says, "We have seen in practice that the leading group of the Party Central with Jiang Zemin at its core is doing splendid work and can be trusted." |
| February 6 | Fuyuan municipality in Heilongjiang province (across from Khabarovsk) is designated an open city. |
| February 10 | The Xinhua News Agency reports that China has established trading relationships with over 221 countries and regions and has set up over 200 state trading organs overseas. |
| February–March | Five localities in Fujian province—Sanming, Nanping, Longyan, Fuan, and Fuding—and Dongying municipality in Shandong province are designated coastal economic development areas. |

| | |
|---|---|
| March | Huangshi in Hubei province is designated an open riparian municipality. |
| March 15 | The State Administration of Exchange Control promulgates "Regulations Governing Management of the Foreign Exchange Adjustment Markets" (*People's Daily*, March 16). |
| March 29 | Premier Li Peng and Vice Premier Zhu Rongji are reelected at the first meeting of the Eighth National People's Congress. |
| April 19 | The State Council undertakes reform of its direct organs, reducing directly subordinate organs from nineteen to thirteen and administrative organs from nine to five. |
| April 29 | Wang Daohan (chairman of the Association on Relations on the Two Sides of the Taiwan Straits) and Gu Zhenpu (chairman of the board of the Taiwan Straits Exchange Foundation) meet for talks in Singapore. |
| May 28 | Eight localities—Hailin municipality; Ningan, Dongning, Fuyuan, Luobei, Suibin, and Siyaohe counties in Heilongjiang province; and Urukona Banner in Inner Mongolia—are opened to the outside. |
| June 3 | At a symposium on reform and liberalization in the Xiamen special economic zone sponsored by the Chinese Institute of World Affairs (Tong Dalin, director) and *Economic Daily*, the proposal is made to turn the Xiamen special economic zone into a "free port" (Shanghai *Liberation Daily*, June 3). |
| July 2 | Li Guixian, governor of the People's Bank of China, is dismissed. Vice Premier Zhu Rongji takes over the position concurrently. Financial rectification begins. |
| July 5–7 | Zhu Rongji convenes the "National Conference on Financial Work." |
| July 10 | A plenary session of the State Council decides to dispatch ten Central Inspection Teams to twenty provinces, municipalities, and autonomous regions and to strengthen macroeconomic regulation. |
| July 20–23 | Zhu Rongji convenes the "National Conference on Taxation Work." |
| July 26 | Deng Xiaoping writes the bridge name on the Yangpu great bridge over the Huangpu River at Shanghai. |

| | |
|---|---|
| August 20–25 | Jiang Zemin emphasizes combating corruption at the Second Plenum of the Chinese Communist Party Central Disciplinary Investigation Committee. |
| September 18 | Draft of the "Fifty Articles" to be adopted at the Third Plenum of the Fourteenth CPC Central Committee circulated to thirty province-level units, ninety central departments, and sixteen elders. |
| September 23 | Failure of Beijing's bid for the 2000 Olympic Games. |
| October 1 | The forty-fourth anniversary of the founding of the PRC. |
| October 11 | The magazine of the conservatives, *Pursuit of Truth* (October 1993), includes an article attacking the Deng Xiaoping line. (This is viewed as a theoretical challenge by the conservatives in advance of the Third Plenum of the Fourteenth CPC Central Committee.) |
| October 20 | The *China Securities News* espouses "double 13"—loosening money and tolerating 13 percent inflation as long as 13 percent growth can be sustained. (This is based on Deng Xiaoping's remarks in September advocating faster growth.) |
| November 2 | Third volume of *Selected Works of Deng Xiaoping* published. |
| November 11–14 | Third Plenum of Fourteenth Central Committee of the Chinese Communist Party held in Beijing. "Decision on Some Issues Concerning the Establishment of a Socialist Market Economic Structure" (Fifty Articles) adopted. |
| December 1–4 | National Economic Work Conference convened to discuss implementation of the Fifty Articles. |
| December 28–31 | Fifth meeting of the Standing Committee of the Eighth People's Congress approves and promulgates new commercial laws, effective January 1, 1994. These include an individual and enterprise tax law, a value-added tax, an accounting law, a new enterprise law, and new foreign exchange regulations. |

# 1994

| | |
|---|---|
| January 1 | Foreign exchange system overhauled as "official rate" is abolished and trading is unified against the managed |

floating rate, initially about RMB 8.7 to US$1.00. The system of settlements with foreigners in Foreign Exchange Certificates is abolished. All settlements are in RMB. State enterprises are prohibited from holding foreign currency, which must be surrendered immediately to the Bank of China.

February 9–12    Chinese television shows Deng Xiaoping, evidently frail, touring development sites during his annual Spring Festival sojourn in Shanghai, accompanied by his daughter and interpreter, Mao Mao.

# Appendix 1: Chinese Communist Party Central Committee Document No. 2 (1992): Important Talks by Deng Xiaoping

## I

I visited Guangdong in 1984. At that time, Guangdong had just started urban reform and economic structural reform. Eight years later, I again visited Guangdong. I did not expect that it had developed so fast. After seeing what happened there, I became more confident. In the past, we only mentioned developing productive forces under socialist conditions, but we did not mention how reform and openness would emancipate productive forces. In fact, reform and opening up mean to follow the Party's basic line and to carry out the principles, policies, and line since the Third Plenary Session of the Eleventh CPC Central Committee. The key lies in persistently upholding the "one center and two basic points." The basic line should be valid for 100 years, and must not be shaken. Only by keeping this line can we be trusted and supported by the people. If we do not carry out reform and opening up, do not develop the economy, and do not improve the people's living standards, we will then only be on the road to ruin. The common people will not allow anyone to change the principles and policies of the basic line, and those who do may be overthrown at any time. I mentioned this point several times. That is, only by adhering to the basic line can we have a way out.

I can say that if there had been no achievements from reform and opening, we might not have been able to pass the test of the 4 June incident [Tiananmen Square], and if we had failed to pass that test, there would have been a chaotic situation that could have led to civil war. This was the case during the "Cultural Revolution." The reason our country could continue to be stable after the 4 June incident was that reform and opening up had promoted economic development and improved the people's living standards, and that the armed forces and the government also supported this road, this system, and these policies. We should strive to develop more quickly in the next several decades, and this will better

This is the purportedly authentic text of the internal-distribution-only CPC document as published "exclusively" by the *Economic Daily News*, Hong Kong, on March 12, 1992. *Source:* FBIS-CHI-92-050 March 13, 1992.

validate the principles and policies laid down by the Third Plenary Session of the Eleventh CPC Central Committee.

While saying this and that, in one word, we must carry out reform and opening. First of all, this principle and policy must be kept unchanged. Then it should be carried out on a full scale. Only thus can progress be made in the political, economic, diplomatic, cultural, and technological fields, as occurs at present.

The Eighth Plenary Session of the Thirteenth CPC Central Committee was a good meeting. It affirmed that the contract responsibility system on a household basis with remuneration linked to output would be kept unchanged. This is of great importance. Any change on this point will upset the people, and the people may think that the policy of the Communist Party is changing again. At this moment, no change can be made, and any change may be a mistake. There were quite a few such problems. If they were not handled properly, the principle would have been shaken and the overall situation of reform would have been affected. Therefore, urban and rural reform must be kept stable over a long time. Of course, problems may arise in the initial stage of reform and opening up, and some policies needed to be revised. However, even when new policies and revisions are made, it is impossible to completely get rid of the old. With this point being kept, China will have a bright future.

# II

Reform and opening require big leaps forward and courageous experiments, and must not proceed like a bound-footed woman. When making a point, we should boldly, boldly make breakthroughs and boldly advance with giant strides. Shenzhen's significant experience is that without some adventurous spirit and without the courage of making breakthroughs and conducting experiments, one will not be able to blaze a successful trail.

It is impossible to ensure perfection and 100 percent correctness in carrying out reform and opening up. I have never succeeded in doing so. Every year, we should sum up experience, maintain what is right, correct what is wrong as soon as possible, and waste no time in solving existing problems.

Reform and opening may continue 30 to 40 years, so the policies should be maintained more firmly. Day after day we have been increasing our experience in building socialism with Chinese characteristics, but more attention should be paid to originality and creativity. According to reports from various provinces, they all have their own characteristics.

When considering reform and opening, some people just fear capitalism, or are worried about whether its surname is socialist or capitalist in nature. To judge whether socialism is developed, we should take the socialist productive forces as a criterion and should see whether the socialist state is able to improve the people's living standards. For example, from the very beginning there were different opinions on the running of the special economic zones. In Shenzhen, the public economy remains the main body, and foreign funded projects account for only one quarter. However, according to the tax income received from the foreign funded enterprises and the job provided by such enterprises, we should not fear to set up more such enterprises. There still will be large and medium sized state-owned enterprises, as well as township and village enterprises. More importantly, state power is still in our hands. Some people said: The more there are foreign funded enterprises, the more there will be capitalism, and an increase in foreign funded enterprises will lead to an increase in the capitalist factor and the development of capitalism. These people lack even basic common sense.

The reform policies and regulations at the present stage in our country ensure that foreign investors can reap profits, and at the same time, that the state can also achieve large amounts of tax revenue, and the workers can earn wages. We also can learn technology and management skills and further expand our market. Therefore, the advantages will outweigh the disadvantages when the three types of foreign funded enterprises are subject to political and economic constraints. The demarcation between planning and the market is not the substantive difference between socialism and capitalism, and this does not have any inherent link with the choice between socialism and capitalism. The planned economy is not the same as socialism because capitalism also involves planning. On the other hand, the market economy is not equal to capitalism either because socialism also has a market. Both planning and the market are economic means. With the liberation of productive forces as its intrinsic nature, socialism ultimately will reach common prosperity.

Some people say stocks and shares are a capitalist product. We have launched a pilot project in Shanghai and Shenzhen, and the outcome has proved the project a success. It seems that some capitalist practices can be applied to the socialism system. It is nothing serious even if a pilot project fails! If something goes wrong, let us close down the stock exchange and reopen it some days later. After all, there is nothing 100 percent correct in this world.

The idea of common prosperity means that some localities where conditions are ripe will be allowed to develop sooner than others, while localities where conditions are not available are to develop later; those that have developed ahead of others are to support the efforts of those that are trying to develop, and all localities will finally reach common prosperity. We do not mean to let the rich become richer while making the poor still poorer; polarization between rich and poor is absolutely intolerable. Those who get rich first may pay more taxes to support others in their development.

In rural reform, we have introduced the contract responsibility system on a household basis with remuneration linked to output, and have rescinded the system of people's communes. At first only one third of the provinces plunged into this reform. The number of provinces involved in the reform exceeded two thirds the following year, and then in the third year, almost all provinces joined the trend.

Refraining from arguing is one of my inventions. By refraining from arguing we can have more time for practical work. As soon as we start arguing, we will lose time and achieve nothing.

Now we are subject to influence from both Rightist and "Leftist" ideas. In the final analysis, however, we are handicapped by "Leftist" ideas. Rightism refers to "upheaval," while "Leftism" equates reform and opening up to promoting capitalism. Rightism can ruin socialism, and "Leftism" can do the same. We must remain cool-headed; in this way we will not make any great blunders.

# III

For the moment the key to reform and opening lies in economic development. Now that our peripheral countries and areas have the lead on us in economic development, if we fail to catch up with them or if we advance at a slow pace, the public may have grievances when they make a comparison. Therefore, if an idea can help speed up development, we must not stop it but should try to make development still faster. In any case, we must set store on efficiency and quality. We must seize every opportunity to make the country develop quickly. We have a good opportunity now; if we fail to seize it, it will be gone very soon. Slow development simply means to halt. We must strive really hard to upgrade the economy to a new level every few years. Never try to launch any unrealistic reform. In addition, we must pay attention to coordination. If Guangdong plans to catch up with the four little dragons of Asia within 20 years and wants to speed up its development, it will have to quicken its pace further. Shanghai definitely can go faster. By quickening the pace of development, the situation in the four special economic zones, in the Yangtze delta, and in China as a whole will be quite different from what it is at present. From now on, we must speed up reform and development. Now, when I review my work in retrospect, I think one of the great mistakes I committed is that I did not make Shanghai one of the special economic zones at the time when the four existing special economic zones were founded.

Science and technology is the foremost productive force. Economic development relies on science and technology. Without the help of science and technology, we would not have achieved such a high growth rate in the past ten years or so. We definitely must promote science and technology, as China must play a part in this field in the world. In the past, Qian Xuesen, Qian Sanqiang, and other scientists still managed to make some brilliant achievements that astonished the world and did credit to China.

I hope every Chinese studying abroad will return. Everyone is welcome to return home, whatever his political stand. The state will make arrangements for them to work after they return. This policy will not be changed. Let us tell them it is time for them to make contributions. Let us do more practical work and develop science and technology. The higher the standard, the better, and the newer the science and technology, the better. If this is done, I will be happy, the people will be happy, and the state will be happy.

# IV

We must uphold the principle of paying attention to both aspects, promoting reform and opening on the one hand, and fighting all kinds of criminal activities on the other. Both aspects are very important. We must not show any mercy when dealing blows to all kinds of criminal activities and eliminating all ugly phenomena. To catch up with the four little dragons of Asia within 20 years, Guangdong province not only must keep its economy strong, but also must straighten out its social order and cultivate a fine general social mood. Both issues must be handled properly; that is the essence of socialism with Chinese characteristics.

Since opening up, some ugly phenomena have arisen in some parts of China. We must never take a laissez-faire attitude toward such evil things as drug addiction, prostitution, and economic crimes, but must deal with them seriously and crack down on them resolutely. Following the founding of New China, we needed only three years to wipe out all such evil things. This is impossible in some countries and in capitalist countries. Facts have shown that the Communist Party can do away with evil phenomena. In the process of reform and opening up, we must always uphold the strategy of paying attention to both aspects.

Historical experience shows that to consolidate a political regime one must use the means of dictatorship. Democracy is to be applied to the people, and dictatorship to the enemy; this is what the people's democratic dictatorship means. Under the people's democratic dictatorship, consolidating the people's political regime is a just act, and there is no room for hesitation. In the whole process of reform and opening to the outside world, from the beginning to end, it is necessary to uphold the four cardinal principles. At the Sixth Plenary Session of the Twelfth CPC Central Committee I suggested opposing bourgeois liberalization for 20 years. It seems today that the struggle should be carried out for even more than 20 years. If bourgeois liberalization is allowed to spread unchecked, the consequences will be extremely serious. We have spent ten years or so building the special zones to be as they are now. To make them collapse would be a matter of only one night, just as in the case of the Soviet Union.

It is necessary to protect the socialist system by relying on the people's democratic dictatorship. This is a basic Marxist viewpoint.

# V

A correct political line should rely on a correct organizational line as a guarantee. In a certain sense, the key as to whether or not Chinese affairs can be handled well, whether or not socialism with Chinese characteristics can be adhered to, whether or not the economy can be developed more quickly, and whether or not the state can maintain long term political stability lies in "man."

In pursuing "peaceful evolution" hostile forces pin their hopes on the people of several generations following us. People of Comrade Jiang Zemin's generation can be considered the third generation, and there are people of the fourth and fifth generations to follow. When we people of the older generation are still around and have weight, hostile forces are aware that no change can be effected. However, when we old people are dead and gone, who will escort the emperor? Efforts should be made to manage our Army well and to educate the people and youth well.

If something wrong occurs in China, it will come from within the Communist Party. We should be sober about this matter and should stress the training of successors to the revolution. Leaders should be selected according to the four requirements of being revolutionary, more knowledgeable, more professional, and younger in average age. People who have both quality and political integrity should be chosen for leading bodies.

Two people I selected in the past ended in failure. They suffered a setback on issues of adherence to the socialist road and opposition to bourgeois liberalization, and not on the issue of economic work. We should not give way on this point.

It is necessary to select those people generally knowledgeable to adhere to the line of reform and opening to the outside world, and to boldly put them in the new leading organs.

Further efforts should be made to choose young people for leading bodies. Now the average age of the members of the central leading body is a little high. People at the age of 60 or so can still be considered young.

Old people at the advanced age will have difficulties in memory and become stubborn. We should estimate our own strength properly.

Currently, formalism is abundant and articles are too lengthy. In studying Marxism and Leninism, stress should be put on essence and applicability.

# VI

In my opinion, more and more people will agree with Marxism because it brings to light the objective laws governing the development of mankind. Some people say: Marxism will disappear and fail. This is not the case. Socialist China should work hard to practice it.

We should continue to oppose "hegemonism."

Capitalism has developed for several hundred years. Socialism in our country has developed just for a period of time, and moreover, we ourselves have delayed it for 20 years. If we spend 100 more years building our country into a developed one, this will be amazing. From now on to the middle of the next century, our responsibility is very immense and our burdens very heavy.

# Appendix 2: Chinese Communist Party Central Committee Document No. 4 (1992): Multi-Directional, Multi-Strata Liberalization

Beijing, 17 June (*Ta Kung Pao*)—According to informed sources here, the CPC Central Committee recently circulated Document No. 4 to Party members, fully expounding its thoughts on hastening reform, opening wider to the outside world, and stepping up economic development.

The document, known as "The CPC Central Committee's Opinions on Expediting Reform, Opening Wider to the Outside World, and Working to Raise the Economy to a New Level in a Better and Quicker Way," calls on the entire Party membership to conscientiously study speeches made by Deng Xiaoping during his South China tour, further emancipate their minds, and make earnest efforts to create a formula for economic development characterized by high speed and satisfactory economic efficiency.

It is known that the document is to be relayed level by level within the Party. The document is presently being conveyed to Party member cadres at the department and bureau levels. It is estimated that the document will be made known to the entire membership soon.

A person who read the document said the 10,000-character document comprises four parts and covers issues in 19 respects, including transforming the enterprise operational mechanism, further opening to the outside world, restructuring the government, and strengthening macroscopic regulation and control. The CPC-run newspapers and CPC leaders had mentioned those contents sporadically, but the document deals with them in a more detailed and systematic way.

The Document No. 4 which the CPC Central Committee recently circulated within the Party puts forward a series of new measures for opening wider to the outside world.

As disclosed by informed sources in Beijing, the measures include:

Hong Kong, *Ta Kung Pao* "Special Dispatch" from Beijing: "The CPC Issues Document Number Four, Fully Expounding Expansion of Opening Up." In Chinese June 18, 1992. *Source:* FBIS-CHI-92-118 June 18, 1992.

- With the development of Pudong in Shanghai serving as the dragon head, further develop Wuhu, Jiujiang, Wuhan, Yueyang, and Chongqing along the Yangtze River, and adopt the same policies toward them as those applied in coastal open cities.
- Gradually open cities along the borders to the outside world to form a peripheral opening pattern. Apart from four cities including Heihe, open another nine cities and counties in southwest and northeast China to the outside world; Pingxiang and Dongxing in Guangxi; Hekou county, Wanding, and Ruili county in Yunnan; Yili, Tacheng, and Bole in Xinjiang; and Erenhot in Inner Mongolia.
- To actively promote border trade with the neighboring countries and adopt relevant policies for open cities in Harbin, Changchun, Huhehot, Urumchi, Kunming, and Nanning.
- To continue to run well the special economic zones and coastal open cities and open zones and to boldly make use of foreign funds and introduce technologies.
- To select a port city in every special economic zone as well as Shandong, Jiangsu, Zhejiang, and Fujian for establishment of a bonded zone there.
- To strengthen association between coastal and inland areas and the influence of the former on the latter and to give full play to the role of Guangxi as the thoroughfare in southwest China. To accelerate the pace of opening up in the inland areas and, in the projects using foreign funds, to implement the relevant policies for coastal open cities in the capitals of inland provinces and regions.
- To implement the policy combining the preferential measures for certain regions with those for certain industries, expand the spheres for opening up to the outside world, find more ways to make use of foreign funds, and adopt more flexible measures to assimilate more foreign funds and funds from Hong Kong, Macao, and Taiwan. All major projects and high and new technological projects, which have been approved by the state and which are in conformity with the industrial policy, irrespective of their localities, can enjoy the preferential policies for development zones. The spheres for directly using foreign funds should be gradually extended to finance, trade, commerce, communication, tourism, and the tertiary industry through experiments. To allow the approved establishment of one or two foreign funded banks and foreign invested retail firms in certain cities and to allow Shanghai to run a foreign invested insurance company on a trial basis.

According to well-informed sources here, in the latest Document No. 4, the CPC Central Committee put forth a series of new measures to quicken the pace of transforming the enterprise operation mechanism. These new measures include formulation of the provisional regulations on transforming the operation mechanism of industrial enterprises, the resolute closing down and suspension of the enterprises which have incurred losses for a long period of time, and expansion of the pilot project of the shareholding system.

The document also puts forward the related coordinated measures, which include a change in the government functions, perfection of the social security system, and cultivation and development of the market structure.

The document puts forth that it is necessary to make efforts to transform the operation mechanism and to step up the formulation of the provisional regulations on the transformation of the mechanism of industrial enterprises so that the enterprises can really become the producers and operators of commodities. It is essential to exercise the enterprise self-decisionmaking power so that the enterprises can really ensure that they are solely responsible for their own profits and losses and appreciation of the state-owned assets can be guaranteed. The core of the enterprise self-decisionmaking power is the power of personnel labor (sic), the power to distribute wages and bonuses, the power to set prices of products, the power of investment policy decision, and the power of operation of import and export. It is imperative to resolutely close down and suspend the enterprises which have incurred losses for a long period of time, to encourage the development of tertiary industries, to organize and establish enterprise groups, and to carry on international operations. During the period of the eighth five year plan, it is necessary to perfect the contract system and to increase the enterprises which have operated well from one-third to two-thirds.

Document No. 4 states that the shareholding system is "effective" and demands that conditions be created for gradually expanding pilot projects, shares to be issued to society, and meanwhile, shares going to the market be strictly controlled.

Regarding the issue of transforming the government functions, the document puts forth that on the basis of the principles of separating the functions of the government from those of the enterprises, of good macroeconomic management, and of microeconomic relaxation, the functions of the government organs must be integrated with streamlined administration and the government departments must mainly do well in planning, coordination, supervision, and service work.

In the aspect of cultivating the market structure and accelerating the pace of reform of the commercial and material structures, the document says that at present, it is essential to speed up the development of the structures of the commodity market and material market and to deepen reform of the circulation structure. The commercial system must popularize "four relaxations" (operation, prices, distribution, use of labor) so as to enable enterprises to go into the market. The document demands deepened reform of the economic and trade structure, vigorous development of the foreign markets, and acceleration of the pace of trade diversification. On the other hand, it is necessary to simplify the administrative procedure of examination and approval; to reform the quota system; to further the integration of agriculture and trade, and machinery and trade; and to organize and establish operation companies. Production enterprises, enterprise groups, engineering companies contracting work for foreign countries, and commercial enterprises which have favorable conditions must be vested with the power of the operation of import and export; and meanwhile, local trade, border trade, and all flexible trade modes must be utilized to develop export trade with the neighboring countries.

# Appendix 3: Chinese Communist Party Central Committee Document No. 5 (1992): Decision to Speed Up Tertiary Industry

In order to grasp the current opportunity for increasing the pace of reform and opening and concentrate energy on boosting economic construction, it is necessary to effect comprehensive and high-speed development of tertiary industry in light of the requirements of the Ten Year Program and the Eighth Five-Year Plan for National Economic and Social Development.

## First, Speeding Up the Development of Tertiary Industry Has Great Strategic Significance

1. Speeding up the development of tertiary industry is an inevitable result of the enhancement of the productive forces and social progress. The level of tertiary industry is an important yardstick for judging the degree of modern socioeconomic development. Tertiary industry in our country is still developing slowly and remains at a rather low level. This is not suited to the needs of national economic development. The regularity of economic development in many countries shows that, when the economy develops to a certain level, the growth rate of tertiary industry is generally higher than that of primary and secondary industries, and tertiary industry plays an obvious role in promoting the development of the national economy as a whole. Our country has now reached this stage. In order to smoothly achieve the grand objective of socialist modernization, we must tightly grasp this opportunity and raise tertiary industry to a new level.

2. Speeding up the development of tertiary industry can promote the full growth of the market; raise the socialization and specialization level of services; increase the capacity of social guarantees; facilitate the smooth implementation of a series of measures for reform-

Xinhua News Agency report: "Decision of the CPC Central Authorities and the State Council to Speed Up Development of Tertiary Industry (16 June 1992)." *Source:* FBIS-CHI-92-128 July 2, 1992.

ing the labor, wage, price, enterprises management, and circulation systems; benefit the further expansion of opening and the attraction of more foreign investment; promote streamlining of the administrative structure and the enhancement of work efficiency; gradually change the situation in which social services are provided by government offices, enterprises, and other institutions; and create better conditions for the in-depth development of reform and opening in a broader scope.

3. In our country, poor economic results in industry, the low rate of marketable products in agriculture, impediments to the circulation of goods, and financial difficulties have seriously hindered the further development of the national economy. A major reason for the appearance of these problems lies in the irrationality of the economic structure, which is mainly reflected in the fact that the tertiary sector cannot meet the development needs of primary and secondary industries. Tertiary industry requires less inputs, yields quicker returns, and brings about positive social effects. Speeding up the development of tertiary industry will adjust the proportion of the three categories of industry and will optimize the structure of the national economy. It will also effectively mitigate deep-seated contradictions in economic life and promote faster economic development.

4. In the 1990s, a large quantity of new workers and redundant laborers from primary and secondary industries will require job placement each year. Tertiary industry has a unique advantage in absorbing workers and creating jobs: It includes a large number of trades and a wide variety of jobs. There are labor-intensive, technology-intensive, and knowledge-intensive trades, and they can absorb a large number of personnel of all sorts at different tiers. Speeding up the development of tertiary industry is a major step toward easing the increasingly serious employment pressures in our country.

5. By the end of this century, our people's standard of living will reach the level of being comparatively well-off. As compared with the living standard of having sufficient food and clothing, the living standard of being comparatively well-off not only finds expression in citizens' income levels, but also in a more important aspect, that is, the level of services available in society and to citizens. With the development of the economy and the enhancement of the people's income, the masses will not only have more and higher needs in various aspects of their material lives, such as food, clothing, shelter, travel, communications, public sanitation, and living environment, but will also raise more and higher needs in various aspects of their spiritual lives, including entertainment, broadcasting, television, movies, publications, sport and recreation, and tourism. Only by speeding up the development of tertiary industry can we meet the increasing needs of the masses and promote the building of socialist material and spiritual civilization.

# Second, Objective and Key Points of Speeding Up Tertiary Industry Development

6. According to our national conditions, the three categories of industry in our country are defined as follows: primary industry is agriculture; secondary industry is manufacturing and construction; and tertiary industry includes all other trades and industries, which are mainly in the circulation sector, the sector providing services for production and people's livelihoods, and the sector contributing to the enhancement of the scientific and cultural level and providing quality services to residents.

7. The objective of speeding up the development of tertiary industry is: In a period of about ten years or so, we will strive to gradually build up a unified socialist market system, a comprehensive social service system, and a social guarantee system in the cities and countryside, which are in keeping with our national conditions. In the 1990s, it is necessary to speed up the development of tertiary industry while developing primary and secondary industries and promoting the development of the national economy onto a new stage every several years. Therefore, the growth rate of tertiary industry must be higher than that of primary and secondary industries, and efforts should be made to raise the proportion of additional value of GNP produced by the tertiary sector and the proportion of workers employed in the tertiary sector to the average level or a point near the average level for developing countries.

8. The key areas for speeding up the development of tertiary industry are: first, trades which require less investment, yield quicker returns, achieve better results, provide more jobs, and have a closer relationship with economic development and the people's livelihood, such as commerce, material distribution, foreign trade, banking, insurance, tourism, real estate, warehousing, citizen-oriented services, catering, and cultural and public health undertakings; second, new trades related to scientific and technological progress, such as consultancy (including consulting services in the scientific and technological, legal, accounting, and auditing fields), information services, various technical services; third, tertiary industry in the countryside, which mainly refers to trades that provide pre-production, production, and post-production services and trades that raise the quality of the peasantry and the quality of peasants' lives; fourth, basic industries which have a bearing on the overall situation of national economic development and should be developed ahead of other industries, mainly transportation, postal communications, scientific research, education, and public works.

# Third, Major Policies and Measures for Speeding Up Tertiary Industry Development

9. Fully arouse the initiative of all parties with action being taken by the state, collectives, and individuals. It is necessary to give a free hand to urban and rural collective economic organizations, private enterprises, and individuals to run labor-intensive trades which require less investment, yield quicker returns, and provide direct services for production and the people's livelihood. Basic industries that have an advance bearing on the overall situation of national economic development should be run by the state, but it is also necessary to introduce a mechanism for competition. Localities, departments, and collective economic organizations should also be mobilized to run these undertakings according to the unified plan and under unified management. To speed up development of tertiary industry, it is necessary to mainly rely on social forces in all fields and to consistently follow the principle of allowing those who invest to own and benefit from the undertaking. One must not become too dependent on state investment.

10. We are to speed up the pace of tertiary industry development by carrying out reform further in depth and by expanding the opening up process. It is necessary to vigorously launch reform and pilot projects in various forms and boldly make use of foreign funds, technology, and marketing channels; it is necessary to raise funds by issuing bonds and

stocks and through other channels and by other means; it is necessary to vigorously promote enterprise groups' operational modes, break away barriers between different departments, different areas, different trades, and different ownership systems, establish
nationwide and regional tertiary enterprise groups, and speed up the development of tertiary industry. Whatever measures have proven in practice to be effective should be popu-
larized across the board as soon as possible. Those that do not produce rapid, conspicuous
results can continue to be implemented on a trial basis, while those proving unsuccessful
should be replaced by other measures.

11. We will establish a dynamic self-development mechanism for tertiary industry, with
a view to making it a well-established industry. Most tertiary industry establishments
should be developed into economic entities or be run in the form of enterprises so that
they can operate on their own and assume full responsibility for profits and losses. Most
tertiary industry establishments already in existence, which serve as welfare organizations,
charitable bodies, and institutions, must be gradually transformed into business establishments and must introduce enterprise management systems.

12. Aiming for socialization, we will actively push organs, enterprises, and institutions
with potential to open their existing information and consultation, internal service, and
communication and transportation facilities to the public so that they can offer paid services. We are also to pave the way for these establishments to separate from their original
parent organizations so that they can operate on their own and practice independent accounting. Meanwhile, we are to encourage social service organizations to undertake contracts to render supporting services to organs, enterprises, and institutions and to play a
part in the management of services for retired personnel and other affairs. It is necessary to
abolish the "large and complete" or "small but complete" closed self-servicing systems,
thus gradually effecting the socialization of the above-mentioned services.

13. We will encourage tertiary industry enterprises to take over those industrial enterprises in other industrial sectors, in other trades, and in other areas which are about to
shut down, suspend operations, amalgamate with others, or switch to other lines of production. We will offer them preferential treatment and support in terms of asset assign-
ment, debt settlement, credit, taxation, and so on. This must be taken as an important
measure to speed up readjustment to the industrial structure.

14. Administrative staff are strongly encouraged to separate from their original organs
and to shift to service trades. Those who quit their original posts will sever themselves
from their organizations. At the same time, we will vigorously develop trades that serve
production and people's everyday needs and make every effort to accommodate those who
quit their original organizations, thus paving the way for smooth progress in the government's institutional reform and staff rationalization operations.

15. We will expedite reform of the labor and personnel system and vest tertiary industry
enterprises with decisionmaking powers regarding employment. Dismissal and resignation
systems will be introduced step by step to allow both employer and job seeker to make
choices. Those institutions which implement the enterprise management system and are
not recipients of financial appropriations from the state will have a free hand in staff and
labor recruitment; they will be allowed to make their own staffing decisions. Regulations
will be appropriately relaxed on staff numbers in those institutions that are partially supported by state financial appropriations. Redundant personnel in industrial enterprises, especially those with professional technical qualifications, will be encouraged to turn to ter-

tiary industry. College and university graduates and demobilized servicemen will be encouraged to work in tertiary enterprises.

16. It is necessary to observe the law of value, reform the price system, and solve long-standing problems relating to tertiary industry where services have not been reasonably valued. Except for a small number of items for which prices and service standards really need to be set by the state, restrictions must be lifted from most prices and service charge standards relating to tertiary industry, and a system of floating prices, negotiated prices fixed by enterprises within the same trade, or prices set by the enterprise on its own will be adopted on a case-by-case basis so that a set of reasonable price relations will take shape.

17. It is necessary to encourage the expansion of internationalized operations; some state-owned large and medium commercial and material supplying enterprises will be authorized to run import-export trade, and those with potential must try their best to expand operations abroad and actively establish Chinese-funded enterprises overseas. Upon approval, large and medium state-owned foreign trade enterprises will be given marketing franchises in the domestic market. A system will be introduced to effect unified management of domestic and overseas markets. Action will be taken to further simplify examination and approval procedures in applications for overseas business operation.

18. Finance, taxation, and other economic means will be used to promote the development of tertiary industry. Loans for key trades are to be covered by credit plans. Banks and urban and rural credit cooperatives can grant small loans for the purchase of fixed assets and simple equipment maintenance to those collectively run enterprises, private enterprises, and individually run industrial and commercial establishments which promise good economic returns and have the ability to repay debt. For some newly established tertiary enterprises, income tax levies could be postponed or taxes reduced in accordance with industry policy if necessary.

19. Examination and approval procedures will be simplified to reduce the present difficulties hindering the establishment of new tertiary enterprises. Restrictions will be lifted so that tertiary enterprises will enjoy decisionmaking power with regards to business operations and will have greater flexibility to expand their operational scope. Meanwhile, it is necessary to intensify administration and supervision.

20. It is necessary to step up the development of a legal system geared to tertiary industry. We are to speed up formulation of laws and ordinances to regulate enterprises and market behavior. Enterprises will operate according to the law, while administrators for different trades and economic supervisory departments shall administer and exercise supervision according to the law to ensure that tertiary industry develops along the right track under legal regulation.

21. It is necessary to strengthen planning and administration in tertiary industry. Given varying economic structures and development standards in different localities, the focus and speed of development of tertiary industry should vary from place to place. The focus of development should be fixed according to the state's industrial policy in light of local conditions. As far as the development of tertiary [industry] is concerned, factors regarding investment, credit, employment, and land allocation should be covered by the general urban and rural development plan and unified arrangements should be made. Different localities and different sectors must formulate procedures for the implementation of the "Decision," and must revise any policies, ordinances, and regulations that are not in keeping with the guidelines laid by this "Decision" as soon as possible.

The CPC Central authorities and the State Council demand that the Party and government at all levels set great store by tertiary industry. Party and government leading cadres at all levels must try to reach a common understanding, update their concepts, emancipate their minds, give full play to their originality, mobilize the vast number of cadres and masses, and strive hard to fulfill the strategic goal of accelerating the development of tertiary industry.

# References

Chen Baiming, ed. 1992. *Research into the Production and Population Support Capacity of China's Land Resources.* Beijing: Chinese People's Press, February.

Chen Yun. 1986. *Collected Works of Chen Yun 1956–1985.* Beijing: People's Press, June.

*Contemporary Chinese Economic Management.* 1985. Beijing: Chinese Social Sciences Press.

*Customs Statistics Yearbook of China 1990.* 1990. Beijing: Customs Administration of the People's Republic of China.

Deng Xiaoping. 1983. *Collected Works of Deng Xiaoping.* Vol. 2. Beijing: People's Press, July.

———. 1984. *Build Socialism with Chinese Characteristics.* Beijing: People's Press, December.

———. 1987. *Build Socialism with Chinese Characteristics.* Enlarged edition. Beijing: People's Press, March.

———. 1993. *Collected Works of Deng Xiaoping.* Vol. 3. Beijing: People's Press, October.

*Economic Encyclopedia: Planning.* 1990. Shanghai: Encyclopedia Press.

The Economist Conferences. 1993. *Conclusions Paper,* "Roundtable with the Government of the People's Republic of China." Hong Kong: The Economist Conferences.

*Foreign Economic and Trade Yearbook 1991–1992.* 1992. Beijing: Ministry of Foreign Economic Relations and Trade.

*General Theory of China's Natural Geography.* 1985. Beijing: Scientific Press.

Hu Angang. 1989. *Population and Development: A Systematic Investigation into the Economic Problems of China's Population.* Hangzhou: Zhejiang People's Press.

Hu Angang and Wang Yi. 1989. *Existence and Development.* Academica Sinica National Situation Analysis Study Group. Beijing: Scientific Press.

Institute of Political Economy. 1954. *Political Economy.* Moscow: Soviet Academy of Sciences. Chinese edition, Beijing: People's Press, May 1955.

Japan International Cooperation Agency (JICA). 1991. *China: Report of Research Group on Country-Specific Assistance.* Tokyo: JICA, December.

———. 1992. *Report on China: Country-Specific Aid Research Group.* Tokyo: JICA, December.

Li Weiyi. 1991. *China's Wage System.* Beijing: Chinese Labor Press.

Lu Jian. 1992. *Positive Research on China's Economic Cycles.* Beijing: Chinese Financial and Economic Press.

Ma Hong, ed. 1989. *China in the Year 2000.* Beijing: Chinese Social Sciences Press.

Ma Hong and Sun Shangqing, eds. 1993. *Economic Encyclopedia of Modern China.* Vol. 2. Beijing: Chinese Financial and Economic Press.

Ma Yinchu. 1979. *A New Theory of Population.* Beijing: Beijing Press.

Ministry of Agriculture. 1989. *Complete Rural Economic Statistics of China 1949–1989.* Beijing: Agricultural Press.

Mitsubishi Research Institute. 1992. *China Information Handbook.* Tokyo: Sososha Ltd.

*Outline of the Cadre System of the Chinese People's Liberation Army.* Beijing: Military Science Press, internal distribution only.

Qiu Yongsheng and Ni Xiaolin. 1988. *Daoye, Daoye.* Shenyang: Liaoning People's Press.

*Road to Development of the Shenzhen Special Economic Zone.* 1984. Beijing: Guangming Daily Press.

*Seventh Five-Year Plan for Development of the National Economy and Society of the People's Republic of China 1985–1990.* 1986. Beijing: People's Press, May.

Shu Yi and Shen Jingrong, eds. 1987. *Economic Encyclopedia: Finance.* Shanghai: Shanghai Dictionary Press.

*The Standard for China's Being Well-Off.* 1992. Beijing: State Statistical Bureau, September.

State Council Individual and Private Economy Investigation Group, ed. 1990. *China's Individual and Private Economy.* Beijing: Reform Press, November.

State Statistical Bureau, Agricultural Statistics Division, ed. Annual editions. *Rural Statistical Yearbook of China.* Beijing: Chinese Statistical Press.

*Statistical Yearbook of China 1988.* 1988. State Statistical Bureau. Beijing: Statistical Press.

*Statistical Yearbook of China 1991.* 1991. State Statistical Bureau. Beijing: Statistical Press.

*Statistical Yearbook of China 1992.* 1992. State Statistical Bureau. Beijing: Statistical Press.

*Statistical Yearbook of China 1993.* 1993. State Statistical Bureau. Beijing: Statistical Press.

Susumu Yabuki. 1987. *The Economic Level of China: Illustrated.* Tokyo: Sososha Ltd.

*Taiwan Statistical Data Book 1991.* 1992. Taipei: Council for Planning and Development.

United Nations Population Fund. 1992. *World Population Report 1992.* New York: United Nations.

Wang Derong. 1986. *China's Transport System.* Beijing: Scientific Press.

World Bank. 1990. *World Development Report 1990.* Washington, D.C.: World Bank.

————. 1992. *World Development Report 1992.* Washington, D.C.: World Bank.

————. 1994. *World Bank Atlas 1994.* Washington, D.C.: World Bank.

Yang Peixin. 1990. *Inflation: A Catastrophe for the People.* Beijing: Chinese Economic Press.

*Yearbook of Chinese Industrial and Economic Statistics.* 1991. Beijing: Chinese Statistical Press.

Yen Wenguang. 1990. "Causes of the Huge Losses of State Enterprises." *Neibu Wengao* (Internal Distribution Articles). Monthly. Beijing, December 12.

Zhao Bo and Pan Tianshun, eds. 1966. *History of Organizational Work of the Chinese Communist Party.* Beijing: Chinese International Broadcasting Press, June.

# About the Book, Author, and Translator

Susumu Yabuki, one of Japan's leading China experts, presents here a comprehensive and accessible analysis of China's political economy. His insightful explanations are complemented by a wealth of lucid and up-to-date graphs and charts that provide statistical snapshots of economic trends in the PRC.

Placing the issues in historical context, the author considers China's economic growth, industrial and agricultural organization, population, wage policies, foreign investment, energy, transport, and pollution as well as the role of state and private enterprises. Yabuki focuses on concerns central to the PRC's foreign trading and investment partners, such as the evolution of liberalization policies; key open areas; flow, types, and sources of foreign investments; and major development projects, including the Three Gorges Dam.

Useful both as a desktop reference volume for corporations, organizations, and individuals considering the risks and rewards of doing business in China and as an introduction to China's economy and politics for students, Yabuki's unique study fills a genuine gap in the literature.

Professor Susumu Yabuki is well known as one of Japan's leading "China watchers." He is a recognized authority on modern China. Professor Yabuki was born in Japan in 1938. He is a graduate of the faculty of economics of Japan's most prestigious university, the University of Tokyo. He is currently a full professor at Yokohama City University.

Among Professor Yabuki's published works are *Possibilities of Modern Socialism* (jointly with others, 1975); *The Sino-Soviet Conflict* (jointly with others, 1976); *China in the Year 2000* (1984); *China Watching: From Economic Reform to Political Reform* (1986); *The Brain Trust Behind China's Opening* (1987); *China's Economic Level: Illustrated* (1987); *Post–Deng Xiaoping: The Future of Opening and Reform* (1988); *China's Perestroika: Standard Bearers of Democratic Reform* (1988); *The Cultural Revolution* (1989); *Important Documents in "China's Crisis,"* 3 vols. (1989); *The Real Story of the Tiananmen Incident,* 2 vols. (1990). As cotranslator, his publications include *Human Rights Violations in China: The Situation After the Tiananmen Incident,* written by Amnesty International and Asia Watch (1991); *Pekingology: The Situation of China at the End of the Century* (1991); *Mao Zedong and Zhou Enlai* (1991); *Conservatives Versus Reformers: The Power Struggle in China* (1991); *The Economy of China: Illustrated* (1992); and *Deng Xiaoping* (1993).

Stephen M. Harner is president of Yangtze Century Information Services Ltd., a Hong Kong– and Shanghai-based business information and market research company.

Harner was a commercial and private banker with Citibank and Merrill Lynch International Bank in Japan and Taiwan from 1981 to 1993. He was a U.S. Foreign Service Officer from 1975 to 1981, serving in Beijing from 1977 to 1979.

A graduate of the Johns Hopkins University School of Advanced International Studies, Washington, D.C., Harner is the author, with his wife Annie Lai Harner, of *Living and Working in the People's Republic of China,* a 1980 Department of State publication.

# Index

21.c

127390